History of the
Atchison, Topeka and
Santa Fe Railway

Railroads of America

THOMAS B. BREWER
General Editor

RICHARD C. OVERTON
Consulting Editor

HISTORY OF THE MISSOURI PACIFIC
by Thomas B. Brewer and Allen Dickes

HISTORY OF THE
ATCHISON, TOPEKA AND SANTA FE
by Keith L. Bryant, Jr.

HISTORY OF THE BALTIMORE AND OHIO
by William Catton

HISTORY OF THE LOUISVILLE & NASHVILLE
by Maury Klein

HISTORY OF THE CANADIAN PACIFIC
by W. Kaye Lamb

HISTORY OF THE NORTHERN PACIFIC
by Robert L. Peterson

HISTORY OF THE CANADIAN NATIONAL
by G. R. Stevens

HISTORY OF THE ILLINOIS CENTRAL
by John F. Stover

HISTORY OF THE ATCHISON, TOPEKA AND SANTA FE RAILWAY

KEITH L. BRYANT, JR.

Macmillan Publishing Co., Inc.

NEW YORK

Collier Macmillan Publishers

LONDON

Macmillan Publishing Co., Inc.
866 Third Avenue, New York, N. Y. 10022
Collier-Macmillan Canada Ltd.

Library of Congress Cataloging in Publication Data

Bryant, Keith L
    History of the Atchison, Topeka and Santa Fe.

    (Railroads of America)
    Bibliography: p.
    1. Atchison, Topeka and Santa Fe Railway.
I. Title. II. Series: Railroads of America (New York)
HE2791.A83 1974   385'.0978   74–8250
ISBN 0–02–517920–9

FIRST PRINTING 1974

Printed in the United States of America

For
Jennifer
and
Craig

Contents

Illustrations

Maps

Preface

Twelve thousand miles of shining rails stretching from Chicago to Los Angeles and from Houston to San Francisco. Giant locomotives struggling through Raton or Cajon Pass and across the Mojave Desert. Long lines of boxcars filled with wheat in Superior, Nebraska, and flatcars of pulpwood on a siding in Oakdale, Louisiana. Stainless steel passenger cars, Indian Detours, and food by Fred Harvey. Dividend checks from the "Atchison," and trips to California on the "Santa Fe." These are some of the images of the Atchison, Topeka and Santa Fe Railway, one of the nation's largest and most financially sound railroads. For over one hundred years, this rail system has served the southwestern quarter of the United States, and its history is indissolubly linked with the area it traverses. The Santa Fe Railway has become not only an integral part of the southwestern economy, but also a symbol of the basic strength of the rail industry. This is a history of the Santa Fe Railway, its strengths and weaknesses, successes and failures, triumphs and tribulations.

The history of any business or industry can be written in terms of the inner workings of the corporate management and its day-to-day activities, or the study can focus on the interrelationship between the corporation and those who utilize its services. This book represents an effort to use both approaches. The decisions made by the owners and managers are analyzed to understand the motivations involved in the decision-making process. There has also been an attempt to analyze the relations of the railroad with the people it served. Traditionally, histories of railroads have focused on the importance of the industry in furthering the expansion of agriculture in the nineteenth century; and while such analysis is included in this volume, the relationship of the Santa Fe to urbanization in its territory is also discussed. The ATSF played a major role in the growth of Albuquerque, Los Angeles, San Diego and other cities in both the nine-

teenth and twentieth centuries. There has also been an attempt to make
the managers and workers of the Santa Fe "family" appear to be more
than numbers or names, and to portray them at their seemingly mundane,
but necessary, tasks which keep the trains running.

The writing of this book would not have been possible without the aid
and cooperation of the officers of Santa Fe Industries; this is, however, in
no way an "official" history. President John Reed made only one stipula-
tion in approving the project; he asked that the story be brought to the
present time with adequate coverage of the last twenty-five years—the
author agreed without hesitation. Vice President for Public Relations Bill
Burk and his staff provided help at all stages of the project, and the author
is indebted to them and to Chief Engineer W. S. Autrey. Many of the
photographs were provided by the Railway, and Assistant Engineer L. R.
Beattie of the Engineering Department prepared the maps. The interpreta-
tions of events and decisions are my own, and not those of the management
of the Railway or Santa Fe Industries.

Research for the book was facilitated by grants from the Graduate
School of the University of Wisconsin at Milwaukee and by the staff of the
Inter-Library Loan Office of the university library. Stanley Glick served
as my research assistant for a year, and I am very grateful to him for
his labors. Ms. Kathy Poplawski typed, typed and typed the manuscript
drafts, deciphering my script and correcting my spelling. Once again, my
wife Margaret tried to smooth the prose, and raised questions about compound cylinders, convertible debentures and dynamic reverse. Last, I am
indebted to my editors, Professors Thomas B. Brewer and Richard C.
Overton, for their reading of the manuscript and for correcting errors of
fact and judgment. The errors remaining are my own.

History of the
Atchison, Topeka and
Santa Fe Railway

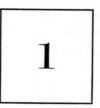

Colonel Holliday's Vision

Although it was only April 26, the sun blazed brightly in the Kansas sky, driving the picnickers under the cottonwood trees which lined Wakarusa Creek. While the men tended to the horses which had pulled the carriages and buckboards from the end-of-track five miles away, the women spread blankets in the shade of the grove and began to display the food brought in large wicker hampers. The management of the Atchison, Topeka and Santa Fe Railroad Company provided a keg of beer and a barrel of crackers, and a large body of men and older boys soon surrounded the place where the keg rested near the cool waters of the creek. The men, led by Colonel Cyrus K. Holliday, discussed the excursion over the new rail line from Topeka to the end-of-track, a trip of seven miles which had taken only thirty minutes. The speed of fifteen miles per hour elicited favorable comment, and there was general agreement that for a new railroad it was a splendid achievement. There were doubters and naysayers; George Noble and Major Tom Anderson of the rival Kansas Pacific Railway joked about this overly ambitious jerkwater railroad that ran from the village of Topeka to the proposed settlement of Cottonwood Grove. It was no joke to Cyrus K. Holliday.

After the picnickers emptied the hampers and drained the keg, and after the sun dropped a few degrees in the sky bringing some relief from the heat, Colonel Holliday spoke to the crowd. Mrs. Holliday, holding daughter Lillie, smiled as her husband, wearing a plug hat and a Prince Albert coat, mounted the empty keg and began to speak. An orator of the old school, the colonel stirred his audience with a brief review of the troubled history of Kansas, and the events which had brought them to this glorious celebration in the spring of 1869. He described the years of work leading to the construction of the Atchison, Topeka and Santa Fe Railroad, and then began to predict the future of the western railroads. "Fellow citizens," he proclaimed, "the coming tide of immigration will flow along these lines and, like an ocean wave, advance up the sides of the Rockies and dash their foamy crests down upon the Pacific." And what railroad would lead in this expansion asked the colonel? None other than the ATSF, which would extend to San Francisco and the Pacific, to Galveston and the Gulf of Mexico, to Mexico City and the Halls of Montezuma, and to Santa Fe, where it would capture the great trade of the legendary Santa Fe Trail. In a burst of enthusiasm he cried, "See, there rolls the broad Pacific, and on its breast are the ships of the Santa Fe riding in from the Orient." That was too much for Tom Anderson who yelled, "Oh, kind Lord, give us a rest!"[1] The colonel quickly concluded his remarks, and the celebrants loaded on the carriages and wagons for the ride back to the end-of-track. Despite Anderson's sally, Cyrus Holliday remained convinced that this excursion marked the beginning of a giant railway network, a transcontinental railroad.

If Holliday's enthusiasm seems unbounded and unrealistic to the reader, it should be remembered that an optimistic belief in progress was a dominant thread in American life in the forty years before and the thirty years after the Civil War. Nationalism and expansionism combined with a sense of adventure and a desire for trade and markets made visions such as Colonel Holliday's commonplace. Thomas Jefferson's purchase of Louisiana and his dispatching of Lewis and Clark to explore that vast domain; the proud place of the American clipper ships in the China trade; the subjugation of Mexico and the seizure of over one-third of that nation; the ongoing movement of the line of settlement to the West; these things stirred the imagination of the American people.

Some dreamers saw the railroad as the avenue of commerce and communication which would stimulate international trade and expedite settlement of the West. In the 1840s the New York merchant Asa Whitney declared that the railroad was the technological basis for western expansion and large-scale settlement. William Gilpin, a man of heroic vision, saw the railway to the Pacific in terms of trade with the Orient. It was America's destiny to subdue the continent and rush over the land toward the Pacific, and that waterway would bring vast riches to the nation. While Whitney and Gilpin published pamphlets and books on these themes, Senator Thomas Hart Benton of Missouri captured the imagination of the common people. Senator Benton spent a lifetime promoting his obsession with a "passage to India" and the East. Throughout the 1840s and early

1850s he urged Congress to subsidize a railway to California to promote trade between the United States and the Orient. The finely spun visions of Whitney, Gilpin and Benton achieved a modest degree of reality on the plains of Kansas in the two decades before the Civil War, and men like Holliday helped to turn the dreams into farms, towns and railroads.

National expansion, territorial and commercial, had been spurred by the California gold rush in 1849, the growing demand for a transcontinental railroad, the desire to subjugate the Indians, and, by the 1850s, the rising tide of sectionalism. The Territory of Kansas, soon to be subjected to the terrors of civil strife, became a major transportation artery long before the discovery of gold. The plains of Kansas had been deeply cut by the iron wheels of heavily laden wagons on their way to Santa Fe. The legendary Santa Fe Trail from Independence, Missouri, to the City of the Holy Faith of Saint Francis crossed the length of the Kansas Territory, and while it made few traders rich, it held a romantic lure far more significant than its meager traffic warranted.

Founded in 1598 by Don Juan de Oñate, Santa Fe became the governmental and economic center for a vast territory north of Chihuahua. Although isolated from the rest of New Spain, except for the long trail south to Chihuahua, Santa Fe developed a significant local economy based on trade with the Indians and farming along the Rio Grande. As stories of the wealth of Santa Fe spread among Americans, attempts were made to establish commercial relations. In 1804 William Morrison of Kaskaskia in Illinois Territory sent Baptiste La Lande to Santa Fe with trade goods; and two years later Captain Zebulon Pike journeyed to the city only to be arrested and imprisoned by the Spanish authorities. Similar treatment of other Americans prevented further developments until 1821, when Captain William Becknell successfully entered Santa Fe and traded with local merchants. Regular commerce commenced, first with pack mules and then with wagons, and Senator Benton began to agitate for a national road to the Mexican city. The commerce was largely one way, as the American traders sold cotton cloth, glass, tools, hardware and paint, and received, in return, gold, silver, furs, wool and Indian crafts. The initial trade route began at Franklin, Missouri, and then shifted to Independence. From there the journey of 775 miles took 70 days although only 38 days were needed for the return trip. Despite the high tariffs and extra "fees" charged by the Mexican officials, the Santa Fe trade proved immensely profitable, with net returns to the trail merchants of 20 to 40 percent.

Following the seizure of Santa Fe by General Stephen Kearney in 1846 and the acquisition of the Mexican Cession by the United States at the conclusion of the Mexican War, business expanded even more rapidly. The once sleepy village of 2,000 people grew quickly, and caravans arriving from Missouri at La Fonda, the inn at the end of the trail, would be greeted by a fiesta. The value of the trade in 1822 had been only $15,000, but by 1860 over 9,000 men, 3,000 wagons and 27,000 oxen were engaged in transporting 16 million pounds of goods, which generated over a million dollars in freight charges alone. Neither wars with the Indians nor civil war in Kansas slowed the growing trade with Santa Fe. The primary negative factor in the operation was the high freight charge of thirty-two cents per pound. Only a railroad could reduce such charges; but construction of a railroad to Santa Fe would have to wait while the residents of Kansas fought with each other over the question of the expansion of slavery.

The Territory of Kansas stood squarely in the path of settlers moving west, and was, therefore, thrust into the center of the slavery controversy. Made a free territory by the Missouri Compromise of 1820, Kansas became a pawn in the struggle between the North and the South as a consequence of the Kansas-Nebraska Act of 1854. That law, providing for popular sovereignty, allowed the residents to decide if the institution of slavery should be legalized in their territory. What followed was not democracy but violence, as proslavery Jayhawkers from Missouri battled settlers sponsored by the antislavery New England Emigrant Aid Society armed with "Beecher's Bibles" manufactured by Sharps. Jayhawkers attacked Quaker settlements, and zealous antislavery forces led by John Brown massacred proslavery settlers. Presidents Pierce and Buchanan pleaded for patience and peace and then sent weak-willed politicians to govern a territory inflamed by violence. Yet, despite the terror and turmoil, most men came to Kansas with ambitions and dreams for economic betterment, and while they passionately felt that Kansas should be a free or slave territory, they did not allow their feelings on that issue to prevent them from seeking their goals. Cyrus K. Holliday was such a man.

Like thousands of other young men, Holliday came west with ambition, imagination and high hopes, and like some he came with a fine education, business experience and a modest amount of capital. Born on April 3, 1826, near Carlisle, Pennsylvania, he was the youngest of seven children. When his father died in 1830, Holliday's family joined a married sister who lived near Wooster, Ohio. Little is known of Holliday's youth until he enrolled at Allegheny College in Meadville, Pennsylvania, in 1848. A Methodist institution with a reputation as a vigorous liberal arts college, Allegheny provided Holliday with a solid education as well as an opportunity to develop his leadership potential. Holliday and his roommate William B. Allison (later a U. S. senator from Iowa) were participants in the Allegheny Literary Society, and in his senior year Holliday served as president of the organization. He graduated in 1852 and joined the George W. Howard Company, a contracting firm engaged

Cyrus K. Holliday, founder of the system. Santa Fe Railway

in building railroads in the Meadville area. In the course of building a line from Meadville southwest to the Ohio border, the company became financially strapped and Holliday, as partner in the firm, received bonds in the aborted venture as compensation for his work. The bonds, guaranteed by the county, proved to be the only valuable securities generated by the company, and young Holliday came away from this experience with nearly $20,000 in capital. With this substantial sum in hand, and a strong sense of adventure and optimism, the young man looked westward.

The year 1854 was momentous for Holliday and the United States. As Congress debated the question of organizing the territory of Kansas and moved toward the legislation to be known as the Kansas-Nebraska Act, national attention focused on this portion of the West. The sectional crisis, which had been growing in intensity since 1819, moved toward a climax as the debate on the expansion of slavery into Kansas drove the free states and the slave states further apart. Holliday undoubtedly followed these events closely, but his immediate concern that summer was his marriage to Miss Mary Dillon Jones, daughter of a Meadville dairyman. The young couple married in Meadville amid antislavery assemblies and conventions organized by supporters of the Western Pennsylvania Kansas Company. A Free-Soiler and antislavery advocate, Holliday determined to investigate the financial opportunities in the West, and in October journeyed to Erie, Pennsylvania, accompanied by his wife. After a tearful farewell in Erie, Holliday traveled on alone in search of a new home in the West.

For the next few weeks he meandered over the Midwest, first to Cleveland, then to Chicago, and on to St. Louis. From St. Louis Holliday took passage on the *Francis X. Aubrey*—a riverboat named for a Santa Fe Trail trader—and moved up the Missouri River to Fort Leavenworth. By stagecoach he journeyed to the frontier village of Lawrence, and on Christmas Day, 1854, he wrote to the editor of the *Crawford Democrat* of Meadville, giving his very favorable impressions of Kansas. Two weeks later he wrote again, praising the territory: "The Creator *might* have made a better country than the Kansas; but so far as my knowledge extends, he certainly *never* did."[2] The climate was mild, the soil rich, the water abundant, and the crop possibilities were virtually unlimited. He decided to stay.

One reason for Holliday's lavish descriptions of Kansas was his desire to sell lots at a town site he helped to create—the new town of Topeka. He had purchased a few shares in the Lawrence Town Company, but as this enterprise was already being developed, Holliday joined a group of men who traveled twenty-five miles farther up the Kaw River to a point where the California and Santa Fe trails crossed the stream. There, on a tract secured by a Wyandotte Indian land warrant, the Topeka Town Company staked out the new town. A born promoter, Holliday wrote to his wife that it was a beautiful site, a future metropolis, perhaps even the future capital of the territory. Despite the fact that the developers were sleeping in tents and a dugout "hotel" and that his choice of a name—Webster—for the site had been rejected for Topeka, he declared: ". . . it proves what I have often said to you—that I could do nothing at Meadville, but let me go off and try my hand among new people and under different influences and I could pursue a different course of action."[3] Elected president of the town company and acting as an agent of the New England Emigrant Aid Society, the promoter began to boom the new "city" on the banks of the Kaw.

While Holliday's interests were primarily economic, no one in Kansas Territory in the years from 1854 to 1861 could avoid involvement in territorial politics, and the young businessman did not hesitate to jump into the fray. In the fall of 1855 he became a writer for the *Kansas Freedman*, helped organize the Free-Soil party in the territory, and was defeated in a contest for a seat in the territorial legislature. The sturdily built young man, meticulously dressed in a Prince Albert coat and stovepipe hat, his uncreased wool pants tucked inside his handmade boots, cut a handsome figure as he entered the mainstream of Kansas society. As the free-state forces organized to fight the proslavery residents, Holliday became a colonel in the free militia. Later promoted to the rank of brigadier general, Holliday took an active role in the fighting in 1855 and 1856. He returned to Pennsylvania in 1856 to visit his family and to campaign for Republican John C. Fremont for president; but the next year found him back in Kansas, promoting Topeka and continuing his fight against slavery.

The next four years were exciting and challenging for Holliday. In 1857 he organized a free-state meeting in Topeka and was elected to the territorial council when the proslavery forces boycotted the election. As a member of the council he worked strenuously to have Topeka designated as the territorial capital. An "abolitionist town," Topeka was inhabited by over 700 people. Holliday reserved a tract of land as the site for the proposed capital building. Though the town company prospered, Holliday's interests shifted in 1857 when he came into contact with Luther Challis, a member of the legislature from Atchison, who had considerable interest in developing a railroad network in Kansas. As early as 1855 a railroad had been chartered in the territory, and by 1857 over a dozen more had been incorporated. Most were projected by town promoters in Atchison,

S. C. Pomeroy, promoter of the railway and Kansas Senator. Santa Fe Railway

Lawrence, Leavenworth and St. Joseph, and several had stipulated their western terminus to be Santa Fe. Indeed, Holliday became a director of one of these schemes, the St. Joseph and Topeka Railroad. But several years would pass and Kansas would continue to bleed before a locomotive whistle would be heard west of St. Joseph.

Even as Holliday continued to participate in territorial politics and promote Topeka, he became convinced that his town needed a railroad, and that such a railway venture could prove very profitable. In late January 1859, he went to Lawrence, and in a hotel room on Sunday and Monday, the 30th and 31st, wrote a charter for the Atchison and Topeka Railroad Company. Completing the charter except for the names of the incorporators, Holliday asked Luther Challis for advice as to which men should serve in the company. Together they filled in the list to include Challis and S. C. Pomeroy of Atchison, Holliday of Topeka and ten other prominent citizens of the two towns. The charter provided for a railroad from Atchison on the Missouri River west through Topeka to the southern or western boundary of the territory in the direction of Santa Fe, and it authorized a branch to the southern boundary of the territory in the direction of the Gulf of Mexico. Holliday was a man of high expectations and dreams. A board of directors of thirteen, at least three of whom had to be Kansans, could issue $1.5 million in capital stock, and when $50,000 had been subscribed and $5,000 paid in, the company could be organized. Holliday introduced the bill in the council on Tuesday, February 1. The bill passed the next day, was sent to the house, and was signed by Governor Samuel Medary on the last day of the session, February 11, 1859.

The scheme languished. A severe drought from June 1859 to November 1860, and then the coming of the Civil War, delayed any action by Holliday and his allies. The drought destroyed crops and the faith of many settlers. Wagons which only several years before had moved westward were seen rolling slowly back toward the East through the seared and tortured land, a mocking slogan painted in tar on the white canvas: "In God we trusted, in Kansas we busted."

Cyrus K. Holliday never lost faith in Kansas or in his railroad, and on September 14, 1860, accompanied by future Senator Edmund G. Ross and two other Topeka residents, took a buggy to Atchison to form the company. Too financially strapped to pay the ferryman at the Kaw River crossing, they forded the river and drove to Atchison. Between September 15 and 17, Holliday called his Atchison supporters to a meeting in Luther Challis's small, brick law office, and there established their corporation. The thirteen directors each subscribed to $4,000 in stock, but only $400 had to be paid immediately. They elected Holliday president, Peter J. Abell secretary and Milton C. Dickey treasurer. The men who met to form the railroad company were short on funds but were the present and

Birthplace of the Santa Fe Railroad in Atchison, Kansas. Santa
Fe Railway

future leaders of the territory and the state. Ross published the *Kansas
Tribune*; J. H. Stringfellow of Atchison edited the *Squatter Sovereignty*;
Jacob Safford would become a district judge; Challis would later move to
New York as a Wall Street banker; Abell served as president of the
Atchison Town Company; and S. C. Pomeroy, an agent for the New England Emigrant Aid Society, would become a U. S. senator and the Republican boss of Kansas. Stringfellow, Abell and Challis were proslavery;
Holliday, Ross and Pomeroy were Free-Soilers; the financial opportunities
of the railroad brought them together. They all agreed that there was no
possibility of building the line without a land grant, and Holliday volun-
teered to begin working toward that end. Ross suggested a territorial railroad convention, and Holliday, seeing an opportunity to boost Topeka as
well, agreed to call such a meeting.

On October 17, delegations from counties and towns in northeastern
Kansas assembled in Topeka's Old Museum Hall to discuss territorial and
federal aid to local railway projects. Samuel Pomeroy presided. An immediate dispute developed over the possible routes to be subsidized, and the
Leavenworth and Wyandotte county men walked out of the meeting. The
remaining delegates voted to petition Congress to provide land grants for
four railways in Kansas, one of which was the route of the Atchison and
Topeka Railroad. B. H. Stringfellow displayed a map of the proposed line
which would follow the Cimarron Cutoff of the Santa Fe Trail. Holliday

then suggested that a committee draft the resolution to be sent to Congress and that territorial delegate M. J. Parrott be asked to push for the land grants. The delegates agreed, and the meeting adjourned. On November 24 the *Topeka Record* proclaimed:

> It is with a good deal of gratification that we are able to announce that the Atchison and Topeka Railroad, which has been a source of so much levity with many of our contemporaries and a prolific theme for prosy disquisitions by the score, the drouth, benevolence, railroads, etc. etc., is in a fair way to realize the expectations of its projectors.[4]

But a few weeks earlier Abraham Lincoln had been elected President; in December South Carolina seceded from the Union; and by April the Civil War had begun. The residents of Topeka would have to be patient for a few more years.

The tide of national politics largely determined the immediate future of the Atchison and Topeka Railroad. The Republican party needed all the strength it could muster at the outset of the Civil War, and Congress quickly admitted Kansas to statehood. The two new Republican senators elected by the Sunflower State, James H. Lane and S. C. Pomeroy, were leaders of the Whiggish wing of the party and staunch supporters of the Pacific Railroad Act of 1862. Through Senator Pomeroy, the organizers of the Atchison and Topeka, particularly Holliday, hoped to secure a federal land grant for the railroad. Holliday sent Pomeroy a handwritten bill providing for the federal government to grant lands to the state of Kansas to aid in constructing a railroad from Leavenworth south to the boundary with Indian Territory, and another from Atchison through Topeka to the western boundary of the state in the direction of Santa Fe, with a branch down the Neosho Valley to the southern boundary of the state. The railroads would receive from the federal government through the state of Kansas every alternate section of land—the odd numbered sections—for ten sections in width on each side of the track. The grant for the railroad to the Colorado state line would be revoked if the railroad were not completed by March 3, 1873. Pomeroy introduced the legislation, and it passed Congress and was signed by President Lincoln on March 3, 1863.

In recognition of Pomeroy's efforts for the railroad the stockholders elected him president of the company at a meeting in the Chase Hotel in Topeka on November 24, 1863. Also on this occasion, the stockholders voted to change the name of the company to make it more descriptive, and perhaps more romantic. The railway became the Atchison, Topeka and Santa Fe Railroad. Over the next few decades, people in Kansas and the southwest came to refer to the company as the "Santa Fe," while eastern investors and the stock exchanges would call the railroad the "Atchison." Although Holliday's official position was only secretary of the proposed line, he remained the prime mover of the railroad. The stockholders appointed a committee consisting of Holliday, Pomeroy, S. N. Wood and Jacob Safford to sell railroad stock both in Kansas and in the eastern money market. In addition, Holliday, Safford and D. L. Lakin began to lobby the state legislature to accept the federal lands, to grant them to the ATSF, and to pass legislation allowing county governments to float bond issues in support of the proposed railroads.

In a vigorous lobbying effort, Holliday and his cohorts, with a behind-the-scene effort by Pomeroy, persuaded the legislature to receive the federal largess. On February 9, 1864, the state legislature accepted the land grant and voted to allow the railroads to select additional lands within twenty miles of the line in lieu of lands already held by settlers through preemption. This was a significant decision, as much of the land grant in the eastern part of the state had been taken by farmers by preemption. The state agreed to transfer the land to the railroads when the ATSF and the Leavenworth, Lawrence and Fort Gibson Railroad were completed. (The latter line would build the route from Leavenworth south to Indian Territory.) The officials of the Santa Fe achieved another victory on March 1, when the Governor signed a law allowing counties to vote subsidies of up to $200,000 to railroads. Further, on February 23, the Kansas legislature petitioned Congress to donate money and bonds to the ATSF as it had for the Union Pacific Railroad. Arguing that the railroad would open new lands for settlement, improve communications, and aid in national defense, the legislature asked for additional subsidization, but it was never granted.

The supporters of the Santa Fe were heartened by their successes. To aid in their stock promotions they began to publish broadsides describing the venture. A map and brochure of 1864 showed a line from Atchison through Topeka southwest to the vicinity of Fort Dodge, where it followed the Cimarron Cutoff to Santa Fe before continuing west via Albuquerque along the 35th parallel to Los Angeles and Santa Barbara. A western branch extended up the San Joaquin Valley to San Francisco, while a branch in Kansas went south from Fort Riley to Fort Smith in Arkansas. How was this railroad to be constructed? The brochure described the land grant, the possible county subsidies, and quoted a letter from Holliday to Pomeroy describing the 3.5 million acres of fertile farm lands in Kansas to be granted to the railroad and the increasing trade with Santa Fe and California. "The prairies are literally white with 'Prairie Schooners,'" Holliday declared. His optimism proved unwarranted.

Problems beset the scheme and prevented immediate construction activity. Holliday went to New York but was unable to raise funds. Pomeroy's influence in Washington and Topeka had been extremely helpful, but when the senator got into political trouble in the state, the railroad suffered because of his prominent position in the company. Nevertheless, in August 1865,-the ATSF ordered 3,000 tons of iron rails from England at $100 a ton, and hired Major O. B. Gunn to survey the route from Atchison westward. On March 1, 1866, Gunn submitted his maps and figures to Holliday. He estimated the cost of construction from Atchison to Topeka at $11,794 per mile including ties, not a great variance from Holliday's earlier guess of $10,000 per mile. Pomeroy and Holliday hired stock agents in the East to sell the company's securities, but to no avail, and the order for rails was voided. The senator and the promoter panicked and made another appeal to Congress. In June 1866, Pomeroy introduced an amendment to the land grant act of 1863, which would have allowed the ATSF to use railless steam traction engines pulling wagons over the route, and reduced the grant from ten sections on either side of the line to six. This scheme received no support in Congress, and it indicates the depth of the financial difficulties faced by the ATSF.

From 1866 until the autumn of 1868, Holliday, Pomeroy and other ATSF officers made numerous trips to Boston, New York, Washington and Philadelphia seeking funds to initiate construction. Their efforts were unsuccessful until they were able to give potential investors some guarantee that the scheme was viable. That guarantee came in the form of county bonds and, more importantly, land. In 1867 the county commissioners of Shawnee County (Topeka) called an election for a $250,000 bond issue to subsidize the railroad. The voters defeated the bond question. Holliday then canvassed the county, selling the residents on the economic benefits the railroad would bring. At a second election in July 1867, the bonds were approved by a vote of 603 to 397, and the commissioners were authorized to issue twenty-year, 7 percent bonds to purchase stock in the project. Using the same house-to-house technique, Holliday subsequently persuaded the voters of Atchison, Osage and Lyons counties to issue bonds in amounts ranging from $150,000 to $200,000. Holliday and Judge Safford returned to New York with the news of this local support, and in May 1868, Holliday reported that construction would start in sixty days. The bonds were helpful in raising funds, but Santa Fe securities became marketable only after the company had acquired an additional 340,000 acres of Kansas farm land.

Once again Senator Pomeroy proved to be a valuable partner in the enterprise. Pomeroy, a member of the Senate from 1861 to 1873 and the model for Mark Twain's Senator Dilworthy in *The Gilded Age*, had a long history of involvement in questionable deals and would later be denied a third term by the Kansas legislature when charged with bribery. But his intervention in 1868 saved the ATSF. Just west and north of

Topeka was the Potawatomie Indian Reservation. A portion of this fertile, well-watered tract known as the Potawatomie Reserve Lands had been sold by the Commissioner of Indian Affairs to the Leavenworth, Pawnee and Western Railroad. That company failed to exercise its option to buy, and the lands again became available. The Atchison entered into discussions with the Potawatomies and the commissioner, negotiating a treaty whereby the railroad agreed to purchase nearly 340,000 acres of the reserve for one dollar per acre. The treaty had to be ratified by Congress. Representative Sidney Clarke of Kansas fought approval of the sale because of the extremely low price. Senator Pomeroy led the fight for ratification, however, and on July 25, 1868, the treaty was approved. The railroad, with six years to pay for the lands, was charged only 6 percent interest on the unpaid balance. The Potawatomie lands proved to be crucial in the early financing of the ATSF. While its original land grant was much larger, and eventually more valuable, the Potawatomie lands were in a well-settled area and could be sold more readily. These lands, and the county bonds, gave the incipient railroad financial credibility.

On August 7, 1868, the railroad contracted to purchase 338,766 acres of the reserve and D. L. Lakin became the company's first land commissioner. Placed on the market at prices ranging from $1.00 to $16.00 per acre, the land brought an average price of $4.41. Lakin offered to sell the land for only 20 percent in cash as a down payment with the balance to be paid in five years in equal installments. Discounts for cash sales were also made. Lands not immediately sold became security for future bond issues and the basis for acquiring financial support in the East. Pomeroy and his brother-in-law purchased considerable land at $1.00 per acre as did several directors of the ATSF. The settlers of the Potawatomie Reserve were being asked to fund the cost of building the railroad, and to many, this land sale came to represent the injustices of federal land policy.

The *Topeka State Record* of October 7 published a letter to the editor by Holliday, who was then in New York City. Holliday announced that the Santa Fe would be built by Dodge, Lord and Company of Cincinnati, which had been attracted neither by the original land grant nor by the county bonds, but by the Potawatomie Reserve. Construction, he wrote, was imminent: "The child is born and his name is 'Success.' Let the Capital City rejoice. The Atchison, Topeka & Santa Fe Rail Road will be built beyond a preadventure. Work will commence immediately."[5]

Some residents of Topeka probably smiled as they read the colonel's letter, for only a few months earlier he had made the same kind of declaration, but no track had been built. On October 12, 1867, George Washington Beach of New York had signed a contract to build the railroad from Parnell Junction, six miles west of Atchison, to the western boundary of the state. Residents and journalists of Kansas greeted the news ecstatically. Beach agreed to obtain the right-of-way, locate, build and construct the line, and, in return, he would receive the land grant, all county bonds, and a mortgage on the railroad. Additionally, as the line was constructed, he would be given capital stock in the company. Although Beach had some backing from several sources, particularly Dodge, Lord and Company, he failed to raise the necessary funds.

Undaunted by this failure, Holliday, Lakin and Safford contacted Dodge, Lord and Company directly and persuaded the firm to send T. J. Peter, one of their executives, to Kansas to look over the route and company lands. Peter came in April, convinced the trip was pointless; but he soon agreed that the project was not only feasible but very promising. Peter, H. C. Lord, General A. E. Burnside of Rhode Island and Henry Keyes of Boston formed a construction company, Atchison Associates, which purchased the Beach contract and agreed to build the line. Lord then succeeded Pomeroy as president of the ATSF after a brief interregnum during which William F. Nast served as acting president. A lawyer and railroad promoter, Lord had rejuvenated several lines in the Midwest, and, with Peter, got the ATSF moving. On September 26, Holliday wrote to his beloved Mary from New York to tell her the good news. He was off to Washington to obtain land certificates from the Interior Department, but Peter was leaving that night for Topeka to initiate construction.

Thomas J. Peter proved to be a most valuable addition to the Atchison management. The company's first Chief Engineer and Superintendent, Peter engaged in a whirlwind of activity as he rushed from New York and Cincinnati, where he raised funds and ordered rails and equipment, to Topeka, where he conducted surveys, hired men and organized his construction crews. A former city engineer in Cincinnati, Peter had considerable railroad experience. A tall, heavyset man with a receding hairline and a walrus mustache, he knew how to work men and had the courage and ability to construct the ATSF. He neither smoked, chewed nor drank, but was capable of the longest and most delicious profanity to be found on the Kansas prairies. His method of operation was simple; he carried all the engineering data in his head—grades, lines and tangents—and subordinates who failed to carry out his verbal orders became victims of his colorful vocabulary. Assistant Chief Engineer John R. Ellenwood, himself a forceful figure, surveyed the line from Atchison through Topeka, and he and his assistant, Fred Lord, began to survey south of Topeka on September 30, 1868. The *Weekly Record* of October 28 carried a notice from Atchison Associates advertising for 500 workmen to be paid $1.75 per day to initiate construction of the railroad.

Senator Edmund G. Ross spoke briefly to a small crowd of Topeka citizens gathered on Washington Street between Fourth and Fifth on October

The Topeka Depot. Kansas State Historical Society

treasurer of the ATSF, was a wood-burning 4–4–0 built in 1869 by the Rhode Island Locomotive Works and sold to the Santa Fe for $11,500. The 60-inch drivers on the "Holliday" gave that locomotive power to move a considerable number of cars of construction materials or coal, but the lightweight "Burnside" could manage only four or five cars. Nevertheless, the ATSF began to operate two mixed trains daily from Topeka to the end-of-track.

Following the Wakarusa picnic in April 1869, Peter's construction crews progressed southwestward. Once Criley completed the bridge across the Kaw, rails, ties, spikes and other materials flowed rapidly to the end-of-track. On May 1, the company issued a timetable showing two trains daily, except Sunday, from North Topeka to Burlingame, where connections were made with Barlow, Sanderson & Company's stage line to Emporia. The train trip took two hours and thirty-five minutes, but it beat walking, riding a horse or the stagecoach. The timetable was premature by several months. When the track crossed the Shawnee County line, however, the ATSF received the bonds approved by the Shawnee County voters and work continued toward Carbondale and Emporia. Grading work, which had been subcontracted, moved forward as men and teams hacked through the rolling hills south of Topeka. With picks and shovels they made deep cuts in the hills and threw up earthen embankments across depressions. Most of

30. They had come to see the first spadeful of earth turned o1
Fe. Senator Ross described the ten-year-long struggle to buil
road, and he took great pride, he told the crowd, in having beer
from the outset. Colonel Holliday, never at a loss for words, follo
and prophesied the beginning of a giant railroad to the Pacific a1
Gulf of Mexico. Actually, the first construction would be from
southwest to Carbondale, the site of large coal deposits.

The decision to begin construction from Topeka rather than from
son came about pragmatically. The Kansas Pacific Railway hac
completed from Kansas City to Topeka along the northern bank
Kaw River, so a connection to eastern lines existed and the KP
be used to bring in construction supplies and equipment. The coal r
southwest of Topeka suggested an immediate commodity of conside1
economic value, which not only would generate traffic but would en
the ATSF to expand both to the West and east to Atchison. The railr
might be ultimately headed for San Francisco or Galveston or Santa
but Carbondale loomed as the immediate target.

In the late fall of 1868, Peter's crews began to construct a bridge ov
the Kaw River in Topeka to connect with the KP. Two pile drivers wer
at work placing eight to ten piles each day. Simultaneously, grading crew
prepared ten miles of roadbed south toward Burlingame. D. E. "Jersey"
Hogbin and J. D. Criley supervised the bridge crews and the pile drivers
borrowed from the KP. Through the winter, teams of oxen pulled huge
timbers to the site. On March 30, 1869, the bridge with its two 150-foot
Howe trusses opened; the 1,400-foot-long bridge cost $50,000.

By March, rails and ties had been brought in over the KP, and Peter's
crews spiked the first seven miles of 56-pound iron rail in place on oak
and walnut ties. The trains over the first few miles of the ATSF were
pulled, or pushed, by locomotive Number One, the "Cyrus K. Holliday,"
a 4-4-0 coal burner. Number One had been constructed by the Niles
Machine Works of Cincinnati for the Ohio and Mississippi Railroad, a
6-foot gauge railway, but when the Santa Fe purchased the locomotive,
the wheels were altered to fit the 4-foot 8½-inch standard gauge track of
the new Kansas line.[6] The locomotive came to North Topeka over the
Kansas Pacific, and on May 30, 1869, engineer George Beach brought her
over the Kaw River bridge and into Topeka with five flatcars loaded with
iron rails. The equipment of the Atchison consisted of the "Holliday," a
used coach purchased from the Indianapolis & Cincinnati Railroad, twelve
flatcars built by Barney and Smith of Dayton and a handcar. Later in 1869,
the ATSF purchased 24 coal cars to haul that commodity from Carbondale, 12 boxcars, another coach, a baggage car, and a second locomotive,
the "General Burnside." The new freight cars were built by Barney &
Smith, while "General Burnside," named for the Civil War hero and

the men were untrained and had no previous railroad experience. Even track-laying foreman Leonard Blood had to be shown by some of the crew how to cut the rails to lay a switch in the line.

The "Holliday" and the "Burnside" brought supplies to Criley and Blood and their crews, but the locomotives operated under serious handicaps. Twelve miles out of Topeka they had to take water at Wakarusa Creek and then run up a short grade to reach Burlingame. This meant backing up from the creek and making a run for the hill; sometimes they didn't make it. The "Holliday" had to be loaded with coal by a bucket brigade, but the "Burnside," when it ran out of wood, could be fed cow or buffalo chips. Clearly, the locomotives were overtaxed, and on May 22, the "Holliday" burst a valve ten miles from Topeka, forcing the workmen to walk into town after a hard, twelve-hour day.

As additional miles of track were laid the newspaper editors and residents of the towns south of Topeka became more enthusiastic about the ATSF, and Colonel Holliday and D. L. Lakin traveled through the area soliciting trade and financial support. The editor of Burlingame's *Osage Chronicle* noted that "The 'Colonel Holliday's' whistle can be heard distinctly when the wind is favorable, and the music thereof accelerates one's spirits and sends the blood tingling to the end of the toes."[7] Simultaneously, the Topeka press reported the construction by the ATSF of a large depot and a shop building, which had produced a modest boom in the town's land market. The arrival of additional passenger equipment allowed the ATSF to turn each train into an excursion, with newspaper men particularly welcomed to ride to the end-of-track to see the progress of the company.

Official operation into Carbondale began on July 1, while track work south of this new town continued. The company built a boardinghouse and station at Carbondale and ordered lumber for a depot at Burlingame. The Santa Fe earned $1,685.14 in July, with freight revenues of $745.94 and passenger income of $939.20. The increasing business meant that the railroad had to expand its roster of permanent employees to eight including a conductor, engineer, fireman, two brakemen, a stage agent, express messenger and newsboy William Beach. From their "commodious" quarters in the Topeka depot the railroad officers directed the operation of this work force.

By September, grading to Burlingame had been completed and residents of the town planned a "blow out" for the 17th to welcome the first train. Editor Murdoch of Burlingame's *Osage Chronicle* celebrated the arrival of the "Holliday" with a demand that the national capital be moved to his city. "Rival papers, please 'toot'!" he declared.[8] Having completed the line 27 miles into Burlingame, the ATSF crews pushed on.

Locomotive No. 5, the "Thomas B. Sherlock," built in 1870. Santa Fe Railway

Undaunted by a financial scare on Wall Street, the Atchison management signed a contract for grading from Burlingame to Emporia, and Senator Pomeroy and Holliday announced that the line from Topeka to Atchison would be built early in 1870. Peter surveyed both routes in November and went east to purchase rails. On December 31, the company advertised for workmen and teams to begin work on the segment to Emporia.

At the end of the first year of operation, the ATSF could show significant progress in terms of construction and revenues. The coal beds at Carbondale began to produce traffic from open pit and strip mining. The company sold coal in Topeka and used it for firing the "Holliday." The Kansas Pacific signed a contract with the Santa Fe to purchase coal from the Carbondale mines for fifteen years. The ATSF charged ten dollars per car to haul coal to North Topeka, and all agent M. L. Sargent had to do to determine how much the company earned each day was to step out of his office in the depot and count the number of loaded coal cars in the yard. By the end of 1870, coal represented one-third of all commodities carried, including construction supplies, as the line hauled a total of 33,598 passengers and 78,917 tons of freight. Not bad for only six months of revenue operation. But despite these figures and the real estate booms in Topeka, Burlingame and Emporia, the financial problems of the Atchison intensified. In late 1869 and early 1870, however, control of the company shifted, resulting in a new infusion of money and enthusiasm.

Atchison Associates was in trouble; formed in September 1868 to build the ATSF, the firm simply ran out of money. Atchison Associates had issued 48 shares of $10,000 par stock with 40 shares to be subscribed immediately. When General Burnside reported that payments were late, two of the associates, Henry Keyes and Emmons Raymond, borrowed money on personal notes to make up the deficit. Peter accepted securities as payment for his construction work during the early months of 1869, reselling the bonds, but sale of the notes became increasingly difficult. The members of Atchison Associates from Cincinnati could not find the cash necessary to fund expansion of the line, and financial control shifted to Boston. The new leaders of the railroad were Henry Keyes, Charles and Carlos Pierce, and the Nickerson family. These men and their financial allies, particularly Kidder, Peabody and Company, tried to rectify the financial chaos created by Atchison Associates.

The associates had sold $960,000 in common stock, $150,000 in Shawnee County bonds, $192,000 in ATSF first mortgage bonds and $768,000 in Potawatomie Land bonds. Although all the bonds paid 7 percent interest and the mortgage bonds were 30 years in term and land bonds 10 years, only $955,700 in cash had been raised from the $2,070,500 in securities marketed. In effect, the sales meant that over half of the securities were "watered." Highly speculative issues, ATSF securities could be sold only with large bonuses, making debt servicing very difficult. Atchison Associates signed a contract with the brokerage house of Kidder, Peabody and Company of Boston providing for that firm to sell large blocks of the railroad company's securities, all at a heavy discount. Kidder, Peabody sold $1,350,000 in bonds, but discounted them by one-sixth, and charged a $50,000 commission. Bond purchasers were given a bonus of $200,000, so that only $880,000 in cash was generated. With that debacle, Atchison Associates terminated its contract with the railroad, and the group of Bostonians who had been purchasing a large proportion of the company's securities exercised their financial interest and took over the management of the Santa Fe.

The shift in financial control of the railroad led to a fortuitous change in the management of the Atchison. Henry Keyes proved to be an excellent president though he served only until September 1870. A prosperous merchant, Democratic politician, and president of the Connecticut and Passumpsic River Railroad, Keyes gave the ATSF an executive officer known for his integrity and shrewd business instincts. Keyes moved the headquarters of the ATSF to Boston, where three of the twelve directors resided, as did Charles W. Pierce, the secretary and treasurer. In addition, three of the directors were also directors of Keyes's C&PRRR. Keyes arranged for Kidder, Peabody to become financial agents for the Atchison and for Baring Brothers of London to become the railroad's European agents.

In order to extend the ATSF to Emporia and west to the Colorado boundary, large sums had to be raised, and raised quickly before the land grant expired. Through Kidder, Peabody and Baring Brothers the company issued $6,855,000 in common stock sold at par with a large bonus of bonds; the bonds supported the stock sale. Altogether $9,294,000 in company bonds and $483,000 in county and township bonds were issued. Kidder, Peabody's sales method proved to be much more successful than selling bonds with a stock bonus. The degree of "watering" lessened as the company's stocks and bonds began more nearly to represent actual assets. This conservative method of financing became a hallmark of the railroad for many years.

Ginery Twichell, who succeeded Keyes as president of the ATSF in 1870, maintained the company's reputation of being shrewdly managed. Twichell, a former stage operator in New England and president of the Boston and Worcester Railroad, served as president until 1873 and as a director until 1877. A member of Congress from 1867 until 1873, Twichell gave the ATSF a voice in that body at the same time Pomeroy served in the Senate. Twichell, Francis Peabody and Joseph Nickerson came on the board of directors in 1871 and, with Thomas Nickerson, set the tone for the railroad. Although one study suggests that these men, particularly the Nickersons, had no large design to develop a transcontinental railway, the Bostonian coterie running the ATSF began an immediate expansion program, and for a few months changed the name of the company to the National Pacific Railway. For over twenty years this New England bloc of basically "developmental" investors sought to create a rail network in the Southwest as a long-range source of economic return. They would seek "opportunistic" investments in land and other railroad auxiliary enterprises, but their view of the Atchison remained largely "developmental."[9]

The first evidence of this new influx of capital came in February 1870, when T. J. Peter completed the survey from Burlingame to Emporia and issued contracts for grading the route. With material and labor costs reaching over $40,000 per month, Peter and Criley drove their crews across the Kansas prairie. Rails from Pittsburgh arrived at the North Topeka interchange to be rushed south to the end-of-track. The pace set by Peter and Criley pushed the management and workers of the company to exhaustion. In Topeka the staff doubled and tripled their functions, with the chief clerk, for example, acting as paymaster, janitor and freight agent. The hours were long, but the wages were good. Santa Fe payrolls represented one of the few sources of cash in Kansas and became increasingly significant to the state's economy. No overtime, no paid vacations, but as the

Ginery Twitchell, the sixth president of the ATSF. Santa Fe Railway

track crews sang, "Its work all day for damn sure pay on the Atchison, Topeka and Santa Fe."

On July 20, Peter's crews reached Emporia. They built the line quickly, cheaply and poorly; the rails were light, and the roadbed lacked ballast. The employees of the company solicited traffic from unpainted wooden depots, but the line was open. The residents of Emporia greeted the ATSF without wild enthusiasm; after all, the Missouri, Kansas and Texas railroad had been there since December 7, 1869. Reaching Emporia was significant for the Santa Fe because access to the cattle trade of the town was gained, and freight schedules were arranged to accommodate this traffic. Not until September 14 did Emporia officially welcome the ATSF, when a large picnic awaited the two hundred travelers who came to the festivities from Topeka on a special train of five passenger cars. Tom Anderson of the Kansas Pacific did not scoff so much when Colonel Holliday gave his usual grandiloquent speech to the throng.

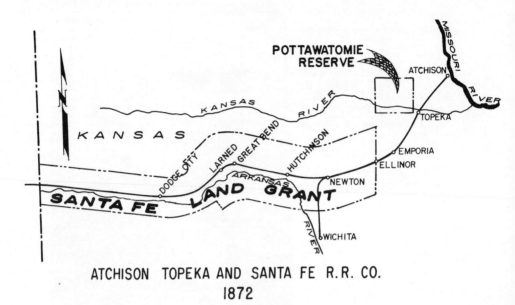

ATCHISON TOPEKA AND SANTA FE R.R. CO.
1872

Atchison, Topeka and Santa Fe Railroad, 1872

In the fall of 1870 a large order of iron rails from Wales arrived at St. Louis, to be delivered to Emporia in January for further construction westward. This news sparked an angry response from the people of Atchison. That city, after all, was to have been the major terminus of the line, and yet all construction was to the west, not the east. Atchison wanted cheaper freight rates, and wanted them immediately, but the directors of the ATSF decided that Atchison would have to wait. The cattle trade, then monopolized by the Kansas Pacific, presented the greatest profit potential in the area. If the Santa Fe could be extended south and west to intersect the cattle drives first, then this trade could be seized from its rival. Tempers flared in Atchison, but limited funds prevented the ATSF from building in both directions simultaneously, at least in the fall of 1870.

Expenditures for construction rose, as did outlays for equipment. Four more locomotives were purchased and named for Tom Peter, Thomas Sherlock, Thomas Nickerson and Joseph Nickerson—the last three being members of the board. Additional flat, coal, box and passenger cars arrived to carry the increasing business. Even though 1870 saw the first serious accidents when a tender axle broke, derailing two cars, and when a train backed into a cow at Burlingame, the road prospered. In the last five months of 1870 gross receipts of $126,960 less expenses provided revenues twice that needed to pay interest on the mortgage.

Kidder, Peabody quickly heralded the good news. A circular advertising the railroad's securities declared that the sixty-two miles of track from Topeka to Emporia had been built "in the most thorough manner." The Atchison could pay 7 percent interest on $28,000 of securities per mile, but was limited by its charter to $15,000 per mile. The remarkable earnings indicated even higher profits in the future as the ATSF would soon be extended west to tap the great cattle trails from Texas and Indian Territory. The vast land grant of the Atchison covered a "healthy and attractive" territory, and land grant bonds at $7,500 per mile of track were also available. Kidder, Peabody asked $850 plus accrued interest for ATSF bonds, which were, the broker declared, a "very safe investment." Rand, Avery and Frye, another investment house, published a pamphlet in 1871 with similar statements. It noted that four of the six members of the Atchison's executive committee lived in Boston, as did both members of the finance committee. Iron rails were stockpiled in Emporia to build the line west to Florence, according to the pamphlet, and new construction would, like that built previously, be of the highest quality. The pamphlet described the area of Kansas traversed by the Santa Fe in glowing terms, and praised the growth of the towns along the route. Both brokerage firms saw increasing potential in sales of Atchison securities.

New England and England were the primary markets for ATSF stocks and bonds in the early 1870s. Stock in the ATSF usually sold at par with a bond and/or note bonus. The Atchison received $6,855,000 in cash for 68,550 shares of stock with bonuses of $5,787,000 in 7 percent first mortgage bonds, $2,960,000 in 7 percent land bonds, $531,000 in long-term 7 percent notes, and $502,000 in county and township bonds. The cash derived from the sale enabled the Santa Fe to build west from Emporia to the Kansas-Colorado state line and from Topeka east to Atchison. A crash construction program would see the railroad grow from 62 miles in length to 469 miles, with a branch 28 miles long. For the next two years Peter, Criley and their crews performed heroically as they pushed the ATSF across the plains.

On November 29, 1870, the ATSF signed contracts to build the line from Atchison to Topeka. The decision by the Bostonian directors, now convinced that the ATSF could no longer afford to turn over its business to the rival Kansas Pacific at North Topeka, delighted the people of Atchison. The ATSF needed additional eastern connections, and in Atchison links could be made with the Hannibal and St. Joseph, the Chicago, Rock Island and Pacific, the Chicago, Burlington & Quincy, and the Pacific Railroad (later the Missouri Pacific). The ATSF would have three options for routing traffic to Chicago, and gain access to a through route to St. Louis. Atchison residents welcomed the news, but work did not commence until 1871, when Alonzo A. Robinson joined the ATSF and began to build from Atchison westward to Grasshopper Falls, and George B. Lake took charge of the crews building from North Topeka east to Grasshopper Falls. Materials for Robinson's men came up the Missouri River to Atchison, while Lake received rails and other materials from the Kansas Pacific at North Topeka. Engineer John Fagan took locomotive Number Seven and a construction train to Robinson at Atchison via the Kansas Pacific to Lawrence, from Lawrence to Leavenworth over what is now the Union Pacific and from Leavenworth to Atchison over the Missouri Pacific. Throughout 1871 grading work continued, but no rails were laid until November.

With a letter in the *Champion* T. J. Peter answered complaints from Atchison residents about the company's inactivity. Peter explained that the long delay was a consequence of English rails being held up in New Orleans. Peter pleaded for patience; the ATSF would arrive soon. Construction took longer than planned because of the delayed rail shipment and because of the several large bridges and masonry culverts which had to be built. By March, rails were being spiked in place and construction of a depot and small shop in Atchison commenced. Robinson's crew met Lake's track layers at Grasshopper Falls in April, and the first through train moved over the line May 13, 1872. The crews were in "high spirits," and all went well as the train proceeded from Atchison to Topeka; but the next day heavy rains washed out three bridges, blocking the eastbound train from Topeka. The line soon reopened, however, and the management rewarded Robinson for his efforts by making him the railroad's Chief Engineer, promoting Peter to the position of Superintendent and General Manager.

As early as the summer of 1870, Peter had dispatched survey crews west from Emporia toward Fort Dodge. At Peter's request, former Governor Samuel J. Crawford asked General John Pope to provide the surveyors with an escort of infantry because of hostile acts by the Indians in the area. The troops guarded the crews as they ran two lines, one west from Wichita, taking a shorter route, and the other west from Newton, following the "great bend" in the Arkansas River. The latter survey, though longer in mileage, would provide lower grades and reduce the cost of construction and future operations. The management selected the longer route for these reasons, not, as critics would later charge, to increase the size of the land grant. From Fort Dodge west the survey followed the river through a flat country where large fills and cuts were unnecessary. By the end of the year the survey crews located the line, and Peter ordered construction materials and hired track gangs.

On December 15, construction west of Emporia commenced. One hundred flatcars of iron rail passed through Burlingame in three days during January, and bridges for the new line began to accumulate in the Topeka

Newton Station in 1871. Kansas State Historical Society

shop. Track layers moved south and west past Cottonwood Falls toward a new railhead in Sedgwick County to be named Newton. There a large cattle yard would be opened to attract herds from the Chisholm Trail. To handle the cattle, fifty stock cars arrived in Topeka with fifty more in transit. Superintendent Peter and Engineer Robinson pushed their crews through the spring of 1871 when over 500 men were engaged in building the line. Simultaneously other crews tore up the old light-weight rails on the Topeka-Emporia track, replacing them with new, heavier English iron. In July the line from Newton to Emporia opened—78 miles of new track—and Criley's men received a brief respite.

The Santa Fe's expansion program began to yield fruit. The Emporia depot alone took in $36,000 during December 1870. As the track crossed three more county lines bonds voted by the counties were given to the railroad in exchange for company stock. The railhead at Newton immediately became the scene of vast herds of cattle moving into town to be loaded on the new stock cars and shipped east to Atchison. By August 1871, two passenger trains each way plied the rails from Topeka to Newton, taking 7½ hours for the trip; stages from Newton took passengers on to Wichita and southwestern Kansas. Yet, despite the progress made, much work remained to be done. If the ATSF was to receive its land grant, 330 miles of track had to be laid from Newton to the Kansas-Colorado state line before March 3, 1873. Chances of making this deadline were considered slight, and so the management requested that Representative Twichell and Senator Pomeroy introduce legislation in Congress to extend the deadline. The proposal received "very cold comfort" in the House of Representatives, as only sixty members voted to suspend the rules to allow debate on the matter. Almost solid Democratic opposition doomed the scheme. Although money became harder to raise, and at least $5,000,000 was needed, construction west of Newton began in the spring of 1872.

Kansas west of Newton consisted of wild, uninhabited prairie known only to Indians, buffalo, trail drivers and the soldiers at Fort Dodge. Robinson followed the easy grades of the survey across the prairie, and Criley used his vast repertory of profanity to urge his Irish crews forward. The 33 miles to Hutchinson opened on June 17, and 74 miles more to Larned on August 12. By September 19 an additional 60 miles of track brought the crews to wild Dodge City. Criley's crews were laying track at a rate of more than a mile per day.

The track gangs of the Santa Fe demonstrated extraordinary endurance. They worked with simple tools and teams of horses, performing hard labor for many hours. Brawn was more important than brains for most tasks, and muscle power largely built the line. Veterans of both armies of the late Civil War and young farm boys drove teams of horses and mules with plows to break the prairie sod, while scraper gangs cut and filled the roadbed. Most of the men slept in tents or shacks built of scrap lumber, and some tents housed as many as a hundred workers. A diet of beans, salt pork, bread and sorghum and sometimes buffalo steaks provided the energy needed for their work. Sunday dinner, prepared by the women cooks hired by the boarding contractors, consisted of dried fruit, store bread, and buffalo meat. Hunters hired by the ATSF shot and butchered the great beasts who roamed the area in vast herds. On Saturday nights the men drifted into the local towns and often into trouble. Sunday was spent in sobering up and mending and washing clothes. The company pay-car moved up and down the line with the payroll, and Pete Criley knew that there would be no work performed the day after the men received their wages of $2.00 per day. The construction camps moved every five to ten miles, attracting a retinue of gamblers and prostitutes. The Indians generally left the camp alone, coming in only at night to steal tools. Sometimes they roamed the track burning bridges or cutting the telegraph line, but the presence of troops at Fort Dodge warded them away. The greatest physical danger for the crews were the Texas Cowboys with whom they fought over rotgut whiskey and painted women in the tent saloons. The most Criley could get from his men on Monday was one-half a mile of track, but that was enough.

End of track west of Dodge City in 1872. Kansas State Historical Society

As the crews raced against the deadline, little could be done by the railroad other than to lay track. Towns sprang up as the line progressed, many of the sites developed by the company, but railroad facilities were meager at best. A few stations were built, but only the stock pens received much attention. Nevertheless, the towns flourished. Within a few weeks Hutchinson boasted five stores with twenty other buildings under construction. The booming economy of Great Bend made money for the Santa Fe and for local speculators, but the town grew regardless of the exorbitant prices demanded for lots. The "iron horse," declared the *Daily Commonwealth* of Topeka, was bound for the Pacific through the richest land in the nation, and the towns along the line were destined to prosper.

Robinson, Peter and Criley suffered several serious setbacks as their men laid the track for the "iron horse." An entire shipload of rails from England was lost at sea when the vessel sank. Cold weather stayed late in the spring of '72 and arrived early that fall. Grades could not be cut through frozen sod, and when the plows refused to move, the crews placed ties on the unturned earth. Although the management of the ATSF and the press repeatedly stated that the railroad represented the highest quality of construction, this was simply untrue. However, the Santa Fe did enlarge its Topeka facilities and the staff of the office increased in size, and, even more indicative of the rapid expansion, a large increment of locomotives and cars was purchased in 1872.

In the spring several new and handsome locomotives arrived at Topeka along with new passenger equipment. The *Railway Review* of Chicago on March 16, 1872, carried one of the first lengthy articles written about the Santa Fe in a national railroad publication, and detailed the recent acquisitions of the company. During 1871 the ATSF had purchased 8 locomotives, 8 coaches, 4 baggage cars, 100 stock cars, 100 combination freight cars, 10 boxcars, 50 coal cars and 4 cabooses to bring the equipment roster to a total of 15 engines, 19 passenger cars and 362 revenue freight cars. All the locomotives except the "Holliday" and the "Burnside" were Taunton-built 4–4–0s of several classes. The *Railway Review* described the machine shop, two engine houses, four depots, and three enclosed water tanks with stone foundations erected by the company to service the new equipment. At Newton the company built a hotel and a cattle yard capable of holding 6,000 head of livestock with facilities to load six stock cars simultaneously. The article lauded the efforts of T. J. Peter who had reputedly "built one of the best roads west of the Mississippi."

Peter drove his crews at a faster pace in the summer of 1872 following the opening of the line to Atchison. Robinson's crews were rushed to the line west of Newton, and the shops at Topeka began to prefabricate bridges for the western extension. The weather failed to cooperate throughout 1872, with serious flooding along the Arkansas River in the spring and extreme heat all summer. But the level terrain west of Hutchinson allowed the track gangs to put down two miles of rails each day. On July 16, Peter's crews set a new record when his Irish gangs laid three miles and four hundred feet of track. Ties for the line were easily acquired on

Locomotive No. 11, the "T. J. Peter," built by the Taunton
Works. Santa Fe Railway

this hot, treeless plain as contractors cut the ties in the Rocky Mountains near Fairplay, Colorado, and floated them down the Arkansas River to a boom stretched across that stream near Great Bend. The 805-foot-long boom collected nearly 200,000 ties, as men in small boats followed the ties down the river to prevent lodging. Disaster struck the construction camp on July 28, when the company herder made off with 75 to 100 horses from the camp remuda, but many were recovered by a hastily organized posse. In Ford County the firm of Wiley and Cutler, a grading contractor, subcontracted their work to Bat and Ed Masterson, who completed four miles of grade that summer. The Mastersons soon abandoned railroad work to become notorious for other types of employment in Kansas and Arizona. Track laying moved forward, and the ATSF reached Larned in midsummer. Regular passenger service from Atchison to Larned began, and the train covered 291 miles in 17 hours and 40 minutes. Passengers paid $16.60 for the privilege of riding the full-length of the Santa Fe.

Those passengers who traveled to Larned probably felt that no other village could compete for the title of "meanest town in Kansas," but they should have waited until October to see Dodge City. Located five miles west of Fort Dodge, the community quickly developed a deserved reputation as the worst of the end-of-track tent towns. A few frame houses, two dozen tents, and a few dugouts and adobe houses marked the location of Dodge. Nearly every large structure housed a saloon, but the busiest merchant in town was the gunsmith. Pete Criley hustled his crews through Dodge as quickly as possible to get them away from a variety of temptations.

Trouble followed the ATSF, however, as additional livestock were lost to rustlers, and a conductor on a passenger train had to engage in a shooting match with a "desperado" to save the U. S. mail. Conditions deteriorated so much that the "good citizens" of Newton, Dodge City, Larned and Hutchinson asked the state legislature for additional legal protection from "roughs" who drifted into their towns. They also pleaded for an end to "murderous proceedings" being used as a substitute for justice. The management of the Santa Fe concurred in these requests, but neither the U. S. marshalls nor the county sheriffs could cope with crime on the plains.

Undaunted by rustlers and desperados, the crews moved westward through the fall of 1872. By December 19, end-of-track stood only 14 miles from the Kansas-Colorado state line. Through freezing rain, snow and drizzle Peter's men laid track across the frozen ground. In 222 days, these tough laborers had constructed an unparalleled 271 miles of track; on December 22, they reached the state line. The crews celebrated; most became oblivious to the cold, many drifted into the tent saloons and houses of pleasure, and Criley rested for the first time in months. Then the federal surveyors who had followed the progress of the line came to Criley's tent and dropped a bombshell; the state line was still four miles away. Quickly Criley gathered up those of his crew sober enough to work, and some who were not. There were neither rails nor ties in the camp sufficient to build the four miles so a locomotive and flatcars went back down the line to gather both, even tearing up sidings to get the rails. With a skeleton crew and a makeshift construction train the four miles of track were laid and the tent city moved to the new terminus.

On December 28, Criley wired Topeka:

> We send you greetings on completion of the road to the state line. Beyond us lie fertile valleys that invite us forward and broad plains lie away in the distance, dotted with mingling herds of bison and cattle, awaiting a further advance. The mountains signal us from their lofty crests and still beyond the Pacific shouts "amen." We send you three cheers of past success, and three times three for that which is yet to come.[10]

The Pacific would have to wait. The management ordered Criley to build to a small trading settlement a few miles into Colorado—Granada—and stop. The Atchison had no more money.

Despite the completion of the railroad to the state line, thus winning the land grant, the company was in trouble. The first *Annual Report*, dated March 31, 1873, showed 497 miles of track, 38 locomotives, 22 passenger cars, 755 freight cars and 255 cars for construction, and net earnings of $423,803. Not only had the railroad run out of cash, but the national economy was about to enter the first massive depression since 1837. The Atchison had developed a huge floating debt of $486,000 by 1873 with no money to pay the interest. Selling 7 percent bonds at a 50 percent discount generated enough cash to pay the interest and retired the floating debt; the price of rapid expansion proved to be very high. Thomas Nickerson arranged a compromise agreement with bondholders whereby a year's interest was deferred; he told them if they refused to accept the delay the company might fail. The Atchison's financial position would remain desperate for two years, and thus Granada remained the end of the line in the West.

Cyrus Holliday, T. J. Peter, the Nickersons and the newspapers of Kansas kept the faith during those two long years. Survey crews worked from Granada to Pueblo, and the company quietly put money aside for future expansion. The editor of Topeka's *Daily Commonwealth* spoke for them all on December 29, 1872:

The road cannot remain on the prairie in the Arkansas Valley, but must be pushed on to a profitable terminus in the cattle regions of southern Colorado, and the silver mines of the territory. It is our opinion, based on our knowledge of the enterprise and resources of the company, that the A.T. & S.F. road will not be completed until it is stopped by the waves of the Pacific, and has been made the fair weather trans-continental route of the nation.[11]

The editor saw the financial problems, but this failed to dim his faith in the ultimate destination of the Santa Fe. Expansion, he agreed, must wait until the line proved profitable. Texas steers and Kansas wheat would provide the ATSF with the revenues needed to conquer the mountains of Colorado and New Mexico.

Texas Cows and Colorado Mountain Passes

The management of the Atchison, Topeka and Santa Fe Railroad built the line from Emporia west to the Colorado state line not only to acquire the land grant, but also to seize the Texas cattle trade from the rival Kansas Pacific. Over the Chisholm Trail from Texas north through Indian Territory to Kansas moved thousands of head of Texas longhorns to the cattle pens of the nearest railhead. Although located in the north-central part of the state, Abilene became the first major cattle town in Kansas, and in 1871 over 600,000 cattle were shipped from there. The officers of the Santa Fe decided to build southwestwardly to intersect the herds before they reached the Kansas Pacific. Even before the cattle trade developed, the company did a booming business in buffalo hides and bones as these giants were slaughtered to open the ranges to Texas beeves.

The killing of the buffalo opened the ranges of Indian Territory and western Kansas to the cattlemen. The slaughter reigned between 1871 and 1875, when the last great herds were destroyed. The railroad construction crews purchased some buffalo meat from hunters for food, but the professional buffalo hunter profited primarily from selling the hides. Dodge City existed initially not as a cow town but as the center of the buffalo trade, and the town soon filled with hundreds of hunters who cut down the great beasts on a grand scale. The hunters skinned the dead animals and sold the hides in Dodge. Fashion in the East dictated the use of buffalo robes in carriages and sleighs, and the prices commanded for the hides made the hunting quite lucrative. Hides brought from $1.00 to $3.00 each, and a highly skilled skinner could prepare 150 hides a day. Soon the prairies around Dodge were littered with the stenching carcasses of thousands of buffalo. Men in wagons followed the hunters and skinners gathering the bleached bones of the animal skeletons. These too were taken to Dodge where they were shipped east to be ground into fertilizer. One hundred buffalo skeletons produced a ton of fertilizer which could be sold for $8.00. Between 1872 and 1874, the ATSF shipped 459,453 buffalo hides, 2,250,400 pounds of buffalo meat and over 10 million pounds of bones. The station area in Dodge was usually surrounded by piles of bones and hides, and both commodities became significant revenue producers.

The extermination of the buffalo proved highly conducive to the range cattle industry, profitable to the ATSF and, of course, devastating to the Plains Indians. Passengers on Santa Fe trains took great sport in shooting the shaggy buffalo from train windows, and tourists were often taken on hunting trips, but the professional hunters reduced the herds with great efficiency. The Indians, losing their primary source of food and shelter, and appalled by the senseless slaughter, were reduced to dependence upon handouts from the agents of the Indian Bureau. Heedless of the plight of the Indians, the hunters successfully opened western Kansas to the great trail herds from Texas.

The extension of the Atchison west from Emporia brought the railroad its first large-scale cattle business. In the spring of 1871 the ATSF reached a site sixty miles south of Abilene and created the town of Newton. The

Ellsworth, Kansas, in 1879. Santa Fe Railway

trail bosses saw the advantage offered by the new railway—the saving of several days' ride—and Abilene began to die. The Santa Fe built large stock pens, loading docks and a hotel in Newton; and saloons, false-front stores and other buildings rapidly appeared. Sand Creek, which meandered through the town, provided water for the herds, and surrounding the site were hundreds of acres of rich buffalo grass. In the summer and fall of 1871 over 40,000 cattle were shipped east from Newton, which became a notorious "hell hole." Down the one and only street in town the Texas wranglers drove their herds, often entering one of the five major saloons on horseback. A dozen men died in gunfights during that first year. Newton's boom ended, however, when the ATSF decided to build farther west and establish a new railhead, and when T. J. Peter decided to answer the pleas of the residents of Wichita and build a branch line to their town.

The town of Wichita sent a delegation to ATSF headquarters pleading for the railroad to build south from Newton rather than west. When the Boston officers decided not to respond to this request, T. J. Peter initiated the project himself. Using his own funds, Peter formed a railroad company, the Wichita and Southwestern, to build from Newton to Wichita. Hoping to encourage Peter, the voters of Sedgwick County approved a $200,000 bond issue to support the first railway to reach Wichita. Aided by Cyrus K. Holliday, Peter organized the railroad on June 22, 1871, and the Sedgwick voters on August 11 approved a bond issue specifically for the Wichita and Southwestern. In May 1872 the railway reached Wichita and a wild celebration ensued. Abilene and Newton were both eclipsed.

Peter's branch line was a creature of the Santa Fe from the outset, and it was soon absorbed by the larger company. The ATSF hired Abel H. "Shanghai" Pierce, a major cattle trader, as its general livestock agent, and on June 8, the first 18 carloads of cattle left Wichita for Atchison. During the first year of operation, over 70,000 head of livestock passed through the Wichita stock pens. The Santa Fe cooperated with the merchants of the town to entice cattle drivers and buyers to use the new line. Cattleman Peyton Montgomery was hired by the ATSF to ride out from Wichita to meet the trail herds and to persuade them to come to Wichita. Montgomery rode down into the Cherokee Strip and soon diverted significant herds to the large stockyard located on the west side of the Arkansas River in Wichita. The town grew to 2,000 souls, and few communities could compete with Wichita's thriving cattle business.

When the Santa Fe built west from Newton, several towns served as temporary cattle markets as the buyers followed the march of the railhead. The railroad encouraged the cattlemen by depositing money in local banks to pay for their expenses. That policy ended when the ATSF deposited $50,000 in a bank in Great Bend which promptly folded. Undaunted, the railroad advertised its services far and wide, even taking a page in Joseph G. McCoy's classic study of the cattle trade. The advertisement stressed the "first class" character of the railroad and its large stock pens and scales at Newton, Great Bend and Wichita. The rates, the ATSF claimed, were always the same to Atchison, Leavenworth or Kansas City.

Certainly the cattle buyers, the trail herders and the packing plants must have appreciated the impact of the extension of the Santa Fe upon railroad rates. While the Kansas Pacific exercised its monopoly over the cattle trade, it charged $100 per carload from Abilene to St. Louis and $150 to Chicago. The ATSF cut rates drastically, and in 1872 charged only $30 per car from Wichita to Kansas City and $100 to Chicago. Both railroads engaged in a series of rate reductions which cut shipping costs even further. The ATSF decided that the only way to permanently block the Kansas Pacific was to locate its principal cattle operation farther west beyond Wichita. When a cattle quarantine law went into effect near Wichita in 1877, the ATSF shifted its interests to Dodge City.

Before 1876, Dodge City had been a minor shipping point, not as significant as either Newton or Great Bend. In 1876–1877, the railroad constructed large cattle pens in Dodge and in the first year of operation 22,940 head were shipped. The small settlement's population grew as an influx of cattle buyers arrived with cash in hand to purchase the Chisholm Trail herds. Dodge City turned into a "roaring hell" again, much worse than when it had been the end-of-track. Reform attempts failed even when the ATSF lent its support to the efforts. The railroad threatened to revoke the status of the town as a divisional terminus and as a cattle shipping point, but to no avail. The ATSF demanded the closing of businesses and saloons on Sunday, that music be banned from the dance halls, and that gambling houses be restricted, but the demands were met for only a brief time. A tough, wild town with a large and growing Boot Hill cemetery, Dodge boomed with the growing cattle trade. Cowboys shot out locomotive headlights and fired at train crews in the yards, and Sheriff Bat Masterson could do little to protect the railroad crews and property. Conductors on passenger trains out of Dodge carried guns in order to collect fares. When a grizzled old prospector boarded a train west of Dodge the conductor asked where he was going and the old man responded, "Hell." "That's 65¢ and get off at Dodge," the weary conductor declared.

Dodge City taxed the spirit of the railroaders and the ATSF's management, but the town produced considerable revenue and the railroad refused to shift its operations. Other communities, such as Caldwell, south of Wichita, asked the ATSF to extend its line to their town, but the ATSF refused. Located closer to Kansas City and Atchison, Caldwell would have meant a reduced haul, and therefore reduced revenues for the ATSF. Not until 1880 did Caldwell get a branch, and even after the ATSF arrived,

Topeka shops and yard in the early days. Kansas State Historical Society

the town failed to compete with Dodge City. The cattle trade in that community reached a peak in 1884 when 800,000 head of cattle and 3,000 men passed through on their way east. But in 1885 the state of Kansas established a quarantine along the border with Indian Territory. The great trail drives then terminated in the Cherokee Strip or went west to Colorado, and Dodge City lost its business and its glamor and romance. Only 3,000 cars were loaded in 1885: an era had ended.

Between 1871 and 1885, one of the main sources of revenue for the ATSF came from the range cattle industry. The cattle trade helped to balance the company's traffic as most commodities moved from east to west, but the beef moved from west to east. The annual reports of the Atchison in the period show the railroad handling an average of 70–90,000 head each year. Technology, particularly the coming of the refrigerated railroad car, altered the operation. Cattle shipped live suffered a severe weight loss, many died, and the company had to provide feed boxes and water tanks for them. By 1875 the shipment of refrigerated fresh meat began to alter the method of transport, and by the 1880s live cattle were rarely shipped east of Kansas City. The quarantines by Kansas and Colorado against "Texas fever" terminated the long drives, and the harsh winters on the Great Plains reduced most ranching operations to more manageable size.

The cattle trade gave the ATSF an excellent source of income. It neither saved the company nor did it become the main commodity hauled, but in the lean years of the mid-1870s it gave the Santa Fe vitally needed business. Travelers passing through Emporia, Kansas, today can witness the continuing significance of livestock to the ATSF, for there one of the most sizable feedlots in the nation is operated by the railway. In Oklahoma, Texas, New Mexico, Colorado, Arizona and California, like Kansas, company agents actively solicit business from ranchers, feedlot operators and packing houses. These men wear Levi's and Stetson's, but the romance is gone. Only children and oldtimers sing verse 362 of the "The Chisholm Trail":

> So we loaded 'em up on the Santa Fe cars
> and said farewell to the old Two Bars . . .
> Come a-ty-yi-ippi-ippi-ay-ippi-ay
> Come a-ty-yi-ippi-ippi-ay.

Few "Santa Fe cars" rolled beyond Dodge City to the end-of-track in Granada, Colorado, as there was little freight to carry, and only a few passengers took the stagecoach from Granada to Pueblo or Santa Fe. The directors of the ATSF reported on June 26, 1873, that the Colorado and New Mexico Railroad Company had been formed to build west from Granada to Albuquerque and on to the Pacific; but they admitted that any expansion plans depended upon the national economic picture, which was not encouraging. In 1873, Henry Strong succeeded Ginery Twichell as president of the ATSF, and Strong, a Scottish immigrant who had become a successful New England lawyer, negotiated with the owners of the fabulous Maxwell Land Grant in southern Colorado and northern New Mexico for trackage rights across their holdings, but no track was laid. During the year Strong served as president, the ATSF deteriorated. The national recession led to declining profits, and no one wanted to invest in a Kansas railroad which terminated in a miserable Colorado town. Clearly, however, the investors in the ATSF realized that the line had to build westward; but Granada would remain the end-of-track until June 1875. The Nickerson brothers, Thomas and Joseph, recognized the need to build westward, and when Thomas became the new president in 1874, plans to build into Colorado were revived.

Cautious, but expansionist oriented, the Boston management of the ATSF saw the economic potential and necessity of extending the line to Pueblo and to Trinidad. Rich coal fields existed at Trinidad and at Cañon City just west of Pueblo. At Pueblo a connection could be made with General William J. Palmer's narrow-gauge line, the Denver and Rio Grande. The DRG operated from Denver to Pueblo, and there were plans

General William Jackson Palmer of the Denver and Rio Grande. Archives and Public Records, State of Colorado

to build from Pueblo west to Leadville in the silver country and south from Pueblo to Santa Fe. Indeed, Palmer came to Boston and tried to persuade the Nickersons to agree not to build competing lines. Palmer feared that the ATSF, halted only temporarily by the depression of 1873, might cut off the DRG by building to Santa Fe. Neither the ATSF nor its rival, the Kansas Pacific, would make a deal with Palmer. The Nickersons and their allies decided to build the extension from Granada to Pueblo, and the Pueblo and Arkansas Valley Railroad Company was formed to construct the new line.

In the spring of 1875 a vast quantity of rails, ties and other materials accumulated at Granada. The shipments arrived largely unnoticed, as there were no towns along the 130-mile route from Dodge City to Granada—only Jerry O'Loughlin's store located in a 20-by-24-foot dugout where buffalo meat was fed to the few passengers on the ATSF trains. In May, Thomas and Joseph Nickerson and several other directors, engineers A. A. Robinson and George B. Lake and the construction crews gathered in Granada. The Nickersons drove a golden spike to initiate work on the new line, and a reporter from the *Pueblo Chieftain* wired his paper: "The Directors have arrived and their engine is branded 'Pueblo.' . . . Everything is lovely and the goose hangs high."[1]

Work proceeded rapidly up the valley of the Arkansas. Track reached Las Animas on September 13, and a few miles west the crews passed the ruins of Bent's Fort, an important trading post before 1852. On February 16, 1876, the PAV reached La Junta and a confrontation with the Kansas Pacific. As the PAV extended westward, it cut off the cattle trade routes which had run northwestward through Colorado to the Kansas Pacific line between Kansas City and Denver. The KP threatened to build south to La Junta and parallel the PAV into Pueblo. In fact, the KP did build a line from its main stem at Kit Carson south to La Junta. The branch proved unprofitable, and when the ATSF, the DRG and the KP later established traffic agreements dividing up the Colorado business, the track was torn up.

Undeterred by the KP's actions, the ATSF management pushed its subsidiary, the PAV, on up the Arkansas River valley. The PAV crews reached Pueblo on March 7, and the arrival of the first locomotive produced the "biggest drunk of the present century," according to the *Chieftain*. That newspaper screamed in a banner headline: "Look Out For The Locomotive." A two-day-long celebration followed with speeches, a parade, and banquets. The citizenry, jubilant over the termination of the monopoly of the DRG, engaged in "eating, drinking, dancing, and general rejoicing."[2] The only event to mar the jollification was the delay in the arrival of two special trains from the East. A massive snow storm in Kansas sent two locomotives and a snowplow into a ditch at Spearville, and the special trains held up in Larned until the blizzard abated. But the snows melted, the trains came through, and the Santa Fe began to boom its "through" line to the foothills of the Rockies.

The company hired J. G. Pangburn to write *The Rocky Mountain Tourist*, a "puff piece" for tourists describing the wonders of Colorado, the "Switzerland of America." This romantic view of the West described the plains of Kansas, the Garden of the Gods in Colorado Springs, and the mineral baths at Manitou Springs. The glories of the Grand Canyon of the Arkansas River (Royal Gorge) were lavishly depicted. To reach this paradise, Pangburn wrote, were the alternative rail routes to Kansas City, where he urged travelers to take "the land hunters', buffalo hunters', and gold hunters' road"—the Santa Fe. From Kansas City to Pueblo the "Pueblo Mail and Express" roared across the plains in only thirty-one hours. The "splendidly organized force" of the ATSF would aid passengers on the "shortest and best route" to Colorado and New Mexico.[3] Tourism

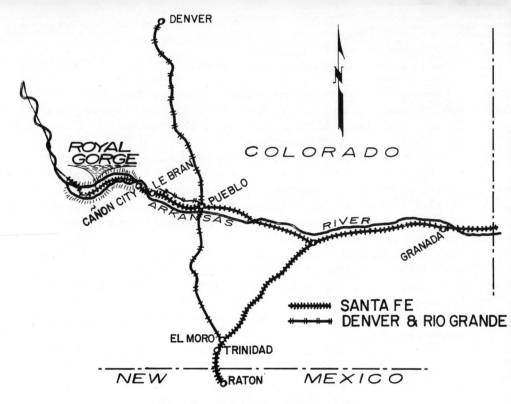

Santa Fe and Denver and Rio Grande

became an immediate source of passenger traffic for the railroad, but the management had larger and more profitable freight trade in mind.

Thomas Nickerson and three other directors arrived in Pueblo on September 6, 1876, and for the next ten days traveled west to Cañon City, over the crest of the Rockies to Lake City and Del Norte, and returned via Alamosa and La Veta Pass to Walsenburg. Sizing up the traffic potential and observing the best routes, the leaders of the Atchison began to formulate plans to enter the mountains. General Palmer panicked. Desperately short of construction funds and realizing the dangers posed by the entry of the ATSF into DRG territory at Pueblo and the KP at Denver, Palmer proposed a two-year contract to divide the Colorado business. In September the three railroads signed the agreement; but to protect himself, Palmer extended the DRG south from Pueblo to El Moro, a DRG townsite only five miles from Trinidad. Trinidadians exploded at this affront, and the few dollars made by the DRG in land sales at El Moro would later cost Palmer's narrow-gauge line dearly. Palmer could not afford to alienate any potential ally, for in 1877 the management of the Atchison hired a new general manager and vice president who would become the nemesis of the DRG.

William Barstow Strong, tenth
president of the ATSF. Santa
Fe Railway

The *Annual Report* for 1877 made the formal announcement that
"Near the Close of the Year the Board elected W. B. Strong, Esq., of
Chicago, Vice President and General Manager of the road. He brings to
your road rare abilities and large experience which cannot fail to be of
great benefit to the Company."[4] This was a gross understatement of the
significance of William Barstow Strong's arrival. Strong came to the Santa
Fe from the Chicago, Burlington & Quincy after having worked for several
midwestern railroads in the twenty-two years after his graduation from
Chicago Business College. Born in Vermont in 1837, but reared in Beloit,
Wisconsin, Strong exemplified the concept of the self-made man and
represented in his conduct and demeanor the virtues of the Protestant
Ethic. Strong would develop the Santa Fe into a major transcontinental
railway before leaving the road in 1889. Dynamic, ambitious, highly competitive, Strong surrounded himself with men of similar attitudes and
complementary skills.

Immediately upon taking over the reins as general manager, Strong
made Albert Alonzo Robinson his right-hand man. Also a native of Vermont who had been raised in Wisconsin, Robinson graduated from the
University of Michigan in 1869 and joined the St. Joseph and Denver City
Railroad. Through a classmate, George B. Lake, Robinson came to the
attention of T. J. Peter who brought him to the Santa Fe in 1871. Pro-

A. A. Robinson, builder of
5,000 miles of track. Santa
Fe Railway

moted to chief engineer during the construction of the line to Dodge City, Robinson began a fabulous career which saw him supervise the construction of over 5,000 miles of railway. A man of unimpeachable integrity and gifted with the ability to select good associates, Robinson became one of Strong's major assets in developing the company. Neither Strong nor Robinson would ever be touched by scandal in the building of the railroad, and their reputations for honesty proved to be a selling point for the management. Strong and Robinson determined that their railroad would expand, that its expansion would not be thwarted, and that the Santa Fe would pierce the Rockies and reach the Pacific Ocean. Colonel Holliday's vision became their own.

The 1877 *Annual Report* also announced that "In accordance with the design of the original projectors of your road the Directors have matured a plan to extend your line into New Mexico, to the vicinity of Santa Fe, in the year 1878, and they trust this movement will be approved and supported by the stockholders of the road."[5] The statement failed to indicate that the directors and the management were not united behind the plan to build south from La Junta along the Santa Fe Trail to Trinidad. Indeed, several of the directors favored building west from Pueblo to the San Juan and Leadville silver districts. The mining companies needed equipment and the towns in the districts desired reduced freight rates on food and supplies. The silver fever even struck Colonel Holliday, who, after a three-week tour of Del Norte and Lake City in June 1878, urged that attention be given to this "remarkable country." In a flamboyant and enthusiastic letter to Nickerson, Holliday praised the area as potentially more profitable than either New Mexico or California.[6] Fortunately cooler judgments prevailed. Thomas Nickerson, the cautious expansionist, also failed to see the urgency of a line to Santa Fe. The wagon traffic to Santa Fe was slight, the major cargo being merchandise, but slowly the ebullient William Barstow Strong and his "advisor," A. A. Robinson, persuaded the Bostonians that the Atchison had to seize and hold Raton Pass, the only practical route into New Mexico. On February 26, 1878, Nickerson allocated $20,000 to initiate construction, and Strong immediately dispatched Robinson to seize Raton Pass.

Company engineers and surveyors had been examining Raton Pass as a potential crossing of the mountains into New Mexico since 1862. Located fifteen miles south of Trinidad, the 8,000-foot pass meandered over the Sangre de Cristo range. In these mountains, called the "snowies" by the fur trappers, only the Purgatoire River and North Raton Creek had carved valleys through the lava masses and coal beds. To the east rose snow-covered Fisher's Peak to a height of 9,600 feet, and to the west stood the Rockies and the twin Spanish Peaks, each over 12,000 feet in elevation. The location of the railroad's right-of-way through the pass was almost as crucial as the actual construction of the line. Fortunately for the Santa Fe, Robinson hired an excellent engineer in the fall of 1877 who located a workable route.

In September 1877, Robinson hired W. R. (Ray) Morley, a former engineer for the DRG and manager of the Maxwell Grant Company. Ray Morley immediately became impressed by his boss, the thirty-three-year-old Robinson, and by their superior, forty-year-old W. B. Strong; it looked like a great outfit for a young man to throw in with. He also liked the sense of adventure and the clandestine nature of his first assignment. Born in Massachusetts in 1846 and orphaned at an early age, Morley grew up in Iowa, where he lived with relatives. After serving in the army during the Civil War, he attended Iowa State University, studying math and engineering. Leaving school at the end of his second year, Morley went west and became a railroad surveyor. For his first ATSF assignment, Morley was sent by Robinson to Raton Pass, an area he knew well, and was cautioned that his work must be in secret. Robinson and Strong feared that any sign of activity there by the Santa Fe would cause General Palmer of the DRG to dispatch men from nearby El Moro to take the pass for the narrow gauge.

To carry out the mission, Morley disguised himself as a Mexican sheep herder, and for several weeks he wandered over the area. When he needed provisions, he stopped at "Uncle Dick" Wootton's house on the wagon toll road over Raton. "Uncle Dick" was one of the foremost living legends in that part of the West. Son of a Virginia planter, Richens Lacy Wootton left home as a boy, traveled west, and became a famous scout and Indian fighter. An associate of Kit Carson and John C. Fremont, a cattleman and sheepman, he made his fortune in 1852 by driving 8,900 sheep from Taos, New Mexico, to Sacramento, California, in 107 days. Returning to New Mexico with $50,000 in gold, "Uncle Dick" built a 27-mile toll road over Raton Pass and constructed a house and hotel at the toll gate. Receiving a charter from the New Mexico territorial legislature, Wootton hacked out the toll road with hand tools, a remarkable feat, particularly as the road crossed the Purgatoire (or Picketwire, as the cowboys called it) 53 times. Barlow and Sanderson stages, wagons from Independence, and trail drivers from Texas used the road. Ray Morley and "Uncle Dick" became good friends, and Morley wrote to Robinson on December 19 that Wootton would sell his toll road to the company for a fair price and that his survey was finished. Morley projected a 2,100-foot tunnel at the summit of the pass, and he urged an immediate reconnaissance survey from La Junta all the way to Albuquerque.

Robinson conveyed Morley's report to Strong, who used it effectively to win Nickerson's endorsement. Although he had earlier favored using the route followed by the Cimarron Cut-off of the Santa Fe Trail south from Dodge City, Robinson became convinced of the economic viability of the Raton Pass line. The large coal fields at Trinidad and at Raton were significant attractions, while the almost total absence of towns limited potential traffic along the Cimarron Cut-off. Strong acted quickly to obtain a railroad charter from the New Mexico territorial legislature to enable the Atchison to enter the territory and build south to Albuquerque and from there west to California and south to El Paso.

Strong, accompanied by Miguel Otero, went to the territorial capital at Santa Fe to obtain the charter. A leading wagon trader and member of one of the territory's prominent families, Otero had excellent contacts in the legislature. He learned that the Southern Pacific Railroad, then entering New Mexico from Arizona near the Mexican border, had agents in Santa Fe trying to block approval of the entry of the Atchison. Seeking to keep the ATSF from building west to California, its private preserve, the Southern Pacific had legislation introduced to require any new railroad in New Mexico to sell at least $1,000 per mile in stock and have 10 percent paid in before construction could proceed. Such a law would have made the New Mexico extension virtually impossible. Otero also learned that a charter could be obtained before the new restriction went into effect. Moving quickly, Strong and Otero produced a charter for the New Mexico and Southern Pacific Railroad Company, a rather strange choice of names, and the charter was approved in February 1878. With the legal problem surmounted, Strong returned to Colorado and ordered Robinson, who was then in Pueblo, to go to Raton Pass and occupy it for the ATSF.

Robinson went to the DRG station in Pueblo and purchased a ticket for El Moro, the closest railroad terminus to the pass. Unfortunately, General Palmer caught wind of the ATSF activity, and when Robinson boarded the train, he found DRG Chief Engineer J. A. McMurtrie also on board with some DRG construction crews. Neither of the engineers acknowledged the presence of the other, and rode south to El Moro. At that DRG townsite, McMurtrie and his men went to the local hotel to spend the night, secure in the knowledge that Robinson had no crew in the area. Robinson, however, hired a buckboard at El Moro and drove to "Uncle Dick's" adobe roadhouse. Robinson told the old scout what the problem was and promised him fifty dollars a month credit for life at the Santa Fe store in Trinidad for the toll road. Angry with the DRG, like most other residents of nearby Trinidad, "Uncle Dick" shook hands on the deal and began to hustle up a makeshift crew for Robinson. When the sun rose at five that morning it shone on Robinson, "Uncle Dick," a handful of men from Trinidad, and some local drifters and cowboys armed with picks and shovels working on the new railroad through the pass. Thirty minutes later, McMurtrie and the DRG crews walked up to find Robinson's men already at work. McMurtrie told Robinson the location was his; the DRG had surveyed this route when the ATSF was still at Wakarusa Creek. Robinson stood firm. McMurtrie then said he knew a better route farther west anyway, and left. The Santa Fe won a major victory.

The destinies of both the ATSF and the DRG were settled by Robinson's midnight buckboard ride. The DRG was effectively blocked from building south, and the ATSF now had two options: to build into New Mexico or west from Pueblo into the Rockies. General Palmer had misjudged Strong's resourcefulness and suffered as a result of his earlier mistreatment of the town of Trinidad. The directors of the ATSF declared that the DRG "retreated" from Raton, but General Palmer was not defeated.

Seizing the route over the pass was one thing, building a railroad over it was something else. From February until the following December, Robinson's crews labored to construct the line from La Junta to Raton. From La Junta to Trinidad the land rose gradually and while some problems were incurred, the first Santa Fe train rolled into Trinidad on September 1. The opening of this 80-mile segment allowed the railroad to bring in heavier equipment to work in the pass itself. From Trinidad to the station called Morley the grade rose 800 feet in 10 miles; from Morley to the summit of the pass, located at the west portal of the tunnel, the grade climbed another 861 feet in 6 miles. Even the 2,000-foot-long tunnel stood over an ascending grade. The small 4–4–0s which the ATSF brought in could not cope with the grades. Robinson then ordered a new, heavier locomotive, from the Baldwin Locomotive Works, a 2–8–0 named "Uncle Dick," which, with its added traction, could pull as much as two of the 4–4–0s. "Uncle Dick" jumped the track constantly the first two weeks it worked the shoofly switchback around the uncompleted tunnel, but eventually the engineers learned how to control the "monster." The switchback stood 7,800 feet in elevation on a 6 percent grade and a curve of 16 degrees, and even the new locomotive could handle only a few freight cars over the pass. On December 7, 1878, the first train entered New Mexico. The tunnel crews met inside the mountain in July, but the switchback remained in use until September when the giant excavation became operative. Even as construction proceeded, Ray Morley surveyed south another 120 miles toward the town of Las Vegas.

Many observers in the East and in the West felt that the Atchison, in its triumph at Raton Pass, had abandoned plans to build westward from Pueblo up the Arkansas River to Leadville, and possibly on to Salt Lake City or Ogden. *The New York Times* had noted a year earlier that such an action could potentially challenge not only the DRG but also the Union Pacific and the Central Pacific, then enjoying a monopoly on the central transcontinental route. Surely, the *Times* suggested, this upstart railroad from Kansas would not challenge the DRG, the UP, the CP, and the Southern Pacific in New Mexico all at the same time. Such a view provided cold comfort to General Palmer. He tried to counter the ATSF by building west from Pueblo 37 miles to the Cañon City mines, but he upset the residents of Cañon City by failing to construct into the town proper. He sent McMurtrie and his crews west across La Veta Pass, and by June 1878 the DRG opened a line to Alamosa. These efforts strapped the DRG. Traffic from Pueblo was being taken away by the ATSF, and the coal and coke trade at El Moro failed to develop. The loss of Raton Pass to Strong and Robinson forced Palmer to act to save his line.

General Palmer and his narrow gauge were "floundering," as the "officials at the Atchison Road hovered about like vultures, waiting for a chance to swoop down upon its weakened rival."[7] Palmer tried to play the Atchison against the Union Pacific and the Kansas Pacific, and in an overtly friendly gesture, proposed a pooling agreement to Thomas Nickerson. Despite this attempt to woo the Santa Fe, Palmer was rebuffed when W. B. Strong insisted on a division of the Colorado traffic highly unfavorable to the ĐRG. Strong even went so far as to suggest that Palmer lease the DRG to the ATSF. Caught in a terrible bind, Palmer attempted to placate both the Atchison, with whom the DRG exchanged traffic at Pueblo, and the KP-UP, with whom traffic was exchanged in Denver. Fearing an open rupture with either line, Palmer evenly split his east-bound tonnage between his major connections. Strong refused to accept this arrangement, and a rate war ensued, with the ATSF taking much of the former DRG business in the Pueblo-Trinidad area. Conditions deteriorated rapidly when the Santa Fe announced that it intended to build west from Pueblo to Leadville and the San Luis Valley and north from Pueblo to Denver. The Santa Fe hinted broadly that this new adventure had the support of its principal eastern connection, the Chicago, Burlington & Quincy, which it did. General Palmer found that his little narrow gauge had been thrust into the center ring of a Trans-Mississippi West railroad war; and William Barstow Strong, who loved a good fight, dragged the reluctant Nickerson into the fray.

The silver booms at Leadville and Silverton promised a handsome traffic, as the isolated and desperate mining towns begged for a railroad connection across the Rockies. The most feasible route, and one surveyed several times by both the Santa Fe and the DRG, lay through the Grand Canyon of the Arkansas River, or the Royal Gorge. Located southeast of Cañon City, the Gorge slashed through the mountains, its sheer rock walls rising 3,000 feet on either side of the 30-foot-wide river channel. A narrow shelf along the river provided enough space for a single track railroad to be built west to the valleys on the other side of the mountains. In building toward Royal Gorge, the DRG line to the coal fields had been constructed seven miles short of Cañon City, and for four years the residents of the town nurtured their grudge against the DRG. At the request of the DRG the town provided $50,000 in cash and $50,000 in real estate as a subsidy to complete the line, but the narrow gauge was extended only to a point three-quarters of a mile from the center of the town. Now the anger of the residents reached a feverish pitch.

In 1876 the people of Cañon City pleaded with the ATSF to construct a railroad paralleling the DRG west from Pueblo. Concentrating their energies elsewhere, Strong and Nickerson politely declined. The citizens of Cañon City then formed their own railroad company, the Cañon City and San Juan Railway on February 19, 1877, and hired H. R. Holbrook of the Santa Fe to make a survey for this incipient enterprise. Holbrook staked a line through the canyon and prepared and filed the plat with the General Land Office in June 1877. Simultaneously, the Leadville boom grew in intensity, and General Palmer's interest in Royal Gorge revived.

Traffic to the silver country moved across the mountains by freight wagon, pack mules and stagecoaches at prohibitive rates. That a railroad could be profitably built in the area seemed evident to Palmer and McMurtrie, who spent over a week in the mining district in the fall of 1877. Then too, Palmer saw a line to Leadville as only a short segment of a longer route west to Utah and a connection with the Central Pacific from California. News of his ambitions or, perhaps, grandiose scheme, reached both the Santa Fe and the Union Pacific. Strong and Nickerson acted to block the extension of the DRG even as the leaders of the narrow gauge moved cautiously to seize Royal Gorge.

In April 1878, Strong watched the movements of Palmer, McMurtrie and the DRG crews, while the rival leaders closely followed the actions of Strong, Robinson and Morley. Strong's line of communication with the Cañon City and San Juan Railway, an ally of the ATSF if not an affiliate, consisted of a telegraphic code which Palmer's agents broke. Knowing that the Santa Fe crews were busy at Raton Pass, on April 16 Palmer ordered McMurtrie to entrain his crews at El Moro, move them to the end-of-track at Cañon City, and build rapidly into Royal Gorge. A. A. Robinson observed McMurtrie loading his construction train and notified Strong, who ordered Morley, then at La Junta, to get to Cañon City first and organize the CCSJ men into action before McMurtrie got there. Knowing that the DRG agents were listening to ATSF messages, Morley quietly put a construction train together and rushed to Pueblo. He went to the DRG station at Pueblo and asked to charter a train to Cañon City. The DRG agent refused the charter, and declined to send ATSF telegrams to Cañon City. Undaunted, Morley saddled his own black gelding, "King William," and raced off into the night on this huge hunter. King William brought his owner into Cañon City shortly after midnight, having covered the forty-odd miles from Pueblo in record time. An oft-repeated story claims that Morley rode his horse to death, a story which does disservice to Morley's memory and the strength and speed of King William. Morley roused the people of Cañon City to action. The local leaders of the CCSJ were awakened and warned of McMurtrie's imminent arrival. Just prior to Morley's night-long ride the CCSJ had named Strong its general manager and Robinson its chief engineer, so that Morley acted as a member of the railway organization. That was really unimportant, for the people of Cañon City despised the DRG and turned out of bed at Morley's call. Gathering at a local mercantile store, the townspeople were given shovels and picks, and under Morley's direction moved out to the entrance of the gorge.

Half an hour later the episode at Raton Pass was replayed. McMurtrie and his men arrived to find Morley directing his ad hoc crew in the gorge. McMurtrie pointed out to Morley that the old survey stakes that he was using were placed there by DRG surveyers five years before; Morley did not need to be reminded, he had been a member of McMurtrie's crew in 1873 when they drove the stakes. Morley then informed McMurtrie that the DRG had failed to file a plat after it had made the survey, and therefore, the DRG had no prior claim. McMurtrie refused to back down, and his crew went to work a few yards away.

Strong followed Morley's actions through the use of a company "pony express" to Pueblo, as the DRG continued to refuse the Santa Fe use of the telegraph line. The ATSF subsidiary, the Pueblo and Arkansas Valley, formally absorbed the CCSJ to give the Santa Fe the legal right to enter the fray, and Strong sent 300 men, some armed with rifles and pistols as well as shovels, to Cañon City. He also ordered rails and materials to build the line from Pueblo to Leadville. The DRG countered by hiring some of the 300 men to whom they offered better pay; the ATSF then raised its pay scale. McMurtrie constructed some forts above the Santa Fe grade, placed armed men in them, and then ordered his crews to set off dynamite charges above the rival line, sending rocks and boulders roaring down on Robinson's forces. Strong reacted by hiring 100 gunmen in Dodge City, loaded them on a special train and rushed this army to the construction site. Bat Masterson captained Strong's gun hands in Royal Gorge. Unintimidated, the DRG hired additional gunmen in Denver and in the mining towns and put them in the stone forts and trenches. Located only a mile apart, the two construction crews stole equipment from each other and threw it into the rushing waters of the Arkansas River. Tension increased, tempers flared, and additional trenches and forts were built. Both Strong and Palmer feared a real war, and sought to end the sham and pretense in the canyon by turning to the courts.

Palmer contended that the DRG had legal title to the gorge by prior survey and occupancy. Yet he failed to recognize the animosity of the local residents and the hostility of the local courts toward the DRG. When Morley beat McMurtrie to the gorge, the *Colorado Chieftain* of Pueblo threw a banner headline across its front page, screaming: "Catching Weasels Asleep, Or How Morley Outflanked McMurtrie."[8] Local judges and juries reflected this point of view. Nevertheless, Palmer went into court arguing that his men had staked a route through the gorge five years before Holbrook and the CCSJ. The ATSF filed a countersuit, and Strong got an injunction against the DRG, ordering McMurtrie to stop work. McMurtrie refused to obey the injunction and vacate the forts, and he was arrested. Palmer then obtained a counterinjunction ordering Morley and Robinson to cease construction. Crews from both camps brought work to a halt by acts of vandalism and sabotage. Both Palmer and Strong appealed to the governor for support from the Colorado militia, but to no avail. An appeal by Palmer to a federal court produced a stay order against both railroads which commanded them to stop all work and post bonds of $20,000 each.

The federal court took the case under advisement, and the proceedings moved slowly through the docket. An initial ruling favored the Santa Fe, but the court declared that both lines could reach Leadville by using joint trackage in the narrower portions of the gorge. This decision, on August 23, 1878, upset General Palmer, who insisted upon sole occupancy. Any joint trackage would have to be built with three rails because of the difference between the 3-foot narrow gauge DRG and the 4-foot-8½-inch standard gauge ATSF. Strong immediately let contracts to build a line from Pueblo to Cañon City, and Palmer appealed the decision to a higher court.

Fighting broke out in the canyon when the rival crews began to crowd each other as they sought the best and easiest grades. Clearly the most economical route lay on the north side of the river where the DRG was located, and the DRG fought to keep the Santa Fe on the south side. Strong ordered more men to the gorge; Nickerson merged the CCSJ into the PAV, and he increased the capital stock of the PAV to $6 million. Plans for an extension to Leadville with branches all over central Colorado were announced by the Atchison. Strong wanted to kill off the DRG once and for all, but Nickerson decided to turn to the courts for support. He favored a peaceful settlement and thought a lease of the DRG by the ATSF would provide the best solution.

Nickerson, considered an "ultra conservative" by Strong's aides, knew that the fight at Raton and the gorge had driven Palmer and the DRG to the wall financially. Many of the bondholders of the DRG favored leasing the line before the company failed. And, perhaps more significantly, larger amounts of DRG bonds were owned by Bostonians, men with close ties to the Atchison. These investors leaned heavily on Palmer who reluctantly traveled to Boston to make the arrangements. Under the terms of the lease, which Nickerson personally prepared, the Atchison would take over the 337-mile DRG on midnight, December 13, 1878. The Santa Fe would initially pay the owners of the narrow gauge 43 percent of the gross receipts of the DRG, though the percentage would gradually decline during the term of the lease. Palmer signed the thirty-year lease on October 19, and the bondholders issued a sigh of relief. DRG bonds, which had been falling in price, rose almost immediately from 74 to 94. Palmer, who felt morally responsible to the DRG investors, returned to Colorado to hand the narrow gauge over to his arch-rival Strong.

Strong still opposed the lease, and to the surprise of no one in the Centennial State, the agreement failed from the outset. Palmer and his associates immediately accused the ATSF of using the lease to its advantage.

Strong bled the DRG of traffic, diverting it to the Santa Fe. DRG traffic links to the KP and the UP at Denver were closed, and freight from Denver was routed south to Pueblo to move east over the ATSF. Pueblo boomed and Denverites rose up in a wrath; merchants in the capital city who had never liked the DRG became its most staunch supporters. The Santa Fe raised rates to Denver from Pueblo, Colorado Springs and Cañon City to divert additional traffic eastward over its own line causing DRG income to fall below that needed to pay interest on its bonds. The *Rocky Mountain News* of Denver became the "mouthpiece" for the DRG and General Palmer. Palmer used the pages of the *News* to voice his demand that Strong stop giving all the long hauls to the ATSF. Strong ignored him and the protesting Kansas Pacific, and even used the DRG to send construction materials to his crews at Royal Gorge. Palmer, incensed, pushed his original suit to the U.S. Supreme Court. There was nothing the ATSF could do to stop the legal action, but Robinson and Morley continued to build westward from Pueblo up the Arkansas River with 1,000 men and 100 teams. Robinson constructed twenty miles of railway into the gorge, including the famous "hanging bridge" which supported the track when the shelf along the river became too narrow. Palmer's old crews kept up the vandalism, and Bat Masterson returned to the gorge to "keep the peace."

On April 21, 1879, the U.S. Supreme Court rendered a decision in the Royal Gorge case. The Court ruled that both railroads could build through the gorge, but that the DRG had the prior claim. The DRG authorization of 1872 set precedent, and the injunction against the DRG was withdrawn. If only one line could be built, it would have to be used by the DRG and the ATSF. The Court gave Palmer the legal victory.

General Palmer immediately sought to regain control over the DRG by having the lease vacated. A Colorado court, only six days after the Supreme Court decision, ruled that the Santa Fe, a Kansas corporation, could not legally lease the DRG, a creature of the state of Colorado. The Supreme Court of Colorado delayed the order, however, and soon Palmer and the DRG flooded the court with appeals. Meanwhile, both railroads sent more men into the gorge, where fighting broke out again. Palmer urged immediate action by the courts; DRG bonds were holding well on the market; and Palmer claimed that the ATSF had violated the lease. The Colorado Supreme Court ordered the lease terminated.

Strong, Robinson and Morley prepared for the worst, as Palmer and his associates accumulated carbines, shotguns and rifles throughout May and June. The ATSF management knew that the arms had been sent to McMurtrie at Pueblo, and Strong deployed his troops there and at other strategic points on the DRG. Strong hired Ben Thompson, the famous frontiersman, Indian fighter and lawman, for $5,000, and placed him in charge of defending the Pueblo roundhouse. Thompson selected his own men, who turned the roundhouse into a fort. June 11, the ATSF–occupied DRG station at Colorado Springs came under seige and soon capitulated to Palmer's men. The DRG crews moved south over the narrow gauge to Pueblo, and aided by the local sheriff and armed with a court order, demanded Thompson and his Texans leave the roundhouse. He refused. Palmer, according to Thompson, offered him $25,000 to surrender, but again the gunfighter refused. Cooler heads suggested the futility of a fight, and the law officers escorted Thompson and the ATSF men out of the facility, which the DRG then seized. The transition proceeded peacefully elsewhere, and Palmer soon recovered his railway.

Palmer's victory was short-lived, and Strong probably had a good laugh, for in July, the DRG was thrown into the hands of a receiver, Louis C. Ellsworth. Like Palmer, Ellsworth claimed that the Atchison was bleeding the DRG through the lease, and that the receivership had become neces-sary because the ATSF had allowed the property to deteriorate. The Santa Fe returned the lease to Ellsworth in August, and the DRG resumed con-struction in the gorge. Strong countered by announcing that the Santa Fe planned to build a standard-gauge line paralleling the DRG from Pueblo to Denver. Indeed, Strong wanted to get the lease renewed through the receiver, but Nickerson favored termination. In late summer, a new ele-ment entered the contest as the financier Jay Gould began to purchase the now low-priced DRG bonds. Gould, who also controlled the merged UP and KP, desired an end to the fighting which hurt all three of his lines. By September, Gould and Russell Sage, with Palmer's blessing, had made very heavy purchases of DRG bonds and trust certificates. Gould planned to use the DRG against the Atchison to benefit the UP and the KP. Palmer agreed to Gould's demand that no traffic agreements be made with the ATSF which did not include equal rights for Gould's properties. Gould and Sage were elected to the DRG board, and the former threatened to parallel the Santa Fe with a new line from Great Bend to Pueblo. Nickerson and Strong agreed to negotiate.

Nickerson, Strong and the ATSF management were eager to end the controversy, too. They wanted to direct their attention to the extension of the ATSF into New Mexico, and the Atchison found itself in a minor financial bind at this time. To facilitate an end to the Colorado imbroglio, on December 20, the ATSF, the UP and the KP established a pooling agreement on Colorado traffic. This alliance led to an out-of-court settle-ment on February 2, 1880, between the Santa Fe and the DRG. The so-called "Treaty of Boston" resolved most of the difficulties between the ATSF, DRG, and UP, and was to prevail for ten years. The Santa Fe canceled the DRG lease, and all litigation stopped. The Court discharged the receiver and the DRG obtained sole right to construct a line from Pueblo through Royal Gorge to Leadville. In return, the DRG paid the ATSF approximately $1.4 million for the work it had accomplished in the gorge. In addition, the DRG agreed not to build a railroad to Santa Fe, and the Atchison agreed to stay out of DRG territory, specifically Denver and Leadville. The DRG would give the ATSF one-half of the southwestern Colorado traffic and one-fourth of the Denver trade. The long war ended, but at a heavy cost to all concerned. The fate and future of the Santa Fe had been resolved at Raton Pass and Royal Gorge, in William B. Strong's private car and the ATSF board room in Boston, and by Ray Morley's King William.

The ATSF won a clear victory at Raton Pass, and the muddle at Royal Gorge and the contest with Jay Gould's Union Pacific and Palmer's Denver and Rio Grande convinced the leaders of the company to look to New Mexico for a line to California, not to the overland route via Salt Lake City. Once again they returned to Colonel Holliday's original vision, and Strong, Robinson, Morley, Lewis Kingman and H. R. Holbrook shifted

Offices of the ATSF in Topeka, 1879 (at left).
Kansas State Historical Society

their attention, crews, equipment and ambitions to New Mexico and the route to Santa Fe and California.

Even as Strong and Nickerson planned to build westward they maintained uneasy eyes on their domain in Kansas. In the 1870s the population of Kansas swelled from 360,000 to 990,000 and railroad mileage leaped from 1,234 to 3,104. Much of the new track was being built by competitors of the ATSF. If the Atchison wanted to maintain its share of the growing traffic in cattle, corn and wheat, it had to make its position secure by building branches into the new farming areas. Another dilemma developed for the management as they noted the declining significance of the town of Atchison as a major railroad terminal. Independence, Westport, Leavenworth, St. Joseph and Atchison declined as Kansas City became the gateway to the West. Kansas City rivaled St. Louis as the dominant urban center in the region, and outstripped its rival in the wheat, cattle, and corn markets. The ATSF had to use other lines east of Atchison, and Nickerson and his Bostonians came to the conclusion that their railroad had to enter Kansas City over its own track. A twofold plan emerged for expansion in Kansas in the 1870s: a series of branches to tap the growing farm areas, and a new line to Kansas City.

In June 1875 the ATSF leased the Kansas City, Topeka and Western, a 67-mile jerkwater line from Kansas City to Topeka, and acquired terminal facilities in the former with the Kansas City and St. Joseph and the Chicago, Burlington & Quincy railways. The KCT&W had a checkered past, having been built in bits and pieces by several different companies. The portion between Topeka and Lawrence, the former Kansas Midland, had been constructed by a notorious con artist, G. C. Chapman. Chapman got the line built and then fled, leaving the railroad in dire financial straits, but taking $125,000 at the time of his departure. The Kansas Midland suffered from washouts, attachments by sheriff's deputies, and constant derailments. The KCT&W operated a circuitous line from Lawrence to Pleasant Hill, Missouri, missing Kansas City by ten miles. Trackage rights over the Missouri River, Fort Scott and Gulf Railroad allowed trains to enter Kansas City. The route was long and the line difficult to operate. When the ATSF acquired the Kansas City, Topeka and Western, it was in wretched condition. The *Annual Report* of 1876 noted that the entire trackage had to be rebuilt because of the very high maintenance costs. Landslides along the Missouri River bluffs had to be prevented; ballast laid down; nearly all the bridges had to be rebuilt or replaced; and the acquired KCT&W equipment needed to be scrapped. A more direct entrance into Kansas City became mandatory, and the portion of the KCT&W to Pleasant Hill was eventually sold. However, even with these additional expenditures, a significant development took place with the entrance of the ATSF into Kansas City, its eastern terminus for the next ten years, for now the Santa Fe had four or five optional routings for freight sent east of Kansas City.

Within the state of Kansas the ATSF built a number of branches, usually forming a subsidiary company to construct and operate the new line as an affiliate of the Santa Fe. The use of subsidiaries kept the management out of some legal problems, and allowed mortgage bond issues which were not obligations of the ATSF. To reach the newly opened farm areas in east-central Kansas, a branch opened from Emporia south through Eureka to Howard, some seventy-five miles. Another new line began at Florence and went north and west to McPherson and west to Lyons, which was reached in the summer of 1880. Nickerson decided that additional cattle trade could be derived from constructing lines south of Wichita; branches were built to Arkansas City via Winfield and to Wellington via Mulvane, and from Wellington a short spur reached Caldwell. Although designed to block rivals from building in the same areas, the expansion program was not always successful. In one instance, the ATSF and the Union Pacific agreed to operate jointly a sixty-mile-long branch from Manhattan through Alma to Burlingame. While the towns along these branches welcomed the coming of the Santa Fe, as did most farmers along the routes, their enthusiasm waned quickly, and soon the legislature in Topeka heard massive complaints that freight rates and passenger fares were too high.

From the mid-1870s on, the farmers and merchants of Kansas and other midwestern and southern states complained of the "excessive" rates charged by the railroads. Indeed, some rates were too high and abuses did exist; for example, rates for short hauls were generally much higher than for longer and more competitive hauls. But without the railroads, the towns and farms would not have existed. William B. Strong made an eloquent plea for his company in 1879 when the Kansas legislature debated a bill setting maximum rates. Strong argued persuasively that a regulated rail tariff would block further railway expansion in the state, for investors would be frightened by such "stringent" legislation. He cited and quoted John Stuart Mill on the legitimate functions of government of which railway rate making was not one. Railroads, Strong argued, must set rates high enough to provide good service and earn a profit; their debts must be paid. Even the present rates, he declared, were less than reasonable, and they were established voluntarily. His pleas went unanswered, and the management began to witness a steady erosion of intrastate rates in Kansas and elsewhere. Sometimes it seemed that both the politicians and the elements were against the railroad.

Operating conditions in Kansas in the 1870s were less than ideal. Passengers in ATSF coaches took delight in firing their pistols and rifles from train windows; antelope, coyotes, buffalo and birds were considered

Locomotive No. 2, the "William B. Strong," built in 1881. Santa Fe Railway

fair game, and when they were sighted, so were Indians. The Indians shot back. The ATSF armed crews west of Newton, but in July 1874 they had to ask the commander at Fort Wallace for troops because the Cheyennes were harassing trains and track gangs. A. A. Robinson asked for protection for his workers after four men were found dead and scalped near Syracuse in August. The state arsenal gave the ATSF arms and ammunition. Other hazards were far more serious than the Cheyennes. Sparks from the wood- and coal-burning locomotives set deadly prairie fires in the summer and fall. The locomotive department tried all types of smoke and spark arrestors on the smokestacks, but these were largely unsuccessful. Too often the devices sent smoke, cinders and sparks pouring into open freight or passenger cars. The cruel Kansas snow storms often blocked the tracks, especially west of Newton; in the blizzard of 1874–75 the line west of Dodge City closed for more than twenty days. To make matters worse, in 1874 a plague of grasshoppers settled on Kansas devouring everything with a starch content, even curtains on windows. Earnings fell as farmers lost their crops, and the Atchison cut wages 20 percent and rates even more. Operations almost stopped as grasshoppers covered the iron rails, turning the bearing surface into a greasy slime. Locomotives slipped and slid, their sanders unable to give the drivers enough traction. Finally Master Mechanic H. V. Faries devised a brush which was mounted in front of the wheels to sweep the "hoppers" off the rails. Wage cuts, long hours, and work hazards produced the first labor problems on the ATSF.

The rapid growth of the Santa Fe meant not only a larger work force but also a greater degree of labor specialization. The operating crews of engineers, firemen, brakemen and conductors swelled as did the maintenance section gangs, yard crews, boiler makers, shopmen and office staff. Wages were relatively good but varied widely over the line, with each man paid largely on merit. Employees in the settled areas of Kansas received less than those working at La Junta or Raton Pass, where living conditions were crude to say the least. Wages generally fell into broad categories with locomotive engineers averaging $3.25 per day and section men $1.00 to $1.10 per day. Conductors were paid monthly, about $60.00 on the average, and brakemen about $15.00 less. Paymaster Jim Moore's special car moved over the line like a rolling fortress, issuing pay as it reached a group of men regardless of the hour. There were a few times in the mid-1870s when Moore arrived late, not because of grasshoppers or snow, but because the management ran out of cash.

A wage dispute led to the first strike on the railroad. In 1877 the ATSF reduced wages 5 percent on August 1, and conductors were slashed drastically from a top salary of $120 a month to $75. They struck, but when the management refused to restore the cuts they returned to work at the lower wage. A second strike occurred on April 4, 1878 when engineers received a 10 percent pay reduction. Most engineers and firemen walked off their jobs, closing down the railroad for five days. At Emporia, where feelings were very high, a mob threatened the depot and other facilities, and at the urging of the ATSF, the governor called out the militia. A militiaman killed an innocent bystander, and in the following mayhem several of the strike leaders were arrested. The railroad hired replacements for the strikers, and in its 1878 *Annual Report* denounced the "tramps and vagabonds" attracted by the strike. The crisis passed, and many of those who had struck returned to work. The management slowly realized that wage cuts were not conducive to good labor relations, and began to deal with labor problems in a less autocratic manner. Under Strong, however, workers on the ATSF would not be allowed to dictate policy on wage or hours. Despite Strong's demands on them, ATSF employees developed a keen sense of loyalty to him and the company. Some employee benefits were provided by the railroad, and Strong established a system of modest cash gratuities. The ATSF was not an "equal opportunity" employer in the 1870s, but in 1874 the first woman employee, Mrs. Caroline Prentis, became a clerk in the Topeka general office. Other labor problems would arise occasionally, such as in 1881, when eighteen section men were arrested for padding payrolls; but the ATSF developed a reputation for fairness among the brotherhood of railway men.

The Santa Fe needed the concerted efforts of its employees in the 1870s to handle the large growth in passenger and freight traffic. Despite the depression following the panic of 1873 and several years of crop failures, business increased. In 1870, gross earnings of $182,580 were produced by 98,917 tons of freight and 33,628 passengers. Within four years the gross increased to $1,250,805 generated by 79,416 tons of freight carried east and 106,894 tons carried west and by 69,659 passengers. The rapid extension of the branch lines in Kansas and expansion to the west caused the gross to almost double from $3,950,868 in 1878 to $6,381,442 in 1879, and to swell to $8,556,976 in the following year. Yet only in 1878 had eastbound cargoes surpassed those westbound in tonnage. The imbalance in ATSF freight traffic would continue for several more years until the new territories being opened could produce more than they consumed. While the coal mines at Carbondale and elsewhere contributed to eastern traffic, as did the cattle trade, in 1874 the Granada depot, then the end-of-track, had almost twice as much business going west as going east. Nevertheless, gross revenue per train mile more than doubled between 1874 and 1880.

The shipment of coal, cattle, sheep, grain, ore and buffalo hides and bones to the east and of manufactured goods to the west created the basic traffic pattern for the ATSF. The through passenger service from Kansas City to Pueblo attracted tourists and settlers, and travelers going west exceeded those going east by over 90,000. The newness of the railroad and the growth in traffic kept the operating ratio (the ratio of operating expenses to gross earnings) at a very low 44.6 in 1874 and 43.4 in 1879. The net earnings of the railroad were good in the depression year of 1873, but rapid expansion soon took its toll. The management also skimped on equipment purchases in 1873 and 1874, thus placing heavier burdens on existing equipment and making future purchases an absolute necessity. Locomotive shortages in 1874 led to seven new acquisitions in 1875 and the leasing of three engines from other lines. The management admitted in the 1875 *Annual Report* that at least ten to fifteen new freight locomotives were needed. Maintenance costs rose as the old iron rails from Topeka to Emporia wore out and as cuts were widened, bridges replaced and the Newton-Granada tracks were virtually rebuilt. Throughout the late 1870s the management poured earnings back into the road for steel rails, ballast, fences, telegraph lines, and new bridges. Earnings, however, rose to cover these expenditures, and on August 25, 1878, the first dividends were paid.

The *Annual Report* for 1879 announced that earnings for 1878 had been excellent and that regular dividends were in sight. The ATSF had grown from 508 miles of railroad in 1874 to 1,167 miles in 1879, and by May 1, 1880, the directors projected that 1,317 miles would be in operation. Net income for 1879 reached $3,454,968, which indicated that most of the water had been wrung out of company securities. Rising profits after 1875 allowed the management to pay off the floating debt and to build up

The Albuquerque depot in 1880. University of New Mexico Library

a modest working capital. In 1875, part of the coupons on notes due July 1, 1881, were paid in scrip, but after that the company began to pay regularly in cash. The Nickersons pursued a very cautious financial program and were able to borrow funds at much lower rates than the 12 percent paid in 1873 and 1874. By the end of the 1870s, ATSF bonds sold widely and even the common stock attracted attention and rose in price. As the decade came to a close, the railroad was worth about $50 million and had issued approximately $24 million in stock and $16 million in bonds. The sale of land and local subsidies helped create this favorable financial picture, but profits from rising traffic provided the bulk of the income. Within ten years of the initial construction of the railroad, the directors declared a cash dividend of 3 percent. Few railways in the West or the East could match this record.

The directors not only reported very good financial news in 1879, but also noted that Engineer Robinson was working with "untiring energy and zeal" on the extension of the ATSF into New Mexico. The tunnel over Raton opened in September, and all New Mexico lay before the construction crews. For two years Robinson had been dispatching Morley and his survey teams into New Mexico to find the best route south from Raton to Las Vegas, Santa Fe, Albuquerque and El Paso. In the fall of 1877 Morley and Lewis Kingman worked from Trinidad south down the valley of the Rio Grande and west to Silver City in southwestern New Mexico. In the summer of 1878 they surveyed west from Las Vegas to the Rio Grande. Although his crew contracted malaria and their work took longer than anticipated, Morley submitted his preliminary report by October. He urged Robinson to persuade Strong to build southwestward from Raton to the Rio Grande Valley, follow the valley to southern New Mexico, and then turn west to California along the 32nd parallel rather than along the 35th. The latter represented little potential in terms of local traffic and posed massive obstacles to quality construction and efficient operations. Robinson concurred, and on January 10, 1879, he and Morley submitted a joint report to Strong urging that the line be built south from Raton through Glorieta Pass to Albuquerque and the Rio Grande rather than through the town of Santa Fe. The trade to Santa Fe was no longer significant, they argued, and even the Barlow and Sanderson stagecoaches had reduced service to Santa Fe. Instead they urged a branch from Lamy to the territorial capital.

Rincon, New Mexico, in 1883. Santa Fe Railway

Robinson and Morley saw several advantages to their proposal, some economic and at least one political. The route through Glorieta Pass would enable the ATSF to reach the valley of the Rio Grande, which had excellent agricultural prospects. Timber and coal deposits in the mountains represented potentially large local revenues. And, to cinch their argument, they noted that the bulk of the members of the territorial legislature lived along this proposed route and that it would "be an advantage to be on the good side of this population."[9] Strong soon agreed to their plan.

Robinson's men labored mightily as they built south from Raton, reaching Las Vegas in July 1879. Construction through Glorieta Pass taxed the minds of the surveyors and the strength of the grading crews. The pass reached an elevation of 7,453 feet in the midst of a large forest. The cool air, which gave the pass its name, "summer house," made the hard work more tolerable, but the thirty-mile segment proved difficult to build and operate. After a long steep climb to the top of the pass, a cut thirty feet deep had to be made as the rails crossed the divide between the Pecos River and the Rio Grande. The railroad followed canyons and creek beds

to the headwaters of Galisteo Creek where, off seven miles to the north-west, could be seen Thompson Peak towering over the Sangre de Cristo Mountains. From the crest of the pass the construction crews built down-grade for forty miles as the line dropped over 2,000 feet in elevation. At the western end of the pass the ATSF gangs worked through Apache Can-yon, site of a battle in 1862 between Union and Confederate armies contending for control of New Mexico. Through this wild and tortured can-yon the railroad broke out to the west, to the banks of the Rio Grande. From that point Robinson's crews built rapidly down the valley of the Rio Grande following the easy grade of the river. The line passed through Albuquerque on April 15, 1880, and by September 16 the railhead reached San Marcial in southwestern New Mexico, 235 miles from Las Vegas. .

The entry of the Atchison into New Mexico dramatically changed the local economy. Isolated from national life and existing on trade provided by the wagon companies, New Mexico had changed very little in the fifty years after the opening of the Santa Fe Trail. With the coming of the railroad, coal mining became a major industry and the sheep and cattle ranches expanded their operations. Farmers in the Rio Grande Valley now had a means to ship their produce to eastern markets. The locomo-tive became a symbol of progress in New Mexico and signified the end of a way of life as it tamed the vast reaches of the "Land of Enchantment."

Strong's expansionist policies had been approved by Nickerson and the board of directors based on the Robinson-Morley reports. The subsidiary New Mexico and Southern Pacific Railroad built the line from Colorado to Albuquerque, some 248 miles, and Robinson's estimated cost of $2,621,000 was not far off the mark. Seven percent gold bonds at a maximum rate of $15,000 per mile were offered to the public. The ATSF leased the NM&SP and guaranteed payment of 37 percent of gross earnings and a rebate of 15 percent on all business delivered to and from the NM&SP at the Colorado state line. The bonds had sold quickly, allowing Robinson to build to the Rio Grande.

There remained the question of a branch into Santa Fe. Initially irate at being bypassed by the mainline, the residents of the capital soon clam-ored for a branch from Lamy. A local bond issue spurred the railroad to action, and the eighteen-mile line opened in February 1880. A fiesta wel-comed the railway with a massive parade around the Old Plaza led by the 9th Cavalry band. A band at the depot greeted the first train which backed in from Lamy because there was no wye to turn around on. Two locomotives, the "A. G. Greely," a Baldwin 4–4–0, and "Marion," a Taunton 4–6–0, hauled in the trainload of ATSF officials and New Mex-ico dignitaries. Governor Lew Wallace, author of *Ben Hur*, drove the last spike at a brief ceremony. The fiesta marked the end of the Santa Fe Trail. Now the iron horse swept the prairies 860 miles from Kansas City to Santa Fe. Undoubtedly Colonel Holliday smiled as he recalled the scoffers in attendance at the picnic on Wakarusa Creek that warm spring afternoon in 1869. In less than a dozen years part of his dream had become reality, and as a director of the ATSF until his death on March 29, 1900, Holliday would see nearly all of his vision fulfilled.

3

Russian Wheat Farmers
and Boston Capitalists

"I never saw finer country in the world," proclaimed an Indiana news-paper editor, "than that part of Kansas passed over by the Atchison, Topeka & Santa Fe road. Corn waist high, wheat in shock, oats in fine condition, and vegetables in abundance."[1] Writing in 1875 after an excursion through the Santa Fe land grant in western Kansas, this Indiana newspaper man reflected the buoyant optimism of the railroad, especially its Land Department. The fortunes of the company were directly linked to the economic growth and prosperity of the Sunflower State—as Kansas boomed, so did the railroad. The growth of agriculture in Kansas in the 1870s and 1880s gave the Atchison a firm base upon which to expand, and, equally significant, helped the railroad dispose of its 2,928,928.54 acres of land.

Kansas witnessed a phenomenal rate of growth in the 1870s and 1880s. The population of the state rose from 364,000 to a million between 1870 and 1880; but this population explosion failed to keep up with the expansion of agriculture. In the same decade the number of cattle doubled, corn production increased by 700 percent and wheat by 1,000 percent. In 1880 the Sunflower State contributed 109 million bushels of corn, and 23.4 million bushels of wheat to the nation's tables. The ATSF *Annual Report* for 1875 noted the size of the bumper wheat crop and declared it to be the "surest and most valuable traffic." Certainly wheat was impor-tant, especially the superior quality wheat, but by 1877 corn supplanted wheat as the major commodity. The spectacular growth in population and agricultural production in Kansas can be traced directly to the expansion of the railway network in the state.

Population growth in eastern Kansas had been substantial in the 1860s, but the area served by the fledgling ATSF grew even more rapidly. Three counties served by the Santa Fe grew five-fold, and in 1874 the railroad reported that 13 of the 18 counties it traversed had grown in population from 64,440, in 1870, to 105,661. In the same period 10 counties increased their cultivated acreage by 149,463 acres. In the land grant counties a population of 2,327 in 1860 grew to only 9,354 ten years later; but by 1875 some 46,440 people were in residence, and by 1880 over 124,000 lived along the line west of Newton. The ATSF made a substantial contribution to the prosperity of the state as the number of farms along its route leaped from 6,000 in 1870 to 21,500 ten years later. The area served by the company surpassed the growth rate of the remainder of the state, and yet all of Kansas grew rapidly as railway expansion gave the Sunflower State the highest per capita rail mileage in the Union.

The extraordinary boom in agricultural production along the ATSF could be partially explained by the way in which the railroad disposed of its land grant. The nearly three million acres stretched westward from near Emporia in alternate sections ten miles wide on either side of the track. As most of the land between Atchison and Emporia had previously been settled, the railroad could take in lieu lands, or indemnity lands, within twenty miles on either side of the line. The railroad had 6,400 acres per mile of track to sell to potential settlers, and the land grant presented excellent agricultural prospects: there was plenty of water and blue stem grass, lands too rolling for row crops could be used for grazing, and the topsoil was deep and rich and capable of producing more grain than any other river valley in the world. From the outset, the ATSF sold the land to family farmers and not to ranchers or to speculators. Large-scale agricultural production seemed to represent the best traffic potential for the railroad. Although only 74,000 acres had been sold by March 1872, a sales boom developed the following year with the Land Department becoming the primary instrument in generating this massive real estate transfer.

In 1868 the Atchison opened a Land Office and named David L. Lakin the first commissioner. An impressive man with a large, dark beard and receding hairline, Lakin proved to be a good worker and organizer. His office began to dispose of the Potawatomie Reserve Lands and then turned to the land grant which had to be surveyed, classified and appraised. In the spring of 1870 Lakin began to survey the grant, a task not completed until four years later. Surveyors found their work extremely difficult, but quick action was necessary as the ATSF had issued a

$3,520,500 mortgage on the lands at a 27 percent discount. Lakin also located indemnity lands in a forty-mile-wide area from Cottonwood Falls to Spearville. A field party of nine men fought the elements, buffalo and Indians to complete their work. Even as the survey team prepared its maps, Lakin established a land office at Cottonwood Falls and prepared to sell farms. Based on the surveyor's appraisals, initial sales began in 1872. Because of Lakin's increasingly poor health and the taxing nature of the position, A. E. Touzalin, formerly land agent for the Burlington and Missouri River Railroad in Nebraska, replaced him and reorganized the Land and Immigration departments.

A native of Jamaica, Touzalin added a new dimension to the Santa Fe land office. He not only completed the Potawatomie Reserve sales, but this dynamic salesman also made the Land Department one of the best in the nation. He commissioned salesmen throughout the Midwest and East to sell ATSF property. He sponsored excursions by newspaper editors and reporters, educators and real estate agents to western Kansas to view the land grant. Land agencies were established in Kansas, staffed with salesmen placed on commissions rather than on salaries to encourage industry on their part. A minimum price of $2.50 an acre made it possible for small farmers to purchase a tract, but the salesmen were told to show customers a wide range of prices. Touzalin's work ended abruptly, however, following a personal difference with Thomas Nickerson. His replacement, Colonel Alexander Johnson, more than filled Touzalin's role.

A. S. Johnson came to the ATSF in 1874, and stayed with the railroad in the Land and Tax Departments until 1890. Johnson carried on with vigor the work initiated by Touzalin. He knew Kansas well because he was the first white child born in the Territory and the son of a missionary to the Indians. The power wielded by Commissioner Johnson can be seen in the fact that at one point 90 percent of the county property taxes collected at Dodge City were paid by him for the railroad. His obligations were many and he proved equal to the task. At the end of 1873 the Land Department had a short-term debt and no capital, but Johnson initiated a vigorous sales campaign which alleviated much of the indebtedness by issuing $700,000 in bonds paying 12 percent interest with land contracts as security. An exceedingly high rate of interest to be sure, but Johnson had confidence that additional land would be sold. A good promoter and salesman, he organized a highly successful campaign, which lasted for a dozen years, and sold nearly the entire tract.

The Land Department used a variety of devices to promote sales. Johnson organized excursions for prospective pilgrims and for publicity purposes. Booklets and broadsides were printed and distributed by the thousands. All suggested that at least several hundred dollars in capital would be needed to establish a farm. Not all of the commissioned agents were as honest as the Land Department, but Johnson tried to prevent fraudulent or misleading claims. A wide variety of plans for purchasing the land were offered, including a no-money-down, four-years-to-pay-at-7-percent-interest scheme. When drought and grasshoppers plagued Kansas in 1874, rival railroads used these natural calamities to ridicule the Santa Fe lands. Johnson countered with a massive delegation of 225 journalists who visited the property and proclaimed it the "Garden of the West."

Promotional pamphlets extolled the virtues of the land, with one of the best examples appearing in 1874: "500,000 acres of the Best Farming and Fruit Lands . . . in and Adjacent to the Cottonwood Valley" described the "famous" Cottonwood Valley and its abundant springs and clear running water. "A better opportunity for obtaining a farm has never been offered, and probably never will be."[2] The following year saw sixty agents distributing these brochures outside of Kansas. Over half of the "foreign agents" operated in Iowa and Illinois. Johnson selected these men and the agents along the line in Kansas on the basis of their salesmanship and integrity. However, trying to coordinate all of their activities from Topeka meant that some were not as honest in their representations as others.

The Philadelphia Centennial in 1876 gave Johnson another opportunity to sell lands and the virtues of Kansas to easterners. The ATSF sent a large display of Kansas crops to the fair, and a new pamphlet was issued for circulation in Philadelphia. Forty-six pages long, "How and Where to Get a Living. A Sketch of 'The Garden of the West,' " sang the praises of the land grant. The pamphlet emphasized corn rather than wheat as a potential crop, and insisted that farmers had to have capital to make a go of a Kansas farm. President J. A. Anderson of the Kansas State Agricultural College praised the land, and urged farmers to see it for themselves because it was "the best thing in the West."[3]

To further induce farmers to make purchases, the railroad held colonization meetings where half-price tickets to visit Kansas were sold. In addition, special trains brought thousands of excursionists to view the land grant. By 1879 the Land Department's operations were so large and far-flung that Johnson divided the land grant into four territories, and hired traveling agents to tour the East, Midwest and Europe. The Land Department now told farmers they would need $800 to $1,000 to start if married, half that if single, as well as "grit." Johnson tried to keep expenditures by the department to a minimum and to spend money on the farmers rather than upon advertising. He allowed farmers to apply excursion costs to the purchase price and then agreed to have their belongings and equipment brought to Kansas at low freight rates, or even for free. The Union Pacific, trying to sell its land, complained about Johnson, and the "luxuri-

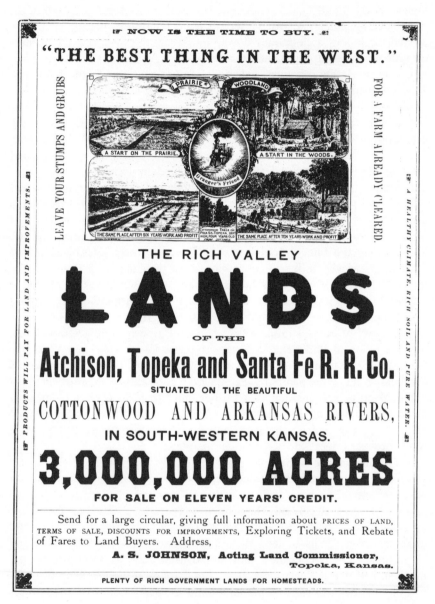

Advertisement for homesteads in the Kansas Land Grant. Santa Fe Railway

ous" immigrant cars used by the Santa Fe. But the ATSF developed a reputation for honest deals and accurate information, and these virtues undoubtedly aided Johnson and his agents in their work.

The sale of the land grant reflected the general economy and the conditions in Kansas at a particular moment. The initial sales in 1872 were modest, but they continued to increase in an irregular pattern until reaching a peak in 1885. A subsequent sharp decline brought an end to sales, and thereafter the Land Department operated only to collect yearly payments from those who had purchased land on credit. Sales rose dramatically from 1871 until 1874 with most land purchased in 160-acre tracts at an average price of $5.00 to $6.00 per acre. Most buyers came from Illinois, Kansas, Iowa, Ohio and Indiana or Europe. After the drought and grasshopper plague of 1874, sales plummeted, but recovered dramatically by 1878. In 1873, lands sold were located largely in Marion, Harvey, McPherson, Reno and Barton counties, but as the better farms were occupied in these counties, buyers began to purchase property further west. Even though the Land Department disposed of fewer acres in 1874 and 1875, the average price remained about the same ($5.59 per acre), and the price did not fluctuate greatly for the next five years. Heavy sales in the years from 1882 to 1886 reduced the ATSF holdings dramatically. In 1885 alone the department sold over one-fourth of the entire grant. The price per acre fell, however, to $2.66 in 1885 and to $2.44 in 1886 because the last areas sold were west of Dodge City, and the land offices at Garden City, Cimarron, Lakin and Dodge City could advertise them only for grazing cattle or for irrigated farming. Thus, the sharply reduced prices. To demonstrate the crop possibilities even where the lands lacked large water supplies, the railroad established six experimental tracts of twenty acres each to be shown to potential customers who toured the property.

Terms of the sales varied over the years with some property sold for twenty percent in cash, with principal payments deferred for 4 years and the balance to be paid in 8 years at 7 percent interest. At other times the mortgages were for 11 years in a period when other railroads extended credit for only 6 to 8 years. These liberal terms also encouraged the rapid disposition of the land grant.

Unlike other railroads, the ATSF surveyed and patented its lands quickly, and thus began to pay property taxes quite early. Although Touzalin and Johnson protested what they considered to be unfair county property levies, by 1886 the Santa Fe had paid $1,172,832.28 in taxes. The counties traversed by the railroad established higher tax rates than their neighbors, largely because the ATSF had patented its lands early, and much of the tax money paid by the railroad was used to build schools in rural areas and to construct county courthouses. While the railroad felt that it was being treated unfairly, its willingness to patent lands made the company far more popular than the Kansas Pacific, which moved very slowly in placing its land grant on the tax rolls. The aggressive sales policies of Touzalin and Johnson not only benefited the local taxpayers, but also introduced to Kansas a significant immigrant group—the Mennonites—who also became major contributors to the state's economy.

The western railroads with land grants, such as the Santa Fe, sought to attract European immigrants to their properties. Working through colonization agencies, steamship lines, and European land companies, the ATSF appealed to Scandinavian, British, French and German farmers to consider Kansas as a place for relocation. European newspaper men were brought to Kansas to see the lands, and the railroad purchased advertisements in their publications. A branch office of the Land Department operated in London, and distributed 300,000 pieces of literature in a variety of languages throughout Western Europe. Sub-offices in Liverpool and Hamburg furthered these efforts. Agents circulated through European cities, giving evening lectures to factory workers on the wonders of Kansas. The man responsible for the success of the foreign operation was C. B. Schmidt, the "General Foreign Agent."

In January 1873, Touzalin hired Schmidt, a native of Saxony who had been educated at the Dresden Commercial College. Schmidt had come to the United States in 1864 at the age of 21 and moved to Kansas in 1868. He worked in the state for several years, and he maintained good ties with European friends through a steady stream of letters and by publishing articles about the United States and Kansas in the German press. Schmidt's letters in the *Frankfurter Zeitung* were read by a Mennonite leader, Cornelius Jansen, who wrote to him for information about the Midwest. Schmidt took the letter to the offices of the ATSF, where, because of Schmidt's connections, linguistic ability, and charm, Touzalin hired him to aid the railroad in wooing the Mennonites, who were sending a delegation to Kansas in the summer of 1873 to inspect farm properties.

The Mennonite observers coming to Kansas represented only a small vanguard of a larger body of coreligionists who would eventually settle in the Sunflower State. Descendants of the Anabaptists of Reformation Europe, the Mennonites had been ill-treated in Switzerland, and so they migrated first to Holland and then to Prussia. Granted lands in the marshes of the Vistula River and exempted from military service, they prospered until the eighteenth century when Prussia placed restrictions on their acquisition of land. Catherine of Russia invited them to settle in the southern reaches of her nation, and from 1789 until the 1840s thousands of Mennonites moved to districts along the lower Volga, Don and Dnieper rivers. They established villages, churches and schools, always maintaining the German language. Becoming wheat farmers, they shipped millions of bushels of grain to the markets of Western Europe. The high quality of their hard red wheat, their use of blooded livestock and crop rotation brought the Mennonites prosperity. Unassimilated by their Russian neighbors, the Mennonites sought and received special consideration from the Russian government. In 1870, however, the Czar abolished their exemption from military service and their right to use German in their schools, and they were given ten years in which to emigrate if they desired. Several of their leaders, especially Cornelius Jansen, urged them to move to the United States. When petitions to the Czar to continue their exemptions were denied, the majority of the Russian Mennonites looked to the United States or Canada for new homes.

A small delegation of Russian Mennonite leaders came to the United States in 1872, visited older Mennonite settlements in Pennsylvania and Indiana, traveled through the Northern Pacific land grant, and toured Manitoba, Canada. Their concerns for freedom of worship, freedom from military service and continued use of the German language prevented them from reaching a decision on relocation. The next year another group came to inspect additional land in the American West.

Touzalin and other ATSF officials wanted to sell land to the Mennonites and make these fine farmers citizens of Kansas. When Cornelius Jansen and the other Mennonite delegates arrived in the United States, Schmidt took them on a tour of the Santa Fe land grant. They visited Marion, Reno, Sedgwick and McPherson counties and appeared favorably impressed. Jansen asked that 100,000 acres be reserved for them, and after returning to Russia and discussing immigration with other church leaders, he notified Schmidt on October 14, 1874, that the land would be purchased. Before the end of the year, thousands of Mennonites began the long trek to the United States. One group of 400 families arrived in Kansas with $2 million in bank drafts to purchase land, animals and equipment. In the first year of large sales, over 3,000 families bought land. Many arrived in the early winter, too late to take possession of their property, and so the ATSF arranged temporary housing for them. They were welcomed to Topeka by Governor Osborn, who held a reception for them before they moved into their temporary quarters located in the old King Bridge Shops in the capital. Large groups of "natives" went down to the Shops to see these bearded and sober folk dressed in their homespun woolens. Traders and merchants soon learned that these families knew good animals and equipment from bad and that they could not be deceived. To bring their household possessions to the United States the railroad chartered a Red Star Line boat, and storage for these goods was provided when they reached Kansas. Touzalin immediately saw the enormous potential represented by the Mennonites who remained in Russia, and he dispatched Schmidt to Europe.

In February 1875, Schmidt entered Russia, his letters of introduction taped to his body to prevent his mission from being discovered by the Russian government, which now had second thoughts about allowing the Mennonites to leave. Traveling to Vilna, Minsk, Kharkov and Alexandrovak, Schmidt made contact with Mennonite colonies, and was given $56,000 in rubles by one bishop to purchase lands. In the fall of 1875 some 6,500 additional immigrants arrived in Kansas, and Schmidt promised that more would come. Opening an office in Europe, Schmidt began a "hard sell" advertising campaign, circulating pamphlets in German among the Mennonites.

Between 1874 and 1883, thousands of Mennonites came to Kansas. The ATSF opened temporary barracks for them in Topeka and other towns, and used special trains to haul the farmers and their household goods to their lands. The railroad set aside land for churches and schools in the townsites settled by the Mennonites. One observer in 1883 estimated that at least 15,000 Mennonite immigrants had settled on ATSF lands, and most were financially solvent. Their primary crop and major contribution to the economy of Kansas and the Great Plains was hard red "Turkey" wheat. A small colony of French farmers in Marion County had introduced this variety earlier and discovered that it grew successfully, but flour mills in Kansas could not accommodate the hard grain. The Mennonites found that the hard red wheat resisted winterkill and the Hessian fly, and planted huge areas with the seeds they had brought with them. Seeing the distinct advantage of the strain, flour mills adapted to the grain by substituting steel rollers for the old burr system. Hard red wheat became the standard seed in Kansas and the Great Plains, and it made the area the breadbasket of the nation. Touzalin and his successors did more than just sell lands for the Santa Fe; they also provided the railroad with a future freight business of enormous proportions.

The labors of the Land Department were not always successful, and conditions—climatic and political—often thwarted their efforts. When the grasshopper plague came in 1874, the railroad carried over a million pounds of freight without charge for the settlers on the former land grant. The company helped organize county relief associations, which distributed food, clothes and free wheat seeds to destitute farmers. The Santa Fe reduced rates on coal and other commodities and, more importantly, declared a moratorium on land payments due from the farmers. Interestingly, as some farmers gave up in the face of drought and grasshoppers, the Mennonites stayed, buying farms, equipment and animals from those with less courage and foresight.

Some failures in the political arena also retarded the Land Department's efforts. The ATSF strongly opposed the temperance movement in

Kansas, with Schmidt arguing that many Europeans would not come to a "dry" Kansas. Yet, while the prohibition law of 1881 remained on the books, temperance failed to deter most immigrants. The Santa Fe and the other railroads which had labored so mightily to bring in these immigrants reminded the people of Kansas that they had not given up on the state even when the government of Kansas failed to treat the railroads fairly. In 1881 the Santa Fe petitioned the state legislature, declaring:

> . . . notwithstanding that the word KANSAS was, in the minds of the inhabitants of all the Eastern States, synonymous with grasshoppers, drouth, and starvation, yet, by the unaided efforts of these railroad corporations, an agent has been placed in every town and village in the United States and every city in Europe to correct this impression and talk and plead for Kansas.[4]

Certainly the railroads had promoted the state, encouraged settlement and boomed its agricultural prospects to create business, and the ATSF also earned some money from its land grant, not as much as critics, especially the farmers, claimed, but a substantial sum.

The Land Department operated under the direction of Colonel Johnson until 1890, when he resigned. His successor, John E. Frost, took over the department until its holdings were liquidated. In 1898 Frost himself bought the last remnants of the land grant in Kansas. When the Interstate Commerce Commission published its evaluation of the ATSF in the 1920s, the ICC concluded that in Kansas, by June 30, 1916, the ATSF had sold $12,435,957 in property, paid taxes of $1,202,976 and had expenses of $1,737,889 for a net profit of $9,495,091 on the land grant. The railroad had by 1916, however, given the federal government a discount of $2,405,761 on freight, passenger and mail rates. Thus the profit on nearly 3 million acres of land was approximately $7 million. In addition to the profits of the ATSF, the federal land in the alternate sections not granted to the railroad doubled in value. The land grant surely benefited the Santa Fe, but it also provided farms to tens of thousands of people. The federal government, through the railroad, made a major contribution to the settlement of Kansas. The profits earned by the ATSF hauling the wheat produced by the Mennonites and other Kansas farmers also encouraged the company's officers and executives in Boston to build westward with renewed vigor. The officers saw Kansas as a continuing source of earnings and a base upon which to expand. Encouraged by the growing prosperity of Kansas, the Boston investors agreed to a massive expansion program.

The Atchison became strongly identified with Boston in the 1870s, and this identification continued until the end of the next decade. When Thomas Nickerson succeeded Henry Strong as president of the company

Thomas Nickerson, president of the Santa Fe from 1874 until 1880. Santa Fe Railway

in 1874, ten of the fourteen directors were Bostonians. Indeed, the Nickerson family came to represent one of the largest financial interests in the railroad. Born in Massachusetts in 1810, Thomas Nickerson entered the Atchison with a substantial purchase of securities in 1870, thus terminating a long career in shipping and the mercantile business. A member of the Massachusetts legislature, church leader and a philanthropist, Nickerson first became a member of the company's executive committee, then served as vice president and ultimately president, holding the latter office until 1880. Nickerson stabilized the company's finances and led the drive to build the Atchison to the Pacific coast and Mexico. From 1880 until 1884 Nickerson served as president of the Mexican Central Railway and the California Southern Railway, and from 1880 to 1881 he presided over the Atlantic and Pacific Railroad. His brother Joseph became a director of the Atchison, while his brother Frederick served as a director of the Union Pacific. By the mid-1880s the second generation of Nickersons entered the ATSF when Albert Nickerson became a powerful member of the board of directors. These men and their allies so tightly held the Atchison's securities that as late as 1883 some 547,000 of the 569,100 shares of stock issued by the company were owned by Bostonians, and for several years only the stock exchange of that city listed ATSF securities.

In 1880 Nickerson stepped down as president of the Atchison, although he remained president of three affiliated lines. Another Bostonian, T. Jefferson Coolidge, succeeded him. Coolidge came to the Atchison after a career in the East India trade. Scion of a distinguished family and Harvard educated, Coolidge knew very little about railroading or the Southwest. He took two trips over the line, seeing the country as barren and profitable only if freight rates remained high. Indifferent and unconcerned, Coolidge thought of the ATSF presidency as only a burden:

> I found the work not only fatiguing but unprofitable, because as director and president I felt that my duty to my *cestius que trust*, the shareholders, prevented me from taking advantage of any facts not known to all, and cut me off from speculations which might have been advantageous. I resigned as soon as I could.[5]

Despite his unusual candor, Coolidge failed to provide the ATSF with aggressive leadership. An "opportunistic" investor, Coolidge purchased $718,500 in Atchison securities only after becoming president. His election and brief tenure did suggest, however, the close relationship which existed between the ATSF and the Chicago, Burlington & Quincy as Coolidge held a large block of stock in the CB&Q and had formerly served as a director of that road.

The Atchison and the CB&Q not only were owned substantially by Bostonians, but their executives were close friends and the two roads exchanged substantial traffic. Operating west from Chicago to Minneapolis, Omaha and Kansas City, the CB&Q served a heavily competitive area. The Santa Fe provided one of its best sources of traffic at Kansas City. Charles E. Perkins, vice president of the "Q" from 1876 to 1881 and president from 1881 until 1901, wanted to merge the two companies. "I wish we had it," he wrote, to block Jay Gould's expansion in the area.[6] The president of the CB&Q prior to 1881, John Murray Forbes, opposed bringing the two railroads together, fearing the size of the combined operation and the financial risks involved. The conservative directors of the CB&Q agreed with Forbes. Nevertheless, both Forbes and Perkins cultivated the executives of the Santa Fe, and the two railroad cooperated with each other on questions of rates and expansion. *The Commercial and Financial Chronicle* and other publications continued to speculate on a merger, and indeed, Perkins still wanted to "hitch" the "Q" to the ATSF in 1880, but to no avail.[7] As long as William Barstow Strong's hand guided the Santa Fe, however, Perkins had little to fear—at least for a few years.

When T. Jefferson Coolidge resigned as president in 1881, the directors immediately named Strong chief executive. The directors of the Atchison had consistently favored limited expansion of the line, but from the time Strong joined the railroad his ardent demand for additional construction had moved the company forward. His persuasive arguments, rising profits, and the successful defeat of the Denver and Rio Grande gave the directors confidence in him and his ambitions for the railroad. When he was general manager and vice president, Strong operated the railroad guided only by the general policies emanating from Boston. Determined to build to California, Strong alternatively threatened, cajoled and persuaded the directors. Not personally wealthy and with a limited financial voice in the firm, Strong moved nevertheless with boldness and decisiveness. He gave the directors a solidly professional management, which reflected his personality and drives. Strong stated his policy of expansion in an often-quoted portion of the 1884 *Annual Report*: "A railroad to be successful must also be a progressive institution. It cannot stand still if it would. If it fails to advance, it must inevitably go backward and lose ground already occupied."[8] Under his direction the Santa Fe would quadruple in length and become a major transcontinental railroad.

Strong dramatically altered the goals of some of the stockholders and directors as he persuaded them to follow Holliday's dream. Many of the original investors were largely motivated to purchase securities because of the prospects for immediate profits—largely from the land operations. In time, however, the situation altered, as the Santa Fe expanded to Colorado and the investors had to extend their financial commitments. The management presented to them a picture of increasing competition and the absolute necessity of further expansion; an expansion which could be neither planned nor orderly. In effect, Strong told men like Coolidge that they should abandon their opportunistic goals and see their investments as developmental entrepreneurship. His arguments, supported by the threats presented by other railroads and other investors, and by increasingly positive financial reports, won them over. The Atchison became an open-ended rail system which reinvested its increasing profits in new mileage.

The *Annual Reports* from 1880 through 1884 showed ever-increasing prosperity. Nickerson's conservative financial policies gave Strong a substantial base from which to work. In 1880 the solid credit rating of the ATSF enabled the railroad to market securities at a 5 percent interest rate even though the 8¼ dividend that year was in stock. The following year shareholders received 6 percent dividends in cash plus 50 percent in stock, and the shares hit 154¼ on the New York Exchange. In that same year the gross rose 47 percent and mileage by 23 percent. A net of $8,037,826 provided a surplus of $1,132,071, and the directors declared three cash dividends. Both Coolidge and Strong noted the rising cost of expansion in terms of heavy locomotive and equipment purchases, replacement of iron rails with steel, new roundhouses and shops, and large maintenance costs, and to pay for these items the ATSF successfully issued $6 million in stock at par of which $2.5 million was for rolling stock and locomotives.

Strong acknowledged the immediate and favorable response by investors to the security issue in the *Annual Report* for 1882. He thanked the stockholders for their confidence:

> Thirteen years ago, the Atchison, Topeka & Santa Fe Railroad, a line then twenty-eight miles in length, under the same general direction which now governs its affairs, asked the confidence and support of the Massachusetts public in the execution of the project it contemplated. Through good and evil times, that support has always been readily given and that confidence has never been broken; and, as a result, those who have followed the fortunes of the Company have shared in its prosperity.[9]

Then Strong announced additional good news. He reported that the gross had risen by $2,188,796 to a new high of $14,733,305, and that the net of $6,136,048 generated a surplus of over $1 million. Further, there was "no floating debt" despite the addition of 136 miles of new track to raise the total to 2,620.

The Atchison continued to enjoy prosperity in 1883 and 1884, giving the stockholders greater confidence in Strong's expansionist policies. As the steel-rail mileage swelled to 1,700 out of 2,620, maintenance costs began to fall. A darkening cloud, Strong warned, was the action by the state of Kansas setting maximum freight rates at three cents per mile per hundred weight, but he expressed faith that the people of Kansas would treat the company fairly. There had been virtually no new construction, but operating expenses fell, reducing the operating ratio from 58.46 the year before to an incredibly low 47.80. The following year the ratio rose because of increasing operational costs, even though the gross income had also risen. Costly floods occurred in New Mexico, and falling freight rates began to take their toll.

Strong again warned the stockholders that increasing competition and rate making by the states were proving very harmful. Reluctantly Strong took the railroad into the Transcontinental Traffic Association in 1883, a pool which hoped to stabilize rates and divide freight shipments. The pool gave member roads a percentage of the Mississippi River–Pacific Coast traffic, but the Southern Pacific Railroad received the largest share, an unwarranted share, Strong believed. The pool paid the Atchison over $200,000 in 1884, but the agreement soon collapsed. This was not Strong's method, and the ATSF management determined to oppose both pooling and state regulation, a policy soon adopted by many other lines. The board of directors noted Strong's warnings concerning the decline in rates, but they continued to provide substantial sums for his expansionist program.

On April 27, 1882, Charles Crocker, vice president of the Central Pacific, wrote to Collis P. Huntington of the Southern Pacific that the Atchison had "strong backers in Boston [who] do not seem to want for money."[10] One reason Strong seemed to be able to raise virtually unlimited sums was the success of his early expansion program. In six years the ATSF grew from 868 miles to 3,600; gross earnings rose from $4 million to $16.3 million; and the net increased from less than $2 million to $7,315,000. The funded debt climbed from $4,175,000 to $46 million, but capitalization reached only $38,576 per mile. The capital stock issued skyrocketed from $8,615,000 to $57 million, but in 1876 no dividends were paid and yet by 1884 stockholders received 6 percent on their investment. The ATSF earned an excellent credit rating, and Strong could borrow at very low rates of interest.

Kidder, Peabody and Company handled most of the security issues. The Atchison became increasingly dependent upon this banking house, which played a major role in floating the railroad's stocks and bonds. Where early issues of securities had sold at a discount, the strength of the railroad soon enabled Kidder, Peabody to sell securities at par. The initial offering of New Mexico and Southern Pacific $1,000, 7 percent bonds sold at $900 plus a bonus of nine shares of stock. Shortly thereafter, an issue of 20,000 shares of stock sold at 100. After 1880, the directors established a policy of selling stock rather than bonds, and as the Atchison established a dividend level of 6 percent, the sale of stock brought in considerable capital. Where Nickerson had been forced to plead for capital at lower rates, Strong obtained money almost too readily. Kidder, Peabody expanded its market to include England and Holland, selling securities of the ATSF and its affiliates. The Atchison controlled its subsidiaries by stock ownership while selling their bonds through collateral trusts to obtain lower interest rates. Nickerson and Strong acquired smaller railroads by exchanges of securities (rarely by a cash payment), and until 1887 the prosperity of the railroad allowed larger and larger issues of such securities. Yet problems grew as balance sheets failed to indicate consolidated profits and losses of the subsidiaries. Clearly, net earnings were not growing as fast as capitalization, but this increasing financial problem did not deter Strong in the salad days of expansion in the early 1880s.

Strong viewed expansion as the only means to counter competition and block the invasion of Santa Fe territory by other lines. The Union Pacific and Missouri Pacific represented grave threats in Kansas and could be

Collis P. Huntington of the Southern Pacific. Southern Pacific Lines

countered only by an independent transcontinental line, Strong contended. Collis P. Huntington's Southern Pacific was racing across southern Arizona and New Mexico toward El Paso and a connection with the Texas and Pacific; Huntington threatened to build on to New Orleans and to permanently block the Atchison from California. Strong's response came in a letter to Kidder, Peabody, on April 15, 1882: "It has been found in the United States that the power of a Railroad to protect and increase its business depends much upon its length, and the extent of the territory it can touch."[11] In the fall of 1880 the ATSF extended to south-central New Mexico at San Marcial, and Strong had to decide on the ultimate terminus of the line. Despite A. A. Robinson's opposition, Strong decided to build to a connection with the Southern Pacific at Deming, New Mexico, and open a second national transcontinental rail route.

The *Annual Report* for 1880 announced that construction crews would soon reach Deming and that the railroad could "Expect large business from California and the mining districts of Arizona." On March 8, 1881, the track gangs met at Deming, and, at a brief ceremony, Dick Coleman of the Santa Fe and three Southern Pacific officials drove a silver spike.

The first through train for California left Kansas City on March 17 at 10:15 in the evening. Engine Number 85, two express cars, a baggage car, three coaches and two Pullmans inaugurated service to the Pacific coast. The Deming transcontinental connection proved to be an immediate disappointment. Huntington did not intend to route freight through Deming to the ATSF when he could send it over his own line to Texas or even over the Central Pacific to Ogden, Utah, and the Union Pacific. Few trains would pass through Deming; while this was physically a new transcontinental line, it was not economically viable. Within a week of the opening, the Santa Fe announced that no coast-bound freight would be accepted over the route.

Strong never believed that the Deming connection would become valuable, and as early as November 1878, he sent Morley to survey another route from central New Mexico south and west to Guaymas, Sonora, Mexico, on the Gulf of California. Morley's survey ran from Albuquerque to Rincon and then diagonally to Hermosillo and Guaymas. The sleepy fishing village of Guaymas represented to many Americans a splendid port and a future metropolis. Imperialistic aspirations to seize more of northern Mexico, grand designs to capture the "China trade" and the geographical fact that Guaymas was closer to Kansas City than was San Francisco supported this romantic dream. A tactical consideration very important to Strong was the simple threat such a railroad would present to Huntington.

On February 27, 1880, *The New York Times* announced that the Boston capitalists supporting the Atchison were forming a new scheme to reach a Mexican port on the Pacific in order to capture a large share of foreign trade to the South Pacific, Latin America, New Zealand and Australia. *The Times* reported that the Sonora Railway Company would immediately build from Deming, New Mexico, to Guaymas and that 300 miles of rails were on their way from England. The route was several hundred miles shorter than the New York–San Francisco rail connection, and it would become a major new transcontinental route according to the article. Strong traveled to Mexico City and entered into negotiations with President Porfirio Díaz for a charter and subsidy from the Mexican government. They signed an agreement on October 14, 1880, granting the Sonora Railway a 99-year concession to build from Guaymas north to Nogales, Arizona, a distance of 260 miles, and providing a subsidy of 7,000 pesos per kilometer of track laid, a sum equal to $11,270 per mile. In the summer of 1881 Ray Morley commenced construction at Guaymas. As chief engineer of the Sonora Railway, he surveyed from Guaymas north to the border and constructed a dock to receive rails, cars and locomotives. Supplies came from England around Cape Horn, or from San Francisco, and construction proceeded slowly northward through difficult

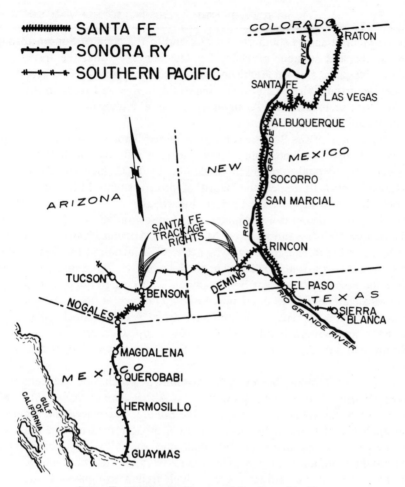

Santa Fe, Sonora Railway and Southern Pacific

terrain. In November 1881, Morley completed the line to Hermosillo and pushed construction north toward Nogales. With 10 locomotives, 7 passenger cars, 181 freight cars and gangs of Mexican laborers, the Sonora crept toward the Arizona border.

Morley's work at Guaymas convinced Huntington that Strong meant to complete the line, that it had not been an idle threat. When Strong announced plans to parallel the Southern Pacific from Deming southwestward to Nogales, Huntington agreed to lease to the ATSF for two years the SP line from Deming to Benson, Arizona. Strong immediately formed the New Mexico and Arizona Railroad to build the 90 miles between Benson and Nogales, where a connection would be made with the Sonora Railway. The Santa Fe advanced $1.3 million to its newest subsidiary, and crews labored across southern Arizona and in the state of Sonora through the spring and summer of 1882. On October 25, 1882, the track gangs met at Nogales, and the Atchison announced the opening of its 1,700-mile main line from Kansas City to Guaymas, the longest rail route in the world under one management. A silver spike in a mahogany tie symbolized completion of the line.

The leaders of the Sonora Railway included Thomas Nickerson, Arthur Sewall, Benjamin Cheney and other Atchison officials and directors; and most of the capital was raised in Boston by these men. In 1881, three Mexican nationals joined the board of directors, but little capital came from Mexico to support the project. Indeed, the subsidy promised by the Mexican government did not materialize for several years. The fiction that the Sonora Railway and the New Mexico and Arizona Railroad were independent ended in March 1882, when the ATSF acquired the Sonora Railway in a two-for-one stock exchange. In addition, the Santa Fe guaranteed the Sonora's 7 percent bonds amounting to $4,107,000, and pledged the Mexican subsidy to bond purchasers. *The New York Times* reported that the announcement of the purchase drove Atchison stock up from 79 to 83⅞ and Sonora bonds rose from 89 to 99. Clearly, said the *Times*, Strong had subverted the Southern Pacific monopoly of rail traffic in the Southwest.

Within ten months, however, the wisdom of purchasing the Sonora, or even building it, came into question. The ATSF *Annual Report* for 1883 admitted business remained poor on the Sonora, but placed the blame on an epidemic of fever in Mexico. Almost a quarter of a million dollars in repairs had to be made on the line, and the Mexican subsidy stood almost $1.5 million in arrears. The line lost $93,495 in 1883, and $33,123 in 1884. In order to attract more through freight to Guaymas, the Santa Fe purchased a seven-eighths interest in a steamer, the "City of Topeka," to operate from Guaymas to other Mexican ports. Its operation failed to generate additional traffic. During the next fifteen years it became increasingly evident that the Sonora Railway was a serious strategic error and a financial disaster. Eventually the Sonora would be traded away, but remarkably, the major investors continued to seek wealth and financial glory in Mexico.

The now more daring Nickerson and his associates formed the Mexican Central Railway in February 1880, to build a railroad from El Paso south to Mexico City. The Santa Fe opened a branch from the Albuquerque-Deming stem at Rincon to El Paso in July 1881—the so-called "Horned Toad" line—and Nickerson saw the Mexican Central as another extension of the ATSF. He raised some $31 million in capital to construct the Mexican Central, which became an "intimate ally" of the Atchison, although they were not legally related. Nickerson wooed Ray Morley away from the ATSF to build the Mexican Central, but this young and vigorous engineer died as a result of a rifle accident near La Cruz, Mexico, in 1883. Nickerson's hope that the Santa Fe would absorb yet another Mexican stepchild went aglimmering, and only a traffic agreement held the roads together. In this instance Strong exercised unusual restraint when an opportunity for expansion presented itself—perhaps because he had committed the Santa Fe to build from Albuquerque to the Pacific over the 35th parallel.

Shortly after the ATSF entered New Mexico, Strong had dispatched Ray Morley, Lewis Kingman and A. A. Robinson to survey routes to the Pacific. Their survey teams made vast sweeps across New Mexico and Arizona, and they sent back to Boston voluminous reports which analyzed locational possibilities and the potential traffic on each route. After determining the route from Raton through Albuquerque to Deming and El Paso, Strong then asked his crews for recommendations for building to the West Coast. On November 28, 1878, Robinson filed a report urging use of the 32nd parallel from southern New Mexico to southern California, passing through Yuma and Tucson. He argued strenuously against the 35th parallel route from Albuquerque west, believing that the Grand Canyon sealed off all potential traffic from the north. The 32nd parallel route would enable the ATSF to reach either Guaymas or San Diego, and it could be operated more efficiently. Within a brief period of time, however, Collis P. Huntington's Southern Pacific preempted the 32nd parallel route as it built eastward from Los Angeles to El Paso. Further, Lewis Kingman reported that the territory between Albuquerque and Tucson was "hopeless" both for locating an operable line and for potential traffic. Strong and Nickerson decided that the best possibility for their own independent route to California was the 35th parallel.

Lieutenant Amiel Weeks Whipple and a federal party first surveyed the 35th parallel route in 1853. In the pre–Civil War era the federal government dispatched a number of expeditions to find the best transcontinental rail route, and the survey of 1853 had orders to follow the 35th parallel to the Pacific. Whipple's party gathered at Fort Smith, Arkansas, in June of that year, and moved west to locate a rail route. The twelve men on Whipple's team included representatives from various technical and scientific fields including botany, geology, astronomy and meteorology, as well as an artist and an engineer. They followed the Canadian River through west Texas and continued westward to Albuquerque. Accompanied by a military escort they journeyed into the San Francisco Mountains of northern Arizona, passing through the vast forests of pine beyond Canyon Diablo. For a month they worked to find a suitable route through the mountains between the present site of Flagstaff and the Colorado River. Their magnetic instruments failed when volcanic rock reversed the poles of their compasses. Though their mules had died of starvation, they reached "The Needles," three pinnacles of rock on the California side of the Colorado River, on February 20, 1854. Entering California, they moved across the Mojave Desert to Cajon Pass, and on March 21 arrived in Los Angeles. Whipple reported that a railroad could be built along the route, and estimated the cost at $90,000 per mile. Whipple's report received widespread attention, particularly in St. Louis, where it was hoped that the eastern terminus of the first transcontinental rail route would be located. The national struggle over the expansion of slavery, however, would postpone any decision on the 35th parallel route until 1865.

The termination of the Civil War produced a revival of many transcontinental railroad schemes, and a number of railroad companies were formed to link the Midwest with California. General John C. Fremont and a handful of speculators had a bill introduced in Congress on December 11, 1865, to charter a railroad from Missouri and Arkansas to the Pacific along the 35th parallel. The railway would begin in Springfield, Missouri, and reach Albuquerque via the Canadian River valley. From Albuquerque the route proceeded across Arizona to the Colorado River and then up the San Joaquin Valley to San Francisco. To further the work of this new transcontinental line, the federal government would provide a 200-foot right-of-way and a land grant of twenty odd-numbered sections of land per mile on each side of the track in territories and ten sections per mile in states. The line was to be completed by July 4, 1878. President Andrew Johnson signed the bill on July 27, 1866, creating the Atlantic and Pacific Railroad with capitalization of $100 million. A minor clause in the law, which would become a major problem in the future, authorized the Southern Pacific Railroad to meet the Atlantic and Pacific near the California border, thus preserving the SP's monopoly in the Golden State. Undaunted by this "modest" provision, General Fremont and his supporters began to sell securities in the A&P, and to build to California. Progress was slow, however, and by 1872 the A&P extended only from Pacific, Missouri, near St. Louis, to Vinita in northeastern Indian Territory, a distance of 361 miles. Three years later the A&P fell upon hard times and went into receivership.

A new railroad company emerged to revive the A&P. The St. Louis and San Francisco Railroad was formed on September 11, 1876, to take over all but a few miles of the A&P in Indian Territory. This preserved the fiction that the A&P, with its enormous land grant, still existed. The Frisco, as the new company became known, announced that it would build to the Pacific along the 35th parallel route and that branches would be built into southern Kansas. The Santa Fe recognized that a threat to its home base existed and that both the 32nd and the 35th parallel routes were now in the hands of other companies.

The Frisco moved aggressively during the next four years. It built a branch west from its main line across Missouri into southern Kansas. The city of Wichita and surrounding Sedgwick County voted a bond issue to attract the new line. Frisco officials hoped to reach Wichita and a connection with the ATSF and then use the Santa Fe to Albuquerque where a railroad would be built westward under the A&P charter. Strong and Nickerson opposed this upstart which was invading ATSF territory in Kansas, and they were outraged when rumors spread in 1879 that Jay Gould, or perhaps Collis P. Huntington, was about to seize the Frisco. Nickerson acted quickly to turn the Frisco into a cooperative ally and forestall the rumored action by Gould or Huntington.

Nickerson entered into negotiations with James D. Fish, president of the Frisco, in the fall of 1879; and on November 14, they signed the Tripartite Agreement. This agreement brought together the interests of the Atchison, the Frisco, and the A&P to build a transcontinental railway under the A&P charter. The Frisco agreed to stop invading southern Kansas and to terminate construction at Wichita. Further, several Bostonians would be added to the Frisco board to represent the Atchison. The Frisco would use the ATSF from Wichita (later changed to Halstead) to Albuquerque, and from that point a jointly owned line would be built to California. The A&P would issue first mortgage bonds at the rate of $25,000 per mile and income bonds of $18,750 per mile, with both the Santa Fe and the Frisco obligated to pay half of any unpaid interest. Eastbound traffic of the A&P would be divided at Wichita, with the Frisco to receive St. Louis freight and the Santa Fe that which was designated for Kansas City and Chicago. In a substantial coup, Fish agreed that Nickerson would be president of the A&P, and that three trustees would control all A&P stock. The Atchison and the Frisco would jointly sponsor an initial A&P issue of $10 million in 30-year, 6 percent mortgage bonds. The boards of the two railroads ratified the agreement on January 31, 1880, and *The New York Times* of the following day announced what had been the talk of Wall Street for months. Writing in the 1879 *Annual Report*, Nickerson declared: "The current year has been one of great activity, and more than usual progress," because the negotiations with the Frisco had made the year "one of notable events in the history of the Corporation."

A. A. Robinson wasted no time in preparing to build the A&P. Even as Fish and Nickerson established the agreement, he sent a small crew 180 miles west of Albuquerque to seize a strategic location in an effort to

The "Kansas," Locomotive No. 27 of the Atlantic and Pacific. Santa Fe Railway

block Southern Pacific designs. Lewis Kingman and W. A. Drake moved into Arizona to survey the route, and shortly after the agreement was ratified they were joined by H. R. Holbrook and J. E. Early. They used the notes from Lieutenant Whipple's party of 1853–1854 and from a survey made by General William J. Palmer in 1867–1868 for the Union Pacific. The rugged terrain prevented Kingman and Holbrook from preparing the detailed work Strong and Robinson usually demanded of their men. There were few settlers in the vast reaches between Albuquerque and the Colorado River; scattered ranches, some Mexican herders, the army post at Fort Wingate, and large numbers of Navajo Indians occupied the land. Water was hard to find, and food supplies were precarious. Kingman and Holbrook tried to maintain peaceful relations with the Navajo and shared their meager foodstuffs with them; but on May 3, 1880, Strong approved requisitions for 8 Colt revolvers, 12 carbines and 700 cartridges which the surveyors had purchased in February and March. Because they were forced to bring water to their temporary camps from springs fifty or sixty miles away, Kingman and his crew rationed water at the rate of one pint a day while they moved toward the Colorado River. By the fall of 1880, their work largely completed, Kingman and Holbrook sent their reports to Robinson. Based upon the surveys, Robinson wrote to Nickerson on August 31, recommending that the town of Isleta, twelve miles south of Albuquerque, serve as the initial construction point, since building directly westward from Albuquerque would be more costly and would mean much heavier grades. Nickerson and Strong concurred, and construction began.

Lewis Kingman took charge of the track gangs, and by February 1881, 100 miles of line were completed, of which 80 miles were in operation. Kingman stockpiled huge quantities of construction materials to build the 600-mile segment, with over 800 carloads of rail gathered at just one point. Construction crews encountered some minor problems with the Indians, who tore up portions of the track at night; but the Indians were persuaded to stop by Father Dourchee of Mission Isleta. By September, Kingman's crews had laid 236 miles of track and were well into the forests of northern Arizona. Yellow pine, junipers and piñons covered the mountain tops to the 8,500-foot level, where the larger water supply allowed firs and aspens to grow. Grading subcontractors for the forest areas included a group of Mormons led by John W. Young, one of Brigham Young's sons. Initially Kingman's crews were mostly Irish, but he hired Mexicans as well. The A&P paid tracklayers and graders $2.25 per day, and spikers and iron layers received $2.50. The enormity of the project meant that addi-

Atlantic and Pacific Railroad

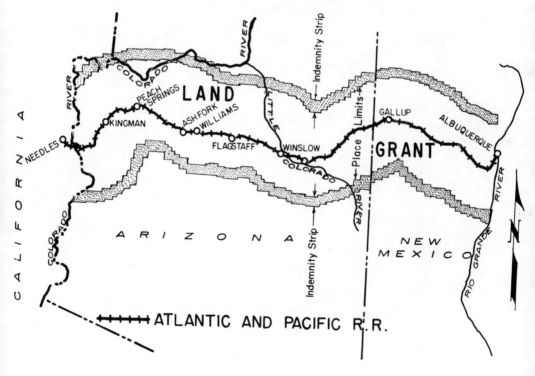

Canyon Diablo Bridge in Arizona. State Historical Society of Colorado, William Jackson Collection

tional labor had to be acquired, and so Kingman hired local Apaches and Navajos and Mojaves from California as shovelers and day laborers. The Indians soon became the heart of many of the crews and were excellent workers. Laying the 52-pound steel rails at the rate of one mile per day, the gangs rapidly approached a serious obstacle to the railroad—Canyon Diablo.

Located twenty-six miles west of Winslow, Canyon Diablo pierced the Plateau of Arizona to a depth of 250 feet, with sheer yellow and white limestone rock walls rising almost perpendicularly from the narrow river bed. Robinson had sent bridge builders to the site months before the rails arrived. The bridge crew hauled supplies to the canyon from the rapidly approaching railroad. The bridge iron, which had been prefabricated in New York, was designed to hold thirty times the weight of the trains it would carry. The iron bridgework soared 222½ feet above the canyon floor, supporting the 560-foot long structure on trestle bents and towers. At a cost of $250,000 and untold agony of the bridge workers, the structure opened in July 1882, two months after rails had reached the site.

Despite increasing friction between the engineers from the Santa Fe and those from the Frisco who were building the A&P, construction progressed rapidly across Arizona. The Johnson Canyon Tunnel between Ash Fork and Williams opened after a period of difficult work, making the 250 miles of track from Canyon Diablo to the Colorado River operable. A pile bridge across the river to Needles, California, opened on August 3, 1883; and the A&P crews laid rails over the bridge and up the river to the town. Even as the A&P crews built across northern Arizona, Huntington announced that he would build a branch of his SP from the main line at Mojave to Needles to connect with the A&P as provided by the charter of 1866. The SP assembled a small army of Chinese laborers at Mojave and constructed the connection across the searing desert to the new terminus. Another transcontinental route now existed, but once again Huntington thwarted the ATSF—it still did not have an independent line into California. The 1883 *Annual Report* of the ATSF noted ominously that although the company had enjoyed a prosperous year, the opening of the Needles connection proved to be a disappointment. The ATSF had not received traffic from the Southern Pacific at Needles, for Huntington continued to direct freight through Ogden or El Paso.

William Barstow Strong took on one of the giants of American railroading as he pushed the Sonora Railway to Guaymas and the A&P to the California border at Needles. Collis P. Huntington planned to use any means necessary to keep the ATSF out of California in order to maintain his monopoly in the Golden State. The acknowledged leader of the Southern Pacific's "Big Four," Huntington worked tirelessly to extend his SP

Altantic and Pacific roundhouse in Needles, California. Santa Fe Railway

to New Orleans and to protect his transcontinental connection with the Union Pacific at Ogden. A shrewd, calculating man with few friends, Huntington could be narrow, vindictive and domineering, but like Strong he also possessed great energy and persistence. As the Santa Fe marched toward California and the Pacific, Huntington sought and found an ally to stir up trouble for Strong in the Midwest. While the A&P expanded westward, its other parent, the Frisco, continued to invade Jay Gould's territory. The Frisco built steadily southwestward from Missouri through Arkansas and Indian Territory into northern Texas. Gould's wrath rose with his temper, and he acted to protect the territory of his Missouri Pacific and Texas and Pacific. The expansionist policies of the Atchison and its partner brought Gould and Huntington together in an alliance against the upstarts.

In the late fall of 1881 Gould and Huntington agreed to jointly purchase control of the Frisco, and thereby block the extension of the A&P beyond Needles and end the construction program in Texas which threatened Gould's properties. Large purchases of Frisco securities were reported by *The New York Times* and *The Commercial and Financial Chronicle*, but Strong and the ATSF directors remained calm. Gould and Huntington did not attempt to keep their actions secret, and word of their purchases spread rapidly. On January 24, 1882, they announced that together they held just under half of the stock of the Frisco, and they soon gained seats on the board of directors. The new Frisco board voted to terminate construction of the A&P at the Colorado River and to curtail any further expansion in Texas.

Recognizing the futility of fighting both Gould and Huntington, and simply desirous of saving the A&P, Strong accepted the arrangement and agreed to connect with the SP at Needles. In turn, the SP agreed to give the A&P through-freight service from Needles to San Francisco. But Huntington refused to send eastbound freight through Needles, and Santa Fe freight often became lost or delayed rather mysteriously between Needles and San Francisco. Strong refused to accept defeat. He announced that the Atchison intended to build a line into California which would parallel the SP all the way to San Francisco Bay if necessary.

A bluff, and Huntington knew it, but in 1883 Collis P. Huntington found himself in financial trouble. He had overextended his personal fortune, and he determined that a modest retreat was in order. Strong and Huntington entered into negotiations in early 1884 over the Needles-Mojave line. Strong offered to purchase the 242-mile-long property, and Huntington agreed to sell, but at an outrageous price. Strong reported to the finance committee of the Atchison board of directors that Huntington wanted $40,000 per mile for the connection and an additional $6 million for $3 million in stocks and bonds issued against the property and $3 million in Frisco bonds; the securities were grossly overpriced at par. When the ATSF refused to purchase the Frisco securities, Huntington removed them from the package and lowered his price to $35,000 per mile. Then his partner Leland Stanford balked at anything less than $40,000 per mile. The finance committee told Strong to try to obtain a better deal.

Under increasing financial duress, Huntington and Gould accepted a much more moderate offer. In April 1884, they sold their interests in the Frisco, and Huntington agreed in August to a temporary lease of the Needles-Mojave line, a lease which would lead ultimately to a purchase of the property. The A&P purchased the line for $30,000 per mile; but until a clear title could be obtained, a lease at 6 percent of the purchase price per year would exist. Further, the Santa Fe obtained trackage rights from Mojave to San Francisco at a rate of $1,200 per mile per year. Huntington also dumped $3,096,768 in A&P securities on the Atchison for $1,524,356, a price far higher than their true value. The California rail monopolist knew the A&P was in serious trouble and unloading these securities only made matters more difficult for Strong. The leader of the Santa Fe obtained the long-sought entrance into California and through-service to San Francisco could now be offered; but such traffic as the ATSF won failed to help the A&P, whose bookkeepers continued to use large quantities of red ink.

Jay Gould of the Missouri
Pacific. Missouri Pacific Lines

From the very beginning of the ATSF-Frisco expansion of the A&P
there had been serious financial problems. In January 1882, the Frisco
failed to sell its half of an A&P bond issue. Vast cash advances had to be
made to build the line, which cost far more than anticipated to construct
and operate. Both the Frisco and the ATSF were hard pressed to pay the
interest on the A&P bonds which they had guaranteed. Even when the
line opened, the fastest express train took 24 hours to travel the 574 miles
from Albuquerque to Needles over the rough, unballasted track with its
heavy grades and sharp curves. Between November 1, 1883 and June 30,
1897, the A&P lost $13,890,275 on a gross income of only $7,564,764.
Local revenues on the A&P were virtually nonexistent, and through-traffic
failed to materialize. Both New Mexico and Arizona levied heavy taxes
on the A&P and its land grant, thus adding to the railroad's burden. Service
deteriorated so badly that in 1886 the *Arizona Journal-Miner* of Prescott
charged the Santa Fe with "almost criminal neglect."[12] A new, large,
permanent bridge over the Colorado River opened on July 29, 1884, but
few trains used the expensive structure. Only by selling one million acres
of land had the January interest been paid in 1885. The management of
the A&P tried to put the best face on its *Annual Reports* in the mid-1880s,
but an unfunded debt of over $6 million hung over the property like a
dark cloud. Without the massive land grant which the A&P had acquired,

the Atchison might have actually abandoned the A&P in 1884, as the parent company's *Annual Report* hinted.

The A&P had gotten 14,325,760 acres of land from the federal government after completing the line from Isleta to the Colorado River. A high percentage of the property consisted of desert wasteland with only limited ranching possibilities. This land of low mesas, erosion valleys and dry washes supported stands of yellow pine and Douglas fir at higher elevations; but a rainfall of less than three inches per year failed to attract many buyers in the nineteenth century. The A&P Land Office discovered that farmers, ranchers and timber operators had preempted over a million acres, and so lieu lands had to be taken. The railroad right-of-way and other facilities took a very modest 8,000 acres, leaving an enormous tract to sell. Land offered for ranches attracted a few buyers, but problems with squatters, preemption entries and "Mexican" land grants snarled attempts to clear titles to the property. The Land Department insisted that potential buyers see the land, and wagons and teams were available at the land offices to take prospective customers to the sites. From 1883 until 1889 the Santa Fe and the A&P offered land buyers free transportation to the property. Sales were meager, however, even at 50¢ to 75¢ per acre. A major sale in 1884 to the Aztec Land and Cattle Company of one million acres at 50¢ per acre generated a large share of the total land sales. The Land Department finally turned to leases rather than sales to generate income from the property, but by 1897 the A&P had received only $3,853,336 from its land grant.

In the mid-1880s the general public's attitude toward land grants for railroads became quite negative, and the federal government responded by canceling many grants, including portions of the original A&P subsidy. In 1884 and 1885, bitter debates in Congress ensued over the forfeiture of the land grants, and one Senator denounced the A&P as a wholly unprofitable railroad built across a wilderness, without traffic or profits. The critics demanded that the A&P grant along the uncompleted route be forfeited. On July 6, 1886, the federal government took from the A&P the lands which had been granted on the central division from Indian Territory to Isleta and from the Colorado River to San Francisco. The New Mexico–Arizona property remained to the A&P, but neither land sales nor traffic were significant enough to pay operating expenses let alone interest and dividends. Strong realized that if the A&P were to be saved, a massive increase in through-traffic had to be generated, and a truly independent line from Needles to the Pacific coast at Los Angeles or San Diego was the only means to develop such traffic.

The officers of the Atchison acknowledged that the line to Guaymas had been a flanking movement and that the A&P route to Needles repre-

Williams, Arizona, along the A&P. Santa Fe Railway

sented basically a feint. They further contended that only a direct assault on Huntington's California monopoly would succeed. Therefore, as early as 1879, they began to encourage a revolt among Californians, especially in San Diego, against the Southern Pacific. The southernmost potentially large port in the state, San Diego possessed a salubrious climate, a huge natural harbor, and several enterprising businessmen and local boosters, but San Diego did not have a railroad. From the decade preceding the Civil War until 1879, San Diegoans dreamed of their city's becoming the Pacific terminus of a transcontinental railroad. The predecessor of the Texas and Pacific was to have terminated there, and a half-dozen other schemes were proposed, with several miles of grading having been actually completed at one point; but the town failed to attract sufficient interest from the outside and lacked sufficient capital locally to initiate a railroad on its own. In 1879 Frank Kimball, one of San Diego's most prominent citizens and owner of the large Rancho de la Nacional south of the city, traveled to the East in an attempt to stimulate interest in the city among railroad builders; neither Jay Gould nor Tom Scott was interested. Kimball went to Boston and found Thomas Nickerson and the directors of the Atchison more than modestly tempted by San Diego's offer of 10,000 acres of land. Nickerson dispatched Ray Morley to run a survey from Needles west to San Diego and sent Morley and two other officials to San Diego on October 8, 1879, to talk civil leaders into a larger grant-in-aid. Morley reported that a railroad could be constructed to San Diego through Cajon Pass, and the city fathers of San Diego added to Kimball's earlier subsidy proposal. While Nickerson found the new offer attractive, the ATSF had decided by February 2, 1880, to build west on the A&P charter and the 35th parallel, much farther north than the 32nd parallel route into San Diego. There would be a lengthy delay in reaching San Diego, Nickerson wrote to Kimball.

Frank Kimball, the people of San Diego and the residents of San Bernardino did not give up in their efforts to attract the Santa Fe. San Bernardino, which had been bypassed by the SP, hoped that the ATSF would build a line through that community and then south to San Diego. Kimball returned to Boston and again sweetened the original offer. Nickerson, the Atchison directors and Kidder, Peabody were persuaded.

On July 10, 1880, Frank Kimball, representing Kimball Brothers (his own realty firm), and the San Diego Chamber of Commerce and Board of Trustees, and Thomas Nickerson, as president of the California Southern Railroad, signed a contract to connect San Diego with the Santa Fe. The California Southern, organized by Kidder, Peabody and Company, Nickerson, and three other Atchison officers, agreed to build a railroad from San Diego north and east through San Bernardino to meet the A&P line. Kimball Brothers and other residents of San Diego gave the California Southern some 17,356 acres of land (primarily the old National Ranch owned by Frank and Warren Kimball south of the city), two miles of harbor frontage, 486 city lots for depot and terminal space, and $25,410 in cash. The California Southern set July 1, 1882, as a deadline for building at least 116 miles of track from San Diego to San Bernardino. Kimball's seemingly personal generosity in donating 10,000 acres of property was tempered by a clause in the contract which established the San Diego Land and Town Company, a joint interest of Kimball Brothers and the California Southern, which received 6,000 acres of land in its own

San Diego harbor with California Southern construction materials. Historical Collection, Title Insurance and Trust Company

right. The California Southern agreed that for five years its 10,000 acres would be sold only through the Land and Town Company. A syndicate of Kimball Brothers and ATSF/CS officials purchased another 10,000 acres for speculative purposes. It is only reasonable to assume that Nickerson and the Atchison officials were motivated to form the California Southern and to enter into the fray against Huntington again because of the potential profits of San Diego real estate.

Nickerson and his associates incorporated the California Southern Railroad Company on October 16, 1880, with capitalization of $2.9 million. Benjamin Kimball of Boston, not related to the Kimballs of San Diego, held the largest block of stock; and while most of the capital came from Boston, the board of directors also reflected San Diego's contribution of land and enthusiasm. Nickerson resigned as president of the Atchison to devote his energies to the CS, and he began to solicit his friends for stock purchases. He distributed a circular in January 1881, declaring that San Diego possessed the greatest harbor on the West Coast and the finest climate in the country and that it was a land of "wine and honey." Aiming the circular toward investors in the Atchison, the Frisco and the A&P, Nickerson declared, "Parties largely interested in the Atlantic and Pacific and the Atchison, Topeka and Santa Fe Railroad Companies, have organized the California Southern Railroad Company for the purpose of building a standard-gauge railroad and telegraph line from the port of San Diego to a connection with the Atlantic and Pacific Railroad in California."[13] He noted that the citizens of San Diego had donated $1 million in land and that the California Southern interests would be well served by the San Diego Land and Town Company with its capitalization of $1.5 million. The California Southern offered 6 percent, 40-year bonds at a rate of $25,000 per mile with $7,000 per mile to remain in the CS treasury. Each subscriber of $1,100 would immediately receive 10 shares of the $100 par value stock in the CS, a $1,000 bond, one share of the Land and Town Company and, when the railroad reached San Bernardino, two additional shares. With the land profits as a substantial lure, Nickerson sold enough bonds to initiate construction.

Chief Engineer Joseph Osgood arrived in San Diego on October 11, 1880, and established the CS headquarters. He surveyed a route from National City, the terminal to be built on the old National Ranch, through San Diego to San Bernardino. All equipment and rails came to San Diego around Cape Horn, and in March 1881, the four-masted British sailing ship *Trafalgar* arrived with a cargo of German and Belgian rails. Steam towboats and lighters unloaded the rails and brought them to the CS wharf. Osgood organized construction crews and began to build from National City north through San Diego. The 55 miles north and east along

Excursion train in Temecula Canyon. Historical Collection, Title Insurance and Trust Company

the Pacific Ocean to Fallbrook Junction opened January 2, 1882, and work through Temecula Canyon proceeded through the spring and summer. Ignoring the warnings of natives of the area that the canyon was subject to flash floods, Osgood pushed on. A cargo of rails from Cardiff, Wales, arrived on August 1, 1882, and were used to complete the line to Colton on the sixteenth. There the CS had to cross the SP main line in order to build on to San Bernardino.

The Southern Pacific had attempted to block construction of the CS at every opportunity, and when the CS reached Colton, the SP refused to allow Osgood's crews to lay a crossing to enable the railroad to proceed.

Huntington proposed to Frank Kimball that the CS sell out to the SP, but Kimball refused and threatened to withdraw his land subsidy if the other CS owners accepted Huntington's offer. The SP then "persuaded" the sheriff at Colton to seize the CS crossing which had been prefabricated at the National City shop. After the CS crews took the crossing back by stealth, CS lawyers got a court order requiring the SP to allow the crossing to be laid. The SP then placed three locomotives in a row at the crossing site and refused to move them. The residents of Colton and San Bernardino became so incensed that the threat of riot provoked an additional court order which was served on the president of the Southern Pacific at San Francisco. The SP backed down, the locomotives were moved, and the crossing was installed. The CS proceeded on to San Bernardino, and service began on September 13. The residents of the towns along the route, especially San Diego and San Bernardino, wildly celebrated the opening of their "independent" railroad, but there remained to be built the 250-mile connection with the A&P at Needles.

CALIFORNIA SOUTHERN R.R. AND CONNECTIONS

California Southern Railroad and Connections

By the fall of 1883, the CS and its supporters had no more money. A second prospectus issued by Nickerson in 1882 produced some additional capital, but the CS was in serious trouble. It could not survive on local traffic, and the management could not raise money to complete the link to the A&P. Construction of the first 116 miles had been estimated to cost $10,000 per mile by Kimball and $18,000 by Nickerson, but Osgood spent between $25,000 and $26,000 and, therefore, was fired. Then when the winter rains arrived, the CS came to further grief. Heavy rains fell for four weeks in January and February 1884, and flash floods swept through Temecula Canyon washing thirty miles of CS rails, ties, and bridges out to sea, providing little consolation to the investors who were now told that restoration of the line would cost $319,879. For nine months the CS remained closed. The California Southern, which had issued $7 million in securities, had an income of $19,000, expenses of $24,000 and a net loss of $57,000. New construction remained out of the question, for no earnings were being generated, and in July 1884, the CS defaulted. William B. Strong, who had succeeded Nickerson as president of the Atchison, determined not to allow the CS to enter bankruptcy and fall into the hands of the Southern Pacific.

From April until November 1884, the ATSF, CS and SP jockeyed for position in southern California. On April 15, Nickerson issued a plea to the CS stockholders to raise $300,000 to repair the flood damage, but they subscribed to only $114,500 in new securities. Strong simultaneously negotiated with Huntington for the Needles-Mojave branch; as has been seen, Huntington capitulated and agreed in August to sell the line to the Santa Fe. Next, Strong turned to the California Southern, and through Kidder, Peabody, announced plans for the Atchison to purchase the CS. A circular dated November 7 described the arrangements: the bondholders of the CS surrendered their first-mortgage bonds to Kidder, Peabody and received 6 percent income bonds; a new issue of 6 percent first-mortgage bonds was sold to the Atchison at the rate of $10,000 per mile; and the ATSF also received half of the capital stock of the California Southern. With the money raised from the Atchison bond purchase, the CS would construct a connection from San Bernardino north 81 miles to Barstow (then called Waterman) on the newly-acquired track between Mojave and Needles, and rebuild the Temecula Canyon line. This agreement, following rather quickly the deal with Huntington for the Needles-Mojave property, produced considerable negative comment in several financial journals, which noted the vast debts of the A&P, Sonora and California Southern. Strong responded by keeping dividends at $6.00 per share.

The purchase of the California Southern marked the final stage of Santa Fe expansion to the west coast as it sought independent transcontinental status. A circular from Kidder, Peabody declared on October 25, 1884,

San Diego depot, built in 1887. Historical Collection, Title Insurance and Trust Company

that the CS represented a "Key to the Pacific business." The purchase of the CS gave the Atchison a port on the Pacific not controlled by Huntington and the SP; only the 81-mile link between Barstow and San Bernardino needed to be completed to give the Santa Fe a through line.

The terrain between Barstow and San Bernardino presented some of the most difficult problems for railroad engineers in the state of California. Ray Morley and Fred Perris, an excellent railroad engineer and a pioneer surveyor in California, both went over the ground and declared that a rail route through Cajon Pass was feasible. South of Victorville the survey placed the line on a long climb of 1,000 feet into the mountains along the south slope of the Mojave Desert. Yucca and Joshua trees covered the foothills, to be replaced by thick brush as the grade climbed to the summit. Juniper and piñon supplanted the shrubs as the line reached the divide at 3,823 feet of elevation. The engineers then sent the grading crews plunging down from the summit into the San Bernardino Valley in a winding course through deep cuts to the valley floor. Chinese and Mexican laborers worked through much of 1885 laying the 61-pound rails through Cajon Pass, and on November 15, 1885, they drove the last spike.

The first through passenger train east from San Diego departed on

November 16, and a large celebration welcomed the travelers in San Bernardino. On November 26 the first Pullman train arrived in San Diego from Kansas City, and the *San Diego Union* predicted "a period of moderate expansion" for the city.[14] Officials of the ATSF were far less sanguine in their view of the opening of the line. While San Diego offered considerable potential as a harbor, it was not going to rival San Francisco or even Los Angeles. Coastal vessels could be utilized to take cargoes from San Diego to San Francisco, but at enormous expense. Shipments from Kansas City to San Diego failed to materialize, the California Southern continued to lose money, and the shops at National City were not expanded because the Santa Fe decided to build its major facility in southern California at San Bernardino. Angry San Diegoans were further incensed when news arrived on September 24, 1885, that Strong had signed a lease with the SP to use that company's tracks from Colton into Los Angeles; the Santa Fe now entered a second and more significant California terminus.

Collis P. Huntington simply could not cope with Strong's aggressiveness. By leasing the Colton–Los Angeles line, Huntington hoped to forestall further Santa Fe expansion in southern California; but Huntington had lost in his bid to hold Strong at Needles, he had failed in his attempt to prevent the Atchison from linking up to the California Southern at San Bernardino, and now he gave Strong entrance into Los Angeles, albeit over SP tracks. To further mollify Strong, Huntington established the Pacific Coast Association to pool and divide California traffic, and he invited the Santa Fe to join the association. At a meeting in February 1886, the representatives of the Atchison demanded a larger share of the pool and Huntington tried to arrange a compromise to prevent an all-out rate war, but Strong refused to accept less than a full share. Huntington publicly claimed that he "even agreed to give the Atchison some of our earnings for the sake of peace, but it wanted more than it had earned or could earn."[15] There would be no peace in southern California—for Strong had already decided to enter Los Angeles over Santa Fe rails and, further, to interlace the area with a network of branches from San Diego to Los Angeles and San Bernardino. No quarter for Huntington and the Southern Pacific.

On January 1, 1887, President J. F. Crank of the Los Angeles and San Gabriel Valley Railroad came to New York City to arrange for an expansion of his railway. William Barstow Strong immediately invited him to Boston to visit with the ATSF board of directors. Crank also received an invitation from Leland Stanford, then president of the Southern Pacific, to come to Washington and visit with SP executives. Mr. Crank bought a ticket for Boston; the SP had fought his small railway at every turn and

Los Angeles and San Gabriel Valley train near Pasadena. Historical Collection, Security Pacific National Bank

he would not sell out to "the Octopus." Although originally chartered as a narrow-gauge railroad in 1883, the LA&SGV operated a standard-gauge line from Los Angeles to Duarte in the San Gabriel Mountains, a distance of thirty-one miles. The early developers of the LA&SGV had asked the Los Angeles common council to grant considerable right of way along the Los Angeles River with the railroad to serve as a levee, and in addition the city fathers were asked to give $20,000 to the railroad and grant the company considerable city property for station, yard and engine facilities. The council denied this request, but, in 1885, gave the LA&SGV a 50-foot-wide right-of-way to a point near the First Street bridge in the business section. The LA&SGV built slowly eastward from Los Angeles, reaching Pasadena on September 11, 1885. The SP refused to help the LA&SGV, forcing the company to bring rails, locomotives and equipment to Los Angeles at exorbitant rates. When Crank met with Strong and the directors of the Atchison in Boston he agreed to a "bargain" price and sold his shortline to the Santa Fe. Strong then ordered construction crews to San Bernardino where they built the short section of track from that city to Duarte in the mountains. On May 31, 1887, the first Santa Fe train to travel over Santa Fe owned and operated trackage arrived in Los Angeles, and the railroad war Huntington feared began.

Until the 1870s the area around the little town of Los Angeles consisted

The Overland Limited on the desert. State Historical Society of Colorado, William Jackson Collection

of substantial ranches with large herds of cattle interspersed with a few small farms. The census of 1870 listed only 5,728 people living in the one- and two-story adobe houses surrounding the Main Street commercial area of Los Angeles. Drinking water and sewerage moved along open ditches in the undeveloped community. The area possessed an agricultural economic base with wheat, grapes, wine and fruit marketed in Los Angeles. Changes came with the arrival of the SP on September 6, 1876, but extremely high freight rates retarded large-scale development. The population had risen to only 11,183 by 1880, but the arrival of the Santa Fe set off an unbelievable population and real estate boom. Cutthroat competition between the Atchison and the SP drove passenger rates from Kansas City to Los Angeles to an unbelievably low $1.00 on March 6, 1887. The magnificent climate, substantial advertisements by the town and the railroads, and the low fares brought thousands of people to the burgeoning city. The real estate boom came almost immediately after the arrival of the ATSF, and county property values soon soared to $41 million, while local banks held $6 million in deposits. Three years later the population passed 50,000, and even the collapse of the real estate market failed to slow the spectacular growth rate.

Strong, local California businessmen and the directors of the Atchison saw the vast potential of southern California; the Santa Fe began to build a substantial rail network both to promote and to take advantage of the boom. The Atchison built a second line into the city from San Bernardino through Riverside and Orange County. This seventy-mile line opened on August 12, 1888. That same year a branch was built from the second Los Angeles entrance south to Fallbrook, giving the Santa Fe a direct route from Los Angeles to San Diego. This branch along the coast became the main line to San Diego, enabling the Santa Fe to abandon the difficult and troublesome route through Temecula Canyon. Fred Perris, who had served as the chief engineer of the California Southern, supervised the construction of these lines. Because nearly all of the branches were built independently, a collection of Atchison officials and California business-men served as directors or officers, though the operations were clearly controlled by the Santa Fe. In the Los Angeles area, the company built a branch to Redondo Beach to capture additional tourist trade and to gain a harbor facility. A similar line to Santa Monica did not include a harbor facility, but reached another beach resort. During the years 1886–1892

On the surfline to San Diego. Historical Collection, Title Insurance and Trust Company

many other short branches were constructed, and in September 1889 most were consolidated with the California Southern Railroad into the Southern California Railway, a corporation with capital stock of $16,935,000. The Santa Fe interlaced the greater Los Angeles region with branches in order to sell town lots and passenger tickets; but this trackage would prove of even greater value when the boom of 1887 paled in comparison with those of the 1920s, 1940s and 1960s. The Atchison stood to profit from the industrial and population explosions in southern California, and thousands of travelers would reach the region on Santa Fe passenger trains, attracted by the low fares, good service and "Meals by Fred Harvey."

Fred Harvey and His Girls

The "Sage of Emporia," William Allen White, wrote that Fred Harvey "had more friends west of the Mississippi than William McKinley and Bob Fitzsimons together."[1] And why were the people served by Fred Harvey and the Atchison, Topeka and Santa Fe Railroad so indebted to him? The Kentucky humorist Irvin S. Cobb provided the answer:

> The original Fred Harvey is dead—has been dead in fact, for several years, but his spirit goes marching on across the southwestern half of this country. Two thousand miles from salt water the oysters that are served in his dining cars do not seem to be suffering from car sickness. And you can get a beefsteak measuring eighteen inches from tip to tip. There are spring chickens with the most magnificent bust development I ever saw outside of a burlesque show, the eggs taste as though they might have originated with a hen instead of a cold-storage vault. If there was a cabaret show going up and down the middle of the car during meals, even the New York passengers would be satisfied with the service, I think.[2]

Service by Fred Harvey came to represent the finest in food, the most efficient waitresses, and hotel accommodations equal to the best in America's larger cities. But before the coming of Fred Harvey, the traveler in the West suffered grievously.

Railroad station lunch counters and restaurants in the Trans-Mississippi West served terrible food in a slovenly manner to passengers who raced through their meal to avoid missing their train. The cooks in the stations formerly worked in mining or logging camps, or perhaps on cattle drives.

Menus consisted of rancid bacon, canned beans, or three kinds of eggs—eggs from the East aged and preserved in lime, ranch eggs from local farms, and yard eggs laid near the depot. The soda biscuits served with the eggs were known as "sinkers" by the patrons. Diners could choose either cold tea or bitter black coffee to accompany their meal. The tables lacked napkins and were covered by dirty cloths on which were placed chipped and broken crockery by the "hash slingers" who waited on the customers in the "dining room." Lunch stops of twenty minutes left no time for leisurely dining, and many times the train would whistle just as the meal arrived. The owners of the restaurants and the train crews divided the profits generated by the untouched meals left behind by anxious travelers.

Passengers hoping to avoid the chronic dyspepsia produced by station cafés brought box lunches or purchased sandwiches from the "butcher boy" on the train. Forty or fifty people eating box lunches in a passenger coach crossing Kansas on a warm July day created an unbelievable odor which attracted swarms of black flies.

The railroads and their employees despaired of the situation. Trainmen suffered more than passengers from the absence of tolerable eating facilities, and even more from a lack of clean hotels in the towns at the end of their runs. Dining cars operated on a few railways in the East, but not in the West, where the lunch stop survived well into the twentieth century on some lines. Often the engineers and crew men cooked their own food at the end of the day in the roundhouse or boiler room, but they still needed a decent place to sleep. The railroad companies encouraged local businessmen to provide acceptable facilities, but with little success. Even the Santa Fe operated a small food service on the second floor of the Topeka depot in 1874, but company employees found it distasteful. Their attitude changed abruptly in 1876 when Fred Harvey leased the Topeka lunch counter.

Born in London, England, on June 27, 1835, Frederick Henry Harvey migrated to the United States at the age of fifteen. Nothing is known of his childhood, except that his parents were of English-Scottish extraction. Upon arrival in New York, Harvey obtained a job at the Smith and McNeill Café as a busboy, receiving two dollars a week. Finding the work taxing and financially unrewarding, he left New York for New Orleans, but contracted yellow fever in the Crescent City. After recovering his health Harvey journeyed on to St. Louis. There he entered the restaurant business in 1856, and three years later married a seventeen-year-old Bohemian girl, Barbara Sarah Mattas—his "Sally." During the Civil War Harvey contracted typhoid, and shortly thereafter his partner disappeared taking all the funds from the restaurant. Harvey left St. Louis, becoming first an employee of a packet boat company, and then mail clerk for the

Fred Harvey, purveyor of fine food. Santa Fe Railway

Hannibal and St. Joseph Railroad, and ultimately an employee of the Chicago, Burlington & Quincy, performing a variety of jobs. By 1876 Harvey's hard work and tenacity paid off and he became general western freight agent for the CB&Q. The Harveys resided in Leavenworth, but Fred's work took him all over the Midwest.

Not only did Harvey's travels keep him away from his home and growing family, but his journeys also exposed him to the foul food and wretched hotels which plagued the small towns he visited. The Harveys lost two children to scarlet fever, and that experience, plus Harvey's bouts with yellow fever and typhoid, caused him to react even more negatively to the disgusting food and sleeping facilities he found on his travels. When he arrived home in Leavenworth he could count on being welcomed by his growing brood of children—Ford, Byron, Sybil, Minnie, and Marie—and enjoying the pleasures of his wife's fine cooking and the comforts of their clean, well-furnished home. Feeling that other travelers must react to their maltreatment just as he did, Harvey decided to provide something better.

In 1875 Harvey and Jeff Rice formed a partnership to operate restaurants on the Kansas Pacific line at Wallace, Kansas, and Hugo, Colorado. Maintaining his position with the CB&Q and supervising the daily operations of these distant eateries proved almost impossible, particularly when he and Rice disagreed on the "standards" to be maintained. The partnership terminated quickly. Harvey remained convinced, however, that depot restaurants could be profitable and yet offer decent food in pleasant surroundings. He took his ideas to the management of the CB&Q, but they were unconvinced. Harvey decided to present his concept to another railroad. As general freight agent for the CB&Q, Harvey knew many of the second-level executives of the connecting lines, including Charles F. Morse, superintendent of the Atchison. Early in 1876, Harvey called on Morse to explain his concept of railroad eating facilities. The tall and wiry, nervous Englishman presented himself to Morse. Dressed in conservative business suit, consisting of a long coat, tight pants and string bow tie, Harvey cut a distinguished figure and favorably impressed the Santa Fe superintendent. Morse contacted President Nickerson who agreed to give Harvey a try by leasing the Topeka lunch counter to him. No contract was needed, Morse and Harvey agreed—both were gentlemen.

Harvey hired Guy Potter of Leavenworth to manage the counter under his close, personal supervision. They cleaned up the room, prepared a new, larger and more moderately priced menu, and gave good, efficient service. When the small counter could no longer handle the booming business, they expanded the facility without lowering their standards. The counter's success frightened the management of the Santa Fe, which feared that all passengers would detrain at Topeka and find the food so good they would travel no farther and leave the Kansas plains empty of settlers! Harvey would have to open additional facilities farther west.

Morse urged Harvey to operate the eating house and provide sleeping accommodations at Florence, where a restaurant and hotel carried on a good business in new quarters located on railroad property. The owners had expanded the size of the Florence facilities, but Morse favored Harvey's style of operation. Harvey borrowed money to pay $4,370 for the building and $1,000 for the furnishings, and then sold the building to the railroad. On January 1, 1878, he contracted with the Santa Fe to operate the restaurant and provide hotel rooms for company employees at Florence. This was the last contract signed between Harvey and the railroad until 1889; all other operations were "gentlemen's agreements." Harvey hired a new manager for the Florence hotel and restaurant, the former head chef of the Palmer House in Chicago, for the unheard-of salary of $5,000 a year. He refurnished the hotel—called the Clifton—and soon

Fred Harvey lunchroom, Deming, New Mexico. Santa Fe Railway

the magnificent food and lodgings in this small Kansas town became famous in the region. The chef bought local pheasant, quail and prairie hen and produced magnificent European cuisine. Farmers near Florence found that Harvey paid the highest prices for their produce, but would buy only the very best and the most fresh. As business boomed at Florence and Topeka, Harvey resigned from the CB&Q to become a full-time restaurateur.

Operating out of an office in a small room at the back of the Hannibal and St. Joseph depot in Leavenworth, Harvey presided over his rapidly growing chain. In 1879 he opened a restaurant in Lakin, and as T. J. Peter's men built westward, Harvey followed close behind. Lunch rooms and hotels sprang up at Newton, Hutchinson, Dodge City, La Junta, Trinidad, Las Vegas, Lamy, Albuquerque, Gallup, Winslow, Williams, Ash Fork, Seligman, Kingman, Needles and Barstow. The first "Harvey Houses" lacked the picturesque charm of the later houses, but they served fine food. Before "El Vaquero" opened in Dodge City, the Harvey House operated in two old boxcars on stilts; one served as the dining room, the other the kitchen. The architecture was crude, but the food and service were not. Fred Harvey ordered that pies would be cut in four pieces, not the traditional six. Water for the coffee would be brought to the restaurants by tank car and not from nearby alkali-laden streams. The reputations of his dining rooms attracted not only train passengers and crews, but also townspeople; and for a brief period Harvey put up signs saying his places were open only to travelers. Public pressure forced him to rescind the rule. Local hotel and restaurant operators objected bitterly to his decision, but the policy remained. When Harvey refused to purchase inferior food from merchants in Trinidad, Colorado, they organized a boycott of the Harvey House, but the boycott soon collapsed as the superiority of Harvey meals and service won his customers back.

Fred Harvey always maintained his English aplomb, never giving into excessive demands but always "maintaining the standard." Visiting one of the Harvey House kitchens he heard a great clamor in the dining room:

> "What caused all of the trouble?" Mr. Harvey asked the Steward.
> "Oh, that man is an out and out crank. No one can please him."
> "Of course he is a crank," agreed Harvey, "but we must please him. It is our business to please cranks, for anyone can please a gentleman."[3]

Harvey's philosophy applied to customers who ordered only coffee and pie as well as guests at his magnificent resort near Las Vegas, New Mexico.

Six miles west of Las Vegas, in a beautiful valley, flowed numerous hot mineral springs. Used by the Indians, Spanish explorers, trappers, scouts and the U.S. Army, the springs reputedly possessed curative powers similar to the waters of the fashionable spas in Europe, particularly in Germany. As early as 1846 the Army built an adobe bath house at the site for treatment of Mexican War wounded. The management of the railroad saw the springs as a possible tourist attraction and invited Harvey to develop a resort there. The Santa Fe constructed a branch line six miles long from Las Vegas into the valley where Harvey built an elaborate hotel named the "Montezuma." Constructed entirely of wood in the "Queen Anne" style, the hotel stood on the side of the valley. It was a four-story structure over 300 feet long, with a massive tower of eight or nine stories which connected the balconies that ran along the front of the building. The largest frame building in the United States, the Montezuma contained furnishings rivaling the hostelries at Saratoga Springs in New York. The Atchison hauled in electric generators, pianos, billiard tables, mirrors and gas and water works for the hotel. Connected to the main building were bath houses capable of housing 500 health seekers each day. On April 17, 1882, the $200,000 Montezuma opened with great fanfare, and its 270 rooms soon filled with passengers exercising their "stopover" privileges. Las Vegas became a major health and pleasure resort with four trains each day carrying passengers to the Montezuma, where Fred Harvey guaranteed first-class service.

Shortly after the Montezuma opened, Harvey sent one of his assistants, Charles Brant, to Guaymas in Mexico to arrange for a supply of fresh produce during the winter months; no canned foods were served at the

Montezuma. Brant also arranged for fresh shell fish, sea bass and sea celery to be shipped to Las Vegas over the Sonora Railway and the Santa Fe. The thirty to forty sea bass Brant ordered each week were accompanied north by four live green turtles supplied by the Yaqui Indians. Brant believed the sea bass to be similar to North American black bass, but he discovered they were enormous and subsequently reduced the order to two per week. The four turtles, weighing around 200 pounds each, cost $1.50. A small pool in the Rio Gallinos held the turtles while they were fattened, and the Montezuma dining room menu always listed fresh turtle soup and turtle steak served with giant sea celery salad. The grandeur of the site, the assumed powers of the waters and the gourmet cuisine of the dining room attracted hundreds of guests to the Montezuma. Alas, on January 18, 1884, the giant frame building burned. A new hotel, the Phoenix, replaced the Montezuma; but in the 1890s resort traffic declined and the hotel was eventually sold. The concept of fine lodgings and excellent food in a beautiful setting would be tried again at other sites by Harvey with more lasting success.

Some guests at the Montezuma witnessed one of several situations in which the cool, autocratic Harvey established his reputation as a man not to be trifled with. One evening a group of drunken cowboys entered the Montezuma and began to shoot up the billiard room. Harvey left the dining room where he was eating and followed the cowboys into the bar, where they began to destroy a collection of Indian relics and shoot the bottles of liquor behind the bar. Harvey came in and demanded, "Boys, put up your guns!" "Who the hell are you?" "My name is Fred Harvey. I

Hotel Casteñada, Las Vegas, New Mexico. L. E. Seitz Associates

am running this place and I will not have any rowdies here. You are welcome to come here as often as you please and stay as long as you behave like gentlemen, but if you don't behave like gentlemen you can't stay here and you can't come again. Now damn you, put up your guns and take a drink with Fred Harvey!" One of the drunks began to curse. Harvey grabbed him by the collar, jerked him over the bar and held him down on the floor. "You mustn't swear in this place," Harvey declared. A cowboy not as drunk as the others stepped in and said, "Fred Harvey is a gentleman." The cowboy on the floor and his companions quieted down, and the "show" ended. Harvey treated them to a drink, breakfast, and a huge quantity of black coffee. They gave the Montezuma no more trouble.[4]

Not all of the toughs of New Mexico could be handled as readily, and Harvey seemed to have more difficulties there than in any other territory. In Lamy, reputedly the roughest town served by Harvey, a gang of gamblers and confidence men took over the town, robbed the Santa Fe employees of their salaries, and refused to pay for food at the Harvey House. When Harvey's manager declined to serve them any more, they ordered him to leave town. He wired Las Vegas for instructions, and Harvey and the Montezuma cashier, John Stein, came to his aid. The next morning a dozen toughs entered the Harvey House, demanded breakfast, ate, and called for the manager. Harvey asked what they wanted with the manager, and they said they were going to hang him. Harvey responded that he hoped they wouldn't because he needed the manager to run the place. But, he said, pointing to Stein, I don't need him and you can hang him as often as you want. However, he concluded, as long as he lives you must pay for your food or you don't stay. Stein, a huge bull of a man, stared at the men without flinching. They threw some money on the table and left. The Lamy manager continued to collect his bills after Harvey and Stein returned to Las Vegas.

Harvey, his managers and his waitresses "civilized the West," providing railroad passengers and local residents with wholesome food served in a graceful style. Harvey's managers arranged a system with the railroad crews whereby food stood ready as passenger trains pulled into the depot. The house and depot were usually connected, and the station agent kept the manager informed of the progress of the trains. Two, three, or four times each day the Harvey House received, fed, and sometimes bedded large numbers of passengers. Before the train arrived, a brakeman or conductor went through the cars with a notebook and inquired of each passenger if they preferred the lunch counter or the dining room. "Dining room six bits, lunch counter pay as you eat." His tally was telegraphed ahead allowing the manager to allocate his resources. A gong sounded while the train was still one mile away so that when the passengers poured off of the train all was in readiness inside and the first course was on the dining room tables. Harvey's dictum that no customer needed to be rushed was followed, as was the rule that no traveler be allowed to miss his train. The table d'hote menu offered limited choices, but food of very high quality. For interest, the menu was rotated every four days throughout the system, and even in the desert areas passengers were served salads and fruit and fresh water fish. Speed in serving made the twenty- to thirty-minute stop seem longer to all but the hurried waitresses and managers. An elaborate system of signals told the "drink girl" whether a customer wanted coffee, tea or milk. The waitress placed the customer's cup either up, down, or tilted on the saucer, and woe to the passenger who fiddled with the china before the "drink girl" arrived. In all of the houses Harvey's chief rule always prevailed—maintenance of standards regardless of cost.

The Harvey employees endeavored to provide the services their employer demanded. About half of the Harvey employees were men—the managers, chefs, buyers, and commissary superintendents; the female employees were largely the "Harvey Girls," the waitresses. The "Harvey Girls" came from "back East," particularly from the Midwest and New England, recruited by advertisements in newspapers and young women's magazines. The Harvey matrons and managers sought young women between 18 and 30 years of age who were attractive and intelligent. Recruiters tried to avoid schoolteachers because the managers thought they were not suited to the routine of the restaurants. The "Girls" agreed to refrain from marriage for one year, but the turnover rate remained high. They received a starting salary of $17.50 per week plus tips, room and board. Following a vigorous training period the young ladies were sent to their houses in the West and came under the supervision of a matron who ran the dormitory. The matrons maintained strict rules concerning hours and dates, and established a high moral tone. The presence of a large body of attractive single women, however, did not go unnoticed by the local merchants, cowboys, miners and railroad crewmen, and some matrons felt they actually ran matrimonial agencies.

Dressed in black shoes and stockings, plain black dresses with an "Elsie collar" and a black bow, and a heavily starched white apron, their hair plainly done with a white ribbon, the "Harvey Girls" stood in sharp contrast to the "painted ladies" of the nearby saloons. Their neatness, modesty, and manners attracted the attention of the "locals" and the travelers. Courted ardently, many of the "Girls" married well, and one former Harvey employee estimated that at least 4,000 babies were named Fred Harvey something or other. Some "Girls" stayed with the system—Bridgett Malone served as head waitress at Las Vegas for thirty years—and the "Harvey Girls" achieved widespread fame for their work and char-

Menu cover from 1888. Fred Harvey, Inc.

acter. Novelist Edna Ferber wrote: "my father used to say that those Western railroad brakeman and Harvey lunchroom waitresses were the future aristocracy of the West. Fine stock he used to say. . . ."[5] The "Girls" were treated well by Harvey, receiving relatively good pay for the times. When they were transferred, the "Girls" received passes and free meals. Some Houses were more desirable as assignments than others—Needles, California, and Rincon, New Mexico, were considered the Houses where "bad" girls were sent—but most of the waitresses stayed in the same locations.

The Harvey employment office at 18th and Wentworth streets in Chicago labored mightily to select only the "best" young women. Many of the "Girls" were well educated, but all became highly trained under the watchful eyes of the matrons, managers, superintendents and Harvey himself. One "Harvey Girl," Laura White, saw her compatriots as female counterparts of the Santa Fe man, "a railroader at heart."[6] On her first assignment at Ash Fork, Arizona, Laura White learned to serve full meals to sixteen people in twenty-five minutes, to keep the cutlery and china polished, and coffee cups always full. There would be no frayed napkins, nicked cups, bent silver, broken toothpicks or conversation with customers while a train waited. The "Girls" displayed coolness and diplomacy, even when parents shoved protesting fourteen-year-olds into high chairs in order to get the half price for children. Life for the "Harvey Girls" could be romantic, and their lives consisted of more than the usual drudgery connotated by work in a restaurant. It is doubtful, however, if they would have seen themselves as happy-go-lucky as actress Judy Garland in the Metro-Goldwyn-Mayer film of 1945, "The Harvey Girls." Yet the customers developed a sense of loyalty and, indeed, gratitude to these young women. One "poet" in the West wrote: "But the fairest of all sights, it seems to me, was a Harvey girl I saw in Albuquerque."[7] Fred Harvey recognized their contribution to the development of his business, and while he had no pension plan, each long-term employee could anticipate that the firm would provide for her retirement.

Fred Harvey's operations aided the railroad immeasurably. Labor-management relations eased as crewmen on the line received excellent food and lodging, something lacking on other railroads. Passenger-traffic promotion benefited greatly as the reputation of "Meals by Fred Harvey" spread across the nation. When Thomas Nickerson and William Strong decided to make the Atchison a transcontinental railroad they persuaded Fred Harvey to follow the track gangs to California. The eating facilities on the old Atlantic and Pacific were deplorable; Harvey sent his associate David Benjamin to Arizona and California, where he turned the former saloon-like eateries into "Harvey Houses." The house at Holbrook, Arizona,

California Limited at Laguna Pueblo. State Historical Society of Colorado, William Jackson Collection

opened in 1884 in five old boxcars, their exteriors a kaleidoscope of peeling paint and bleached boards. But inside, the walls were painted in muted colors, and the tables were covered with Irish linen and set with English silver. Pitchers of ice water and bouquets of desert flowers greeted the hot, dusty traveler at Holbrook. The 75¢ menu included blue points on shell, whitefish with Madeira sauce, young capon with hollandaise sauce, roast beef, English-style baked veal pie, and prairie chicken accompanied by seven different vegetables, four salads—including lobster salad au mayonnaise—and a wide variety of pies, cakes and custards, followed by cheese and coffee. Even in an isolated town like Coolidge, Kansas, a Harvey customer could report that "Without a butcher, or grocer, or gardener, within hundreds of miles, here was an elegant supper, which might be said to have been brought from the ends of the earth and set down in the middle of the American desert."[8]

Part of Harvey's success derived from his own good taste and close inspection. When Harvey inspected a restaurant he wiped his pocket handkerchief across the tops of the doors and windows checking for dust, a chipped plate would be smashed on the floor and a poorly set table overturned. He visited Europe nearly every year to order china, silver, and linens for his houses, purchasing the best and most serviceable. Even while abroad he received daily reports from his superintendents, and he urged them to "keep up the standard" while he was away.

The relationship between Harvey and the Santa Fe management allowed both to profit and have confidence in their joint operation. The railroad supplied the buildings, and Harvey equipped them. The railroad provided coal, ice and water, and hauled Harvey employees and supplies for free. When Harvey found good water hard to obtain in the West, the railroad brought spring water to the houses in steel tank cars. Harvey and his staff carefully planned their menus, based largely on a systematic procurement program. Some of Harvey's most trusted employees were the buyers who called on selected farmers for fresh produce, eggs and meat, and Harvey dairies at La Junta, Las Vegas and Temple, Texas, supplied the system with milk, butter and ice cream. The railroad delivered the fresh produce to the houses along the line. Many of the houses operated at a substantial loss, but the managers were never allowed to reduce the quality of the food or service to make them profitable. In the houses where hotel facilities existed the same rules of quality prevailed, and Harvey selected the furniture and decor with an eye for service and beauty. In return for Harvey's contribution, the Santa Fe operated no dining cars west of Kansas City until 1892. Before that, all trains stopped at the Harvey Houses, and Harvey had to operate even where losses were entailed. When the railroad built from Kansas City to Chicago in 1888, Harvey took over dining car operations between the two cities; but not until 1892 and the inauguration of the California Limited from Chicago to Los Angeles did diners go west of Kansas City over the Santa Fe, and then only on the Limited. By the end of the 1880s, the sheer size of the relations between Harvey and the railroad forced them to abandon their "gentlemen's agreement" and sign a contract.

On May 1, 1889, Fred Harvey and the Atchison signed an agreement legalizing their previous arrangements. Harvey received first choice of locations as the railroad expanded, and for a brief period close relations continued to exist. The management which followed that of William Barstow Strong did not appreciate Harvey's services, however, and tried to establish a system of railroad-owned dining cars west of Kansas City. When Harvey went to court to protect his houses, the railroad backed down. In 1893 another contract gave Harvey the dining car service, too. The railroad furnished the cars and Harvey the food and manpower, and when the diners lost money, as was always true, the railroad reimbursed Harvey for his losses. Harvey and the Santa Fe quickly learned that even increased sales in dining cars did not create profits because the labor costs remained high and constant. But Harvey food on Santa Fe diners sold passenger tickets and the advertising department turned "Meals by Fred Harvey" into a company slogan. In 1896, when Edward P. Ripley became president of the Atchison, Harvey found an ally as positive in his regard for the restaurateur as William B. Strong had been. A new contract combined the houses, diners and hotels into one operation based on a profit-sharing system. With Ripley's full cooperation, blessing and enthusiasm, the Harvey system entered into a second period of expansion.

Prior to 1900, the Harvey system along the Santa Fe represented a utilitarian approach to meeting the needs of travelers and railroad company employees. Only with the Montezuma Hotel in Las Vegas had an attempt been made to capture the carriage trade or even to entice the average passenger to stay longer than one night in a Harvey hotel. After the turn of the century the Harvey organization and the Ripley management sought to enhance the already solid reputation of the Harvey Houses by providing more luxurious surroundings and actively seeking tourists who would make the Harvey hotels their central locale for extended periods of time. Under the direction of President Ripley of the railroad and Fred Harvey's sons, the Santa Fe and Harvey sought to attract tourists with a chain of resorts and quality hotels.

The immediate expansion of the hotels meant larger units and new construction. Harvey and the Santa Fe hired Mary E. J. Colter, an interior decorator, to design the buildings and select their furnishings. An authority on southwestern art and archaeology, Mary Colter developed a structure which combined the traditional Spanish and Indian styles. The "mission" Spanish and Indian mode employed many porches carried by heavy wooden beams, adobe faces supported by large buttresses, subtly colored tiles, and subdued earth colors of red, brown, blue and orange. The first large structure in the Colter style was the Alvarado Hotel in Albuquerque. A massive "adobe" structure located adjacent to the ATSF depot, the Alvarado (named for Hernando Alvarado, one of the first whites in the area) included a restaurant, 89 hotel rooms, and a museum which sold Indian artifacts and crafts. The Spanish names selected for the new hotels linked the chain to the romantic period of Spanish rule in the Southwest —El Ortiz in Lamy, La Fonda in Santa Fe, Bisonte in Hutchinson, El

Alvarado Hotel, Albuquerque, New Mexico. Santa Fe Railway

Vaquero in Dodge City, Castaneda in Las Vegas, Fray Marcos in Williams, El Garces in Needles and Casa del Desierto in Barstow. The hotels ranged in size from The Havasu with accommodations for 19 in Seligman, Arizona, to the 147 rooms at La Fonda. Each hotel maintained a separate identity and charm, but all set the same high Harvey standards.

One of the small "gems" in the chain, El Ortiz in Lamy, opened on May 8, 1910, and soon won a reputation far larger than its small size suggested. An adobe hacienda in style, the building surrounded a tile patio filled with flowers. The interior was furnished with heavy Spanish-style furniture, Navajo rugs and other Indian art. The western novelist Owen Wister visited El Ortiz shortly after its opening and proclaimed, "I found a little gem of architecture, a little clean haven of taste and comfort."[9] The Harvey system displayed not only good taste but also a growing flair for publicity and good public relations.

The Atchison and its purveyor of fine food and lodgings enhanced their growing venture in tourism in 1903 with the establishment of services at Grand Canyon. The railroad built a branch from the main line at Williams to the rim of the canyon, where the company constructed Bright Angel Lodge and El Tovar at a cost of $500,000. Located among stands of Ponderosa pine in a magnificent setting, the two lodges became an extremely popular "stopover" for tourists. Despite the isolation of the area —the Santa Fe had to haul water in by tank cars—travelers flocked to the canyon. The famous artist Thomas Moran came to the lodges at Harvey's request and painted remarkable pictures of the grandeur of the canyon. Lithographs of Moran's works were widely distributed by Harvey and the Santa Fe to schools, hotels, railroad depots and offices, and tourist bureaus. The hotel operation flourished, as did Harvey's growing line of Indian art.

One of the Harvey system's bright young men, Herman Schweizer, operated the lunchroom at Coolidge, New Mexico. Schweizer purchased rugs and jewelry from the local Navajos and sold them to travelers who visited his eating facility. His enthusiasm for Navajo arts and crafts came to the attention of Minnie Harvey Huckel and her husband, John Huckel, a Harvey executive. Huckel and Schweizer decided to make Indian arts and crafts available at other locations, and Minnie Harvey Huckel suggested the development of the museum shop at the Alvarado. When Mary Colter designed the hotel, she set aside space for the craft shop and museum, and Schweizer toured Navajo villages and pueblos purchasing goods to be sold by Harvey. When El Tovar opened, a special shop, Hopi House, sold the crafts of the Hopi tribe. The Harvey system demanded the very best in rugs, jewelry, blankets, turquoise, beads and silver work, and the large orders created employment for the Indians and

Interior of the Indian Shop at the Alvarado. L. E. Seitz Associates

helped to preserve their ancient crafts. So successful was this Harvey promotion that the railroad soon incorporated the Indian motif into its passenger operations, so much so that the railroad's passenger service and the
Harvey system became synonymous to southwestern travelers.

In the midst of the expansion program Fred Harvey died. Often ill the
last sixteen years of his life, and quite seriously sick for three years before
his death on February 9, 1901, Harvey gradually turned over the management of the system to his sons and son-in-law. The business operated
smoothly through the transition period, and his sons Byron and Ford ably
presided over the expanding operation. A closed corporation, the Fred
Harvey system could be described best as "family owned and operated."
At Harvey's death the chain included 15 hotels, 47 restaurants, 30 dining
cars, and food service on the ferries across San Francisco Bay. The Atchison had even agreed to Harvey's operating off-line food services at the
giant St. Louis Union Station. The death of the founder did not interrupt
the growth of the system, and the family carried on the traditions established by Fred Harvey.

Fred Harvey's contributions to the eating habits and comforts of the residents of the Southwest were considerable. His patrons learned what good food tasted like and demanded equal quality elsewhere, forcing his competitors to upgrade their restaurants in order to survive. Harvey Houses served as "normal schools" for the training of cooks, managers, and waitresses, and often supplied personnel to other hotels and restaurants. Many former Harvey employees managed other properties after serving an apprenticeship with the system. As one critic wrote shortly after Harvey's death, "Harvey eating-houses served as schools to all the Southwest, bringing about a general reform. The rival railway systems and other competitive lunch rooms could no longer persevere in their barbarian ways."[10]

The Harvey services enhanced the passenger traffic of the Atchison, Topeka and Santa Fe Railroad; and as the railroad grew, the Harvey houses and diners followed. With the close cooperation of Harvey and his sons, the executives of the Santa Fe made the railroad famous for its passenger services. William B. Strong and Edward P. Ripley found in Harvey a significant asset, and both the railroad and Harvey profited. Even when Strong and his successors took the railroad too far too quickly, Harvey dutifully followed. "Meals by Fred Harvey" became available in a growing number of towns and cities as William Barstow Strong expanded his railway.

5

Headlong Expansion

During the 1880s the American railway network expanded throughout the nation, interlacing urban centers and their hinterlands. The railroads consumed vast quantities of iron and steel, lumber and coal, and other construction materials. Large groups of men built and operated the railway system, which soon encompassed nearly the entire country. In the process of expansion the railroads overbuilt, giving some states—such as Iowa, Illinois and Kansas—far more rail mileage than could be operated profitably. This legacy of excess railway, which still exists, albeit for different reasons, in the mid-twentieth century, came to haunt the managers of the railroads, and it saddled the companies with debts they could not service and with lines they did not need and should not have operated. Yet the prevailing philosophy of the 1880s was to meet competition not only by cutting rates but also by invading the "territories" of rivals. William Barstow Strong subscribed wholeheartedly to this concept and expanded the Atchison, Topeka and Santa Fe Railroad to meet the challenges, real and imaginary, presented by its competitors.

A patriarchal figure with long white hair and sideburns which flowed into a massive white beard, Strong adopted the Atchison as his child and dominated the company as it grew from adolescence into maturity. His philosophy of expansion was in keeping with the mood of the times and the goals and aims of the company's investors. He told them what they desired to hear, and he supported his philosophy with deep personal convictions and dividend checks, at least for the moment. He presented a succinct statement of his beliefs in the *Annual Report* for 1888:

The history of Western railroad construction for the past quarter century has demonstrated that successful results can only be attained by occupying territory promptly, and often in advance of actual business necessity. This was the policy of the Atchison Company from the first. It led the way. It built, not upon assured returns of profits, but upon a faith which time has absolutely vindicated, . . . that the great Western and Southwestern regions of the country were rich in possibilities.[1]

Strong won the support of the stockholders and the directors with his dominating personality and the strength of his arguments. He told the directors that "railroading is a business wherein progress is absolutely necessary. . . . A railroad must make new combinations, open new territory, and secure new traffic." And what happened if this led to conflicts with rivals? "Costly as a war always is, peace can be bought at too great a price."[2] Peace would not prevail in Kansas or elsewhere in the Southwest as long as Strong ran the Atchison and Jay Gould controlled the Missouri Pacific.

In the mid-1880s the Missouri Pacific built over 1,000 miles of new track into ATSF territory, a total surpassed only by the 1,300 miles of line built by the Chicago, Rock Island and Pacific. Strong reacted to this invasion of Kansas by expanding the Santa Fe within the Sunflower State. Gould sent his Missouri Pacific into the southern half of Kansas, long an ATSF monopoly, and ultimately built all the way to Pueblo, Colorado, before he stopped. The MP reached Wichita in 1882, and three years later began to take a large portion of the cattle business in western Kansas. While the Santa Fe had arranged a truce with the Frisco, no such agreement could be made with Gould or his MP. Aided by town and county subsidies, Gould pushed the MP through the cattle and wheat country, and Strong countered with a vigorous construction program of his own. From 1883 until 1887, the Santa Fe, Missouri Pacific and Rock Island built thousands of miles of branches in Kansas, which by 1890 had the second largest rail mileage in the Union. Strong's initial steps to meet his rivals came as early as 1880.

Strong and the Boston management became increasingly concerned about their Kansas holdings in the late 1870s. A large independent system in eastern Kansas, the Kansas City, Lawrence and Southern Kansas Railroad, operated over 365 miles of track in the area between Lawrence, Independence, and Hunnewell. Strong decided to purchase the KCLSK, and did so for $3,743,000 in 5 percent Atchison bonds. He explained to the stockholders in the 1880 *Annual Report* that "In unfriendly hands, it might have interfered and seriously with our business, while it could, under proper management, become a valuable property."[3] The purchase also terminated a rate war with the KCLSK. *The Commercial and Finan-*

cial Chronicle agreed that the purchase was necessary to halt the threat that such an independent line presented; the Atchison had to defend its Kansas territory, which still produced most of the company's profits.

To protect the Santa Fe's position, Strong built short branches into the expanding agricultural areas of the Sunflower State. A. A. Robinson constructed new lines from Lyons to Ellinwood (20 miles), El Dorado to Douglass (24), Sedgwick to Halstead (9), Olathe to Holliday (14), Wichita to Kingman (45), Chanute to Girard (40), Harper to Attica (12), and Ottawa to Emporia (56). This expansion program continued through the mid-1880s, creating a vast network serving a relatively small area. The new branches led to temporary local land booms, and townspeople rejoiced when the first locomotive arrived; but as it turned out, the long-term economic effects were negative.

Strong recalled his construction crews for a brief period in 1884–1885, but in 1886 the Atchison announced that 450 miles of new track would be built in Kansas at a cost of $5.6 million. A subsidiary, the Chicago, Kansas and Western Railroad, constructed the new routes, and within the year was operating 401 miles of line. By the end of 1887 the CK&W grew to include 903 miles of track. The CK&W received local subsidies of $700,000, but funds for the company came largely from the sale of 5 percent bonds at $14,000 per mile, and 6 percent income bonds at $10,000 per mile. The Atchison held all the stock of the CK&W and agreed to give its subsidiary a 10 percent rebate on gross earnings as long as necessary to pay interest on CK&W bonds. The CK&W securities sold rapidly, and branches were built from Hutchinson to Kinsley (84 miles), Great Bend to Scott City (120), Independence to Cedarvale (55), and elsewhere. The Hutchinson-Kinsley shortcut across the "Great Bend" of the

Locomotive No. 132, built by Baldwin in 1880.
    H. L. Broadbelt

Arkansas River aided the ATSF greatly because it substantially reduced the mileage along the old main line.

While Strong fought Gould throughout Kansas, he also sought to block the growth of independent lines in the cattle country of the Texas Panhandle. In 1886 the Atchison announced that another subsidiary, the Southern Kansas Railroad, would build 200 miles of new track from Kiowa, Kansas, southwest through Indian Territory to Panhandle City in the Texas high plains. The vast cattle ranches and the agricultural prospects of the high plains motivated the ATSF as did the potential threat represented by the expansion of a local Texas railway, the Fort Worth and Denver City. The FW&DC extended from Fort Worth northwest into the plains, and planned to connect with the Colorado and Southern, then building south from Denver, to provide a direct route from Denver to the Gulf of Mexico. Strong did not want to see Texas beef hauled to Galveston or Denver, and he began to push the Southern Kansas Railway into the Panhandle. An act of Congress on July 4, 1884, authorized a railroad across Indian Territory from Kiowa through Camp Supply and across Wolf Creek to Texas. No lands were granted, but the railroad received a 100-foot right-of-way. The act stipulated that the Indians would be compensated for the loss of land and that freight rates would be the same as those in Kansas. Strong lost no time in dispatching surveyors into the area. Construction crews followed rapidly, reaching Shattuck in Indian Territory in late 1886 and Canadian, Texas, in 1887. In January 1888, the Southern Kansas arrived in Panhandle City and made a connection with a fifteen-mile branch from the FW&DC's main line. For a brief period the Southern Kansas operated into Amarillo over the FW&DC, but eventually the company built its own track into the town. Strong's instincts had been correct, for his new line quickly developed a large-scale cattle business. Indeed, Lewis Kingman wrote to Alonzo Robinson on April 7, 1888, that the Southern Kansas should be extended southwestward toward the Pecos River valley and perhaps to the El Paso–Albuquerque line, but this project would have to wait for twenty years; Strong decided to reach the Gulf of Mexico first.

When Colonel Holliday spoke at the Wakarusa Creek picnic in April 1869, one of the termini he projected for the Santa Fe was the Gulf of Mexico. Thomas Nickerson and William Barstow Stong shared the Colonel's view that the company needed to tap the gulf market and enter central Texas. In so doing, the ATSF would also cross that vast virgin tract called Indian Territory, a land with enormous agricultural potential and unknown mineral wealth. Even more compelling for Strong was the growing competition with Gould's Missouri Pacific, which enjoyed a strategic, almost monopolistic, position in the Texas transportation network, and Strong felt that the Santa Fe should seek a portion of the traffic from

Texas to the Midwest. Therefore, in the mid-1880s, Strong began to examine potential entrances into the Lone Star State, and, in particular, a struggling independent railroad in Texas—the Gulf, Colorado and Santa Fe Railway Company.

The early history of the GCSF and the urban rivalry of Galveston and Houston are closely intertwined. Galveston dominated the trade of the Lone Star State from the period of the Republic of Texas to the 1860s. Cotton, lumber and cattle made Galveston rich and complacent, and they spurred the incipient metropolis of Houston into action. The existing railroad system moved freight to Galveston through landlocked Houston. The urban promoters of Houston aided the Houston and Texas Central Railway and the Texas and New Orleans Railroad as they built from their city into the interior of the state, and, simultaneously, the Houston boomers began to develop the Houston Direct Navigation Company. The latter enterprise constructed a ship channel from the gulf at Galveston Bay to Houston in order to bypass the docks, wharves, and middlemen of Galveston. The Houston strategy paid off, and commerce through Galveston began to dry up. Complicating Galveston's economic problem was the recurrence of yellow fever; in 1867 some 1,150 people in the city died in an epidemic. The town of Houston, fearing the disease would spread, embargoed all traffic between the two cities, and it was immediately discovered that the embargo strangled commerce on the only railway into Galveston. If the embargo worked so well, and it did, concluded Houston businessmen, why not use it more often? For the next few years the most remote hint of fever in Galveston became a pretext for Houston to embargo the rail line between the two cities, forcing merchants to transship their goods in Houston rather than at Galveston. The business leaders of Galveston realized, almost too late, that they had to build another railroad to the interior of Texas which would go around rather than through Houston.

On May 28, 1873, the commercial community of Galveston obtained a charter for the Gulf, Colorado and Santa Fe Railway. The state of Texas authorized the GCSF to issue $2 million in capital stock, which could be increased to a maximum of $7 million by a two-thirds vote of the stockholders. Only $200,000 needed to be subscribed and only 5 percent paid in, however, in order to initiate work on the railroad. The charter provided that the company could build from Galveston northwest to Santa Fe, New Mexico, via Cameron, Belton, and the Canadian River valley. The legislature aided the GCSF by granting state lands equal to sixteen sections per mile, or 10,240 acres per mile, to a maximum of 3,554,560 acres. The lands granted were in an undesirable area in the western part of the state, and the GCSF simply sold its rights to the land without locating it, realizing only $211,168 or 6¢ an acre from the huge tract. When the government of Galveston County agreed to support the GCSF by subscribing to $500,000 in bonds, the project began to move forward. By November 14, 1873, over $750,000 had been subscribed and plans to initiate construction were being formulated by the GCSF's first engineer, General Braxton B. Bragg, who had been commander of the Confederate Army of Tennessee.

The leaders of the GCSF hired Bragg to build their railroad in the midst of great enthusiasm for the project. The prime movers of the railroad were the elite of Galveston's business community—men such as Albert Somerville, Henry Rosenburg, W. L. Moody, C. R. Hughes and George and John Sealy. They gathered at the corner of 37th and Mechanic Streets on May 1, 1875, at 1:00 in the afternoon to see Rosenburg turn the first spade of earth on the GCSF. A giant party followed with the celebrants partaking of crackers, cheese and champagne provided by the GCSF. Galveston would soon be freed from the threat of Houston's "quarantines," and would have its own railroad to the interior—or so they believed.

General Bragg came to the GCSF as the hero of Shiloh and Chickamauga and won the confidence of President Somerville of the GCSF, but this strict disciplinarian and two-fisted drinker knew little about the building of a railroad. He privately admitted to his wife that he "shuddered" at the responsibility, but he set his crews to their tasks. By July 1874, he had laid out the first 125 miles of line and planned the causeway from Galveston across the bay to the mainland, but he moved very slowly. In the fall of 1874 Bragg made a significant decision when he hired Colonel J. P. Fresenius as chief of his field parties. A German engineer with considerable railway experience, Fresenius got the GCSF moving. The sharply contrasting abilities of Bragg and his associate led to the former resigning in June 1875, allowing the directors to make Fresenius the chief engineer.

During the next two years the GCSF proceeded slowly north and west from Galveston. Fresenius built a causeway across the bay using 5,000 red cedar piles, only to find that the *teredo*, or sea worm, loved the cedar and devoured it rapidly. Within three years all of the timber had to be replaced, requiring the constant presence of a pile driver and a dozen bridge carpenters. The company replaced the cedar with much cheaper native elm, but only the eventual replacement of timber with concrete pilings resolved the problem. At the end of three years the GCSF extended only sixty miles, offered irregular service and had consumed gallons of red ink. The Galveston County government tried to withdraw its investment, and the railroad faced immediate bankruptcy.

The directors offered the GCSF for sale on April 15, 1879, and George Sealy bought the line for $200,000. Sealy, who already had invested some

$250,000 in the company, took over the railroad, and infused the scheme with vigor and capital. A native of the Wyoming Valley of Pennsylvania, Sealy came from an Irish family of ten children. After working his way through school, he became a station agent for the Delaware, Lackawanna and Western, but at the age of twenty-two joined a cotton brokerage firm. Although Sealy opposed slavery, when the Civil War began he joined the Confederate army, serving without pay. He moved to Galveston at the end of the war, entered the cotton and banking businesses, and made a small fortune. To Sealy must go the credit for developing the GCSF.

First, Sealy reorganized the railway. A new charter issued on March 8, 1879, required that 80 miles of track be built within the next year, and 50 miles more had to be constructed each year thereafter. Sealy then paid $10,000 to Galveston County for its $500,000 in securities and began to raise new funds. Bernard Moore Temple replaced Fresenius as chief engineer, and he initiated a massive construction program. The Virginia-born Temple sent surveyors into the interior of Texas, and when they had located the line, Temple followed rapidly with construction gangs. On August 1, 1880, the GCSF reached Brenham, and that same day obtained trackage rights into Houston. Laying 60-pound rail across central Texas, Temple's crews reached Belton in March 1881 and started a branch northward to Fort Worth. The main line reached Lampasas in 1882, and another branch opened from Alvin to Houston, giving the GCSF its own line into the city. Later that year Sealy purchased the Chicago, Texas and Mexican Central, a poorly built, jerkwater line from Cleburne to Dallas. The CTMC gave the GCSF entrance into Dallas, the fastest growing city in the state. Sealy also arranged an exchange of stock with the Central and Montgomery Railway, which operated from Navasota to Montgomery in the piney woods of East Texas. The timber in East Texas promised future freight shipments as well as immediate access to a supply of ties for Temple's crews. This branch was extended to Conroe in September 1885.

Sealy and Temple could take considerable pride in the GCSF, which by 1885 operated a significant rail system from Galveston and Houston to Dallas, Fort Worth and Lampasas. The company received financial support from counties and communities along the new line, with subsidies ranging from the $70 supplied by Nickleville to the $85,000 contributed by Fort Worth. Small towns such as Weatherford, Paris, Ladonia, Honey Grove and Farmersville raised $10,000 to $15,000 for the GCSF. The railway also profited from townsite development. The towns of Rosenburg, Sealy, Somerville, and Fresenius were developed by the GCSF, but its greatest success was Temple, which became a division point. With money from local subsidies and the sale of securities the GCSF marched on to Brownwood in 1885.

Chief Engineer Temple directed most of this large-scale expansion of the GCSF, but was succeeded by a Yankee engineer in the mid-1880s, Walter Justin Sherman. Sherman found working conditions in central Texas to be very difficult, especially in the hot summer months. As the track moved across the waxy, black soil of the Texas prairies, members of Sherman's crews "deserted," and replacements were difficult to recruit. In desperation the GCSF authorized a daily "whiskey ration," and Sherman dispensed a dipper of liquor to each man at the end of the day. The operating department also had labor troubles in 1885, when the Knights of Labor led a strike against the GCSF. The train crews took critical parts from locomotives to keep the management from running trains. Townspeople along the line, especially at Temple, sympathized with the strikers, forcing the GCSF to agree to arbitration. The rapid expansion of the railroad under Sherman's direction, the strike, and intense competition with the Missouri Pacific weakened the financial condition of the GCSF, causing William Barstow Strong, Jay Gould and even Charles Crocker to think about acquiring the line.

As early as 1881, the GCSF attracted the attention of several railroad magnates, including Charles Crocker, who urged C. P. Huntington to buy the GCSF because of its strategic location and the threat it represented to Jay Gould. After Huntington decided not to purchase the company, he organized a pool to divide the Texas traffic with the independent line and Gould, but when the management of the GCSF demanded 75 percent of the freight to Galveston, the pool collapsed. Jay Gould's railroad monopoly in northern Texas hurt the GCSF badly; Gould controlled not only the Missouri Pacific but also the Missouri, Kansas and Texas, the Texas and Pacific, and the International Great Northern, cutting off the GCSF from independent connections to St. Louis and Kansas City. A rate war in 1882 harmed the GCSF far more than it hurt Gould's lines; Sealy, Rosenburg, and the other leaders of the GCSF felt that their railroad had to have a new connection north out of Texas if the company was going to survive. Strong soon offered just such a possibility.

In the spring of 1884, A. A. Robinson sent surveyor H. L. Marvin into Indian Territory to find the best rail route from southern Kansas to northern Texas. Marvin surveyed three possibilities: Coffeyville to Gainesville, Arkansas City to Gainesville, and Arkansas City to Red River Station. In his report, dated May 20, Marvin favored a line from Arkansas City south through the "Unassigned Lands" to Gainesville, where branches could be extended to Fort Worth and Dallas. In the central portion of the territory a large area was not "assigned" to any tribe, and it appeared to be the first tract which might be opened to white settlement. Strong accepted the report and agreed that Marvin's choice appeared to offer the greatest potential for future traffic and a route which could be built cheaply and

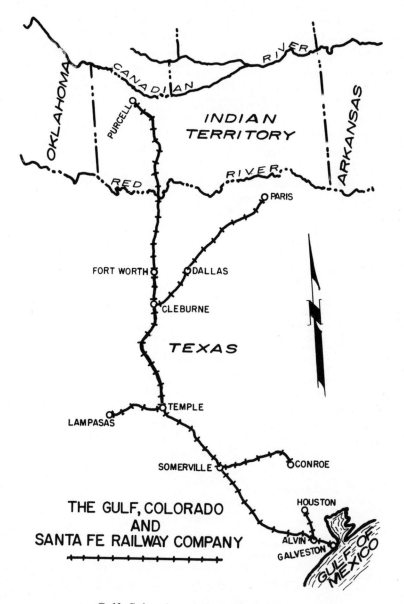

OKLAHOMA

CANADIAN RIVER

INDIAN TERRITORY

ARKANSAS

PURCELL

RED RIVER

PARIS

FORT WORTH DALLAS

CLEBURNE

TEXAS

N

TEMPLE

LAMPASAS

SOMERVILLE CONROE

HOUSTON

THE GULF, COLORADO
AND
SANTA FE RAILWAY COMPANY

ALVIN

GALVESTON

GULF OF MEXICO

Gulf, Colorado and Santa Fe Railway

operated efficiently. In July, Congress approved the request of the Santa Fe to build across Indian Territory along Marvin's survey. Strong then contacted George Sealy to arrange a connection with the GCSF.

Strong's overtures to the GCSF were cordially received, and for two years quiet negotiations proceeded. When the directors of the GCSF found the road in deep trouble in 1885, Sealy began to press Strong for a definite decision. On March 25, 1886, the stockholders authorized Sealy to arrange an exchange of stock with the Atchison on the best terms he could get. Both Strong and Sealy saw a merger as the best means to thwart Gould, and Strong initiated hard bargaining with a firm offer. His proposition appears very generous at first blush. The Atchison offered to pay $8,000 per mile in stock for all shares of the GCSF—the railroad had 625 miles of track in operation and 70 miles more under construction. The main line extended 345 miles from Galveston to Brownwood, with branches from Alvin to Houston (24 miles), Somerville to Conroe (74), Cleburne to Dallas (54), and Temple to Fort Worth (128); and crews were building westward from Brownwood to San Angelo and east from Conroe into the Piney Woods. But Strong offered to purchase 1,000 miles of track; he demanded that the GCSF build north from Fort Worth to Purcell in Indian Territory to meet the ATSF, north from Dallas to Paris to connect with the main line of the Atchison's ally the Frisco, and from Cleburne to Weatherford, all within one year. Sealy could hardly believe that Strong wanted Sealy's financially desperate company to construct 375 miles of line, and do so immediately. To placate the GCSF stockholders, Strong sweetened the proposal, once Sealy agreed in principle to the terms, by offering to finance the additional construction.

Sealy accepted the deal and returned to Galveston to make the necessary arrangements. Help came from several sources. The citizens of Fort Worth heard of the Santa Fe's offer and raised a subsidy of $30,000 and donated right-of-way through the city. Sherman agreed to supervise the new construction program, and on April 16, he began to survey north from Fort Worth to Purcell, a distance of 172 miles. Sealy obtained an amendment to the charter of the GCSF to allow construction into Indian Territory, while Sherman hired crews to build the line. The indomitable chief engineer later recalled that Sealy asked him if he could construct 300 miles of track in 300 working days; Sherman responded yes, all he wanted was money and Sealy's backing—he got both.

Within a hundred days Sherman surveyed the three routes and hired 100 engineers, 2,000 teams and 5,000 men to grade the roadbed and build the bridges. Each day at 7:00 A.M. track-laying crews received one mile of rail and the necessary ties and spikes to lay it, and another mile of rail at 1:00 P.M., and when the second mile had been laid, they could call it a day and receive their cup of whiskey. The flat prairie terrain crossed by the three lines allowed the crews to lay track rapidly. The only significant barrier for Sherman's men was a pass through the Arbuckle Mountains in southern Indian Territory. Marvin's survey called for a one percent grade following the valley of the Washita River. Sherman's men began blasting out the limestone rock with hand drills and dynamite, hauling their supplies to the site by wagon from Gainesville. When the track layers arrived, the deep cut through the mountains had been opened. Sherman's crews proceeded rapidly toward Purcell even as Robinson's ATSF track gangs built south from Arkansas City. As the crews moved across the largely unsettled territory, stations were established every ten miles. The GCSF survey crew chief came from Philadelphia, and across Indian Territory he named stations as though it were the "Mainline"—Overbrook, Wynnewood, Paoli, Wayne, and Ardmore. On April 26, 1887, four hours ahead of schedule, Sherman's men reached Purcell, beating the Santa Fe crews. The GCSF now had an independent outlet from Texas, and a generous offer of purchase. On June 18, 1887, through-trains began to operate from Kansas City south to Galveston.

The contract signed on March 3, 1886, by Strong and Sealy called for the transfer of the entire capital stock of the GCSF to the Atchison in exchange for $8 million in Atchison stock. The Santa Fe also assumed the $12,000 per mile in first-mortgage bonds and $5,000 per mile in second-mortgage bonds of the GCSF for a total security exchange of $25,000 per mile. On March 23, the stockholders of the GCSF elected representatives of the Atchison to their board, and the next year on March 8, the officers of the Atchison became the officers of the GCSF, thus completing the merger.

The Santa Fe gained an excellent strategic position in the acquisition of the GCSF. It obtained a direct route from Kansas City and Wichita south to Galveston with access to Fort Worth, Dallas and Houston. The branch from Dallas to Paris provided a through-route for the Frisco from St. Louis to Texas points. The ports of Galveston and Houston gave the Santa Fe access to wharves and warehouses serviced by ship lines to New York and Europe. Kansas grain could now flow southward over the Atchison to enter international commerce. More importantly to Strong and Sealy, Jay Gould's stranglehold on Texas had been broken. But at what price? Charles Perkins of the Chicago, Burlington & Quincy and other railroad leaders felt that Strong paid far too much for the GCSF. And, while Gould had been thwarted, a renewed rate war followed. Strong held firm, despite the criticisms, defending the acquisition: "It will secure to the Atchison Company independence against any attempt of rival lines to close the doors of trade against us or to cripple or embarrass our business."[4] Strong could have added that the new line through Indian Territory, then largely unoccupied, represented an asset of enormous potential.

When Robinson and Sherman built the connection between Arkansas City and Gainesville their crews found much of the land a wilderness. Some ranches existed in the Cherokee Strip along the Kansas border, and small farms dotted the Chickasaw Nation between the Canadian and Red rivers, but most of the new line crossed the tract known as the "Unassigned Lands." The only "towns" existed around Santa Fe facilities at Guthrie, Purcell and "Oklahoma," the future Oklahoma City. The depot at "Oklahoma" served the troops and the Indian agency at nearby Fort Reno, and stationmaster J. W. Hughes built the first house in the "town" from old ties. Two years later President Benjamin Harrison opened the "Unassigned Lands" for settlement, and on April 22, 1889, the first "run" into Indian Territory quickly populated the area. The Santa Fe ran eleven special trains into the "Unassigned Lands" on April 22, each carrying over 1,000 people. In one day Oklahoma City grew from a small station surrounded by shanties to a tent city of several thousand. Trains from Kansas and Texas continued to bring in more settlers, and within a brief period the prairies were converted into farms, and townsites into bustling communities. Strong's decision to build across this virgin territory proved to be fortuitous; his decision to build from Kansas City to Chicago was less so.

The Atchison trunk lines extended from Kansas City west to Los Angeles, San Diego and Guaymas via Kansas, Colorado, New Mexico and Arizona, and south from Wichita to Houston and Galveston on the Gulf of Mexico. The Atchison exchanged traffic in Kansas City with the Chicago, Rock Island and Pacific, the Alton, the Chicago, Burlington & Quincy, and several other Granger lines. In the mid-1880s, these companies began to expand westward into Kansas and even to Colorado, causing Strong to question the policy and strategy of relinquishing Santa Fe traffic to these invaders at Kansas City. Railroad strategy in the Midwest shifted dramatically during the 1880s as managers acted and reacted to the expansion of other railroads. Kansas City also became less and less a terminus and more and more an independent industrial and commercial center. When evidence of Strong's changing attitude reached Charles Perkins of the CB&Q, he tried to dissuade his long-time friend. Perkins argued, correctly, that there were already too many lines from Chicago to Kansas City, but Strong remained adamant. When Perkins failed to persuade Strong, John Murray Forbes of the CB&Q pleaded with the Atchison's president, and then, when Strong refused to change his mind, Perkins and Forbes threatened to build additional mileage in Kansas. They urged stockholders in the CB&Q who also held Atchison securities to use their influence with Strong and the Atchison board of directors, but to no avail. Even a proposal to merge the Atchison, the CB&Q and the Alton fell on deaf ears.

Strong dispatched surveyors from Kansas City to Chicago as early as 1883, and he began to stockpile data on local traffic, bridge sites and small, independent railways along the routes surveyed. A. A. Robinson sent a memo to Strong on November 11, 1884, urging construction of the line but cautioning that such action would result in a loss of traffic connections at Kansas City, and predicted that competition would intensify. Strong deferred action while the lines to California were completed and the negotiations with the GCSF continued. In the spring of 1886, he sent Robinson over the territory between Chicago and Kansas City to make a final location, and Robinson's report of August 9 urged immediate action to forestall additional invasions of Kansas by the Missouri Pacific, Frisco, and CRI&P. Strong and Robinson hesitated for only a moment to consider purchasing the Alton, which had an excellent Kansas City–Chicago route, but the purchase price seemed far too high. Strong told Robinson to start purchasing right-of-way as quickly and quietly as possible, and he asked the board of directors to approve the creation of several new subsidiaries to construct the line; they approved the scheme immediately.

Robinson laid out virtually a straight-line route between the two cities. So heavily interlaced was the area by other railroads that Strong and

Gulf, Colorado and Santa Fe No. 75, built by Schenectady in 1888. Santa Fe Railway

Robinson decided to forgo any opportunity to develop local traffic. The only major town located along the route was Fort Madison, Iowa, until Strong shifted the location a few miles to enter Galesburg, Illinois. The decision to enter Galesburg came only after that community raised almost $100,000 and donated twenty acres of land for the depot and right-of-way. Robinson's survey avoided curves and grades as much as possible because he and Strong agreed that the Santa Fe wanted the shortest and fastest track between the two termini. While Robinson purchased right-of-way for the "airline," Strong organized the finances.

On December 3, 1886, he chartered the Chicago, Santa Fe and California Railway Company in Illinois, and on January 24, the new subsidiary offered $15 million in 5 percent gold bonds on the Boston, New York and London markets. The Atchison guaranteed the interest on the 50-year bonds and took $30 million in CSF&C stock. The CSF&C then made a purchase of its own: it bought the Chicago and St. Louis Railway, "two streaks of rust" which operated 154 miles from Chicago to Pekin. The new Atchison "airline" could use almost 100 miles of the C&StL from Chicago to near Streator and would also be able to use its entrance into Chicago. Built by Francis E. Hinkley, and known as the "Hinkley Road," the C&StL was planned as a Chicago–St. Louis line, but the management ran out of funds when the track reached Pekin. The tough rail competition in northern Illinois drove the C&StL into Strong's arms, and he consummated the sale on December 15, 1886. By assuming the $1.5 million lien on the C&StL, Strong acquired the poorly built road with its light rails, heavy grades and frame depot located at 23rd Street in Chicago. Robinson immediately sent track gangs to the C&StL to initiate a massive reconstruction program.

Robinson stood ready to rebuild the C&StL and to connect it to the Atchison via the "airline." The Santa Fe owned a portion of the Kansas City Belt Line and could use it to reach a point eight miles east of Kansas City. From there Robinson had to build 350 miles of new line to Streator, including two major bridges across the Missouri and Mississippi Rivers and 100 miles of deep cuts and heavy grades from Bucklin, Missouri, to Fort Madison. The bridges represented the most serious obstacles with regard to speed of construction, and Robinson initiated work on these giant structures very early. He retained Octave Chanute, the internationally known bridge designer, and together they developed plans for the two major crossings and three smaller bridges over the Illinois, Des Moines and Grand rivers. Smaller in these instances was a relative term, because the Illinois River crossing two miles east of Chillicothe consisted of a channel structure 752 feet long, but the approaches brought the total length to 1,417 feet; the Des Moines bridge stood 900 feet in length; and the Grand

CHICAGO, SANTA FE AND CALIFORNIA RAILWAY COMPANY

Chicago, Santa Fe and California Railway

River crossing extended some 459 feet. The two major bridges across navigable waterways required Congressional approval, which was received; and their construction was financed by toll bridge subsidiaries whose securities were held by the CSF&C, which guaranteed the interest. The Mississippi River bridge at Fort Madison cost $580,000 and ran some 2,963 feet on 8 spans. The draw span alone was 400 feet in length. The Missouri River bridge at Sibley, though shorter, was considerably more difficult to build. The channel had shifted over 1,800 feet in less than 10 years, and bedrock could be located only at 42 to 47 feet below the waterline. Chanute favored a high bridge on 8 masonry piers, and drew up the plans. Through the winter of 1887, the bridge crews hauled supplies to the Sibley site from the nearby Wabash Railway, and though three lives were lost in the process of construction, the first train crossed over a false work on January 26, 1888. On May 1, the bridge opened; it had cost $770,000. Meanwhile, the track gangs were also busily at work.

Robinson purchased materials months in advance and stockpiled them at strategic points on the proposed line. He scattered his experienced engineers and track gangs along the 350-mile route, and he supplied them with machinery, teams and 72-pound rail for the track. Construction proceeded rapidly as Robinson's crews increased in size from 5,000 men to 7,000. The chief engineer moved up and down the line directing his men, who laid the rails at a rate of four miles per day. Near Medill, Missouri, on December 31, 1887, at 6:00 P.M. the last spike was driven. Blizzards during the winter and delays on the bridges prevented the ATSF from opening the route to through-traffic. Accommodation trains moved over the line in January, but not until April 29, 1888, did through-revenue service begin. In one year Robinson rebuilt 100 miles of track, constructed 350 miles of new line and erected 5 bridges totaling 48,106 feet in length. Rapidly and efficiently, this excellent engineer put together Strong's "airline."

Strong's belief that entering Chicago would generate a massive infusion of new traffic for the Atchison meant that the old C&StL terminal facilities had to be abandoned and new properties acquired and developed. Another subsidiary, the Atchison, Topeka and Santa Fe Railroad in Chicago Company, authorized to issue $5 million in stock and $10 million in bonds, sold $5.5 million in bonds to build two miles of track, terminal buildings and a freight house. In 1887 the Atchison spent $3,316,000 on real estate for yards and additional terminal facilities. The new tracks gave the Atchison access to Dearborn Station, where it became the most significant passenger operation. The new freight facilities were utilized almost immediately, and Strong soon put the Dearborn entry to good use.

The finest passenger trains then available initiated passenger service over the Kansas City–Chicago line. On a schedule of 13 hours and 45 minutes, the longest vestibule trains in the world—some 600 feet in length—raced between the two cities. The trains consisted of a mail car, baggage car, second-class chair car, two first-class coaches, a parlor-smoker, a diner, and two sleepers, all of steel-girder construction. A generator in the baggage car provided electric lights, and steam from the locomotive heated the train. The interiors of the coaches were trimmed in carved mahogany and maroon plush, while the parlor contained antique oak paneling with golden brown sofas and wicker settees cushioned in silk. The Pullman Company decorated the sleepers in Louis XV style, with bronze hardware, French oak trim and peacock blue upholstery. The diner, soon to provide "Meals by Fred Harvey," contained small rooms for private

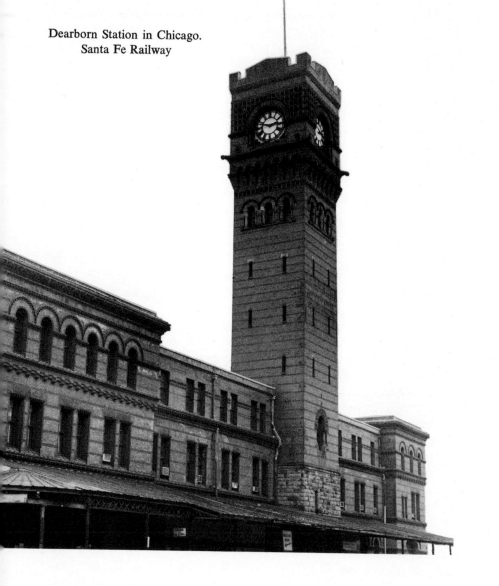

Dearborn Station in Chicago.
Santa Fe Railway

dining. Strong intended to give the Alton, CB&Q, and his other competitors a run for their money.

The new Chicago line enabled Strong to pull the Santa Fe out of the Southwestern Railway Association and to disown the pooling and traffic agreements at Kansas City. The move badly hurt the Alton and the CB&Q because of the loss of the Atchison's traffic. Former Santa Fe allies became rivals, or indeed, enemies. Strong cut rates between Chicago and Kansas City, and in 1889 the Atchison announced it would make through-rates on livestock only over its own line between these two points; there would be no exchange with the Milwaukee Road or the Alton. A rate war ensued, and all the lines in the area suffered losses in revenues. Why had Strong been so obstinate in building this expensive and highly provocative new segment? He explained: "The people along our whole system, above all other things, want direct, rapid and unobstructed communication with Chicago, with only one carrier to deal with in the entire transaction; and they will patronize the road which furnishes it."[5] There may have been some shipper demand, as Strong argued, but the real drive for independence came from Strong himself; and he continued to build more track even when it was strategically unnecessary and economically unsound. But to criticize Strong is to criticize the railroad industry in general in the 1880s.

Strong built or purchased a number of branches at the same time that he acquired the GCSF and constructed the "airline" to Chicago. A seventeen-mile branch from Atchison gave the Santa Fe entrance into St. Joseph, Missouri, and the purchase for $800,000 of a Wabash line east from St. Joseph seventy-six miles to Lexington Junction tied the Missouri city to the new Chicago track. Additional branches were built in Kansas and in southern New Mexico in the newly opened mining areas northwest of Deming. The GCSF extended its main line in West Texas from Lampasas to San Angelo in 1888; and Lewis Kingman sent his assistant Phillip Smith to survey additional routes in southwestern Kansas, northwestern Indian Territory and the Texas Panhandle. Despite Smith's favorable reports, Strong held off building in the area because once again he had tangled with Jay Gould.

In 1887 the Missouri Pacific opened its line from Kansas to Pueblo, Colorado, drastically altering the traffic arrangements in the Centennial State. Strong pulled the Santa Fe out of the old "Treaty of Boston" and formulated plans to enter Denver either by new construction or by the purchase of the Denver and New Orleans railroad then being built by former Colorado Governor John Evans. The D&NO hoped to build to the Gulf of Mexico via Fort Worth, but the Atchison, DRG, and Union Pacific fought Evans and his independent line. When Strong offered to purchase the D&NO, Evans refused to sell, and so Strong ordered the Pueblo Yard to stop exchanging cars with the D&NO. Strong had previously gained entrance into Denver over the DRG in 1882 by laying a third rail on the narrow-gauge line, but this operation became increasingly difficult and expensive. When Evans turned down a second offer of $2 million for the D&NO, and when the Missouri Pacific opened its line to Pueblo, Strong determined to enter Denver over his own rails. In March 1887, he formed a new subsidiary, and constructed 116 miles of track north from Pueblo. In Denver the Atchison purchased the Denver Circle Railroad for $800,000. The Denver Circle operated an eight-mile-long terminal line in the Mile High City, giving the Santa Fe strategic traffic connections. In September 1888, Santa Fe passenger trains began to operate from the Denver Union Depot.

When Gould disrupted Colorado traffic arrangements for the Atchison, Strong moved to destroy Gould's "monopoly" in St. Louis. On January 26, 1887, *The New York Times* announced the purchase by the Atchison of the St. Louis, Kansas City and Colorado Railroad, a fifty-mile-line from St. Louis to Union, Missouri. Further, reported *The Times*, the Atchison planned to extend the StLKC&C from Union to the new Kansas City–Chicago "airline," giving the ATSF entrance into St. Louis; the residents of St. Louis were "tickled." Gould then discovered in April that Robinson's surveyors were in the field between Pekin and St. Louis with unannounced plans to build to St. Louis from Chicago. Strong gave an additional indication that the Atchison meant business when he bought the St. Louis County Railroad that summer. The St. Louis County operated a five-mile-long switching and terminal line in the city. Gould became convinced that Strong would counter every new piece of construction, and an unwritten truce soon prevailed; both men brought their construction programs to a halt. The Atchison's orphan line in St. Louis remained isolated until it was sold in December 1899. Years later the Santa Fe would again seek entrance into St. Louis; but in the late 1880s the battle shifted from construction to the rate structure.

Overexpansion heightened competition, which led to the formation of pools and traffic agreements that soon collapsed to be followed by wholesale rate cutting. When the Denver-Pueblo pool fell apart in July 1883, the rates between these two points were slashed almost 60 percent. The same pattern developed in transcontinental rates, but on a grander scale. As early as 1881 the Union Pacific and the Atchison agreed to a $66\frac{2}{3}$–$33\frac{1}{3}$ split of traffic bound for California. Completion of the Texas and Pacific to El Paso in 1882 led to a division of 60–20–20, whereupon the Southern Pacific cut rates. Huntington reduced tariffs on his steamship lines between New York and California, and soon captured over two-thirds of the transcontinental business. Traffic over the Atchison between Albuquerque and Needles diminished to virtually nothing. A new Transcontinental Pool Association was formed to stabilize rates; but Strong refused to join, and tariffs fell again. The association pleaded with Charles Perkins of the CB&Q to persuade Strong to join. Perkins felt that Strong was a reasonable man who would accept a redivision giving the Atchison a larger share, but he was wrong. Strong remained belligerent and organized a systematic campaign to obtain traffic for the Atchison. Large companies like E. I. Du Pont De Nemours were solicited by letter and by Atchison representatives, and the railroad began to increase its share of transcontinental traffic. The Southern Pacific then offered Strong 23 percent of the business between the Missouri River and the West Coast, but Strong held out for 50 percent of the traffic to southern California and 28 percent to the remainder of the state; Huntington said no. In the rate war which followed, passenger fares from Chicago to the West Coast fell from $115 to $70. Tickets from Kansas City to San Francisco declined from $24 with a rebate of $3.00 to $16.00, and for a very brief period, to $1.00. Rates rose briefly in early 1887 when a new "understanding" was achieved, but the Atchison still opposed pools and agreements as "uncertain" at best. Strong wanted the railroad presidents to establish a permanent tariff structure to which all companies would adhere; the sharp decline in rates had to be stopped.

Farmers, small shippers, and many consumers complained that freight rates were too high, especially west of Chicago. Yet rates in the West fell drastically in the 1870s and 1880s. Atchison rates in Kansas declined substantially between 1875 and 1890, but the Kansas Board of Railroad Commissioners ordered a 26 percent cut in 1886, citing much lower rates east of Chicago. The commissioners expressed no concern for the differences between operating costs in the East and West, in the extreme variance of total tonnage carried, or the type of cargoes transported. Atchison freight rates compared quite favorably with those of other trans-Mississippi railroads, but all were hurting by 1887 as the freight charges were reduced. The average ton-mile rate on the Santa Fe fell from .0243¢ in 1880, to .0188¢ in 1884, to .01258¢ in 1888, and to .01228¢ two years later. Strong argued that something had to be done immediately to prevent the major roads from falling into bankruptcy.

Strong retained the staunch support of the Nickerson family, Kidder, Peabody, and the board of directors through the vast expansion program and during the rate wars; but as revenues declined, and as it became increasingly difficult to cover all of the new fixed charges, the stockholders began to pressure Strong to reach a compromise with Gould and Huntington. The Atchison, that "splendid child of Boston energy and enterprise," according to the Boston Herald, needed a respite. The Commercial and Financial Chronicle had editorialized at the beginning of the decade that the Atchison was the "only formidable competitor of the Gould system," and that in these Bostonian investors Gould had no mean antagonists, for "they are enterprising, alert, energetic, aggressive, and are backed by abundant capital."[6] The growing financial obligations of the Atchison, the Gould system, and Huntington's Southern Pacific, however, brought the leaders of the three systems together.

In November 1888, Strong, Gould and Huntington met to settle the rate war. They established a clearing house system which led to the creation of the Southwestern Railroad and Steamship Association. The association regulated rail and water transport west of the Missouri River and south of Kansas City. The three major partners controlled a majority on the five-man executive committee of the association, which not only established rates but also limited new construction and extensions. The spring of 1889 saw the establishment of the Trans-Missouri Freight Association, which covered the region between the Missouri River and the Rocky Mountains, and once again the Atchison joined. These agreements halted, at least temporarily, the decline in rates and the construction race; but Strong had waited too long to achieve peace. By 1888 the Santa Fe was in deep financial trouble, trouble which had been brewing for half the decade.

Charles Francis Adams, the Boston business leader, political figure and president of the Union Pacific, expressed the view held by most investors, trade publications and business analysts when he wrote in 1883 that Strong, the Nickersons and Kidder, Peabody had made the Atchison into "one of the most brilliantly successful [railroads] in the business history of the country."[7] Certainly the financial history of the Atchison until 1883 suggested that such praise and confidence were well placed. Between 1879 and 1883 the railroad grew in length from 470 miles to 2,620. It issued $48 million in par-value stock, of which $15,447,600 was sold for cash; $11,381,900 was issued in exchange for stock of acquired lines; $18,077,150 was distributed as dividends; and $3,391,500 was exchanged for ATSF bonds. In addition, the railroad had sold $45,780,500 in bonds by 1883. Such a massive issue of securities might have been questioned had not the profits in 1881 and 1882 been so large. Income rose as the freight carried leaped from 250,000 to 1,360,000 tons. After 1883, however, rates fell and the national economy began to slide. Strong paused very briefly to digest the first major period of expansion, but in 1886 he once again had launched a program which took the Santa Fe to the Gulf of Mexico and to Chicago and which sent branches over Kansas and Texas.

The Atchison management and Kidder, Peabody tried to continue their earlier conservative method of finance—primarily the selling of stock rather than bonds. The stock sold at par with frequent stock bonuses as dividends. Branches were often leased by guaranteeing rental fees equal to the annual interest on the bonds. This scheme worked well as long as the branches earned their way, but by 1888 the Atchison had paid out $2,361,300 to cover defaulted interest on the leased lines. That same year the railroad carried as an asset on its books $13,558,678 due from the branch lines; but there was no hope of recovery. The ATSF also had to maintain the branches and provide them with equipment, and the burden grew heavier each year.

Investors might have raised objections to Strong's expansion policies—only a few did—had not the securities of the Atchison continued to appreciate in value. In 1879 Atchison stock sold at 82, but in 1882 it peaked at 96⅛. The fluctuation on the New York Stock Exchange was substantial; in 1884 the low mark was 59½ and the high 80, but highs of 119⅞ in 1887 and 99⅝ the next year kept investors happy enough. The number of stockholders swelled to over 6,000. So widely held were the securities that both Jay Gould and Collis P. Huntington tried to obtain control through the purchases of moderate blocks of stock, though neither was successful. When latent criticism of the expansion program became verbalized in 1887, Strong and Robinson defended both the extension of the line and its financial operations. Robinson told *The New York Times*:

> The Atchison never begins or plans a piece of work until it has the money to carry it through. We arranged for all of the money we are going to want abroad and at home before we began our extensions. Within two years by the end of this year we shall have built 3,000 miles of new road.[8]

Robinson confidently described the financial methods and the expansion program, but he then admitted that the vast new mileage meant heavy outlays for equipment and reconstruction of some of the older track now being used to maximum capacity.

Not only did the Santa Fe expand throughout much of the 1880s, but it also improved its physical plant and made massive purchases of new, heavier locomotives and rolling stock. The maintenance and improvement budgets grew larger and took an ever-increasing portion of the company's income. As early as 1881 the management noted the need for more steel rails, tie replacement and ballasting. New and larger yards, terminal facilities, depots, roundhouses, shops and offices had to be built. Beyond Newton the water facilities needed to be improved and bridges rebuilt to carry the larger locomotives and cars. Kidder, Peabody began to sell millions of dollars of stocks and bonds to pay for these improvements.

One of the most noticeable improvements on the Santa Fe occurred in the rebuilding of its trackage. In the late 1870s the company began to replace the worn iron rails with new steel. Maintenance crews sent usable iron to branch lines to be relaid. The new rail was rarely much larger in size, especially on the branches, but section crews relaid the main line with 62–70-pound steel. By the mid-1890s all but a few hundred miles of the main line had steel rail. As the track gangs replaced rails they also put in new, treated ties. Tie plates were not in general use, and so the wood wore rapidly, especially in areas of heavy moisture. The Santa Fe pioneered in the use of treated, or creosoted ties, establishing a plant in 1885 at Las Vegas, New Mexico, which received its supply of soft pine from East Texas or Arizona. Ties which formerly lasted only four years could now be used as long as fifteen years. The new ties and rails needed ballast, and the Santa Fe's plant at Strong City, Kansas, supplied the track crews with crushed rock. Burnt-clay ballast on the Illinois and Missouri lines worked well also; but ballasting was costly, and as late as 1896 few miles of non-main line were protected; even the A&P line still operated without the benefit of ballast. While some work could be deferred, bridge replacement and grade and curve reduction could not.

Throughout the system the first bridges were constructed largely of untreated wooden piles. In the 1880s and the following decade bridge crews erected steel and masonry replacements. Similarly, culverts had to be installed where fills replaced trestles. The load capacity of many bridges needed to be increased, just as sharp grades had to be reduced. In Colorado and New Mexico, particularly, curves were straightened and cuts deepened to reduce the grades. Little was done, however, on the A&P, as traffic simply did not warrant large expenditures. Elsewhere, section gangs roamed over the system laying new rails, installing treated ties, replacing bridges and doing other work to prepare the track for heavier motive power and rolling stock.

The equipment of the Atchison increased rapidly from 5,530 units in 1880 to 32,293 in 1895. The numbers grew impressively, but even more significantly, the tractive power of the locomotives jumped markedly, as did the capacity of the freight and passenger cars. The Santa Fe purchased most of its locomotives from the Taunton, Hinkley, Baldwin, or Manchester Locomotive Works, with most of the initial orders being for 4–4–0s. In the mid-1880s, larger engines came from Baldwin and Brooks in fleets of 2–6–0s and 4–6–0s. The latter, with tractive efforts of over 20,000 pounds, eclipsed even "Uncle Dick" in size. These new locomotives pulled freight cars of ever-increasing length and capacity. The ATSF also began to diversify its freight car fleet to meet shipper demands, adding refrigerator cars and special gondolas and hoppers for minerals and stone. Improvements were made on the rolling stock, and in the mid-1880s men like George Hackney and Benjamin Johnson traveled over the ATSF, explaining the new automatic air-brake system being installed on the equipment. Years would pass before the installation was completed, but this marked a major advance in safety for crewmen and the reduction of damaged freight. Simultaneously, the Santa Fe purchased improved passenger cars with larger seating capacities. Vestibules replaced open platforms and electric lights were installed instead of gas. This massive acquisition

Riding to California in style. Santa Fe Railway

program and the improvement of existing equipment meant that additional shops and offices had to be constructed.

The Atchison corporate headquarters remained in Topeka, although the executive offices were located in Boston. In 1880 the general office in Topeka consisted of a large two-story wooden building and a few rented rooms nearby. A three-story masonry building replaced the wooden structure, and in 1884 a large four-story building at the corner of Jackson and 9th streets became the general office. When a disastrous fire badly damaged that structure in 1889, it was rebuilt and another floor added. The people of Topeka had lobbied vigorously to keep the offices and the major shop in their town. In 1872 the voters approved a bond issue of $100,000 to guarantee that the facilities would remain; and when, in 1881, the shops were doubled in size, many Topeka residents breathed easier, especially when the railroad began to build its own locomotives in the new facility. Locomotive shops at Cleburne, Albuquerque, San Bernardino, Fort Madison and Chicago served other areas of the system. These locomotive facilities required cranes, heavy tools, large stores, and ever-increasing manpower, as did the car repair shops which sprang up along the Santa Fe to service the growing fleet of freight and passenger equipment. Even a modest facility as in Nickerson, Kansas, required a twenty-eight stall roundhouse, a small shop, and a freight car repair track. Every year Strong earmarked more capital for equipment and for facilities to keep it in good order.

To operate its expanding lines the Atchison management constantly increased the size of its work force. The decade saw generally peaceful labor-management relations because the railroad paid relatively good wages. The average Santa Fe employee in 1885 received $581 yearly, which increased to $660 in 1888, but most of them worked dreadfully long hours. Benjamin Johnson, a graduate of Cornell University, worked on a switch engine crew at Newton in 1882 from 7:00 A.M. to 8:30 P.M. six days a week and for a slightly shorter period on Sunday. When the crew received an extra assignment to switch the southbound Wichita passenger train, Johnson asked for a pay raise, which he got. Johnson was just one of the 4,391 Santa Fe employees in Kansas. Their wages varied enormously; engineers earned $3.44 per day for a twelve-hour day; firemen $1.93 daily; passenger conductors $3.41; freight conductors $2.47; and machinists $2.43; but section hands were paid only $1.32 and laborers $1.39. The wages were generally decent, although the hours were long. Most complaints from the men were about the high incidence of accidents. In 1884, for example, 7 employees in Kansas were killed and 585 were injured in accidents. Only the coming of the safety coupler and the air brake would reduce this fearful toll. However, Santa Fe employees did not participate in the great railroad strikes in 1885, but some joined a brief sympathy strike three years later. On March 15, 1888, a wildcat strike by Santa Fe engineers and firemen threatened to close down the company, but Strong refused to be intimidated. He stopped all trains, including those carrying U.S. mail, and defied Postmaster General Dickinson's order to resume Postal Department service. The management hoped to use nondelivery of the mail to win public support against the strikers, but the Cleveland administration pressured Strong into operating the mail trains. The strikers could not take advantage of the situation, however, and returned to work very shortly. The management which took over the Atchison in 1889 instituted new labor policies, making more benefits available to train crews. In addition to wage increases, the railroad provided a seniority system, new rules for overtime and pay for turn-arounds. Unlike other companies in the 1880s, the Santa Fe did not suffer from intensive labor strife, but the railroad had enough troubles in other areas to make up for it.

The Indian, New Mexico and Arizona territories were still part of the "Wild West" in the 1880s, and Atchison crews and trains suffered from robberies and acts of vandalism. The Atlantic and Pacific line west of Albuquerque witnessed an increasing number of holdups, but the most spectacular robberies occurred around Raton, New Mexico, and in southwestern Colorado. In June 1882, six men, including a Santa Fe engineer, died during a holdup near Raton. Two months later, armed men seized a westbound passenger train a mile west of Granada. The passenger train had been waiting on a siding when two of the gunmen mounted the engine. Conductor Dees went forward to see why the train remained stopped, and when he discovered the cause he began to fire at other members of the gang who were rifling the express car. Back in one of the coaches the sheriff from Las Vegas, New Mexico, and a deputy sheriff from Raton heard the shots and joined Dees to drive off the gang, which fled with $5,000 taken from the express car. The trainmen and law officers saved some $10,000 contained in the express car safe, and the train proceeded on to Trinidad. Life for Atchison crews was never dull, and the same could be said of the management in the late 1880s.

From 1885 through 1888 the Atchison's traffic ebbed and flowed as rates continued to fall. The Kansas corn and wheat crops determined whether the railroad made a large profit or skirted the brink of financial disaster. Operating revenues declined in 1885 and again in 1888 when the Midwest suffered crop failures and drought. Total revenue in 1888 was slightly less than that of three years earlier, and the operating ratio leaped from 53.40 to 70.63. The financial burdens of the system grew more rapidly than its ability to produce earnings. Some 2,799 miles of track in 1884 produced a net profit of $5,147,883, but in 1888 some

A 4–4–0 from Baldwin in 1887. H. L. Broadbelt

7,010 miles of line generated a deficit of $2,933,197. The deficit can largely be explained in terms of the huge indebtedness of the entire system. Where in 1884 the Atchison had issued $60,673,150 in stock and sold $48,258,000 in bonds, by 1888 the stock grew to $75,000,000 while bonds outstanding soared to $163,694,000. The blame fell squarely upon Strong's over-exuberant expansion program.

In the *Annual Reports* of the late 1880s the management noted, though without alarm, the slide in earnings, the reduction in rates, and the interest payments demanded by the Sonora, A&P, and other deficit-ridden branches. By 1887 Strong acknowledged shortages of motive power and rolling stock, and increasing competition. In that year alone the Atchison spent over $40 million for real estate and construction, and Strong began to discount company securities in order to sell them. When the operating ratio rose sharply the following year, and several of the subsidiaries showed heavy losses, some stockholders and security analysts began to raise questions about the company's fiscal well-being. Most of the directors remained calm, and several issued positive statements about the Atchison's financial position. Indeed, in 1887, the Atchison increased its dividend rate from 6 to 7 percent.

Opposition to Strong's expansion program by some stockholders began as early as 1885, and several filed law suits to block acquisition of the Gulf, Colorado and Santa Fe and the construction of the line to Chicago.

Railway Age raised some doubts about the Atchison's fiscal position in 1887, but concluded, "The career of this company has been one of the marvels of the railway enterprise, and it would be unsafe now to attempt to fix a limit to its expansion or to the ambitions of its Napoleanic president and its bold and enterprising directors."[9] And even one year earlier *The Commercial and Financial Chronicle* accused the Atchison management of being too conservative in expanding to meet competition. In response to this rising chorus of criticism, Strong admitted that the increase in the dividend rate had been an error, but only because projected revenues failed to materialize.

Yet, criticism mounted. Security analyst S. F. Van Oss later declared: "Within six years a most prosperous property had become an utter wreck, burdened with debt, and not able to pay a dividend." Van Oss blamed ". . . those in power [who] had by a wrong policy contributed as much to the decay of the railway as commercial depression and competition, and perhaps even more."[10] He cited the "indiscriminate" and ambitious expansion program as the primary reason for the Atchison's plight, especially the line to Chicago, which had alienated former friends. *Railway Review* agreed that the expansion "mania" had produced financial disaster. Defenders of Strong's program pointed to the absence of fraudulent construction companies controlled by "insiders," the quality of construction, and the need to build lines in advance of settlement. Competition, drought, rate reductions, and the economic "necessity" of lines to the Gulf of Mexico and Chicago were cited by Strong and Robinson to defend their policies; but while basic truths were to be found in these statements, a financial crisis had developed.

When the expansion program terminated, the Atchison's debts totaled $158,891,820, not including those of the A&P. Fixed charges ran to $8,487,045 yearly. In one year the Sonora lost $355,915, the GC&SF $1,328,791, the A&P $1,578,404, and the Kansas City to Chicago line $441,555. The company's cash holdings dwindled, and the operating ratio hit 93. The recently increased dividend rate was cut, and then on November 15, 1888, dividends were terminated. The floating debt grew from $3,317,446 to $8,076,059, forcing the directors to issue $10 million in three-year "guarantee fund notes" at 6 percent, but only $7 million could be marketed. Economy measures followed with salaries cut by 10 percent. Confidence in the company collapsed as Atchison stock, which had been selling at 99⅝, fell to 26⅜. Despite the optimism which permeated the *Annual Report* for 1888, clamors for a change in management grew in intensity.

The coterie of Bostonians and security houses which had dominated the Atchison's board of directors could not cope with the crisis. The Nickerson family held 17,000 shares and Benjamin Cheney with 12,755 was the largest single stockholder, but they lacked the financial resources to keep the Santa Fe afloat. Kidder, Peabody complained that Albert Nickerson dominated the board, but no one man or family could control such a large operation. The brokerage firms affiliated with the Atchison held large blocks of stock (Baring Brothers, 22,300; Kidder, Peabody, 8,470; and Lee, Higginson, 2,397), but more importantly, they also controlled access to additional capital. The three firms supported the expansion program and had raised the funds to pay for it; but by 1888, they became frightened and persuaded Strong to agree to market no new securities. Then, when they discovered the huge floating debt in 1888, they joined those calling for new leadership.

In January 1889, Atchison stock hit a new low. Stockholders forgot the $28,756,387 in cash dividends they had received, and they flooded the market with Santa Fe stocks and bonds. On January 20, over 70 percent of the business on the Boston stock exchange was in Atchison securities. When the market failed to improve, the management issued a sixty-page analysis of the health of the company, but the large publication contained no statements, only tables, charts and graphs. When the Atchison held its annual stockholders meeting on May 9, the firms of Kidder, Peabody and Baring Brothers led a majority of the stockholders who voted to replace five members of the board. Thomas Baring, Oliver Peabody and three representatives of their houses, plus George Magoun of Kidder, Peabody, who had been on the board since the previous October, constituted a new majority. These men stripped Strong of most of his power, although he remained president of the Atchison. George Magoun, as chairman of the new board, took over the financial and policy-making responsibilities, while Strong retained control only over daily operations of the rail system.

Demotion to "errand boy" for the board proved more than the proud Strong could accept. He resigned as president on September 6. Many stockholders blamed him personally for the plight of the company, failing to recognize his extraordinary achievements; the Atchison was, after all, largely his creation. Few of the critics took cognizance of the fact that the Atchison's financial trouble was the product of overoptimism, and perhaps carelessness, and not the result of stock manipulation or corruption. Yet only in the future, as the Santa Fe prospered and the territory it served boomed, did Strong appear vindicated.

Allen Manvel of the St. Paul, Minneapolis and Manitoba succeeded Strong as president. Born in New York in 1837, Manvel had a long career in railroading before joining the Atchison. A frugal, hard working man who put in fourteen-hour days, he faced grave problems. The old hands on the Santa Fe resented him at the outset, blaming him for Strong's resignation, but Manvel paid them, and Strong, the high compliment of retaining nearly all of his predecessor's former assistants. Recognized as Kidder, Peabody and Baring Brothers' appointment, Manvel tried to restore confidence in the Atchison. He instituted stringent economic restrictions and formulated a scheme to fund the floating debt, but earnings did not increase and fixed charges had to be paid. The Atchison had gone too far too fast, and either new financing had to be found or drastic surgery had to be performed. During the next eight years the Atchison would be reorganized, and the process would be painful to the investors, management and employees, but from this experience a giant of a railroad would emerge.

6

The Captains of Industry Reorganize

The new leaders of the Atchison, Topeka and Santa Fe Railroad realized that immediate action had to be taken to save the company. The financial crisis deepened in 1888 and early 1889, and the new management installed by Kidder, Peabody and Company and Baring Brothers sought to diminish the heavy cash flow for fixed charges and to increase profits by more efficient operations. On President Allen Manvel fell the burden of implementing William Barstow Strong's efficiency plan and the obligation to increase traffic and revenues. Vice President Joseph W. Reinhart began to devise a scheme to refinance the heavy obligations of the Atchison, and Chairman of the Board George Magoun tried to persuade the investors in the company that all was well with the railroad. During the next four years these men had the opportunity to revitalize the railroad and improve its financial position. As will be seen, they failed miserably.

The principal factors which brought the Atchison to financial grief were overexpansion, some extravagances in operations, and an overly generous if not reckless, increase in dividends. The vast expansion program, financed by larger and larger issues of securities, became more than the system could bear. In September 1889, Magoun and Reinhart and the Atchison's financial committee studied various plans of reorganization. They reported that the Atchison had $163,006,660 in bonds and car trust certificates outstanding with an annual interest obligation of $9,075,769, plus additional obligations in the form of rentals and taxes to create a yearly fixed burden of $11,157,769. The bonds on the Atchison amounted to $56,498,000 at 4½ to 7 percent interest rates, plus an additional

$104,288,000 in bonds issued by 32 subsidiaries. The financial committee urged that the total security issue be increased and simplified. This would, they hoped, decrease fixed charges and pay off the floating debt. As the Atchison earned only $6.3 million the previous year, the committee proposed an immediate voluntary reorganization. Amid rumors of bankruptcy and a continuing decline in the price of Atchison stock, the committee proposed a massive restructuring of the company's debts.

The committee urged that the forty-one issues of bonds be replaced by two classes: 4 percent general mortgage bonds amounting to $150 million and 5 percent income bonds of $80 million. These new bonds would be exchanged for previously issued notes and provide $13,750,000 in cash to pay the floating debt. The Atchison would replace $163 million in notes with bonds amounting to $230 million, but the inclusion of income bonds reduced fixed charges appreciably. Had the plan been in operation in 1888, the committee noted, there would have been a profit rather than a loss. The committee hoped to avoid foreclosure and a voting trust, and they urged that the bondholders accept the plan. They reminded the owners of the Atchison of the railroad's history of generous dividends and stock bonuses.

Although the plan received the immediate endorsement of most bondholders, the proposal drew sharp criticism in the press. *The New York Times* and several financial journals condemned the plan for its failure to levy an assessment on holders of common stock. The income bonds were placed ahead of the common stock, but the stockholders were not asked to make any immediate sacrifices. During the next three years this aspect of the plan was thoroughly condemned by many railroad analysts, and the London *Times* declared that bondholders were forced to make "cruel sacrifices" by the common stockholders who, "if equity had been observed would have been wiped out . . . unless they had paid assessments."[1] The committee rejected the criticism and presented its plan to the board of directors. Kidder, Peabody and Baring Brothers, now in complete control of the board, approved the plan. The reduction in fixed charges seemed to be the primary consideration in making the decision. Joseph Reinhart defended the proposal, and he argued that together with the new economy measures he had placed in effect the voluntary reorganization would save the Atchison. On October 15, the management presented the plan to the bondholders, and Atchison common stock rose in price on the exchanges for the first time in months. An affirmative response by the security holders allowed the directors to announce on November 23 that the plan would become effective on December 15. The bond exchange proved to be an outstanding success as investors submitted all but a very small amount. The exchange cost only $1,440,772, which included a fee of $125,000 for Kidder, Peabody. While the funded debt jumped appreciably, the fixed charges declined, and the average interest rate fell by 1.35 percent.

In most respects the reorganization could be described as a success, at least for the immediate future. A possible bankruptcy had been avoided and the system had not been disrupted. The reorganization did create a major obstacle, however, in that no provisions were made for future capital requirements for improvements; it became impossible to raise additional capital by issuing bonds. Superficially the plan seemed to have merit, and combined with prosperity on the Great Plains, bumper crops, and an increase in traffic it augured well for the future. But the failure to provide for working capital through assessment of the common stockholders added to the problems faced by Manvel, Reinhart and Magoun. Yet, these three men soon fell into the same trap which had caused the crises of 1888–1889; they initiated a huge expansion program.

Frisco Railroad

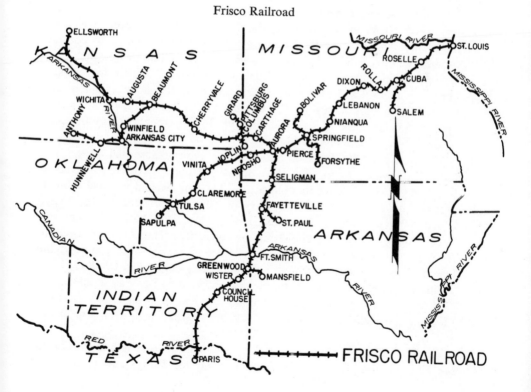

The St. Louis and San Francisco Railroad continued to be a trouble-some partner throughout the 1880s. The arrangement for joint develop-ment of the Atlantic and Pacific Railroad did not appear threatened; but the StL&SF, or Frisco, did continue to build branches in territory con-sidered by the Atchison to be its own. In 1887, relations between the A&P's partners deteriorated further when Frisco stockholders approved additional expansion in Kansas. Only negotiations between the executives of the railroads prevented a deeper rupture, and harmony returned with the completion of the Gulf, Colorado and Santa Fe branch from Dallas to Paris, Texas, opening a through-route for the Frisco from St. Louis to southern Texas via the Paris Gateway. The roads continued to exchange traffic in Kansas, and the Frisco gave the Atchison an ally in St. Louis. The management of the Santa Fe feared, however, that the Frisco might fall into unfriendly hands, and as early as 1888 speculation grew that a merger was imminent.

Magoun, Manvel and Reinhart saw several advantages in the acquisi-tion of the Frisco, not the least of which included securing an entrance into St. Louis. Reinhart opened negotiations with the Frisco management, and on May 23, 1890, they reached an agreement. For the 1,442-mile Frisco, the Atchison paid $22,511,688 of its own common stock, or three shares of Atchison for four of the Frisco. Santa Fe executives were reportedly jubilant over the "bargain price," but they failed to consider the heavy bonded debt of the Frisco—some $31 million. While the Atchi-son management stressed the mutual advantages of merger in terms of operating efficiency and geographical harmony, the heavy funded debt loomed like a giant albatross. In 1889 the Frisco lost $277,000 and devel-oped a floating debt of over $2 million. Frisco stockholders, therefore, readily accepted the favorable terms offered by the Santa Fe.

Within a year, the Atchison admitted that the purchase had been a mis-take. The *Annual Report* for 1891 noted that the Frisco had not paid its way and could not cover its obligations. The line needed massive rebuild-ing, new yards and depots. To carry out these improvements the Frisco issued a large quantity of bonds, and the Atchison had to purchase a sizable share when they could not be marketed. The Atchison tried to revitalize the Frisco with new equipment and made some progress; the Frisco's operating ratio declined, but the floating debt grew. In 1891, when $7 million in Frisco notes matured, the Atchison had to pay a substantial sum to gain an extension. A terrible mistake had been made, but Manvel, Magoun and Reinhart acquired yet another railroad with even less justifi-cation.

On September 5, 1890, the Atchison announced that it had purchased the 327-mile-long Colorado Midland Railway for $4,355,200 in common

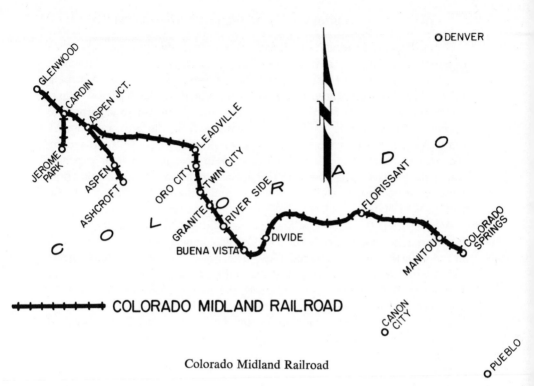

Colorado Midland Railroad

stock and $1,955,424 in cash, and had guaranteed the CM's funded debt of $11,244,866. The CM extended from Colorado Springs westward through the Rockies to Glenwood Springs. The builders of the CM hoped to construct further westward, eventually reaching Salt Lake City or Ogden and a connection with the Central Pacific. The CM and the Denver and Rio Grande fought for the meager traffic in the South Park of Colorado, and each sought to find friendly eastern connections. The Chicago, Rock Island and Pacific built to Colorado Springs and was rumored to want the CM. The Atchison leaders feared that either the DRG or the CRI&P would acquire the CM and hurt the Santa Fe's new line from Denver to Pueblo by diverting traffic. The CM lost money consistently, had a terrible line to operate, especially in the winter, and its floating debt grew yearly. The CM represented only a threat to a stable rate structure; its line offered no real competitive threat to the ATSF. Nevertheless, the Atchison acquired the CM, paying far more than it was worth. The purchase of the Frisco and the CM flooded the stock markets with Atchison securities, the price of which kept falling as Manvel failed to develop the traffic the company so desperately needed.

When Kidder, Peabody and Baring Brothers established the new management in 1889 they did so under certain conditions. One requirement was the appointment of Reinhart and the institution of a new bookkeeping system based on the procedures used by the Pennsylvania Railroad. Reinhart installed the new accounting methods, and attempted to separate the accounts of the subsidiaries. To control cash outflow, the brokerage houses also required that all expenditures of more than $25,000 be approved by the finance committee. These "reforms" were designed to limit expenditures and to clarify the company's financial condition. Much of this effort became an exercise in futility after the acquisitions of the Frisco and the Colorado Midland.

Manvel tried to economize and increase the Atchison's earning power. He moved the presidential office to Chicago and consolidated the offices of subsidiaries and the merged lines. The new accounting system caused the *Annual Report* to be issued at the end of June rather than the end of December, but the first report utilizing the new procedures did not contain encouraging news. Heavy expenditures on the California and Chicago lines for ditching, filling, side tracks and buildings reduced earnings, and

the Paris-Dallas branch had to be rebuilt to accommodate Frisco traffic. Manvel reported that the huge equipment purchases of 1887 and 1888 were only beginning to be absorbed. In 1887 the Atchison purchased 157 locomotives, 198 passenger cars and 3,108 freight cars, and the next year 115 locomotives, 97 passenger cars and 5,664 freight cars were added. Much of this equipment had been placed in storage when it arrived because of the traffic slumps. Business had revived, however, and Manvel concluded the report on an optimistic note.

No sooner had the report been issued than rumors began to circulate that the Atchison was again in serious financial trouble. Reinhart denied the rumors categorically. He claimed that crop estimates from Texas and Kansas looked very promising and that traffic reports in general were favorable. He noted the rise in the price of Atchison common from 26½ in October 1889 to 58 in January 1890; investors had no reason for alarm.

The results of the following year's operations did not support Manvel's optimism or Reinhart's positive prognosis. Gross earnings rose only slightly over $2.5 million, agricultural traffic slumped, and the net actually fell by more than $9 million. Maintenance costs rose, and Manvel purchased

Shops and roundhouse, Nickerson, Kansas, in the 1890s. Santa Fe Railway

additional rolling stock, including 87 locomotives, 2,250 freight cars and 11 passenger cars. While the agricultural tonnage continued to fall, the Santa Fe did increase its traffic in other categories, especially in manu-factured goods and minerals, thus creating a need for the new equipment. The 1891 *Annual Report* sought to justify the purchase of the Colorado Midland and argued that the Frisco was improving its earning power; but the heavy financial drain continued as the Atchison sought to support its affiliates.

The failure of the Kansas corn crop in 1890, falling rates, large losses on the Atlantic and Pacific and Colorado Midland, and huge discounts to refinance notes began to take a heavier toll on the Atchison. Company bonds fell in price to 83¼, and the presence of the income bonds prevented the floating of new securities for capital needs. Manvel and Magoun decided to suggest yet another financial restructuring. In 1892 they pro-posed to exchange the income bonds for fixed-interest bonds, creating, in effect, a second mortgage. In the 1892 *Annual Report* Manvel urged stock-holder approval of the plan, maintaining that it would enable the Atchison to issue additional bonds for improvements and to pay for more equip-ment he had purchased. The new second-mortgage bonds would be of two types, Classes A and B. Class A bonds, totaling $80 million, would be issued at par in exchange for the old income bonds. Their interest rate would begin at 2½ percent in 1892, increase to 4 percent in 1896, and maintain that rate until maturity. The Class B bonds would be issued in series at the rate of $5 million a year for four years and pay 4 percent interest. The bondholders accepted the new Class A bonds readily, and some $78 million were exchanged, but only $5 million of the Class B bonds were marketed. The plan can only be described as a total disaster. The Atchison now stood obligated to service $222 million in securities, and the system was worth about half of that figure. As President Manvel sought to keep the Atchison going he strained himself to the limit, and on February 24, 1893, he died. The board named Reinhart his successor. The elevation of Reinhart to the presidency upset many Santa Fe veterans, especially Vice President and General Manager A. A. Robinson. Twice passed over by the board, Robinson soon resigned to become president of the Mexican Central. When he departed, Robinson let it be known that he strongly disagreed with Reinhart's accounting methods; investors should have heeded his warning.

The new second mortgage with its heavy fixed charges fell on the Atchison at a time when the entire railroad industry was experiencing falling revenues. In addition, the Atchison suffered from labor strife, rate wars and political attacks. As part of his economy drive, Manvel reduced the total number of Santa Fe employees, but cut the working day from twelve hours to ten. In 1892 the telegraphers on the GCSF struck, and a telegram containing a fake strike call on October 17, 1892, brought on a walkout by telegraphers all over the Atchison system. The next year Santa Fe shopmen went on strike when Reinhart refused to raise their wages to levels established by other railroads. The shopmen demanded higher wages, shorter hours and restriction of work performed by apprentices. When Reinhart agreed only to raise wages, the shopmen responded by asking for greater authority on hiring, firing and work schedules. The strike became increasingly bitter, and only a compromise arranged by the railroad brotherhoods brought about its resolution on April 22, 1893. Reinhart then turned his attention to the continuing rate wars.

The Atchison, when under Strong's guidance, tried to avoid pools, stabilize rates, and limit state regulatory legislation. Manvel and Reinhart followed the same course. In 1890, when the Chicago–Kansas City pool ordered the Atchison to divert traffic to other roads at Kansas City, Manvel refused. Only when the Atchison received an equal amount of westbound traffic would he surrender eastbound cargoes. As a consequence of the Santa Fe's position, the pool collapsed. Just when Manvel felt some relief east of Kansas City, the Denver and Rio Grande slashed rates in Colorado, and the Missouri River–Los Angeles passenger fare fell from $50 to $20. Reinhart pledged to maintain fair rates and reasonable profits, and he sought support from Collis P. Huntington. When rates continued to fall, Reinhart took the Atchison out of all pools and traffic associations in the spring of 1894, charging that secret cuts and rebates by the Santa Fe's competitors had destroyed their effectiveness. When a general demoralization of the industry followed, Reinhart announced an end to the rate war with the Southern Pacific. The Atchison restored rates to the September 1, 1893, level, and the war terminated, if only briefly. Nevertheless, the average ton-mile freight rate on the Atchison fell from .0113¢ in 1892 to .0107¢ the next year, and to .0098¢ in 1894. Ironically, just as rates sank to an almost ruinous level, the political attacks on the Atchison reached a new climax.

Since the days of the Pottawatomie land deal, some Kansas farmers had criticized the Santa Fe, and in the 1880s the chorus of criticism grew louder and louder. Farmers attacked the railroads in general, and the Santa Fe in particular, because of their land grants, "high rates," and political power—real and alleged. Many believed that the state government of Kansas responded affirmatively to every whim of the railroad. This protest movement became sharply focused in Kansas in 1890 and 1892 when the Farmers' Alliance and the Populist party made the Atchison and its "power" the central campaign issue. Mrs. Mary E. Lease, famous for her remark that farmers should raise more hell and less corn, charged that "Kansas suffers from two great robbers, the Santa Fe Railroad and the loan companies. . . ."[2] In 1892 the Populist candidate for governor, Lorenzo Lewelling, lashed out at the railroads, singling out the Santa Fe for particular abuse. Another Populist leader, "Sockless" Jerry Simpson, accused the Santa Fe of exercising a transportation monopoly in Kansas. The idea of an Atchison monopoly came as a shock to the company, which had witnessed a wholesale railroad invasion of Kansas and sharply declining rates as a result. But the voters of the Sunflower State responded to the Populist charges and elected Lewelling governor. At his inaugural, Lewelling declared:

> Fellow citizens, we have come here today to remove the seat of the government of Kansas from the Santa Fe offices back to the statehouse where it belongs. You have beaten the Santa Fe railroad and you must organize the legislature tomorrow, and I wouldn't let the technicalities of the law stand in the way.[3]

The Populist government of Kansas did not affect the Atchison's operations, though the depression of 1893 did lead to further rate reductions. Most of the charges against the railroad faded from view, and by 1901 Jerry Simpson could be found in New Mexico selling Santa Fe lands. The verbal abuse the Atchison suffered in the 1890s did not vitally harm the railroad, but the depression of 1893 proved more than the company could stand.

In 1893 the United States entered into the worst depression since 1873 and the most catastrophic until 1929. The stock market collapsed, industries closed, banks failed, and the economy ground to a halt. President Grover Cleveland refused, however, to use the resources of the federal government to alleviate the misery brought on by the depression. Thousands of miles of railroad fell into the hands of receivers as business declined precipitously. The Atchison, already in serious financial trouble, could not remain solvent despite the flood of optimistic statements issued by President Joseph Reinhart.

When Reinhart succeeded Manvel as president of the Atchison, the financial journals and the company stockholders indicated solid support for him. Born in Pittsburgh in 1851, Reinhart graduated from the Western University of Pennsylvania and became an employee of the Pennsylvania Railroad. He worked for several other railroads prior to becoming an independent consultant and efficiency expert and joining the Atchison. Considered a "good, practical railroad man," Reinhart sought to end the rumors circulating about the financial condition of the company. In June 1893 he persistently denied that the Santa Fe had any floating debt and reported that assets more than equaled liabilities. He even declared that the Atchison could take care of the floating debts of the Frisco and the Colorado Midland. As the national depression worsened, rumors circulated that the Atchison might seek the protection of a bankruptcy court. In October Reinhart denied emphatically that the railroad was seeking a receivership. Near the end of the month he issued a positive financial statement showing a substantial increase in earnings, and the board of directors indicated they were satisfied with Reinhart's management of the railroad. Magoun declared that the financial panic had been anticipated by the company and that previously enacted economy measures enabled the road to meet the traffic losses. One wonders what kind of economy measures Magoun referred to in light of the delivery to the Atchison in April of two luxurious business cars from the Pullman Palace Car Company. Even more revealing was Reinhart's hasty departure for England on October 28.

Reinhart went to England seeking money from Baring Brothers and their allies. The English holdings of Atchison stocks and bonds had grown to a sizable amount since the Barings entered the railroad in 1883. Indeed, many American analysts believed that the Atchison acquired the Colorado Midland only to save the investments in that company by Baring Brothers and their friends. Reinhart sought money from the English investors to cover interest payments due on January 1, 1894. In November he cabled news that English security holders had confidence in the Atchison and had agreed to take $3 million in bonds. A meeting of Atchison stockholders lauded his achievement and declared that he had saved the company.

Reinhart returned to the United States in early December still assuring investors that all was well. But rumors that the English bond purchase had fallen through caused an attack on Atchison stock, and the price fell to 15¼. Reinhart reluctantly admitted that he had received only assurances of purchases, not actual cash, and the speculative assault worsened. On December 20, George Magoun died, and the bottom dropped out from under Atchison securities. *The Commercial and Financial Chronicle* lamented Magoun's death and tried to reassure investors that the $4 million in cash and $14 million in securities in the Atchison treasury would cover the $9 million in current liabilities. But who would purchase the securities, even with a sharp discount? Reinhart discovered that the Atchison had absolutely no credit left, and so he took the necessary step of requesting a receivership. Although the usually reliable *Financial Chronicle* on December 22 still reported that the Atchison could easily weather the depression, the previous day the directors had secretly dispatched Santa Fe lawyers to Topeka to apply for a receivership.

On December 23, at Little Rock, Arkansas, Judge Caldwell of the U.S. District Court appointed Reinhart, John J. McCook, and Joseph C. Wilson receivers at the request of the Union Trust Company on behalf of

Atchison bondholders. In announcing the receivership, Reinhart still maintained that the company was sound; he blamed the receivership on the depression and Magoun's death which, he said, had terminated negotiations with English investors. Reinhart's announcement provoked great hostility in the press and from stockholders. *The Commercial and Financial Chronicle* expressed only disappointment, but *The Economist* accused Reinhart of gross deception. The last *Annual Report* had been misleading, *The Economist* stated, and cast doubt on the integrity of the management and the receivers. The appointment of Reinhart as a receiver provoked further negative comments.

Following the appointment of receivers for the Atchison, the Frisco and the A&P, several protective committees of security holders were formed. Committees in Boston, New York and London began to draft plans to refinance the Atchison. The London committee largely represented the Class A second-mortgage bondholders who wanted a plan to maintain their interest in bonds rather than convert them to common stock; but such a feature of any reorganization would have been not only selfish but merely a palliative. Edward King of Union Trust represented the Boston committee, Robert Fleming came from London to defend the English interests, and Hope and Company sent agents from Amsterdam to speak for the Dutch investors. They formed a General Reorganization Committee and hired Stephen Little to carry out a thorough examination of the Atchison's books. A nationally recognized accountant, Little began to try to analyze the railroad's financial condition. While Little carried out his investigation, a proposal to issue a new, larger second mortgage, more income bonds, and assess the common stockholders $12.00 per share failed for lack of support. The stockholders refused to accept an assessment and any plan which protected the bondholders almost exclusively. The London committee pushed the proposal, but the New York committee said absolutely no. Then Little reported his findings, producing a bombshell.

Little presented his preliminary analysis in July, and he filed a lengthy formal report on November 2, disclosing numerous irregularities—including four years of book juggling. Little charged that Reinhart had overstated earnings by $7,644,451 and had failed to show numerous rebates, a practice illegal under the Interstate Commerce Act. Further, Little claimed that Reinhart carried as an asset uncollectable pool money while overstating the company's cash position and inflating the accounts receivable. As of April 30, Little found the Atchison with a floating debt of $12,834,223, and while Reinhart had reported net earnings of about $12 million for 1893, Little discovered only $8 million. The books of the Atchison had been manipulated to show the most favorable position, and the illegally issued rebates totaled nearly $4 million. Little also charged that Reinhart had carried as an asset considerable worn-out equipment. The Atchison, he concluded, was in far worse condition than previously believed, and he placed the blame almost entirely upon Reinhart.

Reinhart denounced Little and his report. He charged that Little's figures were wrong, but he failed to specify which figures. He refused to comment on Little's allegation that huge advances, some $16 million, had been made to Atchison affiliates. When the press attacked him for refusing to be specific, Reinhart blamed shoddy bookkeeping for the errors; but company treasurer Edward Wilder denied any knowledge of some of Reinhart's transactions. The scandal undermined the confidence of Atchison employees, shippers, and the federal court, which had established the receivership. While no corruption or personal thefts had been discovered, Reinhart's position became intolerable. Even if he had only tried to save the management by manipulating the books, whatever confidence which had remained in him drained away. Blamed perhaps unfairly for the debacle, Reinhart resigned as a receiver on August 8, 1894. He denied all charges of corruption and claimed to be resigning because of ill health and policy differences with the directors; he would be vindicated, he declared. Meanwhile, Thomas Baring and General Counsel John J. McCook denied any knowledge of wrongdoing, but the entire board of directors came under a dark cloud of doubt.

A massive reshuffling of the board followed the appointment of Aldace F. Walker as Reinhart's replacement as a receiver. Reinhart, Robert Harris and B. P. Cheney, Sr., who had already resigned from the board, were joined by Baring, McCook, and three others. A new board including six New Yorkers, four Bostonions—a Cheney and a Nickerson, of course —and three Kansans, including Colonel Holliday, was elected. These changes did not completely diminish the doubts of the investors, for shortly thereafter Reinhart was charged with granting illegal rebates. Though the charges were never proven, and the case was eventually dropped, the hint of possible corruption remained.

Little's report made any previous plans of reorganization obsolete. He demonstrated that earnings for 1890–1893 were much smaller than anyone guessed and that yearly deficits reached a peak of $3,008,242 in 1894. The acquisition of the Frisco and the CM had been financially disastrous, and the A&P's 750 miles of wretched track continued to produce huge losses. Investors had to be called upon to make substantial sacrifices. While the General Reorganization Committee pulled itself together again to devise yet another reorganization scheme, the three receivers operated the Atchison system.

The addition of Aldace Walker as a receiver strengthened the operation and enhanced the reputation of the receivership. Walker had served

Tenwheeler No. 833, built by Baldwin in 1900. H. L. Broadbelt

as an original member of the Interstate Commerce Commission before becoming chairman of the Interstate Commerce Railway Association, and prior to his appointment as a receiver, Walker chaired the Western Traffic Association. He had excellent contacts in the industry, a long career in railroading, and enthusiasm for the task at hand. Walker, McCook and Wilson worked well together and devoted their energies to the Santa Fe, the Frisco and the Colorado Midland. Indeed, the burdens became so heavy, that on September 18, 1895, Wilson collapsed and died shortly thereafter from overwork and fatigue.

The receivers began to put increasingly larger sums into maintenance after a detailed engineering analysis by Robert Moore indicated that the physical plant had deteriorated badly. Moore personally toured 6,192 miles of the 9,344-mile-long system, and he praised the Atchison portion, but the GCSF, A&P, and most of the Frisco were in dreadful condition, he reported. He urged immediate installation of air brakes and automatic couplers on the rolling stock and concluded that almost $14 million in improvements were needed. For two years the receivers struggled to improve the railroad as they sought additional traffic, rate stabilization and higher earnings. The property received the maintenance it so desperately needed, locomotives and rolling stock were repaired if possible and scrapped if not, and new terminal facilities were constructed at several points. Closely following Moore's recommendations, the receivers ordered heavy expenditures for rail and tie replacement, filling in trestles and widening cuts. During the two years and eight days the receivers operated the property they produced net earnings of $9,272,823, but the system lost $1,572,062 because of the enormous expenditures for maintenance. Beginning on December 23, 1893, they labored to save the Santa Fe, performing a remarkable service in the midst of a grave depression, national unrest and turbulence on Wall Street. Their work was facilitated by the active cooperation of the General Reorganization Committee, which devised an acceptable plan to refinance and reorganize the Atchison.

While the security holders of the Atchison, the Frisco and the Colorado Midland had formed numerous committees to protect their interests and to formulate proposals for reorganization, the General Reorganization Committee came to represent the largest body of Atchison investors, and the membership of the committee gave it additional power and prestige. The committee plus additional representatives of the London and Dutch interests formulated a plan which was announced on March 14, 1895, by Edward King, the chairman of the committee. The plan attempted (1) to reduce the fixed charges from $9,232,772 to a safe limit of $4,528,547; (2) to provide for future capital requirements; (3) to liquidate the floating debt; (4) to reinstate the existing securities on an equitable basis; and (5) to consolidate and unify the system. King proposed to foreclose on the Atchison's general mortgage and form a new company to purchase the system at a bankruptcy sale. The new company would issue $102 million in common stock, $111,486,000 in 5 percent noncumulative preferred stock, $96,990,000 in general mortgage 4 percent bonds, and $51,728,310 in 4 percent adjustment bonds. Under the plan the fixed charges would be greatly reduced since only the general mortgage bonds required yearly interest payments. The so-called adjustment bonds were, in reality, income bonds. The plan provided that no additional bonds or preferred stock could be issued without the approval of the majority of stockholders, and it placed a ceiling of $3 million in general mortgage bonds to be issued each year with a total limit of $30 million. The common stock of the old company would be exchanged for new common on a share-for-share basis; but stockholders were assessed $10 per share, and the assessment was guaranteed by a syndicate. General mortgage bondholders of the old company received 75 percent of their holdings in new 4 percent bonds and 40 percent in adjustment bonds. The old second-mortgage and income bond owners were assessed 4 percent and were given a new issue of preferred stock. The holders of $1,000 Class A bonds received $1,180 in preferred stock, and owners of Class B bonds received $1,130 in preferred stock. The lien of the new mortgage covered all former properties of the Atchison, but included neither the Frisco nor the Colorado Midland. The assessment raised $13,567,644 in working capital for the new company.

King's proposal replaced securities carrying heavy fixed charges with issues providing for optional interest or dividends. The $111,486,000 in preferred stock replaced income bonds and went primarily to English holders of the income and second-mortgage bonds. The price of Atchison stock was high enough to insure payment of the stock assessment by the common stockholders. The plan, therefore, received widespread support, and Baring Brothers, a syndicate of New York bankers, and some of the Boston coterie agreed to underwrite the costs of reorganization. *Railway Age*, *The Railway Times*, and *The Economist* of London praised the scheme, as did most financial journals, and only a minority of stockholders refused to support King's proposal. The reorganization of the Atchison, monumental in size, set a precedent for the financial overhauling of several other large systems, as the scheme "unwatered" Atchison securities to a degree that shocked many on Wall Street.

At 2:00 P.M. on December 10, 1895, on the east side of the Santa Fe station in Topeka, Judge J. B. Johnson offered the Atchison, Topeka and Santa Fe Railroad for sale, and Edward King, representing the Atchison, Topeka and Santa Fe *Railway*, bid $60 million. No other voices were raised, and Colonel Holliday's road died, but the "old man" became an incorporator and a director of the new railway.

The most immediate question facing the railway concerned the disposition of the affiliated lines. A three-man committee of E. P. Ripley, E. S. Washburne and W. W. Findley had been established to investigate the question, and they strongly recommended that all but the A&P should be dropped. The Frisco's debt seemed an impossible load to carry, and the directors of the new company decided to write off the $25 million invested in the property. The Atchison recovered only $1,971,550 from the sale of some Frisco bonds. The Colorado Midland showed no signs of profitability, and again the Santa Fe simply wrote off its investment and let the CM go. The A&P remained an unresolved issue although the Reorganization Committee controlled $16 million of the $18 million first-mortgage bonds of the A&P. The new railway offered 50¢ on the dollar for the remainder of the bonds, and in January 1897, a proposal was issued which would relieve the Atchison of part of its obligations on the old A&P securities. On May 4, 1897, the A&P line from Albuquerque to Needles was foreclosed for $12 million, giving the Atchison control. The original system passed safely into the hands of the new railway.

Aldace Walker became chairman of the board of the Atchison; Victor Morawetz was selected general counsel; and on December 12, 1895, the board chose a president for the new railway, Edward Payson Ripley. The selection of Ripley enhanced the already favorable image of the new firm, for Ripley could only be described by using superlatives. Born in Dorchester, Massachusetts, in 1845, and educated in the local schools, Ripley spent virtually his entire life working in the railroad industry. Following several years' experience with the Star Union Car Line and the Pennsylvania Railroad freight department, Ripley joined the Chicago, Burlington & Quincy in 1870, becoming the New England agent of the CB&Q, and

E. P. Ripley, president of the
Atchison from 1896 to 1918.
Santa Fe Railway

by 1888 he had become the general manager. Ripley served in that capacity for only eighteen months when personnel problems prompted his resignation, and he joined the Chicago, Milwaukee and St. Paul Railway as third vice president. Vigorous, dynamic, and civic minded, Ripley took a leading role in developing the World's Columbian Exposition in Chicago in 1893. His reputation for honesty and integrity and his managerial skills attracted the attention of J. P. Morgan and Company, which promoted his candidacy for the presidency of the new railway as did the London and Amsterdam committees. His only rival for the office, D. B. Robinson, the Atchison's acting president, became his first vice president. Ripley selected his other executives with great skill, and he soon created an unusually loyal and efficient staff. The new president made decisions quickly and delegated considerable authority to his subordinates in whom he had great confidence. A plain, unassuming man, Ripley established a paternalistic relationship with the Santa Fe's employees, who referred to him as "the Old Man." An operations expert, Ripley turned the legal and financial problems over to Victor Morawetz and concentrated on revitalizing the company. The Atchison desperately needed an enthusiastic management in 1895.

The Ripley executives surveyed the railway which the receivers turned over to them in 1896, and what they found was not encouraging. The Kansas City–Chicago line needed extraordinary expenditures to turn it into the "airline" envisioned by Strong. The A&P from Isleta to Needles had to be rebuilt, as did the Needles-Mojave track. While the main line from Kansas City to Denver, Albuquerque and El Paso was in good condition, the Ripley team estimated that $250 million spent over 25 years would be necessary to bring the company to a high level of efficiency. Ripley's report to the new board of directors was not pessimistic in tone, however, as he saw enormous potential in the property. The board accepted the analysis without great enthusiasm, but with a determination to make the railway profitable. The bankers who now dominated the board committed the company to the revitalization program Ripley proposed. The two men from Massachusetts remaining on the board, the six New York bankers, plus Ripley, Walker and the four Kansans, made the decision to reinvest any profits in the company.

Within the first six months of operation Ripley turned the Atchison around. The railway's first *Annual Report* on June 30, 1896, showed a net of $3,382,806 and a modest surplus of $141,720. Earnings were up, expenses down, and the operating ratio fell from 82.90 to 75.10. Some of the improvement came as a consequence of the national economic recovery, but much of the credit was Ripley's. He dealt at length in the *Annual Report* with the problem of the A&P. If, as some suggested, the A&P should be abandoned, the Atchison would become just another regional railroad rather than a transcontinental. Ripley argued that California would grow rapidly and produce increasing through-traffic and, therefore, the A&P should be retained. A duplicate line was not feasible, and so the management urged a large-scale rebuilding program. A new corporation, the Santa Fe Pacific Railroad, took over the A&P west of Isleta, and the Atchison committed funds for reconstruction.

Ripley and his staff instituted many cost-reduction programs in the first eighteen months of operation. In 1897 the mechanical department began to convert the coal-burning locomotives to oil, starting with power assigned to California divisions. The discovery of oil in California, Texas and Oklahoma gave the Santa Fe a huge supply of cheaper fuel located adjacent to its main lines. To further reduce fixed charges, he announced in the second *Annual Report* that the Sonora Railway had been traded to the Southern Pacific in exchange for the Needles-Mojave property. The trade made considerable sense to both companies because the Needles-Mojave track was an integral part of the Atchison's main line and of no value to the SP, while the area south of Benson, Arizona, was really SP territory. Both lines were in deplorable condition and the difference in values was less than $200,000. Clearance of titles held up the final transfer until 1911, but the operating departments took over the properties in 1897. Thus Ripley was able to slough off one of the Atchison's major financial liabilities.

The second report also showed continued financial improvement. Ripley declared that "General business is increasing and the earnings for the current fiscal year bid fair to considerably exceed those for the year covered by the report."[4] The 6,479 miles of the system grossed $30,621,230 and produced a net of $7,754,041. The operating ratio fell to 74.68, and Ripley could show a surplus of $1,603,226. Ripley's rebuilding campaign continued as 387 miles of new steel rail were installed and a large new passenger station and headquarters building for the GCSF was erected in Galveston. To increase traffic to and from Dallas, terminal facilities were enlarged and a new freight house and passenger station were constructed. The good news reported by Ripley restored confidence in the investors and the employees; a new era for the Atchison began.

Throughout the remainder of the 1890s Ripley and his associates continued to revitalize the system. In 1898 the company laid 531 miles of steel rail and expanded the shops at Newton, Cleburne and Albuquerque. That year the operating ratio fell to 72.69, the next year to 68.14, and in 1900 to 59.53. This remarkable achievement came about through rising efficiency and the reduction of operating expenditures. Additional steel rails were laid in 1899 (681 miles), and in 1900 Ripley reported that since he had taken over the system 2,493 bridges equaling 38.79 miles in length had been replaced, with many of the new bridges being of steel or masonry. In 1899 the Santa Fe ballasted 250 miles of track and reduced grades on the GCSF, and similar work continued the next year between Fort Worth and Sealy at a cost of $1,650,000. Ripley did not neglect the Santa Fe's deteriorating equipment; in 1899 he added 58 locomotives, 444 freight cars and 12 passenger cars and ordered 48 more locomotives. The following year the system gained 109 locomotives, 582 freight cars and 12 more passenger cars. Not only did the management make new purchases, but it also improved existing equipment. Crash programs to install safety couplers and air brakes improved operations considerably, and the car shops rebuilt freight cars to carry heavier loads. The mechanical department continued to convert coal-burning locomotives to oil, thus reducing fuel costs. The financial consequences of the program exceeded all expectations.

The *Annual Reports* of 1898, 1899 and 1900 tabulated Ripley's progress. In 1898 earnings climbed to $39,214,099, and they continued to grow during the next two years. The surplus of $3,890,424 rose to $9,994,619, and Ripley began to pay off bonds. The board felt so confident that it declared dividends. In June 1899, they voted to pay 1¼ percent on the preferred stock, and then raised the rate to 1½ in December 1899. Wall Street repsonded positively to the "phenomenal" earnings, and the price of Santa Fe bonds rose from 54¾ to 79½, and then to par. Despite huge capital expenditures ($8,590,788 in 1900), the Atchison continued to show rising profits, and the semiannual preferred dividend rose to 2½ percent. The increasing financial stability and the confidence it generated allowed Ripley to undertake a relatively modest expansion program. Only in one area did the Atchison management decide to make a major commitment: Ripley announced in 1898 that the railway would enter San Francisco.

The Southern Pacific Railroad and its rail and steamship affiliates monopolized transportation in the Golden State north of Los Angeles. Throughout the whole of California, only the Atchison challenged "The Octopus," as many called the SP. The SP had established extremely high local rates, much higher than transcontinental rates, and only competition with some independent steamship lines prevented the SP from increasing the tariffs on freight sent out of California. In order to reduce even water competition, the SP charged shippers more to send goods to local ports than for shipping them east on the overland route to Ogden or New Orleans. San Francisco and inland California towns protested, but to no avail. The SP dominated the Transcontinental Traffic Association, which included the major steamship lines, giving Huntington and his successors control of transportation in most of the state. Federal law prohibited foreign flag vessels, with their cheaper rates, in the coastal trade, so that some shippers resorted to an elaborate subterfuge; goods bound from Boston or New York for San Francisco or Stockton were sent via Liverpool or Le Havre in foreign freighters. When the Southern Pacific lobbyists had that loophole closed, merchants, farmers, and other shippers formed the San Francisco Traffic Association to fight "The Octopus."

Beginning in 1891 the association sought to obtain lower freight charges. They persuaded J. W. Grace to initiate steamship service around Cape Horn, and rates fell for a brief period. Then the association began to subsidize local shipping services, but they proved too small to compete successfully with the SP. In 1892 the association turned to the state

"The Emancipator" of 1896. Santa Fe Railway

government and pleaded with the legislature and the Railroad Commission to set maximum freight rates; the SP-controlled government refused to act. The people of northern and central California, particularly residents of the San Joaquin Valley, became increasingly incensed. In 1901, Frank Norris described the machinations of the Southern Pacific in his book *The Octopus*, portraying the plight of San Joaquin Valley wheat farmers who paid more to ship their grain to a port than it was worth. Plows which they ordered from New York came through the valley on SP freight trains and on to San Francisco where they were transshipped back down the valley, allowing the SP to collect freight charges twice. In the novel the president of the SP turned back the pleas of the farmers, declaring he wasn't responsible because "railroads build themselves." Norris took considerable license in his piece of fiction, but the anger and frustration of the farmers was very real.

The traffic association decided in 1893 that the only way to free San Francisco and the San Joaquin Valley from the monopoly was by constructing an independent railway from San Francisco Bay down the valley to a connection with the Santa Fe. Because of the depression of that year, and the large expenditures such a railway would entail, they decided to build from Stockton south 230 miles to Bakersfield and to use ferry boats from Stockton to San Francisco. The association estimated the cost of the railway at $20,000 per mile and began to solicit subscriptions. The depression frustrated their efforts, which soon terminated. Again in August 1894, they solicited for subscriptions, but the response was slight. The association acted in good faith and went to considerable lengths to guarantee the proposed railway's independence. A voting trust would hold the company's stock, thus preventing the SP from buying up the securities and taking over the line. Yet, men were afraid to invest—afraid because of the depression and the power of the SP.

On January 22, 1895, the association held a meeting at the offices of the San Francisco Chamber of Commerce. The officers announced that only half of the $350,000 goal had been subscribed. The gloom of the sponsors indicated yet another failure. Claus Spreckels, a leading San Francisco sugar merchant, rose and denounced the association for its timidity; the project needed $3 million to $5 million, not $350,000. He challenged the other businessmen to stand up and fight with their pocketbooks. He announced that he would put up $50,000 himself, and others pledged an additional $21,000. The capital of the project was increased, at Spreckel's insistance, and he raised his subscription to $500,000 and his sons Rudolph and John D. pledged $100,000 each. By January 30, the association received $1.2 million in subscriptions, and by February 8, the sum had grown to $2 million. On February 25, the state issued a charter for the San Francisco and San Joaquin Valley Railway, and the battle against the SP commenced.

Spreckels and the other supporters of the SF&SJV realized that if and when the railroad was completed it would lack profit potential. The territory through which it would pass was not highly developed, and while rates would hopefully fall, few dividends appeared likely. Therefore they decided to solicit the help of the towns and residents of the valley. To reduce construction costs they asked the towns and the farmers to donate the right-of-way, and, further, the leaders of the SF&SJV told the people of the valley that the railway had to have their financial encouragement. The town of Stockton donated land worth $100,000 and subscribed to $100,000 in securities. Other communities also responded, though with smaller sums. Spreckels insisted that the SF&SJV sell stock in very small amounts to the citizens of the area to broaden the base of support. Mass meetings were called with the railroad spokesmen appealing to the pride of the audience; the "war" with the SP played a major part in the rhetoric of their appeal. Small subscriptions started to come in, and the leaders of the SF&SJV began to call their proposed line "The People's Railroad." *The San Francisco Examiner* proclaimed that stock sales in amounts ranging from $1.00 to $2,500 proved that the railway would be "largely built and owned by people of modest circumstances."[5] The security sales were so successful that the leaders of the SF&SJV ordered rails and hired an engineer to initiate construction.

The SF&SJV hired William Benson Storey as its chief engineer. A remarkably sound choice, Storey had almost twenty years experience as an engineer and surveyor in the West. Born in San Francisco in 1857, educated at Colfax, where his father worked for the SP, and a graduate of the University of California with a degree in mechanical engineering, Storey had been a surveyor for the Central Pacific and the Southern Pacific and had an excellent reputation as a railway engineer. While Storey went to work laying out the route from Stockton south, the directors purchased 2,000 tons of 62½-pound rail, which arrived in San Francisco from New York aboard the Steamer *Washtenow*. Two more ships soon delivered an additional 10,000 tons, and the first rails arrived in Stockton on July 7, 1895. Storey had already awarded grading and bridging contracts, and track laying began immediately.

By December 1895, track crews had laid over 25 miles of rail, and construction down the San Joaquin valley proceeded through 1896. On October 5, 1896, the track from Stockton to Fresno opened, and a special train, "The Emancipator," initiated service. Celebrating their liberation from the bondage of high railroad tariffs, the people in the valley turned out to greet the special train. The six coaches and two combination cars, painted bright yellow with silver lettering edged in black, were pulled by highly polished locomotive Number 50 decorated with flowers and streamers. On board the train the officers of the SF&SJV, San Francisco merchants and officials of the valley towns celebrated their success. At the end of the 125-mile trip, the crowd at a giant barbeque in Fresno gave Spreckels an ovation. "The People's Railroad" began to remove the tentacles of "The Octopus."

The pace of construction slowed in 1897 and 1898, but Storey kept his crews active. He completed the SF&SJV to Hanford on May 21, 1897, and opened a branch from Fresno to Visalia on September 9. Work from Hanford toward Bakersfield continued, and on May 27, the track crews completed the 110 miles from Fresno to Bakersfield. The SF&SJV now stretched 278 miles through the valley including a loop through Visalia. While this represented a substantial accomplishment, Spreckels and the other leaders realized that the SF&SJV needed to connect with the Atchison if a total victory was to be achieved. The state of the SF&SJV treasury in 1898 did not make that prospect appear realistic.

By June 1898 the financial condition of the SF&SJV reached a point where a decision about the future course of the railway had to be made. Of the $6 million in stock authorized by the charter, some $2,464,480 had been issued, $2,671,000 in 5 percent bonds had been sold, and current liabilities stood at $110,928. In 1897 gross earnings rose to $209,133 while operating expenses climbed to $153,102; the following year the figures were $411,179 and $282,326. While prospects for meager profits were good, and some investors felt that the road's independence should be maintained, Spreckels and the SF&SJV management continued to hope for an affiliation with the Santa Fe. Spreckels never intended to operate the

The *San Pablo* of the San Francisco Bay fleet. Santa Fe Railway

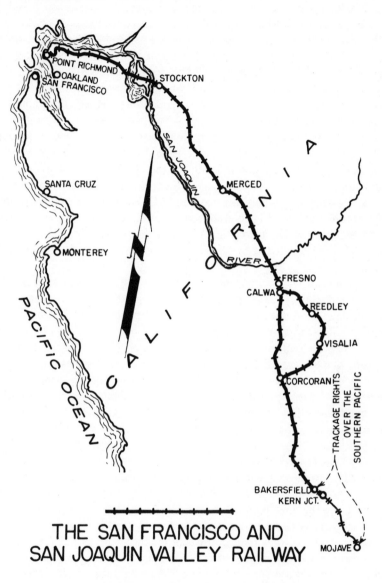

POINT RICHMOND
OAKLAND
SAN FRANCISCO
STOCKTON

SAN JOAQUIN

SANTA CRUZ

MERCED

MONTEREY

RIVER

FRESNO
CALWA
REEDLEY

VISALIA

PACIFIC OCEAN

CORCORAN

CALIFORNIA

TRACKAGE RIGHTS OVER THE SOUTHERN PACIFIC

BAKERSFIELD
KERN JCT.

MOJAVE

THE SAN FRANCISCO AND
SAN JOAQUIN VALLEY RAILWAY

San Francisco and San Joaquin Valley Railway

"People's Railroad," he was not a railroad man, but he hoped to sell the line to the Atchison and thus provide San Francisco with another rail outlet to the East. The primary purpose of the SF&SJV had been quickly achieved, for as the line was extended down the valley, freight rates had fallen to the benefit of all shippers. The nine trustees who controlled the SF&SJV agreed with Spreckles, and while they were prohibited by the charter from selling out to a competitor, meaning the SP, they could and did negotiate a sale with the ATSF.

In the fall of 1898 serious negotiations began. The Atchison agreed to purchase the common stock of the SF&SJV for $2,462,300, and on December 9, at the annual meeting of the Atchison stockholders, they ratified the agreement. Ripley urged them to approve the purchase in order to enhance the Atchison's position in California and to develop more traffic over the old A&P. The Atchison acquired 279 miles of track including the Stockton-Bakersfield main line and the Visalia branch, but a gap of 68 miles existed between Bakersfield and the Santa Fe main line at Mojave.

Ripley did not want to construct a new line from Mojave to Bakersfield which would simply parallel the SP over the difficult Tehachapi Pass. Santa Fe engineers discovered that even if Ripley wanted to build a line, an acceptable second route simply did not exist. After months of futile surveys, Ripley requested the SP to consider leasing their Tehachapi trackage. The SP agreed, and the Atchison received permission to operate over one of the most difficult sections of railroad in the United States. The Santa Fe would pay 60 percent of local revenues and 2¼ percent of the annual valuation of the line and contribute 50 percent of the taxes and maintenance costs. Between Mojave and Kern Junction, two miles from Bakersfield, the track passed through 15 tunnels ranging in length from 121 feet to 1,180 feet, climbed over 2.5 percent grades, and wound around fifty 10-degree curves to reach the summit at 4,025 feet. The engineering marvel of the route, known as "The Loop," carried the track over itself as the line climbed 2,734 feet of elevation in 16 miles. The Santa Fe avoided constructing another line through the granite pass, but Tehachapi would always be a bottleneck on the route to San Francisco.

There remained the matter of building from Stockton to San Francisco. Storey had prepared a survey for the SF&SJV in June 1898, proposing to reach the east side of San Francisco Bay at Point Richmond. He suggested using a flotilla of ferry boats to reach the harbor at San Francisco. His report did not encourage the SF&SJV management because it warned of the geographical obstacles to be encountered along the 77-mile route: the coastal range would be pierced by a long tunnel near Martinez, the tule swamps would require considerable dredging and three drawbridges, and the land at Point Richmond needed massive earth and rock fills before port facilities could be built. Despite the discouraging report, construction began even before the ATSF bought the railway, and James Dun, the chief engineer of the Santa Fe, retained Storey and used his plans after the sale took place. On April 14, 1899, Storey wrote to Dun of the troubles encountered by the construction crews, but Dun and Ripley decided to proceed.

The five tunnels through the coastal range gave Storey nightmares. The lack of stability in the mountains caused unsupported tunnel walls to collapse. The Franklin tunnel, located on a tangent and 5,595 feet long, had to be lined almost solidly with timber. But because of the wet soil the timber swelled and snapped. Storey thought at first that a space could be excavated between the walls and the timber, but he soon concluded that a masonry lining would be necessary. Similar problems were encountered in a shorter tunnel near Pinole, and tunnel crews progressed only six to nine feet per day. Crews also worked rapidly to complete the Alhambra viaduct, which stood 1,600 feet long and 75 feet high, and at the west end of the viaduct the track entered a 300-foot-long tunnel.

The men working on the roadbed through the tule swamps moved forward very slowly. Storey employed three dredges, and then added two more, to throw up an earthen embankment for the track. Over 400,000 cubic yards of peat from the swamp supported 16 miles of track through the tule. The roadbed stood 35 feet above the swamp, which allowed the peat to dry out, and, unfortunately, to become highly combustible. Fires broke out when the steam locomotives dropped sparks as they passed over the track. Storey ordered the roadbed covered with twelve inches of gravel, and the threats of fire subsided. The route through the swamps included a trestle nearly two miles long and several drawbridges over ship channels. The draining of a portion of the swamp and the levee-like effect of the roadbed allowed farmers to reclaim some of the land for use as truck gardens. But despite the mountains and the swamps, Storey's track gangs soon opened the route to the mud flats of Point Richmond.

Before the Santa Fe could utilize the new line, terminal facilities had to be developed on both sides of the East Bay. At Point Richmond workmen labored in 24-hour shifts for two months to fill in the flats and build ferry slips and warehouses. Across the bay the Santa Fe leased "China Basin," an area of mud flats near the harbor, from the State Board of Harbor Commissioners. A new subsidiary, the San Francisco Terminal Company, constructed a stone seawall around the 24-acre property, and filled it in with over 4 million cubic feet of rock. Over the fill the Terminal Company built slips and yards. The slips sagged several times before they were stabilized with additional supports. "China Basin," at the foot of

Passengers bound for San Francisco used the *Ocean Wave* to cross the Bay.
Santa Fe Railway

Fourth Street, became the ATSF freight terminal for San Francisco; but the constricted site placed the company in a disadvantageous position from which to compete with the SP. The bay operation also required the Santa Fe to purchase an extensive fleet of tugboats, ferries and other floating equipment. For thirty years the "flagship" of the Santa Fe fleet was the double-ended sidewheeler *San Pablo.* Her 2,000-horsepower engines moved the *San Pablo* between "China Flats" and Point Richmond, six flags and a tall single stack marking her progress. On May 1, 1900, the Atchison announced that freight service into San Francisco over its own tracks would commence.

Passenger service did not begin until July 6, 1900, when residents of the San Joaquin Valley waited for the first train from San Francisco to Chicago to pass through. At 8:00 A.M. that day the ferry *Ocean Wave* left a Market Street slip and sailed across the East Bay to Point Richmond. There, passengers climbed aboard the waiting train. Number 250, a Dickson 4–6–0, headed the first run, which included a baggage car, mail car, three coaches and a Pullman. Conductor Anderson gave Engineer Com-

stock a highball, and he eased the train out of the terminal. Crowds of
farmers and townspeople gathered at Stockton, Modesto, Merced, Fresno
and Bakersfield as the train passed by. Later that day a westbound train
from Chicago moved through the valley on its way to San Francisco. The
final portion of Colonel Holliday's vision became a reality.

The completion of the entrance into San Francisco in 1900 ushered in
a new era for the Santa Fe. With Ripley's conservative management and
rising national prosperity providing the company with increasing profits,
the Atchison once more initiated a program of expansion, an expansion
dictated not by a competitive urge but by the rapidly growing economy
of the Southwest.

7

Expansion—Conservative and Controlled

When Edward Payson Ripley took charge of the Atchison, Topeka and Santa Fe Railway in 1896, the company had grossed $28,851,841 and had suffered a net loss of $4,433,380 in operating its 6,435 miles of track. By 1915, Ripley and his associates had expanded the railway to 11,000 miles, the gross had climbed to $111,109,770 and the net return had soared to $20,183,965. The hardworking, dynamic Ripley rebuilt the Atchison, almost doubled its length, and made it one of the most profitable carriers in the nation. He purchased or built new track where potential earnings appeared good, and he extended the company's lines into areas without railroads. He refused to duplicate existing railways or construct parallel lines, and, where practical, he favored joint trackage or trackage rights. Unlike William Barstow Strong who built new routes to thwart rivals, Ripley added mileage only when a virgin territory awaited development or when new lines would mean operating efficiency. On this basis the railway became a major factor in the economic expansion of the Southwest and a significant contributor to the growth of Arizona, Oklahoma, Texas, California and New Mexico.

Ripley and his staff reduced the Santa Fe to a basic system in 1896 and sliced away the unprofitable segments which had plagued the company. New construction came slowly and only after lengthy studies and surveys. Ripley's cautious expansionism meant that feeder lines, cutoffs and the rehabilitation of the old main lines would receive his first attention. When an area began to grow or a city or town started to thrive, Ripley was prepared to build—but only if traffic warranted the expense. The Ripley management team scrutinized the potential traffic, the effect of new construction on competitors, and then made their decision. As a recent student of the Ripley management has observed:

> It was in the executive offices of the Santa Fe Railroad [sic] in Chicago that one would find the emerging leadership of American railroads in this new era of professional managership. This rapidly expanding railroad was playing a leading role in the fast-growing Southwest.[1]

The corporate offices in Chicago reflected not only Ripley's dominant personality but also the business acumen of his well-selected associates. Chairman of the Board Aldace Walker knew the industry and the Santa Fe well and had a shrewd eye for future traffic. Victor Morawetz, the general counsel, provided more than legal advice; the urbane, bachelor lawyer contributed a solid background in corporate finance and relations with regulatory agencies. Vice President Paul Morton, President Theodore Roosevelt's future Secretary of the Navy, gave the team a member with bureaucratic skills and an ability to achieve operational efficiency. Ripley and his associates began their construction program with the entrance into San Francisco, but the booming economy of the Southwest caused them to launch an immediate and almost uniformly successful expansion of the Santa Fe throughout the region. Their first project solidified the Santa Fe's position in northern and central Arizona.

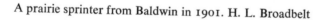

A prairie sprinter from Baldwin in 1901. H. L. Broadbelt

In the late 1880s the long, single track of the Atlantic and Pacific Railroad stretched across northern Arizona from west of Gallup, New Mexico, to the Colorado River at Needles. Territorial Governor Frederick A. Tritle, writing from the capital at Prescott, bombarded officials of the A&P and the Atchison with letters pleading for a branch south from Ash Fork to Prescott, and for passes for himself and his family. President H. C. Nutt of the A&P and A. A. Robinson of the Santa Fe responded with passes and cordiality but no branch line. A group of Arizona Territory business leaders and copper-mining executives made two attempts to construct an independent narrow-gauge line, and in 1886–1887 they built the Prescott and Arizona Central from Prescott north to Seligman. Operating over rugged terrain, and constructed with used rails which were subject to regular collapse, the P&AC offered poor and irregular service. Clearly, a more suitable location and a more substantial branch was in order.

The A&P sent Chief Engineer Samuel Rowe into the area in September 1889, and Rowe located a line from Ash Fork to Prescott and into the town of Phoenix. Rowe wrote the head office that much heavy grading would be necessary, but that the copper mines near Prescott and the Salt River Valley at the town of Phoenix would generate considerable traffic. The climate of the Phoenix area allowed considerable production of winter produce, and the town already had some 7,000 people. Although many structures in Phoenix were of adobe, the community contained five churches, a two-story brick school house, four newspapers, an ice factory, a brewery and a flour mill. A railroad south from the A&P would generate a real boom, Rowe prophesied. He estimated the cost of the branch at $2,356,840, but contended that the route would produce more traffic than the Albuquerque-Mojave main line. For two years Rowe's report received no response, but on May 27, 1891, executives of the A&P and the Santa Fe and some Arizona territorial leaders organized the Santa Fe, Prescott and Phoenix Railway to build a standard-gauge line from Ash Fork to Phoenix, and they agreed to lease the completed project to the Atchison for thirty years.

The SFP&P, or "Peavine," initiated construction at Ash Fork on August 17, 1892, and opened its 57-mile line to Prescott on April 25, 1893. A. A. Robinson kept in contact with the SFP&P management, and supplied the company with advice and construction know-how. The surveyors laid out a route through the winding and twisting reaches of Hell Canyon, and the track gangs worked in some of the most spectacular scenery in Arizona. The line passed through scrub pine forest to reach Prescott and then plunged 23 miles down to Skull Valley. Past Wickenburg the "Peavine" entered Hassayampa Canyon before reaching the Salt River Valley. The route to Phoenix opened on February 28, 1895, and the small agri-

THE SANTA FE, PRESCOTT
AND
PHOENIX RAILWAY COMPANY
AND CADIZ CUTOFF

Santa Fe, Prescott and Phoenix and Cadiz Cutoff

cultural community on the Salt River boomed—as Rowe had predicted. The wide streets of the town were soon lined with trees and houses and even a streetcar system was developed. Phoenix supplanted Prescott as the major urban center, and the seat of the territorial government was moved to the locus of political power. The narrow-gauge Prescott and Arizona Central, which paralleled the SFP&P, proved unprofitable and was soon abandoned. The 197-mile-long SFP&P earned a modest income and maintained a close affiliation with the Atchison through the 1890s. Branches to the copper mines near Prescott and produce from the Phoenix area provided most of the freight.

On October 23, 1901, President Ripley announced that the Atchison had arranged to purchase the SFP&P for $2,889,935. He noted that the line had experienced steadily increasing earnings since 1895 and that it contributed a large amount of profitable traffic to the Atchison. The following year Ripley ordered the "Peavine" rebuilt in the Rock Butte area; 26 miles of track containing 40 bridges and 12 degree curves were reconstructed, thereby shortening the line by 3 miles, eliminating 30 bridges and 7 complete circles of track, and reducing the grades from 3 percent to 1½ percent. Operating efficiency improved and maintenance costs fell substantially.

Even as Ripley extended the Atchison south into central Arizona, he added a feeder north of the main line. In 1897 the Santa Fe granted right-of-way across its lands between Williams and Grand Canyon to Lombard, Goode and Company, which projected to build a railroad to the rim of the canyon. Traffic to the canyon grew as tourists discovered the magnificent beauty of the enormous chasm, but the only means of access was by stagecoach north from Flagstaff. Lombard, Goode organized the Santa Fe and Grand Canyon Railroad, and construction began in May 1899. The SF&GC purchased used 56-pound rail from the ATSF for $41.66 a ton, paying in bonds. Additional supplies from the Santa Fe allowed the SF&GC to build 63 miles of track, but the project collapsed financially in 1900. Ripley then incorporated the Grand Canyon Railway, which purchased the SF&GC, and completed the branch to the canyon rim. The ATSF and Fred Harvey subsequently developed the hotels which housed the hordes of tourists who came west over the Santa Fe.

Ripley then built a few additional branches to mine sites in central Arizona, and in 1902 he inaugurated a significant extension south from Phoenix into Southern Pacific territory at Benson. During the next two years the ATSF built south and east from Phoenix toward Benson, with rumors rife that the line would eventually reach Deming, New Mexico. E. H. Harriman of the Southern Pacific sought to block the expansion, and he chartered a subsidiary to parallel Ripley's new construction. Both companies sought to occupy the best route via Gila Canyon, and the rival track gangs soon came to blows. Ripley and Harriman turned to the Arizona courts for a resolution of the dispute, but a settlement came primarily through compromise and the growing presence of Harriman and his allies as stockholders of the Atchison. By 1904 Harriman owned a large block of Santa Fe securities and strongly urged a settlement favorable to the SP. Ripley and Morawetz balked until Harriman agreed to purchase the branch from Phoenix to Winkelman (some 96 miles in length) for a reasonable sum. Harriman accepted the compromise, and the Santa Fe shifted its attention to improving service from Phoenix to California.

On December 18, 1903, Ripley announced the sale of a large sum of bonds to construct several new lines including a branch from Wickenburg west and north to Cadiz, Caiifornia, on the main line. Service from Phoenix to the West Coast via the "Peavine" was circuitous, and the grades remained excessive. As the Phoenix area grew, the Santa Fe would need a shorter and more economical route. Ripley incorporated the Arizona and California Railway, which built slowly across 100 miles of desert, reaching Parker on June 17, 1907. The crossing of the Colorado River at Parker proved to be enormously difficult, and the bridge did not open until the summer of 1908. Because of the financial constrictions of the national recession of 1907, the 83-mile-long segment from Parker to Cadiz remained uncompleted until the summer of 1910. The opening of the Phoenix-California cutoff completed the basic Santa Fe system in Arizona, giving the company a strong strategic position. Ripley's faith in the future of the state was well placed, and as the population of Arizona swelled from 294,000 in 1910 to 1.3 million in 1960, the Atchison stood ready to serve the transportation needs of its people.

Even while Ripley developed the Santa Fe's position in Arizona, he surveyed the vast potential of the "Twin Territories"—Oklahoma Territory and Indian Territory. Beginning with the famous "run" of April 22, 1889, the federal government slowly opened larger sections of Oklahoma Territory for settlement by white farmers and ranchers. Further, large numbers of whites moved into Indian Territory to develop coal mines, ranches and farms. Czech, Italian, and Hungarian miners joined the work force in the coal country of Indian Territory, and farmers from the Midwest swelled the ranks of agriculturalists in both territories. By 1907 some 1.4 million people resided in the "Twin Territories," and three-fourths of the residents worked on 200,000 farms. Cotton, corn, wheat and other grains poured forth as the virgin soils produced bumper crops. Foreseeing this potential growth and anxious to place Santa Fe lines throughout the territories, President Ripley wrote to Engineer James Dun on January 24, 1899, "I think the time has arrived when we should know more about the possibilities of the Indian Territory and northern Texas, with a view of its further development by our company."[2] Within a month Dun submitted a massive report which urged many new lines to thwart the expansion of the Missouri Pacific and the Missouri, Kansas and Texas railroads. Dun proposed branches throughout central Oklahoma and presented detailed surveys by H. L. Marvin for the routes.

In 1899 the Santa Fe operated two lines through the "Twin Territories": the main line from Arkansas City, Kansas, south through Guthrie and Purcell to Gainesville, Texas; and the panhandle route across the northwestern corner of Oklahoma Territory. Ripley decided that the greatest immediate need was to tap the farm areas on either side of the main line. He chartered the Eastern Oklahoma Railway on July 24, 1899, with $2.2 million in capital; and for the next five years this subsidiary constructed branches of great importance. A new line began at Newkirk in Oklahoma Territory and went east and then south paralleling the main line, which was about forty to fifty miles to the west, passing through Shawnee before regaining the main at Pauls Valley. The new line was designed to carry heavy freight traffic, and Dun ordered culverts to be constructed of stone and masonry with a maximum grade of .6 percent. The Eastern Oklahoma also built a line from the territorial capital at Guthrie east to Stillwater.

Track laying on the plains of Texas. Santa Fe Railway

In 1904 the Eastern Oklahoma bought a line from Pauls Valley west to Maysville and Lindsey, and later acquired the Oklahoma Central, which operated 128 miles of road west from the coal center of Lehigh through Ada to Purcell and Chickasha. Another purchase gave the Atchison a valuable feeder west of the main line and north into Kansas; the Eastern Oklahoma bought the Denver, Enid and Gulf Railroad in 1907, and thus acquired 161 miles of track from Guthrie through Enid to Kiowa in southern Kansas. When President Theodore Roosevelt signed the act merging the "Twin Territories" into the state of Oklahoma in 1907, the Santa Fe had a firm hold on rail traffic through the middle third of the new state.

Another branch in Indian Territory, further to the east and north, also became important. In 1884 H. L. Marvin had reported that a line south from Independence or Coffeyville, Kansas, would be unproductive because the only settlement was the squalid village of Tulsey Town in the Creek Nation. Located two miles from the Arkansas River, the place "is of little importance," he wrote; "The location is not suitable for a large town."[3] The town, which became just plain Tulsa, had only 1,390 people in 1900, but oil soon changed that. Oil was discovered at nearby Red Fork in 1901, and four years later the enormous Glenn Pool came in. The Santa Fe built a line south from Independence through Bartlesville to Owasso; and on May 12, 1905, it extended the branch eleven miles to a connection with the Midland Valley Railroad in Tulsa. As Tulsa's population leaped to 70,000 in 1920 and 140,000 in 1930, Santa Fe traffic grew, and Marvin's analysis of 1884 proved wholly erroneous.

Another area which attracted Ripley's attention was East Texas. The GCSF operated a branch from Somerville through Conroe into the Piney Woods. Only eighteen months after the reorganization of the railway, the GCSF acquired the Texas, Louisiana and Eastern Railroad in the Piney Woods, initiating a program of purchase and construction which would continue for ten years. Texas and Louisiana timber would provide not only cargoes but also ties for the new lines being constructed by the Santa Fe. Ripley's next significant purchase was the Gulf, Beaumont and Kansas City Railway Company which extended from Beaumont north to Rogan, and was being extended north to San Augustine. In order to connect with the GB&KC, the Santa Fe built a sixty-mile extension of its Conroe branch. The entrance of the ATSF into East Texas came at the invitation of John Henry Kirby, builder of the GB&KC and founder of the Kirby Lumber Company. Born in Tyler County in 1860, and a long-time lumberman, Kirby formed his lumber operation in 1901 with some $10 million in capital; his was the first multimillion-dollar industrial corporation in Texas. Kirby worked closely with the ATSF in developing the timber of East Texas between Beaumont and Longview. Kirby operated almost a half-million acres of timberland and fourteen sawmills, and for thirty years the lumber company prospered. After the company entered bankruptcy in 1933, the timber corporation was reorganized, and the ATSF became the main owner acquiring 94 percent of the stock of Kirby Lumber Company. Additional purchases of short timber lines extended the ATSF's East Texas branch north from Beaumont to Carthage in 1904, and to Longview in 1906. That year also saw the opening of a branch from Kirbyville east to De Ridder, Louisiana, and in 1908 that line was extended to Oakdale. Ripley's eye for business created a long, circuitous operation into East Texas and southwestern Louisiana that produced profitable lumber and cotton cargoes which were augmented by petroleum traffic with the discovery and exploitation of the East Texas oil field in the late 1920s and early 1930s. While this section of the GCSF has been treated almost as an orphan and somewhat ignored by the parent company's management, it has contributed its share to the prosperity of the GCSF.

Timber also attracted Ripley's attention to the northern coast of California, and provoked yet another confrontation with E. H. Harriman and the Southern Pacific. Ripley found the ATSF in a most unfavorable competitive position with the SP in the San Francisco Bay area. The Santa

Fe needed a substantial amount of freight going east from San Francisco, and the most obvious possibility was the largely untapped redwood timber country stretching north from the bay some 450 miles in a band from one to forty miles in width. The mature giant redwoods stood 200 feet tall and ten feet in diameter, and each tree respresented a huge quantity of excellent building materials. In addition, the valleys along the Eel and other rivers in the region produced fruit crops and provided pasturage for sheep and cattle. Several shortline railroads and timber lines operated in the area, but no direct link to the bay existed. Ripley bought the 42-mile-long Eel River and Eureka Railroad and the California and Northern Railway, which operated between Eureka and Arcata. He then sought to purchase some shortlines running north from Marin County on the north side of the bay. E. H. Harriman of the SP considered this an invasion of his domain, and he outbid Ripley for the shortlines and initiated his own program of expansion in the area. Ripley sent William B. Storey to survey the territory from the bay to Eureka, and Storey reported that only one railroad was feasible. Harriman, by this time, had begun to exercise his financial position in the Atchison, and he brought about a compromise; the SP and the ATSF would create a joint company to build into the redwood country.

On January 8, 1907, they formed the Northwestern Pacific Railroad to build from Willits to Chiveley, some 103 miles, and absorb the almost 500 miles of track owned by the two parents. Construction of the connecting line, delayed by the panic of 1907, was not completed until July 1, 1915. While the panic caused the parent companies to reduce the flow of dollars needed to build the connection, the terrain crossed by the NWP also retarded construction. The unstable mountains received heavy snowfalls in the winter, and spring thaws turned the Eel River and its tributaries into raging torrents; the Eel often rose 20 to 30 feet overnight. Wagon roads were few, and construction crews found it very difficult to haul in supplies for the massive tunnel work. Thirty tunnels, one 4,000 feet in length, connected the deep cuts and fills along the route. When the NWP opened in 1915, it stretched from Sausalito on the bay, north to Trinidad near the Oregon line. The ATSF used tugs and ferries to move freight from the Sausalito terminal to the Santa Fe slips at Point Richmond, but the water connection did not function smoothly, and in 1928 the Atchison sold its half of the NWP to the Southern Pacific. Only the NWP portion of Ripley's expansion program failed to provide a long-range return.

Other extensions in California during the first decade of the twentieth century gave the Santa Fe a firm base when the Golden State commenced the economic and population explosion which would continue for sixty years. In 1904 Ripley bought the narrow-gauge California and Nevada

Railroad, which extended north and east from Oakland. One "Borax" Smith had founded the C&N and projected it across the mountains from Oakland to Bodie and Death Valley. "Two streaks of rust" when acquired by the Atchison, the new owners used only 11 of its 24 miles of track to reach the port of Oakland. The track was rebuilt to standard gauge, and the first ATSF train entered Oakland on May 16, 1904. During the next five years the Santa Fe built branches from Bakersfield to Sunset to reach the oil field there, and other lines were constructed to Taft and Maricopa, but the basic system remained the same. The only other significant development came in 1905, when Ripley granted the Los Angeles and Salt Lake Railroad (later the Union Pacific) trackage rights from Daggett to Colton over Cajon Pass. But the urge to enter virgin territories, such as the redwood country, kept Ripley's program moving; and his eyes turned to the vast agricultural potential of the Pecos River valley of New Mexico and Texas.

Extending from southeastern New Mexico into Texas north of the Big Bend country, the Pecos River wound some 700 miles through the Llano Estacado (Staked Plains) and the Permian Basin. The Pecos flood plain was largely unoccupied in 1890, except for some Texas cattle herds. Irrigated farming along the river offered hopes for substantial profits, but the absence of railroads precluded such development. The nearest railroads formed an enormous triangle around the valley; the Colorado and Southern cut across northeastern New Mexico providing the eastern leg; the Santa Fe extended from Colorado to El Paso creating the western leg; while the Texas and Pacific between El Paso and Fort Worth served as the base. This huge isolated region attracted two developers who realized the agricultural potential of the Pecos River valley.

James J. Hagerman and Charles B. Eddy proposed to develop irrigated farming in the valley. After having made a fortune in Great Lakes iron mining, Hagerman moved to Colorado Springs, where at the age of 44 he retired because of poor health. Unable to remain inactive, he built the Colorado Midland, which he later sold to the Santa Fe, and developed extensive ranch holdings in Arizona and New Mexico. In 1889, Hagerman met Charles Eddy, a Pecos rancher, who persuaded him to help develop the valley by building a railroad connection to the Texas and Pacific. The Pecos Valley Railway, formed on August 27, 1890, built north from Pecos, Texas, on the T&P, to Eddy (later Carlsbad), New Mexico. The first 89 miles became operative in 1891, and three years later the PVR opened another 70 miles to enter Roswell. Hagerman and Eddy spent millions of dollars on wells, irrigation ditches and small dams, only to be devastated by the depression of 1893. A flood ruined much of the canal system, and few buyers were found for the farm lands. Hagerman went to the Atchison for help, and in 1895, the new railway's managers agreed to extend credit to the PVR to build from Roswell north to a connection with the ATSF. As early as 1893 Chief Engineer James Dun of the ATSF had argued for aiding Hagerman, and two years later the Atchison loaned the Pecos developer some $750,000.

The Santa Fe saw the Pecos Valley Railway as a natural extension of its Southern Kansas line from Panhandle City through Amarillo to the Texas–New Mexico cattle country. Aided by the ATSF, Hagerman formed the Pecos Valley and Northeastern Railway, which built 113 miles up the valley from Roswell to Portales and Texico on the border. The PV&NE acquired the PVR in 1898, and with renewed aid from the Santa Fe, a connection from Texico to Amarillo was constructed in April 1899. The ATSF reached Amarillo from near Panhandle City over the Fort Worth and Denver City until 1908, when it built its own line to connect with its Pecos Valley affiliate. The Santa Fe now had a 370-mile-long feeder from Amarillo to Pecos. To prevent another railroad from gaining control of the Pecos Valley by purchasing the securities of the struggling line, the Santa Fe acquired 96 percent of its stock and two-thirds of its bonds in 1901 for $2,675,902. Ripley then directed Dun to rebuild the branch for heavier freight service, and passenger operations were initiated from Amarillo to Pecos.

The Santa Fe and Hagerman and his associates pushed land sales in the valley through widespread advertisements in the Midwest and in Texas. By 1900 the 8,000 farmers living in the valley were producing bumper crops of alfalfa, sugar beets, peaches and tomatoes. Soon, long lines of reefers moved over the line carrying produce to Kansas City and Chicago. The valley towns began to grow, and the discovery of Carlsbad Caverns in 1901 brought an influx of tourists. Hagerman's Pecos Irrigation and Investment Company failed, however, and in 1904 President Theodore Roosevelt took over the operation under the Reclamation Act. A 25,000-acre reclamation district became the heart of the Pecos valley agricultural development, and the Santa Fe profited greatly from the resulting boom. At the same time, the portion of the branch from Amarillo to Texico became part of one of Ripley's pieces of grand strategy—the Belen Cutoff.

For Ripley, as for William Barstow Strong, the chief bottleneck in transporting goods on the ATSF was Raton Pass. The track rose 1,661 feet in sixteen miles over Raton, and the rate of ascension was not much less over Glorieta Pass, where the track climbed 158 feet in one mile. The 3 percent grades limited the size of freight trains even with newer, larger power plus helper locomotives. The pass created exorbitant operating costs and limited efficiency, a situation anathema to Ripley. The Santa Fe

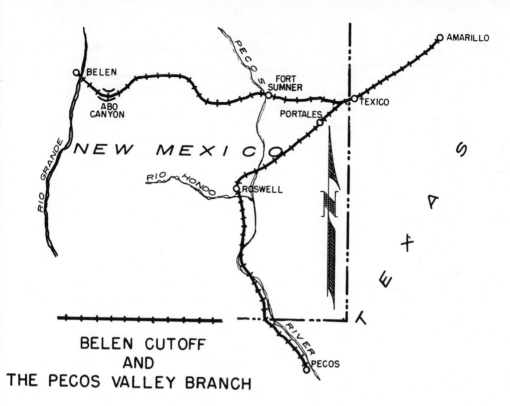

BELEN CUTOFF
AND
THE PECOS VALLEY BRANCH

Belen Cutoff and Pecos Valley Branch

needed a low-grade, all-weather route between Albuquerque and Kansas, and plans for such a cutoff developed slowly between 1878 and 1902. Lewis Kingman surveyed the central and eastern portions of New Mexico in 1878 looking for a new route, and Ripley sent surveyors over the same ground twenty-four years later. For seventeen months Ripley's men worked the area and reached the same conclusion as Kingman: a new cut-off should be built from Amarillo west to Belen via Texico, Fort Sumner and Abo Pass. Located thirty miles south of Albuquerque and twenty-five miles southeast of Belen, Abo Pass crossed the Continental Divide at a much lower height than Raton with a maximum elevation of 6,508 at Mountainaire. The route quickly became known as the Belen Cutoff, the answer to the operating department's dreams.

The route incorporated that portion of the Pecos valley line between Amarillo and Texico, then struck almost due west. The maximum grade of 66 feet per mile seemed miniscule compared with Raton Pass. (The difference in distance was slight; from Chicago to Rio Puerco Junction near Belen was 1,362.5 miles via Raton, and 1,356.6 miles via Texico.) But the ruling grade of only .6 percent and the pusher grade of only 1.25

percent meant significant savings. When the Atchison announced plans for the new cutoff, the press greeted the news by noting that millions of dollars were being spent to avoid less than one-quarter of a mile of Raton Pass—but that one-quarter of a mile was in elevation, not distance. Chief Engineer Dun expressed concern about the operational problems posed by Abo Pass and the need for a high level crossing of the Chicago, Rock Island and Pacific at Vaughn; but the advantages of the route outweighed the construction difficulties. On October 1, 1902, Dun informed Ripley that the field surveys had been completed. Ripley responded by forming the Eastern Railway of New Mexico on October 30 and by issuing contracts initiating grading on the route.

Early in 1903 large quantities of construction materials accumulated at Belen, and soon crews moved into the pass to blast out the right of way. Belen became the focal point for construction efforts, and near the end of January the new grade reached the Rio Grande where a temporary pile bridge aided the movement of supplies to the construction crews in the pass. Some seventy-five freight teams distributed materials to the five work camps east of Belen, but by July, a tightened money market brought construction to a halt. The uncompleted grade to the summit of the pass remained undisturbed until August 1905, when work resumed. By December, the track gangs had laid 108 miles of rail eastward, leaving a gap of only 142 miles. Crews on the eastern end laid 69 miles of rail west from Texico to Sunnyside, a wild end-of-track tent town which proudly possessed seven saloons. The residents of Sunnyside renamed the town Fort Sumner and sought a railroad facility, but the management decided to push on to Vaughn, which became the division point. At Vaughn an enormous fill and an overpass lifted the track over the Rock Island, and crews continued building westward toward Abo Pass. The first train did not move over the completed route until December 18, 1907, but as crews began to ballast the track, install fences, and construct depots and side tracks, Engineer William B. Storey telegraphed the project engineer, "Stop all work on Belen Cutoff." A follow-up letter on February 18, 1908, noted the collapse of the money market and indicated that Storey trusted that the line as it stood was good enough for freight traffic. The operating department could not take over, however, until June 30, 1908.

The benefits of the cutoff accrued slowly. For several years work to improve the cutoff and its eastern and western connections continued. Nineteen miles of new track from Belen west joined the cutoff to the Chicago–California main line at Dalies, and the connection with the Pecos branch was shifted from Texico to the new division point of Clovis. The greed of the city fathers of Portales discouraged the Atchison's plan to locate the junction there, and so the railway created the new town of

Crewmen at the old Harvey House at Needles, 1907. Santa Fe Railway

Clovis, which acquired a large shop and roundhouse. Further to the east the Santa Fe built a new line from Panhandle City into Amarillo, and the entire trackage from southern Kansas across northwestern Oklahoma into the Texas Panhandle was rebuilt. The Santa Fe erected a new bridge across the Canadian River two miles east of Canadian, Texas, in 1908. The old 2,441-foot-long, single-track trestle built in 1887–1888 by the Southern Kansas Railway needed to be replaced because it could not support the heavy freight drags moving over the cutoff. Four through-truss spans, each 260 feet long, could withstand the pounding of the Santa Fe's long freight trains and heavier motive power. The opening of the Belen Cutoff and the upgrading of its connections gave the ATSF two routes from Chicago to Dalies: one line via Raton, the other via Amarillo. The Belen Cutoff became the main freight route for the Santa Fe, even developing a modest, if unspectacular, passenger traffic. Full utilization of the potential of the Belen Cutoff would not come, however, until the

ATSF penetrated the High Plains of Texas and built a new main line from Clovis to Brownwood, giving the Santa Fe a competitive route from Houston and Galveston to California.

Atchison subsidiaries extended throughout much of the developed area of Texas, and they entered all of the Lone Star State's major cities, except San Antonio. But freight bound from Houston, Galveston, Dallas or Fort Worth to California moved north on a lengthy route through Oklahoma to Newton or another Kansas point, and then west. The Southern Pacific, with its "Sunset Line" from Houston to San Antonio, El Paso, Tucson and California, had a distinct competitive edge, and the Texas and Pacific, with its main line from Fort Worth and Dallas west to El Paso, captured much of the California trade of north-central Texas. Ripley looked over the notes collected in an earlier survey of West Texas, in 1888, and then ordered his location crews into the field. From 1903 to 1906 survey parties moved over Llano Estacado and the Edwards Plateau. Only a few farms and ranches existed in this vast area largely inhabited by coyotes, rattlesnakes, blue quail, prairie chickens, jack rabbits, prairie dogs and antelope. Traveling by wagon, sleeping in tents, and covering ten to twelve miles a day, the parties moved frequently across the arid plains. Wrapped in blankets and tarpaulins, the men slept on cots in canvas tents and dressed in sheepskin coats and several pairs of woolen pants, as they fought the frigid winds of the plains during the winter months. Their accumulated reports on the terrain and its agricultural potential began to arrive in Chicago, and Ripley formulated a massive invasion of the High Plains and the Edwards Plateau.

The Staked or High Plains included 30,000 square miles of Texas and New Mexico from the headwaters of the Canadian River south to include most of the Texas Panhandle, the Pecos River valley and the Permian Basin. Below the plains extended the Edwards Plateau centered on San Angelo and continuing south and west to the Rio Grande. The High Plains at the turn of the century was a sea of grass possessing agricultural possibilities for cotton, maize and wheat. Only the small towns of Amarillo, Plainview and Lubbock interrupted the sweeping plains. The Edwards Plateau, largely a broken tableland with topsoil too shallow for farming, represented potentially prosperous ranching country. The plains were treeless and only slightly eroded, except for a few deep canyons, and were nearly perfectly flat. The winters were cold, but dry, and the summers hot, windy and dry. Charles Goodnight had established the first large ranch on the plains in 1876, and other cattlemen followed in the 1880s and 1890s. The coming of the railroads to the Texas Panhandle attracted a few farmers, and by 1900 wheat and cotton began to replace cattle on the ranges.

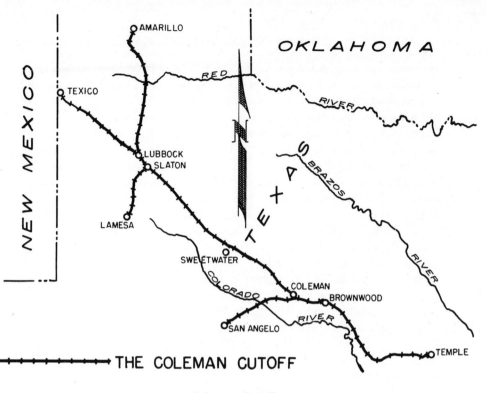

THE COLEMAN CUTOFF

Coleman Cutoff

The opening of the Santa Fe's line to Roswell, and the growth of Amarillo, attracted cattle buyers and farmers from the Midwest. A group of Kansans settled near the town of Canadian and initiated winter wheat production in the Panhandle. Landseekers began to pour into Amarillo, and ranchers carved up their domains into smaller units for sale as farms. North of Palo Duro Canyon wheat became the main crop, while south of the canyon cotton was the principal staple. As land values soared and other railroads, especially the Fort Worth and Denver City, began to survey the area, Ripley decided to move.

Using the amended charter of the Pecos and Northern Texas Railroad, which had built the Amarillo-Texico line, Ripley authorized the first railroad construction into the southern plains with a branch from Canyon on the Amarillo line 57 miles south to Plainview. On February 18, 1907, the branch opened, and the Atchison's invasion of the plains began. Ripley moved cautiously, constantly seeking the advise of Chief Engineer Dun, and, after Dun's death, Chief Engineer Storey. Several routes appeared feasible, such as connecting San Angelo with Roswell, or building from a point west of Brownwood to the Pecos valley branch, but the lack of local revenues discouraged the development of these surveys. The Ripley management then sought the best possible route from Plainview south and east to connect with the San Angelo branch of the GCSF northwest of Brownwood at the town of Coleman.

Every town between Brownwood and Lubbock sought to be on the new line, or Coleman Cutoff, as it became known. Delegations came to Chicago to see Ripley, Dun and, later, Storey, who were also bombarded with letters and telegrams; local subsidies of various amounts were promised if only their town could be on the cutoff and become a division point. Highly influential in making the final decision were the entreaties of C. W. Post, the "Cereal King." Post purchased the 200,000 acre Curry Comb Ranch in Garza County, southeast of Lubbock, and founded Post City as its "urban center." Experimenting with a variety of grains which he hoped to use at his cereal plant in Battle Creek, Michigan, Post sought a rail connection to ship his crops and to enhance the value of the farms carved out of the ranch. Ripley agreed to locate the cutoff through Post City in return for a subsidy of $50,000 from Post, plus an additional $25,000 to be raised locally, and the donation of right-of-way through the ranch. With assurances of financial support, Ripley inaugurated additional construction.

In December 1908, Ripley signed a contract to extend the Plainview branch an additional 45 miles to Lubbock. That community provided a $53,000 bonus and the right-of-way through the town. Work proceeded sporadically, but the line opened on January 9, 1910. Ripley subsequently announced the location of the cutoff from Lubbock to Coleman, some 205 miles. He selected a route from Lubbock through Slaton, Post City, Snyder and Sweetwater to Coleman. The irate citizens of Abilene sought help from the governor of Texas when their town was bypassed, but to no avail. Even Lubbock became incensed when the division point was located at the new "company" town of Slaton, only 17 miles south. Ripley selected Slaton because of the modest mileage between Lubbock and the nearest division point, the profits to be made from lot sales at the site, and because he had authorized a branch from Slaton to Lamesa some 54 miles to the south. Ripley wrote to Storey on February 7, 1910, that Slaton would be a "company" town, but that no officers of the Santa Fe would profit from land sales at the development. By July 1911, the Santa Fe had sold $125,000 in lots, and Slaton had some 1,000 people. Unlike Lubbock, the town of Sweetwater reacted enthusiastically to Ripley's announcement and raised a subsidy of $45,000. Construction of the Coleman Cutoff began on September 30, 1909.

Construction across the plains did not present obstacles of the magnitude of Abo Pass, but the crews labored for months to make the cuts and

High-drivered passenger power from Baldwin in 1903. H. L. Broadbelt

fills necessary to cross the undulating terrain. Mexican laborers living in long construction trains provided the main work force, and an immense body of cars carrying rails and ties accumulated at Lubbock and Coleman. The only significant obstacle encountered by the grading crews was the Cap Rock in Nolan and Taylor counties where, despite local rumors, no massive tunnel project became necessary. Horse or mule teams and scrapers did much of the heavy work, with blasting crews removing some of the rock for deeper cuts. Meanwhile, bridge crews erected numerous steel bridges in advance of the grading gangs. Track crews laying 75-pound rails west from Coleman reached Augustus on April 30, 1910. Aided by their Hurley Track Laying Machine, crews working east from Lubbock reached Augustus on May 1, 1911, and in December the Coleman Cutoff via Lubbock and Amarillo became operative. Trains used the Amarillo-Plainview-Lubbock line to reach the main, as Ripley temporarily abandoned plans to build a shortcut from Lubbock northwest to Texico or nearby Farwell.

Ripley sought additional subsidization from Lubbock or from John Farwell, owner of extensive land holdings near Texico. He sought $200,000; and when no subsidy materialized, he ordered Storey to stop all work. The operating benefits of the shortcut came to outweigh Ripley's distress at the lack of financial aid, and on May 1, 1912, he ordered Storey to proceed. Track laying on the 88-mile-long extension across the sand hills began on March 4, 1913, and rails reached Texico on November 12. Further improvements, such as the construction of stucco and tile depots, fencing and ballasting, delayed the completion of the Coleman Cutoff until March 1, 1914. The cutoff reduced the mileage from Galveston to San Francisco over the ATSF from 2,666 to 2,192 and to Los Angeles from 2,355 to 1,881. The Santa Fe could now give the Southern Pacific and the Texas and Pacific some strenuous competition.

During the same period Ripley also initiated an invasion of the Edwards Plateau sheep country. In 1911 the Santa Fe built a 98-mile branch from the Temple-Brownwood line at Lometa westward through Brady and San Saba to Eden. The towns along the route put up $90,000 in subsidies. The plateau became the center of an enormous wool industry and a source of substantial freight for the ATSF; but not until the late 1920s would the Santa Fe come to dominate the Edwards Plateau as it did the Llano Estacado.

Not even E. P. Ripley could have foreseen the rapid development of the plains which followed the construction of the new ATSF lines. The boom in farm lands accelerated as ranches, such as the "XIT," were subdivided. The population of the plains increased by 350 percent between 1900 and 1910, and farm production rose even more rapidly. Wheat production in some plains counties went from nothing in 1910 to 500,000 bushels by 1919. By 1925 over one-fifth of the Texas cotton crop came from west of Forth Worth, and some 1,130,713 bales were produced that year in West Texas. A dramatic shift from raising cattle and sheep to growing cotton and sorghum using dry-farming methods gave the Santa Fe substantial traffic in the decades which followed. The urban centers grew also, and from Amarillo to Lubbock and Brownwood towns and small cities began to thrive. Ripley's goals of operating efficiency and the generation of traffic in noncompetitive areas were more than achieved by the Coleman Cutoff and the invasion of the Texas High Plains.

The money for Ripley's expansion program came from the sale of securities and from earnings, a remarkable fact considering that the company had only recently emerged from a strenuous and painful reorganization. Ripley and his staff achieved such a high level of efficiency, and captured so much additional freight from the growing Southwest, that the Atchison became one of the darlings among the "Blue Chips" on Wall Street. The physical rebuilding of the Santa Fe and the financial recovery of the company are two of the most fascinating achievements of the Ripley team.

Between 1896 and 1912, Ripley worked a virtual miracle on the Santa Fe. As mileage operated leaped from 6,435 to 10,627, the total revenues soared from $13,656,899 to $110,322,328 and the net reached $33,321,100, up substantially from the $2,432,870 of 1896. This achievement came as motive power increased from 962 units to 2,081 and freight cars grew in number from 27,719 to 63,068. Not only did the Santa Fe acquire more equipment, but the locomotives were heavier, had greater pulling power and operated at a lower per-mile cost. Freight car capacity increased, and the newer equipment had modern safety devices and a longer life span. As the Santa Fe's income rose, Ripley plowed earnings back into the company in a massive improvement effort. Appropriations per mile for maintenance between 1900 and 1906 increased by 70 percent, while traffic rose by only 40 percent. In six years the management spent $15,859,500 on improvements, a sum quite comparable to the efforts of E. H. Harriman to improve the Union Pacific and the Southern Pacific. While some security analysts complained about the costs of the rebuilding program, Ripley urged stockholders to be patient; they would be rewarded by even larger profits in the future, he maintained.

When he took over the Santa Fe, Ripley reviewed the report of Robert Moore, which called for substantial redevelopment, and then he made a number of personal inspections. One of the first results of this survey was the rebuilding of much of the main line. Ripley issued orders to reduce curves and grades and for relaying the route with heavier steel rails. The few miles of double track between Emporia and Florence grew to include a dual system from Chicago to Newton by 1911. Heavier rails and increased traffic magnified the need for track improvements. Beginning in 1902 track gangs installed tie plates on the main lines, and engaged in a massive ballasting program. Crushed rock, gravel, or cinders supported the track and protected the roadbed. The creosote tie plant at Las Vegas was supplemented by plants at Somerville, Texas; Albuquerque, New Mexico; and National City, California. Although a scheme to use eucalyptus trees grown at Rancho Santa Fe for ties proved unsuccessful, the Santa Fe experimented with a variety of hardwoods to find the most long-lasting and rot-resistant ties. Rail weights on the system increased steadily, and from 1896 to 1916, the average weight rose from 60–62½ pounds to 85 pounds. The track improvement program increased the capacity of the system and allowed the operating ratio to decline markedly.

Ripley's concern for cost reduction naturally turned to the problems of Raton Pass. Even with the opening of the Belen Cutoff, the pass remained an operating nightmare. In 1907 Ripley authorized the appropriation of $429,800 for construction of a second, larger tunnel. The new bore extended 2,787 feet on a .5 percent grade and was lined with concrete. The timber lining of the old tunnel represented a potentially dangerous fire problem, and the narrow clearances of 18½ feet in height and 14 feet in width restricted the movement of outsize shipments. The new tunnel was 24 feet high and 17 feet wide, and its completion created a double track from Trinidad to Raton. At 9:35 A.M. on July 9, 1908, Locomotive 1212 and helper 893 moved the first train through the new tunnel. This type of improvement, while costly, raised the level of efficiency and increased the speed and size of freight operations.

Bridges on the main line also needed work, and "Mother Nature" hurried Ripley along in this area. In June 1903, the Kaw and Missouri rivers

Mallets for the Cutoffs—the largest locomotive in the world in 1909. H. L. Broadbelt

near Kansas City went on a rampage, washing out miles of track and several bridges, and in the Kansas City yard four locomotives and several passenger cars were simply swept away. Even before the losses from the flood, considerable work had been done on the major river crossings with rip-rap erected along the Washita, Canadian and Arkansas rivers. Major repair work in the Kansas City area restored normal operations; but in 1914 the ATSF retained the services of Octave Chanute and John W. Wallace, who designed a new bridge at the Sibley site. The major crossings were double tracked or improved to eliminate bottlenecks along the main.

Signaling and communications also concerned the operating department as it sought to improve service and reduce costs. In 1898 Ripley ordered the first installation of block signals, and during the next fifteen years the Santa Fe acquired 891 automatic block signals and 188 interlocking plants. The improvement of the communications network figured strongly in the minds of the management, but greater progress awaited future technological advancements.

The entire physical plant of the ATSF changed under Ripley's tenure as he enlarged shops, built new depots and stations, purchased modern tools and machinery, and erected water-treatment facilities and storage tanks on the western lines. The new depots were of two styles; in the West the structures were generally of stucco in a modified Spanish-Indian motif, while from Texas to Illinois most new structures were wood frame of several standard designs. The Santa Fe participated in the construction of large union stations at Joliet and Wichita, and the company joined in the planning and building of Kansas City's monumental Union Station. The headquarters buildings in Topeka received additions in 1906 and 1907, and a new building was erected in 1909. The Texas subsidiaries of the Atchison—the GCSF and the newly formed Panhandle and Santa Fe—acquired office buildings in Galveston and Amarillo. Texas law required separate Texas railroad corporations, and so the ATSF created the P&SF to operate the Panhandle-Plains lines. These new shops, stations and offices reflected the growth in traffic and the expanded rolling stock needed to carry the cargoes. All these improvements paid off, just as Ripley maintained that they would.

In 1915 the *Railway Age Gazette* reviewed Ripley's work over the previous nineteen years, and asked what the stockholders had received from the $298 million spent by the company, including $217 million of new bonds which had been issued. The editors noted that revenue per train mile on the ATSF was $3.55 compared with $3.07 on the Milwaukee Road and $3.50 on the CB&Q. The traffic was quite diverse; the Santa Fe loaded 57 percent of the California citrus crop and shipped 48 percent of it east; High Plains farms were beginning to contribute agricultural shipments; and the cutoff program speeded deliveries of manufactured goods to the West Coast. A startling comment attracted the interest of investors —the *Railway Age Gazette* called attention to the fact that capitalization per mile had *declined* from $61,500 in 1896 to $57,000 in 1915, and one-half of the total capitalization was in stock. The miraculous financial recovery after 1896 can be attributed to Ripley's policies and the conservative fiscal wizardry of Victor Morawetz and the board's finance committee.

Between 1896 and 1916 the revenues of the ATSF increased with virtually unbroken regularity. Only the panic of 1907 slowed the growth of the corporation's income and profits. Freight rates per mile stabilized somewhat, although the average rate of .0112¢ in 1896 declined to .0097¢ in 1900 and to .0093¢ in 1906. The great increase in average tonnage per train, which climbed from 142 in 1898 to 498 in 1916, compensated somewhat for the decline in rates. Another compensating factor was the average distance freight was carried which rose from 251 miles to 342 miles. The nature of Santa Fe traffic changed also as the economy of the Southwest matured. The percentage of freight represented by agricultural products and livestock declined while the tonnage for minerals, lumber and manufactured goods increased. Still, much of the freight moved one way —food to the East and grain to the Gulf of Mexico. Ripley did reduce the number of "empties" carried; but until the population of the Southwest grew larger and began to "import" more goods, this problem would remain unsolved. The diversification of the Santa Fe's business allowed greater flexibility in time of national economic distress and greater income in prosperous times.

Signs of Ripley's success came in 1906 at the end of the first decade of his tenure as president. In ten years, mileage rose from 6,479 to 8,433, but the gross more than doubled from $30,621,230 to $78,044,347. Significantly, the gross per mile, even as the line expanded, increased from $4,752 to $9,253. While the company had no net after charges at the end of 1897, in 1906 some $18,270,000 remained in the treasury. Between 1896 and 1906 Ripley and the board paid out $60 million in dividends to Atchison security holders, and at least one analyst felt that this policy had been too conservative. While the amount of stock issued ($216,199,530) and bonds outstanding ($280,378,300) seemed large, the capitalization per mile was less than that of the Union Pacific or the Southern Pacific. The conservative fiscal and expansion policies made the Atchison a "blue chip," and not a speculative venture. It had become "the Pennsylvania of the West."[4]

Ripley's policies continued throughout the next decade, further enhancing the company's financial position. The adjustment bondholders received regular interest payments as did the owners of the 5 percent preferred stock. Common stockholders received dividends at a rate of 4 percent, which was later increased to 6 percent. As early as 1901 the common stock doubled in price on the New York Stock Exchange, and the *low* of 18 in 1900 seems unbelievable when compared with the *low* of 83 in March 1907. Much credit for the fiscal solidarity must be given to Victor Morawetz. He utilized "scientific management principles" at a time when such concepts were only being introduced in much of American industry. Ripley and Morawetz operated facilities at peak capacity while maintaining a frugal management. When Ripley's expansion program took more funds than provided by earnings alone, Morawetz developed a borrowing plan which generated capital funding at low interest rates.

Beginning in 1902, the Atchison again embarked on a large-scale borrowing program. The company sold $30 million in 4 percent unsecured bonds, to be paid in twelve annual installments. This novel and frugal policy attracted bond buyers who would make additional purchases of debentures during the next dozen years. To pay for double tracking the Chicago–Kansas City line, for new cars and locomotives, and for the new branches, the Atchison needed from $6 million to $11 million per year. A substantial issue of $50 million 4 percent convertible debentures in 1904 sold very quickly, many to common stockholders who could buy up to 15 percent of the value of their holdings. The next year the stockholders voted to increase the annual limit on borrowing to allow for more expansion. When borrowing reached an even higher limit in 1907, the stockholders approved a $98 million issue of capital stock. The new stock and $10 million in convertible bonds previously authorized moved very slowly on the market because of the panic of 1907. Ripley and Morawetz could only have been disappointed when by 1910 they had sold less than two-thirds of the stock. Once again they turned to earnings for one-third to one-half of their capital needs. Their disappointment must have been tempered, however, as the Atchison easily weathered the national economic troubles while other railroads reduced or omitted dividends and a few entered receivership.

Ripley went back to the board and the stockholders in 1908 and succeeding years with requests for additional capital. Nearly all bonds carried 4 or 4½ percent interest rates, and many were convertible issues. The company raised substantial sums in 1909 ($28,258,000) and 1910 ($14,378,383), and bond owners converted many of these and earlier issues into common stock. The rising price of the common stock made the convertibility feature very popular on the bond market. In 1910 stockholders voted to authorize an additional $100 million in convertible bonds and $100,289,000 in common stock to pay for expansion in Texas and to purchase the Mojave-Needles line, then being operated by lease. The last of the old high interest rate bonds, those of the Chicago and St. Louis Railroad, were retired in 1915. By World War I, only about 10 percent of Atchison bonds paid more than 4 percent interest. The conversion of bonds to stock caused the bonded indebtedness to fall by $54 million between 1912 and 1917, while company assets rose by $124 million. The management easily paid interest and dividends, retaining large sums for improvements.

The Ripley-Morawetz fiscal policies, supported by Walker Hines when he became chairman of the board, received considerable attention from financial journals and railroad analysts. As early as 1901, Lee, Higginson and Company issued a circular containing a positive recommendation to purchase Atchison securities. The financial editor of *The New York Times* offered some mild criticism the next year when Ripley raised dividends and simultaneously asked for a large bond issue; but the editor admitted that the request was justified because of the road's "remarkable improvement." As maintenance expenses, the cost of conducting transportation, and fixed charges declined proportionately to gross income and as the surplus grew, financial reports became even more positive. Carl Synder called the Atchison a "magnificent property," while John Moody lauded the conservative managerial policies. Moody agreed that general national prosperity and the growth of the Southwest had aided the management in their attainments, but much credit had to be given to Ripley and his associate. A most revealing analysis of the Atchison and Ripley by Albert Atwood in 1914 concluded: "the company's bonds are splendidly safe, especially in view of their great buffer of stock, and are among the best of obtainable investments."[5] Atwood described future prospects in most terms, and he shared the general confidence of the financial world.

Nearly all the reports about the Atchison stressed the independence of its board and the diversity of its stock ownership. But the strategic position of the Santa Fe, its financial solidity and Ripley's aggressive expansion program brought representatives of E. H. Harriman and the Rockefeller interests onto the board, threatening, if only temporarily, the company's independence. Fresh from his exhilarating experience in the Northern Securities Case, and still strongly supported by William Rockefeller and other Standard Oil men, Harriman entered the stock market in 1904, purchasing blocks of securities in the Baltimore and Ohio, the New York Central and the Atchison. Harriman controlled the Southern Pacific, the Union Pacific and the Illinois Central, and he sought "cooperation" with the Atchison to eliminate costly rivalries in the Southwest. In the summer of 1904 he approached Ripley and Morawetz and offered the Santa Fe two seats on the SP board in exchange for two places on the ATSF board, adding that Morawetz could sit on the SP executive committee. Ripley responded with a straightforward, "No!" Harriman, again, urged "harmony" and then entered the market.

Through the summer of that year, Harriman, using Rockefeller money and his own, purchased 300,000 shares of Atchison stock. Exercising the power gained by the purchase, Harriman elected two of his associates, Henry H. Rogers and H. C. Frick, to the Santa Fe board in February 1905. They represented Harriman and his other allies, Otto H. Kahn, William Rockefeller, and James Stillman, who held 14 percent of Atchison common stock worth $30 million. Harriman did not push Ripley too far, however, and recognized the strenuous objections Ripley and Morawetz raised—the cumulative voting system actually allowed Harriman to take as many as four seats on the board if he had so desired. Harriman sought cooperation rather than competition, as did his allies Rogers and Frick, who served on the UP board. Frick was also a member of the board of the Rock Island, and Rogers of the Milwaukee Road. Their presence on the Atchison, and Harriman's desire for peace, led to a series of significant compromises which diminished territorial conflicts.

The Santa Fe and the SP met head-on in Arizona and northern California, and reconciliation in these areas must have been influenced by the Harriman men on the Atchison board. As has been noted, the Atchison terminated its invasion of Arizona east and south of Phoenix, while north of San Francisco the SP and the ATSF formed the Northwestern Pacific as a joint venture. Further, the SP, ATSF and UP "pooled" the highly important California citrus crop, thus ending the costly rivalry for that traffic. The Atchison also granted the UP joint use of the Daggett-Colton line as an entrance into Los Angeles. By 1906 Harriman had obtained the "harmony" he had sought, and he and his allies sold their interests in the Atchison. Another Harriman property, the Oregon Short Line, subsequently acquired $10,395,000 in Atchison preferred, which it held until 1909. This brief interlude marked the only period in which the independence of the Atchison seemed threatened.

Ripley's fears of Harriman should have been more tempered. The Atchison had 17,523 stockholders in 1905; only the Pennsylvania Railroad had more. By 1913 the number of stockholders grew to 36,341 with an average holding of only 83.9 shares. Dutch and English interests held large blocks of stocks and a substantial investment in Santa Fe bonds, and several insurance companies were primary investors. Prior to World War I the Equitable Life Assurance Society held nearly 10,000 shares of common stock, and with the New York and Mutual Insurance companies Equitable owned some $25 million in bonds. The board of directors represented this diffuse holding, and the Harriman men could not control the Atchison. Ripley avoided merger discussions, sought strong men for the board who favored the Atchison's independence, and found a prominent group of business leaders willing to serve. Arthur T. Hadley and Walker D. Hines, nationally prominent railroad authorities, served on the board as did industrial leaders Ogden Mills, Paul Morton and Augustus Julliard. But it was Edward P. Ripley whose personality molded and shaped the Atchison.

The hard-driving, hard-working, tough-minded Ripley demanded total loyalty to the Atchison, freedom from government interference, limited rate making by regulatory agencies, and no role for labor unions in employee relations. A "progressive" writer of the period found Ripley's views "medieval" on public questions,[6] but a more recent defender of the American railroad system argues that Ripley saw the growing problems of the industry long before other railroad executives perceived them.[7] Ripley used Santa Fe *Annual Reports*, newspapers, magazines, public conferences and railroad regulatory hearings to carry his message to the American people. He noted rising costs in the form of higher wages and employee benefits, and increasing property and other taxes. He then contrasted these costs with attempts by state agencies to reduce rates and the refusal of the Interstate Commerce Commission to grant requests for higher tariffs. These conflicting phenomena undermined the confidence of investors, who refused to risk capital where there was no guarantee of long-range rate stabilization. Ripley contended that railroads would have to restrict services and halt expansion plans until the government restored investor confidence and public officials stopped attacking the railway industry. He denounced the efforts of "progressives" to achieve "scientific" rate making, but also denounced railroads which granted rebates to favored shippers. He wanted open rate structures, equitable to all, based on free competition and an adequate financial return to investors.

Ripley's views brought him and the Atchison into conflict with several state governments, particularly those of Kansas and Texas. The state gov-

Fast freight power for the Plains—a 2-6-0 from Baldwin in 1901. H. L. Broadbelt

ernment of Kansas attempted to establish a 2¢-per-mile passenger rate in 1906, and Ripley launched an all-out assault. He argued that Kansas passengers produced a meager return for the railroad, and yet the Santa Fe spent millions of dollars in the state; he pleaded for maintenance of the present rate structure. Kansas political leader W. R. Stubbs accused Ripley of interfering in Kansas governmental affairs, of issuing free passes to officials and clergymen, and he launched a campaign for the governorship on the issue. Ripley responded that the Santa Fe was not a disinterested observer and was, after all, the largest taxpayer in the Sunflower State. Stubbs charged that ATSF stock contained massive amounts of "water" and that consumers needed lower rates. Kansas voters agreed and sent him to the statehouse. Stubbs and the legislature enacted the 2¢ fare, which became applicable on all intrastate travel. Despite Ripley's pleas for relief, the low rate remained in effect.

A similar battle in Texas solidified Ripley's opposition to state regulation of the industry. Texas required all railroads operating within its boundaries to have their corporate headquarters in the state, hence the Gulf, Colorado and Santa Fe at Galveston and the Panhandle and Santa Fe at Amarillo. Further, in 1905 Texas enacted a full-crew law enlarging train crews, and four years later the state passed a law requiring new depots in many smaller communities. When the governor and the legislature then threatened to cut freight rates, Ripley exploded, and work on the Panhandle and Plains extensions was stopped. The Texas government got the message, and the proposal was dropped. With this threat removed, construction proceeded.

Ripley's outspokenness and blunt manner often got him and the railroad unfavorable publicity. At an ICC hearing in Chicago in 1910 Ripley testified that a low rate of return prevented the railroad industry from obtaining additional capital. He declared that the ATSF earned only 4.75 percent on its investment, that its capitalization was less than true value, and that rates had to be maintained to secure adequate capital for improvements and expansion. When asked what reasonable rates were, Ripley's answer proved most embarrassing in its candor:

> There never was any better definition than that which was given many years ago by somebody and which has been used as a by-word and a reproach ever since, namely, "What the traffic will bear." That does not mean all the traffic will bear, it does not mean all that can be extorted or squeezed out of it, but what the traffic will bear having regard to the freest possible movement of commodities, the least possible burden on the producer and the consumer, the middleman can take care of himself.[8]

The damage was done. "Charge what the traffic will bear!" Reporters ignored the explanation which followed, and few heard Ripley's charge that rates were unreasonably low. While one member of the ICC called Ripley's testimony "most statesmanlike," the "progressives" had all the evidence they needed to prove "greed and avarice" on the part of railway management.

In the first two decades of the twentieth century a number of individuals and pressure groups sought to cure the general and specific ills of society by the expansion of regulatory and bureaucratic government, by the more efficient use of resources, and by applying the "laws of scientific management." For the railroad industry that meant evaluation by the ICC to establish the exact worth of the property and, thereby, the legitimate rate of return. Further it meant reduced rates, greater efficiency, eight-hour days for crewmen, additional safety devices, precise shop rules, and, for many, unionization. Some "progressives," like William Jennings Bryan, felt that the only alternative was nationalization. Ripley stood foursquare against these notions and for regulation—limited regulation—at the federal level, no role for the unions and a fluid, market-based rate structure. Company benevolence, a free market, and competition would give consumers and shippers the best service and lowest rates, and the workers the highest wages and broadest benefits. His position, once again, received little favorable notice other than among Atchison stockholders and other railroad executives.

The management of the Atchison proceeded very cautiously after 1909, completing the extensions underway, but planning no new major projects. The failure of the ICC to grant rate increases, especially in 1914, caused Ripley to vent his wrath at the commission and to denounce the hostility of Congress toward the railway industry. Very despondently he reported to the stockholders in 1913 that "Our troubles are with various government bodies."[9] In September 1914, he and several other railway executives went to Washington and spoke with President Woodrow Wilson of their plight, urging him to stop the administration's verbal abuses, which were destroying sources of credit. While Wilson agreed to help, his Jeffersonian principles and basic agreement with his antirailroad advisors, such as Louis Brandeis and Bryan, did not allow for a shift in federal executive attitudes.

Ripley continued to plead for cooperation between the industry and government. He sought a system of regional boards to regulate the industry with a federal veto over the boards' decisions. He wanted rates which would provide a guaranteed return equal at least to the previous five-year average plus 6 percent on improvements. Such a scheme, he argued, would bring about efficiency and eliminate waste. He tried to convince public bodies that consolidations and mergers were not necessarily evils even though the Atchison was not a party to or interested in any major mergers. He told the Chicago Conference on Trusts that competition was not necessarily restricted by consolidation; although competition could be lessened at one point, it was possibly enhanced at another. Ripley's strongly articulated views might have received a more positive response had the company's reputation not been tainted by charges of granting rebates—anathema to "progressives" and nonprogressives alike.

In January 1905, at the annual meeting in Boston, some stockholders demanded that Ripley respond to charges that the ATSF had granted $400,000 in rebates to the Colorado Fuel and Iron Company. The Caledonian Coal Company of Gallup, New Mexico, had charged the ATSF with discrimination in favor of CF&I, and it accused former Santa Fe Vice President Paul Morton, then President Roosevelt's Secretary of the Navy, of having granted the rebate. The Santa Fe had leased its coal operation near Trinidad to CF&I in 1896 and bought its coal from the company. Morton, CF&I's vice president and traffic manager, joined the ATSF as second vice president, and three years later the railroad stopped buying coal from Caledonian. Caledonian further claimed that the ATSF had increased its freight rates while those for CF&I were reduced. As evidence, Caledonian published copies of an ATSF rate sheet headed by the notation: "This publication is for the information of employees only, and copies must not be given to the public." The ICC found the Santa Fe guilty of granting rebates while Morton had served with the company, and in June 1905, Morton resigned from the cabinet. President Roosevelt accepted the resignation but defended Morton, who, he said, opposed granting rebates. The U.S. attorney general proceeded to investigate the ICC findings as preliminary to the filing of criminal charges against several second-echelon Santa Fe officials. The case was never pressed, however, and the charges were unresolved. One former ICC member later wrote that President Roosevelt failed to pursue the matter after Santa Fe Traffic Vice President Edward Chambers told Roosevelt that he had ordered the men to issue the discriminatory rates and that they had only carried out his orders. The attorney general did not press the indictments, but the Atchison's image had been substantially tarnished.

Deeply troubled by the rebate charge and by the bad press generally, Ripley inaugurated a campaign to sell the Santa Fe to its customers and the people who lived along its routes. He said that the railroads had to tell their story to the people and present their side of the rate and labor questions. He felt that certain politicians abused the railroads to get votes and that the industry had to fight back. The Atchison, he decided, would go to the people, ask and answer questions, and listen to shipper complaints. One week each month the Santa Fe executives boarded a "Harmony Special" and toured part of the system. The president, vice presidents, freight and passenger agents, agricultural experts, and men from the industrial division traveled from town to town talking with businessmen and farmers about mutual problems. Informal meetings in town halls, churches and schools became open forums for debate and exchanges. Civil engineers from the engineering department provided communities with advice on water, sewerage, and other technical problems. Representatives from the colonization and agricultural departments met with farmers and their wives to discuss crops, new methods and better seeds. Ripley declared, "The friendship of the people living along the line is regarded by Santa Fe men as one of the company's most valuable assets," and he meant it.[10] The image of the railroad did soften, and the editor of the *Ottawa Herald* of Kansas could write: "The Santa Fe is the people's kind of railroad,"[11] and not fear a massive decline in subscriptions.

Ripley also used the good offices of the company to aid communities in times of natural disaster, and if the Santa Fe appeared to be the cause of an accident, the management helped the victims and then let the lawyers and courts establish liability. On September 27, 1915, a tank car of gasoline rested on a spur at the Ardmore Refining Company in Ardmore, Oklahoma. The safety valves on the car began to whistle as heat caused rising pressure in the tank. Refinery workers removed the car's dome cap, and escaping vapors permeated the air 300 feet around the car. A spark! Ignition! A terrible explosion caused buildings to collapse and reduced large portions of the town to rubble. The shock wave and debris killed 48 people and left 450 injured. Even as the rescue work began, the ATSF extended all the aid it could muster. Many townspeople immediately blamed the railroad, although the company thought the responsibility rested with the refinery. Ripley sought to head off lengthy and costly lawsuits and further negative views of the ATSF. He asked Ardmore's mayor to form a committee of citizens to hear damage claims, and said the railroad would pay legitimate damages at the level established by the citizens' committee. Six citizens heard the claims, and Ripley sent some of his legal staff to meet with them. Within a year the vast majority of claims were settled, and only one lawsuit was filed. A billboard near Ardmore, erected by its grateful citizens, proclaimed: "Great Is the Santa Fe! One Corporation with a Soul."

Ripley's policy of better community relations could be observed throughout the system. When the Kaw River flooded Topeka in 1913, the railroad supplied the city with water. In the aftermath of the Galveston hurricane, the GCSF engaged in relief work and used its locomotives as sources of water and power. Community services, damage claims quickly paid, good will and public relations helped Ripley sell his railroad to the region it served.

From Main Street of Ardmore to Wall Street, Ripley's reputation and that of his company became synonymous. He fought for the Atchison and the industry with tenacity, honesty, and blunt language. He devoted late afternoons to eighteen holes of golf; he continued to push for the civic betterment of Chicago; and he appeared before numerous public groups selling his brand of laissez faire economics. But no one or no group would be allowed to interfere with the management of the Santa Fe. Ripley declared in 1914 that: "Between the repressive forces of Government and the demands of organized labor, it is evident that the sum remaining [at the end of the year] as the share of invested capital is in serious danger."[12] His refusal to compromise with regulatory agencies and with the labor unions representing his workers would lead to sharp conflicts during the last years of his presidency, conflicts which would continue during the next administration of the Atchison. These confrontations would reach a climax in the early years of Woodrow Wilson's term and in the period of federal operation of the nation's rail system during World War I.

8

From Teakettles to Mallets

John J. Byrne, general passenger agent for the Santa Fe lines west of Albuquerque, was seated at his desk in Los Angeles on Saturday morning, July 8, 1905, when a nondescript cowboy entered his office and made the most unusual request Byrne had ever received. Dressed in a cheap blue serge suit, blue wool shirt, high-heeled Vaquero boots, a cowboy hat and a bright red tie, the man introduced himself as Walter Scott and demanded to know if Byrne and the Santa Fe could put him in Chicago in the unheard-of time of forty-six hours. Without hesitation, Byrne said absolutely, thinking the man bizarre, if not slightly demented. Scott then asked the price, Byrne responded $5,500, and the cowboy pulled off the cash from a horse-choking wad of bills. How soon could they leave, Scott wanted to know; Byrne told him to be at the Santa Fe's garish, Moorish-style La Grande depot at one in the afternoon the next day, and the famous record-breaking run of the "Coyote Special" would begin.

Walter Scott, better known as "Death Valley Scotty," had been a prospector, miner, and California eccentric for several decades. He had traveled over the Atchison from California to Chicago some thirty-two times, and he decided to set himself a record. Byrne recognized in Scott's challenge a chance for the railroad to gain substantial favorable publicity, and a wire to the Chicago headquarters produced an affirmative response to the scheme. Telegraph keys pounded the remainder of Saturday and into the wee hours of Sunday morning establishing the "Special's" schedule, lining up the best crews available, and arranging for the locomotives to be used. Fred Harvey stocked diner 1407 with provisions, and Chef Beyer

La Grande in Los Angeles. State Historical Society of Colorado, William Jackson Collection

organized his kitchen for the trip. The Pullman Company sent the car "Muskegon" to the depot, and the Santa Fe added baggage car 210 to the three-car train which weighed in at 170 tons. All was in readiness shortly after noon the next day as locomotive Number 442 backed up to the train at La Grande, and the Scott party boarded the "Muskegon."

The Atchison's publicity department had alerted the press Saturday afternoon, and the Sunday morning papers carried the story. Twenty thousand well-wishers descended on La Grande to see Scotty off on his race against time. Scott, his wife, and reporter C. E. Van Loan comprised the party, and Byrne got them in the car and settled for the trip. Van Loan set up his typewriter and prepared to issue a series of continuous reports as the special shot across the West. Engineer John Finlay eased his Baldwin 4–6–0 out of La Grande, slowly opened the throttle, and his steed began to race over the 141 miles to Barstow on the first leg of the run.

From Los Angeles to Barstow, Finlay took his train over Cajon Pass and its 116-foot-per-mile grade. Aided by a helper on the 25-mile run to the Summit, he averaged 48.5 miles per hour. At Barstow he turned the train over to T. E. Gallagher and 2–6–2 Number 1005 for the second leg of the trip. Between Barstow and Needles, some 170 miles, Gallagher averaged 51 miles an hour, but Chef Beyer went into a rage when the lovely dinner he had prepared went to the floor as the train careened around a curve just west of Needles. F. W. Jackson had Number 1010 ready at Needles, at 7:17 P.M. and the 2–6–2 made the 150 miles to Seligman in three hours and thirty minutes over some of the worst grades on the Santa Fe. As Jackson stepped down out of the cab at Seligman, Division Superintendant Gibson asked, "What detained you?", but Jackson knew he had done an excellent job. Another Baldwin 2–6–2 of the 1000 Class captained by Engineer Woods took the "Special" on to Williams averaging 34 miles per hour over the stiff grades. From Williams a Rhode Island 4–6–0 with D. A. Lenhart at the throttle hauled the train to Winslow in slightly over two hours. The crews in California and Arizona set a new speed record and put Scotty well ahead of all previous fast runs.

The relatively easy grades from Winslow to Gallup and Albuquerque allowed engineers Briscoe and Rehder to show their stuff, and they averaged just under 50 miles an hour. Chef Beyer kept his kitchen operating even as the train hit 60 miles an hour across New Mexico, and Van Loan reported that the salt cellars played Ping-Pong with each other as they bounced on the tables. Beyer maintained the traditional Fred Harvey high standards even under these adverse conditions. For Scotty and his guests, Beyer provided luxurious meals, as one menu demonstrates:

Caviar Sandwiches à la Death Valley
Iced Consommé
Porterhouse Steak à la Coyote
Broiled Squab on Toast, with Strips of Bacon au Scotty
Stuffed Tomatoes
Ice Cream with Colored Trimmings
Cheese   Coffee   Cigars

But Beyer almost had to give up east of Albuquerque as Engineer Ed Sears took the train over Glorieta Pass. A helper cut in from Lamy to Glorieta, and as they raced through a curve one member of the crew stumbled, and his shoulder crashed through the window of a car. Between Albuquerque and La Junta the "Special" operated with the new, larger 4–6–2s from Baldwin, the superior mountain-division passenger locomotives of the time.

The average speed fell as the "Special" climbed over Raton Pass with yet another helper; but from the pass to La Junta the engineers began to pull out all the stops. East of La Junta on the "speedway" Baldwin 4–4–2 Number 536 charged toward Syracuse at speeds of 85 and 90 miles per hour for an average of just under 64 miles per hour. From Syracuse to Dodge City and from Dodge almost to Newton, records continued to fall. Scotty wired President Theodore Roosevelt: "An American cowboy is coming east on a special train faster than any cowpuncher ever rode before; how much shall I break the transcontinental record?"[1] Roosevelt did not respond, and Scotty's brag came too soon, for east of Newton, Number 530 lost a cylinderhead and had to be rescued by 2–6–2 Number 1095. From Newton to Chicago 4–4–2s of the 500 Class not only made up the time lost, but also established new records on each division. Averaging between 55 and 62 miles per hour, the Baldwin Atlantics hit incredible speeds over short stretches. Out of Shopton, Scotty rode in the cab and helped fire Number 510 as she raced to Chillicothe. Ripley's track rebuilding program allowed his engineers to hit top speeds, and between Cameron and Surry, the "Special" peaked at 106 miles per hour. From Shopton to Dearborn the train covered 239 miles in 239 minutes, and Van Loan's reports made the front pages across the nation.

At 11:54 A.M. on July 11, the "Coyote Special" pulled into Dearborn Station, completing the 2,265 mile trip in a record 44 hours and 54 minutes, averaging 50.4 miles per hour. The run tested Atchison crews and equipment and demonstrated the significance of Ripley's maintenance and improvement programs. More importantly, the "Special" signaled a transition in the development of the steam locomotive from the modest teakettles of the 1880s to the rise of the modern twentieth-century engine. The 19 locomotives on the Scott Special included 17 from the Baldwin Locomotive Works and 2 from the Rhode Island Works. The 3 Ten Wheelers, 3 Pacifics, 9 Atlantics, and 4 Prairies symbolized the development of larger locomotives with greater tractive efforts.[2] Locomotives with drivers from 67 to 79 inches in diameter, boiler pressures of 220 pounds per square inch, and larger tenders having greater water and fuel capacities enabled the train crews to set records. The improvements made in the previous decade dramatically altered operations on the sprawling system.

Even before Scotty's "Special," the Santa Fe had become known for its fast runs. In 1889 Nelly Bly, a young reporter from New York, challenged the fictional record of Jules Verne's Phileas Fogg of *Around the World in Eighty Days* and set out from New York. She interviewed Verne in Paris, continued on toward the Pacific, and arrived in San Francisco on January 21, 1890. She boarded a special Santa Fe train which covered the 2,577 miles to Chicago in 69 hours, averaging 37 miles per hour. As her train established new records along the line, Miss Bly presented each division superintendent with a quart of Mumm's Extra Dry. She arrived in New York in 72 days to eclipse Fogg's record. An errand of mercy prompted a similar run in 1895 when Director Benjamin Cheney's son became ill while his father was in California. A Santa Fe train took the grieving parent from Colton to Chicago in just over 57 hours. A similar journey by H. P. Lowe of the Engineering Corporation of America established a new Los Angeles–Chicago time in 1903 of 52 hours and 49 minutes, with Lowe rewarding crews $50 each as the records fell. But

Scotty's train with its improved motive power represented a new era. If the Bly and Lowe trains had left the West Coast at the same time as the "Coyote Special" Miss Bly would have been in Emporia 585 miles away and Lowe would have been at Hart, Missouri, 342 miles west of Chicago when Scotty arrived at Dearborn. The story of the rise of the modern steam locomotive is an integral part of the development of the modern railway system.

Beginning with the purchase of the second-hand "Cyrus K. Holliday" in 1869, the Atchison bought, built or acquired through mergers 3,743 steam locomotives. The first locomotives, like the "Holliday" and its immediate successors, were light in weight, spindly, and able to pull only short trains. As the Santa Fe expanded westward in the early 1870s, the company acquired additional motive power, but the size remained basically the same. Nearly all of the early power was of the 4–4–0 wheel arrangement, known as the American type. The first large locomotive purchases came from the Taunton Locomotive Works of Massachusetts, with four 4–4–0s in 1870, nine more in 1871 and eighteen additional units in 1872. Five beautifully proportioned 4–4–0s from Mason in 1872 terminated further purchases until 1875, when the Atchison began a lengthy collaboration with the Baldwin Locomotive Works. Baldwin would eventually supply the Santa Fe with over a thousand locomotives during the next seventy years, and the Santa Fe became one of Baldwin's best customers. The initial order in 1875 was not large, however, as the Atchison also received engines from Hinkley, Mason and Taunton. The locomotive roster grew, and by 1877 the company operated sixty engines.

The Santa Fe in 1877 owned fifty-six Americans and four switchers of the 0–4–0 type. Thirty-three locomotives were Tauntons; only thirteen were from Baldwin. All of the engines were quite small; most had fifty-inch drivers, wood-frame tenders, and short wheel bases. Operating results of this locomotive stable reflected the limited range of their effort. In 1877 they average 40.93 miles per ton of coal, and the fuel cost $2.98 a ton. Total operating costs per average mile were 20.1¢ with 7.65¢ for fuel, 7.02¢ for labor, 0.45¢ for oil and 4.98¢ for repairs. The average operating costs per mile of the locomotives varied enormously from 10.9¢ to 35.1¢. Yet this small fleet rolled up a total of 1,796,569 miles of service with 601,040 in passenger mileage, 952,459 in freight, 53,553 in construction, and 189,517 in switching. From the outset, the company kept detailed records of locomotive performance as it sought to maximize efficiency and meet its ever-growing motive power needs.

The ATSF motive power department proved to be highly flexible in meeting the needs of the company and altering locomotives to fit particular circumstances and financial exigencies. In 1879, for example, the

Baldwin 0–6–0 switch engine, built in 1911. H. L. Broadbelt

Santa Fe ordered two small 4–4–0s from Baldwin for use on the narrow-gauge Denver and Rio Grande, which it then controlled. The DRG regained its independence before the two engines arrived, and so the ATSF rebuilt them to standard gauge, naming Number 111 "Little Butter-cup" from *H.M.S. Pinafore.* "Little Buttercup" became a favorite on the system because it often pulled Jim Moore's pay car. In 1886 the Topeka shop rebuilt Number 111 and gave it a new number. The rebuilt "Little Buttercup" remained in passenger service, pulling the Kansas City–Topeka local until January 18, 1923, when it was scrapped. For forty-four years the rebuilt engine gave the company maximum service.

The ATSF also cooperated with locomotive builders in experimenting with engine designs. In 1878 Baldwin built the enormous 2–8–0 "Uncle Dick" to conquer the 6 percent grades in the 2¾-mile-long switchback over Raton Pass. The "largest engine constructed by Baldwin" weighed 115,000 pounds, had 20-inch cylinders, 42-inch drivers and a tractive effort of 27,400 pounds. The saddle tank over the boiler contained 1,200 gallons of water, but it was soon replaced by a conventional tender. The low-drivered locomotive, with its first and third pairs of wheels having plain tires, could negotiate the 16 degree curves over the pass. "Uncle Dick" hauled seven loaded cars over the "hump," and in a twelve-hour day could move forty-six cars over the switchback southbound and a simi-lar number northbound. Two 4–4–0s in tandem could shift only thirty-four cars in the same time. "Uncle Dick" represented a giant step forward in terms of size—it had to be shipped west in pieces because much trackage could not support the weight of such a locomotive. Both Baldwin and the ATSF gained considerable insight into the construction of larger units from this successful collaboration.

Not all such experiments met with success. In 1889 the Santa Fe ordered a huge 4–4–2, or Atlantic type, as the wheel arrangement became known, from the Schenectady Works. Number 738 had a cab over its boiler—a Mother Hubbard—and a second cab at the rear for the fireman. A very poor performer, the 738 was soon rebuilt into a simple 4–4–0. The Atchison remained eager, however, for greater, more efficient power; and as the road spread into New Mexico and Arizona, orders were placed for more and larger locomotives.

The bulk of the Santa Fe fleet consisted of 4–4–0s, but each succeeding order saw increasingly larger locomotives utilizing the same wheel arrangement. In 1879 Baldwin built thirteen 4–4–0s with 17-inch cylinders, 57-inch drivers, and an overall weight of 73,000 pounds. Two years later another group of fifteen Baldwins weighed in at 78,000 pounds, the largest locomotives purchased by the ATSF to that time. By the end of the century the road had bought or built 480 Americans, but none was outstanding in design. The 4–4–0s remained in service until September 26, 1946, when the last unit was scrapped in Texas.

Early Atchison motive power came from many builders, including the Topeka shops. In 1881 the shop built a second "Cyrus K. Holliday," a 4–4–0. The next year Topeka constructed a second "William B. Strong," and the "T. C. Wheeler," last named locomotive on the line. The "Strong" cost $8,587 and like the "Holliday" it had six-inch air pumps and driver brakes, and was a coal burner. Superintendent of Machinery George Hackney designed a modified diamond stack for the "Strong," which proved to be a successful advance. Though the costs of building locomotives at Topeka compared favorably with prices charged by the major builders, Santa Fe needs were such that the company had to buy large groups of locomotives from Baldwin, Schenectady, Brooks and other builders.

Locomotive 1010, one of several used on Death Valley Scotty's Special. Santa Fe Railway

In 1880 the Santa Fe ordered forty-five 2–8–0s from Baldwin, fourteen of which were like "Uncle Dick," but with tenders rather than saddle tanks. These Consolidations, as the arrangement was known, became the workhorses of the Rio Grande, Mexico and Pacific divisions. The Lehigh Valley Railroad had begun to use 2–8–0s in 1872, and the design became the most popular type in the United States. In the early 1880s the ATSF purchased additional 2–8–0s from Baldwin, Brooks, Hinkley and Pittsburgh, and eventually owned 499 of the type. The Consolidations could pull the system's freight trains efficiently and reliably at moderate speeds over the mountain divisions, and the Atchison placed additional large orders for 2–8–0s in 1898 and 1900. Baldwin built an additional forty-five units in 1898, and forty more two years later. Initially, they each weighed 156,130 pounds and were the first locomotives Baldwin built with cast-steel frames. Although additional 2–8–0s came through purchases or through mergers with other lines, none was built for the ATSF after 1913. The Consolidation lasted, however, until the end of the steam era, working on branch lines or in switching service.

Just as the 2–8–0 became the backbone of the freight operation, the 4–6–0, or Tenwheeler, became the passenger power on divisions with heavy grades. In May 1879, Taunton delivered ten 4–6–0s for passenger service over Glorieta Pass between Las Vegas and Albuquerque, and in 1880 Pittsburgh supplied another class with the same wheel arrangement. Other Tenwheelers came from Schenectady and Baldwin in 1886–1887, and Brooks delivered a large order in 1891–1892. The Baldwin 4–6–0s were large in size, weighing 114,500 pounds, and had 19-inch cylinders, but the Brooks order of the early 1890s represented the beginnings of modern steam power on the Santa Fe. The Brooks design produced a tractive effort of 20,000 pounds, almost double that of other locomotives then in use. Another Baldwin group arrived in 1899 with cast-steel frames, 69-inch drivers, and a capability of producing 23,000 pounds of tractive effort. While the Atchison Tenwheelers totaled some 478 during the age of steam, most became obsolete very early. No more were built after 1901, and the last one was scrapped in 1939. Unlike the Southern Pacific, which used the 4–6–0 in larger numbers over a longer period of time, the Santa Fe found the Tenwheeler expendable as it sought to improve its motive power.

The Atchison's locomotive fleet grew to 233 units by 1881, and the Topeka shop employed 400 men to service and make heavy repairs on the engines. The average tractive effort reached 14,000 pounds, and the engines increased in efficiency. Major problems remained unresolved, however, as mutton tallow lubricants often failed, and the hard water along the system ruined boilers and flues. The minerals in the water clung to the metal of the flues, and the scale which developed caused the flues to burn out as often as every three months. The superintendents of mechanics and motive power constantly sought to keep the locomotives running, cure the water problem, eliminate fires along the line caused by sparks, and improve the lubricants available. Despite these efforts, the locomotives could pull only short trains at an average speed of 15 to 20 miles per hour. Not until the 1890s did advances in technology allow substantial gains in efficiency. By the nineties, steam pressure increased from 130–140 pounds per square inch in the boilers to 180 pounds; newer, longer lasting lubricants became available; and water treatment, of a primitive nature, increased the life span of flues. By 1898, Superintendent John Player could begin to retire some of the original power and purchase replacements of a modern design.

The motive power department not only developed new designs and initiated improvement programs but also tackled the rebuilding of old power and the salvaging of wrecks. The Topeka shop handled a variety of requests and met even the most difficult tasks. While working on the El Paso line in 1884, locomotive Number 196, a Hinkley 4–4–0 built in 1881, disappeared when caught in a flash flood along the Rio Grande. The quicksands of the river swallowed up 196, and soundings to a depth of sixty feet revealed not a trace. Two years later a crew of Mexican laborers found her as they dug a ditch over a mile away from where 196 had disappeared. The Santa Fe excavated the engine, placed it on flatcars, and sent the prodigal back to Topeka. The shop cleaned the locomotive, rebuilt the damaged parts, and put her back on the line. Just one of the many jobs given to the shop.

Sometimes the motive power department simply could not cope with poor designs or "strange beasts" which found their way to the engine roster. When the ATSF took over the Atlantic and Pacific it acquired nine 4–8–0s. These Twelvewheelers or "Mastodons" were about nine years old and lasted another thirty years, giving the maintenance men continual grief. Used on the Needles-Barstow-Bakersfield lines, the 4–8–0s, or "Tarantulas" as the ATSF crews referred to them, could pull heavy loads, but they built up huge amounts of scale and consumed vast quantities of fuel. The department urged, successfully, that the design not be duplicated. Indeed, much of the motive power ordered after 1895 was of a smaller size but more efficient.

The Mogul type, or 2–6–0, first came to the ATSF in 1880 with the purchase of six units from Taunton. Five more arrived in 1881 from Hinkley, and eventually the company owned a total of 119. Most major railroads invested in large numbers of these fast freight service locomotives. The Southern Pacific, for example, owned many more 2–6–0s than the Atchison, and some were built in their Houston shop as late as 1929. The Santa Fe bought fifty 2–6–0s from Baldwin in 1901, and this class had many modern attributes including larger cylinders, 200-pound boiler pressure, and 62-inch drivers. By the end of the 1920s, however, the Santa Fe scrapped nearly all of the Moguls, and only the acquisition of smaller lines which owned some kept the type from disappearing from the system. While the 2–6–0s were easy to maintain, they had limited starting power, and the Santa Fe found that the 2–6–2 Prairie type met its needs far better.

The Prairies never became one of the basic locomotive designs on American railroads, but the Santa Fe owned the largest fleet—238 units. The Santa Fe, Wabash, Milwaukee Road, CB&Q, and Northern Pacific used them for freight service on the plains and passenger service in the mountains, and eventually on branch and local lines. A Mogul with a set of trailing wheels, the Prairie carried a wide firebox with a large grate area which permitted easy hand firing. Some of the 2–6–2s on the ATSF were utilized in passenger service, but crews found the Prairie unstable at high speeds, and none was built after 1906–1907. Baldwin constructed forty units in 1901, and when delivered they were the heaviest passenger-service Prairies ever built. They mounted 79-inch drivers and yet were capable of operation over 16 degree curves. In 1902–1903 Baldwin delivered 103 units for freight use with smaller drivers of 69 inches. The Prairies soon were seen all over the system, and with their tractive effort of 43,200 pounds they pulled substantial freight over the plains country. Their advanced design allowed them to move short freight trains quickly, and though ultimately replaced by 4–6–2s and 2–8–2s, they remained on the roster until the end of World War II.

The growing need for a high-speed passenger locomotive capable of pulling heavy steel cars between Chicago and La Junta caused the Santa Fe to emulate the success of the 4–4–2, or Atlantic type, on a number of Eastern lines. The ATSF ordered ten Atlantics from Dickson Manufacturing Company of Scranton, Pennsylvania, in 1899, but they were so poorly designed that the ATSF rebuilt them into 4–6–0s. This experience did not frighten off the motive power department, which desired a locomotive with a four-wheel leading truck to provide good tracking and stability at high speeds. Samuel Vauclain of Baldwin designed a unit which the Santa Fe perceived as the answer to its needs. Four Atlantics of the 256 Class arrived in 1903, and their almost total success made the Atlantic the standard passenger locomotive on the ATSF for twenty years. Within the next six years the Santa Fe added 117 additional Atlantics and eventually owned 183. The Santa Fe Atlantics received widespread attention in the industry, and their ability to pull heavy passenger trains at sustained speeds produced favorable comments in the railway journals. Indeed, the

A "Bull Moose" Atlantic of 1910. H. L. Broadbelt

ATSF exhibited one of the Atlantics at the St. Louis Exposition in 1904. The last Atlantics, added to the roster in 1910, were the famous "Bull Moosers" of the 1480 Class. Their peculiarly "leggy," ungainly appearance belied their strength. The seventy-three "Moosers" rested on 73-inch drivers, could produce 24,900 pounds of tractive effort, carried smokebox reheaters and Walschaerts valve gear, and utilized a four-cylinder balanced compound system. In the 1920s they had their boilers shortened and were modernized for branchline passenger use. The Atlantics lasted until 1953, performing yeoman service through two world wars.

Locomotive design changes, new wheel arrangements, and larger, more powerful units met some of the system's needs, but fuel remained a seemingly insurmountable problem. From the outset the ATSF acquired coal properties in Kansas, and coal became the main source of fuel. As the line built westward the company purchased additional coal lands near Cañon City, Raton, and Trinidad. The Santa Fe operated several coal-mining subsidiaries in New Mexico and Kansas—the Cherokee and Pittsburgh Coal and Mining Company, for example. In 1879 the Santa Fe and the Maxwell Land Company formed the Raton Coal and Coke Company to develop coal mines at Dillon and Blossburg, and the railroad built spurs to the sites. The consumption of coal by the Santa Fe reached huge proportions by 1887, when the company mines produced 958,184 tons of which its locomotives burned 452,544 tons. The extension of the system to Chicago gave the ATSF access to large quantities of bituminous coal in Illinois; but west of Albuquerque the fuel problem became increasingly crucial.

Between Albuquerque and California, Santa Fe locomotives consumed vast amounts of coal and water, and neither was available in sufficient quantity or quality. A large coal deposit at Gallup produced inferior coal which had a low heat yield. The Gallup coal also burned poorly and came out the stacks in large cinders creating a constant fire hazard. The long hauls to the West meant that the ATSF had to stockpile coal, and the coal-storage sites and large water tanks were strung out across the desert wastes like irregularly shaped black pearls. Public criticism of railroad ownership of coal mines, bitter strikes by the miners, and low profit yields from the mining subsidiaries caused the ATSF to sell nearly all of its coal properties by 1905. Despite every effort to make coal more efficient—including screening and washing—the transportation costs alone forced the company to look for a substitute. The solution came from a California oil company, an answer to the operating department's prayers.

The Union Oil Company of California operated a refinery at Santa Paula on the Southern Pacific, and asked the SP if it would loan them a locomotive to use in conducting experiments with oil as a substitute for coal. The SP refused, and so Union approached the Southern California Railway, a Santa Fe subsidiary. The Southern California sent 4–4–0 Number 10 to Santa Paula, and some of its mechanics went along. Union worked on the locomotive, but when they fired her up, she could not move her own weight. The mechanics brought Number 10 back, but Union continued to experiment with new burner systems. The Santa Fe's San Bernardino shops cooperated in the experiments, and together they developed a flat nozzle which sprayed oil over a wide area of the firebox. With the new nozzle system in place, Number 10 moved over Cajon Pass, and the conversion of Santa Fe locomotives to oil burners began.

Executives of the Santa Fe saw oil as not only solving the fuel-shortage problem but also enhancing efficiency and profits as well. The discovery of large oil fields in California, Texas, Oklahoma and Kansas hastened the conversion process. By 1905 the company had converted 227 locomotives to oil, and the process did not stop until only the Chicago–Kansas City line remained on coal. The Atchison decided to acquire oil properties to meet its own fuel requirements, and in 1902 it purchased the Petroleum Development Company of California, which had 1,500 acres of Kern County land under lease. The Santa Fe continued to acquire other oil properties, establishing not only a large fuel reserve but also accelerating the railroad's diversification into nontransportation areas.

The conversion to oil symbolized the substantial changes taking place in the Atchison's motive-power holdings. In 1896 the railroad owned 962 locomotives, many of which were lightweight, worn out and in poor or nonoperating condition. During the next twenty years, however, the roster grew to 2,084 engines, most of which were newer and heavier, with greater tractive effort. The advent of modern steam on the Santa Fe came about around 1898. The ATSF reclassified and renumbered the entire roster, and many engines were designated for retirement. The arrival of a large group of 2–8–0s between 1897 and 1902 marked the transition to modern power. The average tractive effort in 1903 stood at 22,526 pounds, but by 1916 the average increased to 34,535 pounds. The average weight shot upward from 75 tons to 99 tons, an increase partially resulting from the purchase and construction of several Mallet types. For the most part the Atchison relied on the major builders for designs, working very closely with Samuel Vauclain of Baldwin. By 1900, the mechanical department began to make the major decisions on design changes, and within fifteen years the department drafted the blueprints and wrote the specifications for all orders. Teams of inspectors went from Topeka to the builder's shop to observe all phases of the construction process to guarantee quality. Baldwin, Pittsburgh, and the American Locomotive Company became the principal suppliers of motive power, but Topeka continued to build or rebuild locomotives. If any builder could be said to have dominated the ATSF engine roster it was Baldwin, which by 1907 had built 1,150 of the system's 1,850 locomotives. Yet Topeka had a mind of its own, and no builder could stand up against its demands, even when the Santa Fe was wrong.

Shortly after the turn of the century the Atchison mechanical department believed that substantial progress was being made toward the development of efficient and productive locomotives. The 4–6–0 became the standard passenger locomotive, but its cylinders were as large as the boiler allowed, and the firebox could not be expanded. The Consolidation became the standard freight locomotive, but it too had limited expansion possibilities, and the cylinders could not adequately service the drivers. The Stephenson valve gear, then common on the ATSF, tended to become overheated, was hard to lubricate, and failed at high speeds. The demands for greater speed and increased power produced metal fatigue and wasted huge quantities of steam. Prices were also increasing; a 2–6–0 in 1897 cost $10,181, but by 1907 the price had risen to $14,111. Whereas the Atchison paid $11,026 for a Tenwheeler in 1897, it laid out $19,580 for a Pacific in 1907. Regardless of rising costs, the company decided to embark on a program of large-scale locomotive purchases and to buy newer types. In order to expand fireboxes, four-wheel trailing trucks became necessary. If boiler capacity was to be increased, the boilers must be lowered on the frames. Walschaerts valve gear replaced the Stephenson, and builders were ordered to utilize a higher grade of steel. John Purcell, then mechanical assistant to the vice president, sought to reduce water and fuel stops to increase operating efficiency. A transcontinental train running from Chicago to Los Angeles required fifteen locomotives and numerous water and fuel stops. Purcell suggested an increase in tender sizes, and eventually 92 water stops and one-half of the fuel stops were eliminated on the run. The period of experimentation produced numerous successes, but one gigantic failure tends to dominate the history of the early years of modern steam locomotives on the Santa Fe—the company's abortive romance with compounding steam.

Stationary and marine steam engines possessed the ability to use steam a second time by compounding it prior to exhaust. A compound locomotive had two or more cylinders so arranged that the exhaust steam passed from one cylinder to another where it performed additional work before the exhaust cycle. As early as 1890 the Santa Fe attempted to adopt this concept for its locomotives. A Schenectady built 4–6–0, Number 440, was given compound cylinders, but the experiment failed. The Santa Fe tried cross-compounding with two cylinders, and later turned to the use of four cylinders, but this method of reusing steam did not prove highly successful either. Nevertheless, Topeka persisted in its determination, and a total of 956 compounds of various types could be found on the line. Samuel Vauclain helped the Santa Fe engineers in their efforts, and several classes of 2–8–2 Mikados, 2–10–0 Decapods, and a fleet of 2–10–2 Santa Fe types were built as four-cylinder tandem compounds. The ATSF tried several compounding methods on all sizes of power from 2–6–0s to Mallets, but none could be called a total success. The compounds could be discovered in engine yards just by listening as their extra set of exhausts produced a heavy gentle breath, but out on the road the sound became a blurred panting as the engineers sought to gain speed. With some strange kind of pathological determination, the Santa Fe continued developing compound locomotives until 1930, when the period of experimentation ended. Only a Mallet could successfully use compounding, but the penalty of a 30-mile-per-hour speed limit made the economics dubious on the Santa Fe's long western hauls.

While the compounding experiment did not produce resounding successes, Atchison innovations in other areas were imitated by much of the industry. J. W. Kendrick became third vice president of the ATSF in June 1901, and as an operations expert with a vast knowledge of locomotives he initiated a series of motive-power improvements. Kendrick pushed the builders hard to develop wide fireboxes supported by trailing wheels. Working in close consultation with Baldwin engineers, he designed locomotives which had many interchangeable parts. Some standard parts could be used by several different classes and by a variety of wheel arrangements. Kendrick also established a system of large folios for locomotive plans and drawings, and he instituted uniform methods of repairs in ATSF shops. The efficiency and effectiveness of the mechanical department reduced drastically the number of locomotive failures; in 1907 the road experi-

Baldwin-built Pacific of 1913—a Vauclain Compound. H. L. Broadbelt

enced one failure for each 4,222 miles traveled, but by 1946 the average was one failure for each 98,887 miles.

Kendrick also decided to purchase larger power, and in 1902 the Santa Fe received the first order of fifteen 2–8–2s. The Mikado replaced the Consolidation in freight service because their trailing wheels supported a larger firebox, which in turn helped develop greater tractive effort. Although originally designed for mountain freight service, the 2–8–2s soon could be found throughout the system hauling main line freights. The original design was conservative and utilitarian, and with minor variations the Atchison ordered 59 more in 1913 and 1916. These solid and dependable locomotives demonstrated the wisdom of Kendrick's program.

Similar needs for larger power in passenger service caused the Atchison to turn to Pacifics, the 4–6–2. The Pacific type represented an improvement and enlargement of the Tenwheeler, for the addition of a pair of trailing wheels allowed for a larger firebox and boiler, which gave the engine more weight for better adhesion. The Atchison became the major user of the 4–6–2 in the West, eventually owning 274 of the type; the SP, by comparison, owned only 166. In 1903 Baldwin delivered 41 balanced-compound Pacifics, the 1200 Class. The 1200s were the road's first modern passenger power, and they had single expansion, Stephenson valve gear. The Baldwin–Santa Fe design limited the wheelbase by coupling all pistons to the second driving axle, and located the pistons in the same horizontal plane. So successful were the Pacifics in handling the new heavy steel Pullmans and coaches that the Atchison purchased four additional classes by 1914. The 1200 Class received superheaters in 1915–1916, as well as new cylinders and Baker valve gear, and emerged as more powerful and handsome units. The Pacific and the Mikado improved operating efficiency, but the Santa Fe had to resort to helpers over the grades at Raton, Glorieta, Abo and Cajon, and Kendrick sought a more powerful locomotive for this purpose.

Kendrick and Baldwin designers drew up plans for a 2–10–0 Decapod which Baldwin built in 1902. The Decapod never became popular in the United States, but the Santa Fe thought the type had possibilities in helper service. Number 940 broke the world's weight record when built and was the most powerful locomotive in service anywhere. It was Baldwin's first tandem compound, and the experiment was not successful. The Atchison then purchased two additional 2–10–0s from Schenectady, but they too failed to meet the road's needs. The Decapod did produce a fortuitous thought in the mechanical department—why not take the Decapod, with its enormous power, add trailing wheels for a larger firebox and for guidance in reverse, and create a 2–10–2 road engine? A significant step forward had been made.

The Santa Fe and Baldwin worked together in 1902 to create an acceptable design, and in 1903 they produced the 2–10–2, or Santa Fe type in the Wythe classification. This direct descendant of the Decapod became the mainstay of the Atchison's freight service. The 2–10–2s carried four cylinders with the high-pressure cylinders behind the low-pressure cylinders, but operating on a common piston rod. Baldwin built 86 units in 1903–1904, the heaviest group of locomotives in the world. Thirty-nine of the 2–10–2s burned coal, the rest oil. They were a total success, and the Atchison purchased 74 more in 1905–1906, and 32 additional units were acquired in 1912–1913. John Purcell, the chief mechanical officer, simplified the design of the last class and ordered that the group receive the first builder-installed superheaters on the ATSF. For several years only the Atchison utilized the 2–10–2, but its enormously successful performance in pulling long, heavy freight drags soon produced orders by other railways. The pleasure of having designed such a useful locomotive did not deter the Atchison from additional experiments, and the mechanical department soon engaged in a brief and unhappy love affair with the Mallet.[3]

"Santa Fe" type No. 1654 for heavy-freight drags. H. L. Broadbelt

The fastest passenger power in the West. H. L. Broadbelt

In 1909 the mechanical department launched a series of efforts to develop huge locomotives capable of operating over steep grades with longer and heavier trains. Orders for Mallets went to Baldwin and the Topeka and San Bernardino shops where units were assembled—or disassembled—in an attempt to meet the requirements of the operating department. The designs utilized were supposed to exert maximum tractive effort, manipulate the curves over the various passes, and do so efficiently. What followed was a lengthy experiment with a variety of wheel arrangements using both coal and oil burners. This phase of motive-power development began with the construction of the two largest and most powerful passenger locomotives then in existence. Baldwin turned out Numbers 1300 and 1301 in 1909, and these enormous 4–4–6–2s produced a number of "firsts." They were the first Mallets with four-wheel leading trucks, and their 73-inch drivers were the largest ever applied to an articulated locomotive. They weighed 376,850 pounds, produced a tractive effort of 53,700 pounds, carried low-pressure cylinders and incorporated a flexible boiler system. Designed for fast passenger service, the 4–4–6–2s could easily pull nine or ten heavyweight cars at high speed. For six years the 4–4–6–2s worked the western lines, but in 1915 they were cut up into two Pacifics. They slipped easily, and the unbalanced sets of drivers just did not work. If articulated Mallets failed in high-speed passenger service, why not give them a try as slow, heavy freight power? Baldwin responded with yet another new design.

In 1909 the Santa Fe received two 2–8–8–2 giants, the largest locomotives of the time. The 1798 Class had 63-inch drivers and a rigid wheelbase of 16 feet but could negotiate curves with a radius of 1,360 feet quite satisfactorily. Superheaters gave them even greater power, and they were placed in helper service in the West. Once again enthusiasm for size outdistanced reasonable operating performance, and the units were cut up into 2–8–2s. Well, if you could split Mallets up into smaller power, why not weld smaller locomotives into Mallets? More orders to Baldwin and the Topeka shops!

Undeterred by failure, the management ordered Baldwin in 1910 to build two Prairie Mallets of a 2–6–6–2 configuration, and Topeka combined Numbers 1051 and 1171 into a homemade 2–6–6–2. These three high-wheeled freight locomotives were followed in 1911 by the 3300 Class, which had articulated boilers with flexible joints, but the pleating leaked steam and caused constant nightmares for crews and shopmen. The deep, wide firebox, mounted entirely behind the 69-inch drivers, rested on an outside bearing radial trailing truck. A highly advanced design for the era, the engine produced 62,400 pounds of tractive effort. The hinged boiler had 50 rings of carbon steel as a pleat, and flexible steam pipes led to the cylinders. Cinders in the pleats raised havoc, and the Santa Fe soon had some more 2–6–2s as the Prairie Mallets were divided. These were the last Mallets purchased; Santa Fe shops produced the remainder.

Topeka and San Bernardino took four 2–8–0s and joined them to Baldwin units to produce four 2–8–8–0s of the 3200 Class. After a few years they too were subdivided; but the "Mallet Mania" continued, and the Topeka shops received an extraordinary order in 1911: build ten 2–10–10–2s!

The shop proceeded to construct the largest locomotives in the world. Ten 2–10–2s of the 900 Class and 1600 Class were brought onto the shop floor and were merged with ten low-pressure units supplied by Baldwin. Baldwin also built ten gigantic "turtleback" tenders. The 57-inch drivers carried 616,000 pounds and produced a tractive effort of 111,600 pounds. Topeka dispatched the monsters to California for duty as helpers over Cajon. In service, they operated twenty to thirty cars behind the road unit and could lift an enormous tonnage. Their extraordinary weight meant significant wear on the track over the pass, and yet their size became a benefit in at least one instance. Engineer Frank McNeil had Number 3003 at the head of a long freight drag over Cajon, and after passing Summit entered the downgrade toward San Bernardino. As the train moved down the pass, the air brakes failed and McNeil had a runaway. But the 2–10–10–2 was so heavy that the freight cars could push it only 30 miles per hour downhill! McNeil's experience could not save the giants, and they were rebuilt into conventional 2–10–2s in 1915–1918.

The mind boggles at understanding why the Atchison, normally a conservative system, continued to pursue the elusive Mallet. In 1915 Baldwin actually drew up plans for a 2–8–8–8–8–2 at the Santa Fe's request, but

The giants of the Mallet era, the 2–10–10–2. H. L. Broadbelt

fortunately, only the plans were completed. This giant would have had four pairs of cylinders, a flexible boiler, two cabs, weighed 442 tons, and had a tractive effort of 200,000 pounds. The Atchison's courtship of the Mallet can only be described as a disaster; all of its Mallets were rebuilt or scrapped by 1934. Somehow the Santa Fe failed to learn from the successes of the Norfolk and Western, the Chesapeake and Ohio and the Baltimore and Ohio in the East or the Southern Pacific and the Union Pacific in the West, where Mallets became highly efficient machines. Like the Milwaukee Road and the Texas and Pacific, the Atchison's experience was almost exclusively negative. The Santa Fe simply did not understand the proper role and use of the Mallet, and much effort and money was wasted in pursuit of huge steam power. Between the "Cyrus K. Holliday" of 1869 and the 2–10–10–2s of 1911, fantastic progress had been achieved in locomotive size, power and efficiency, and after World War I even greater strides would be accomplished. The Atchison would become synonymous with modern steam locomotives operating great distances with maximum utilization. The period of experimentation led to more conservative types, and not even a world war and federalization would deter the course of the management in developing its own standards and designs.

9

Federalization and Normalcy

From the assassination of Austrian Archduke Franz Ferdinand in Sarajevo, Bosnia, on June 28, 1914, until the collapse of Wall Street's stock market on October 29, 1929, the Atchison, Topeka and Santa Fe Railway went through periods of turbulence, transition and prosperity. The onset of war in Europe in 1914 came at a time of significant labor unrest on the Atchison, and the federalization of the railways during the war and new federal laws regulating railway labor-management relations exacerbated the tensions long felt on the Santa Fe. Federal operation of the railway system during World War I was inefficient and costly to both the government and the railroads. With the restoration of peace in Europe and "normalcy" at home, William Benson Storey, the new president of the Santa Fe, sought to continue Edward P. Ripley's maintenance and expansion programs, and he did so in the midst of national prosperity and economic growth of massive proportions in the Southwest. Profits soared, traffic boomed and the Santa Fe savored "Coolidge prosperity." The euphoria of the twenties shattered during October 1929, and "the Crash" ushered in another era of struggle. The decade and a half from 1914 to 1929 found the Atchison management coping with modern railway problems, often with a nineteenth-century point of view, and succeeding, though painfully, in establishing new concepts of labor relations, transportation marketing and territorial growth.

Although one historian of the Atchison has viewed labor relations under Ripley as a golden age of teamwork, happy workers, high spirits and intense worker loyalty, this was not always the case. Labor strife on the Santa Fe was sometimes bitter, and Ripley's demands for ever-increasing efficiency provoked his employees to strikes. As early as 1900, a conflict between Ripley and the telegraphers suggested the deterioration of previously good relations. The strike by telegraphers in December came without the required thirty days' notice, but Ripley broke the strike and refused to sign another contract with the union until World War I. This pattern of action and overreaction continued in 1903 and 1904, when a bitter conflict with the machinsts' union ensued.

In May 1904, the International Association of Machinists struck the Santa Fe shops. The issue was not wages, but work rules. The machinists had demanded in December 1903 that work performed by apprentices and helpers be restricted and that all dismissals be reviewed by both parties. Ripley refused to agree to the demands, contending that they would lead to inefficiency and a loss of productivity. Violence occurred at several locations when the railway hired strikebreakers to replace the men. The strike eventually cost the Santa Fe $1.5 million, and months passed before the restoration of normal relations. Ripley made the situation worse by proclaiming in the 1904 *Annual Report* that "motive power is in better condition than before the strike; and the shop labor is more efficient."[1] He hired guards to protect the "new employees," many of whom were Japanese; the Japanese workers at the San Bernardino shop and the Los Angeles car-repair facility received $1.80 per day when the "regular" wage scale was $3.50. The strike, Ripley claimed, was of "no great importance." This attitude failed to ease the minds of some stockholders, and when rumors persisted that Ripley would be forced to resign, he denounced the machinists' union again. Once the heat of anger subsided, Ripley and his advisors realized that cordial relations had to be reestablished, that small tyrannies and harsh penalties for petty offenses had to be abolished, and that greater flexibility had to be provided for in the work rules. Shop efficiency and reduction of expenses depended upon harmony in labor relations.

Work rules on the Atchison had been based on the "Brown system" since July 20, 1897. The system utilized a "discipline by record" whereby men received merits and demerits for their work; accumulated demerits could lead to reprimands, suspension or even discharge. Merits could be used, however, to offset demerits. Each employee had an account or record with the railway, and foremen entered detailed reports for each man. Though the management maintained that the Brown system produced greater efficiency and gave employees a sense of job security, cost analysis of shop operations suggested otherwise. The average annual repair cost for a locomotive on the Santa Fe was $3,042, double the figure on the

Chicago and Northwestern, $800 more than on the Pennsylvania and $1,000 more than on the Illinois Central. Locomotive repair costs per mile were $9.97 on the ATSF, $7.11 on the Baltimore and Ohio and $5.81 on the IC. The average cost of freight car repairs on the Atchison was $101, while the CNW spent $38 and the B&O only $35. Ripley had to reduce costs and yet assuage the growing bitterness of his employees.

In a new approach to the labor situation, Ripley inaugurated a "betterment" system. Betterment entailed a program of automatic and unlimited pay increases, plus bonuses, for outstanding performance, with pay scales related to the quantity and quality of work produced by each man. Foremen kept detailed records of individual output and the level of performance. Emphasis on productivity without increased costs to the railway would bring greater efficiency to the shops according to the betterment concept. Shop organization almost became an art as foremen sought to maximize worker output and as each man attempted to attain a higher level of production. Tools and parts were standardized to speed the flow of cars and locomotives through the shops, and the department of testing and the chemical department cooperated with the operations and maintenance departments in the betterment program. Stores and the mechanical department worked together to move parts and supplies to the locales where they were needed. Standard times for the performances of tasks

were established, and bonuses were paid for work accomplished in less than the standard. The railway created, in essence, a contract with each shopman and promised better wages, bonuses and improved working conditions for higher levels of performance.

The betterment program worked. Wages of the shopmen rose an average of 10 to 20 percent between 1903 and 1906, and improvements in shop efficiency were even more pronounced. The new procedures saved $1 million yearly in the locomotive shops alone, and, more importantly, labor relations improved markedly. This could be attributed partially to the betterment scheme, but also to a new apprentice program, a system of company pensions and expansion of employee services.

National interest in apprentice training programs became sharply focused in the first decade of the century. "Progressive" educators, efficiency experts, social reformers and secondary-school administrators endorsed apprentice programs, and the Santa Fe responded with its own apprenticeship schools. As early as 1900 John Purcell organized classes for apprentices at the Shopton, Iowa, facility, but the program was quite small. In August 1907, Ripley established a system-wide apprentice school on a large scale. A supervisor of apprentices, reporting to the assistant vice president and chief mechanical officer, recruited young men between the ages of 16 and 22 for the program. They were examined by shop

Olathe, Kansas, yard in the days of steam. Santa Fe Railway

instructors and selected on the basis of previously acquired skills, interest and general knowledge, although preference was given to sons of ATSF employees. The apprentices worked ten-hour days in the four-year program with at least 300 days devoted to shop work. A minimum of two hours each day was spent in class instruction, with each class limited to 25 students. The apprentices received $1.50 to $2.00 per day in wages. The training exposed the apprentices to a variety of work experiences to enable them to select the area they liked best and for which they were most qualified. Apprentice shop boards evaluated their performance and met with each student once a month to discuss his progress. The apprentices organized athletic teams, bands and glee clubs, had access to ATSF reading rooms and recreation halls, but were forbidden to use tobacco or intoxicants. For exceptionally talented young men a one-year "Special Apprentice Course" offered an opportunity for more rapid advancement. Between September 30, 1907, and January 31, 1914, some 803 men had enrolled in the course, and 490 had graduated. The program grew to include 29 schools, 38 full-time instructors and 800 apprentices. Seventy-five percent of the graduates of the program stayed with the ATSF, and 12 percent were in official positions by 1914. Over 8,000 men had graduated from the program through 1950, and most officials in the mechanical department had been apprentices. The apprentice schools supplied the company with skilled labor, trained in its own shops, with a unique sense of loyalty to the firm.

Another venture in employee relations was the *Santa Fe Magazine*. Stenographer Albert MacRae urged the railway to create a monthly magazine to tell its story, and Ripley named MacRae the first editor. The magazine's circulation reached a peak of 80,000 copies as it sought to explain the system and its operations to the employees. The first issues condemned gambling, alcohol and tobacco, but the moral aspect was soon discontinued. A "house" news organ, the magazine became a means to inform and enlighten workers and to establish a sense of "family" on the system.

Ripley also sought to create a greater sense of *esprit de corps* with a pension plan. In December 1906, the board of directors established a board of pensions to administer a company-paid-for program. The ATSF offered retirement benefits to any employee who at age 65 had fifteen years of continuous service, or for any man who became physically incapacitated. The benefits, based on a sliding scale, ranged from a maximum of $75 per month to a minimum of $20, and "special cases" could receive a bonus of up to 25 percent. The Santa Fe funded the plan at no direct cost to the workers; few other roads had such programs. During the next twenty-eight years the number of beneficiaries increased as did the cost to the Atchison.

The Santa Fe also made modest contributions to a system of company-sponsored hospitals. Railroading had long been a hazardous occupation, and the need for a systematic health program became apparent to the management early in the company's history. The ATSF and its workers formed the Atchison Railroad Employees Association. The association hired a surgeon and an assistant, paying them with funds derived from a monthly fee of 25¢ to $1.00 from each worker. The railroad made small donations to the association, which opened hospitals in Las Vegas and La Junta. The railroad gave land for the hospital sites and contributed toward building and equipment costs. Dr. John Kaster became the chief surgeon in 1887, serving in that capacity for forty years. The expansion of the Atchison led to the formation of four regional associations in 1891. These associations operated seven hospitals by 1916, with the largest located at Topeka. The members of the association elected trustees who hired doctors, provided good medical care at a low cost, managed the hospitals and invested the monthly payments to develop additional capital. The ATSF provided free transportation to the association trustees and their medical staffs and encouraged employees to participate.

The Santa Fe also promoted the railroad YMCA along its routes. A. A. Robinson gave the Topeka YMCA its start in 1882 by providing space in an old house owned by the railroad. The YMCA received the support of the railroad because the "Y" kept the men out of saloons and provided "clean" recreation. The YMCAs had small libraries and game rooms, and some contained sleeping rooms and baths. The Santa Fe contributed $22,000 to the Topeka YMCA in 1902, and President Theodore Roosevelt laid the cornerstone for a new building the following year. The YMCA along the Santa Fe reached its zenith in the years before World War I, but then entered into decline.

The decline of the YMCAs occurred as the Atchison expanded its system of reading rooms. On November 1, 1898, Ripley appointed S. E. Busser as superintendent of reading rooms, and Busser began to expand the nearly dormant program. Busser believed that if the Santa Fe would "Give a man a bath, a book, and an entertainment that appeals to his mind and hopes by music and knowledge, and you have enlarged, extended and adorned his life; and, as he becomes more faithful to himself, he is more valuable to the company."[2] Busser established rooms along the system, purchased books and furniture, and formed local clubs to keep them operating. At Raton he converted the old Harvey House into a reading room and added a bowling alley and billiard room. At Needles, in the middle of the desert, some $60,000 was spent on the reading room, which included a gym and a swimming pool. By 1909 the rooms represented an investment of $250,000 in facilities, employed a staff of 46, and cost $75,000 a year to operate. Busser organized Chautauqua-like entertainments for the rooms, and traveling troupes and lecturers performed for the workers and their families. These performances were particularly important to employees living in the remote desert and plains towns.

These company-sponsored programs attempted to establish employee loyalty, a loyalty to the ATSF which would transcend the worker's commitment to the labor unions. The unions would also have less appeal because of the significant changes taking place in the composition of the work force, or so it was felt. The old Irish section gangs largely disappeared, and Mexican-Americans and southwestern Indians replaced them. The *Santa Fe Magazine* reported in 1913 that supervisors and foremen found that the Mexican laborers performed railroad work exceptionally well at first, but that they became less motivated as they became "Americanized." The ATSF issued Spanish dictionaries to the foremen as the Mexican-American force continued to grow.

But if Ripley hoped that more benefits and new groups of workers would dilute support for the unions and reduce their demands, he was wrong. The brotherhoods continued to press for additional benefits and higher wages and for national and state legislation to aid the workers. The threat that Ripley had seen in terms of legislative rate making was paralleled in labor relations. In 1914 he wrote:

> . . . the threatening attitude of the labor organizations must not be lost sight of. . . . Your company has always shown the utmost consideration for its employees, and as a class they are a credit to themselves and the road. Left to themselves there would be little of which to complain, but the organizations as a body have been aggressively demanding increased wages for their members with no regard for the ability of their employers to pay, and have been steadily demanding, and frequently with success, many varieties of legislation, such as full-crew bills, designed to increase operating expenses.[3]

Hoping to offset organized labor's attraction, Ripley announced another company program for the employees. On July 1, 1916, the railway instituted a death benefit plan for employees with two or more years continuous employment. Families of deceased workers received 5 percent of the wages earned the previous twelve months multiplied by the total number of years of employment. The minimum benefit was $250 and the maximum was $3,000. The experimental plan operated for a trial period of two years, and it then became a permanent benefit financed entirely by the ATSF. The program continued until the inception of the Railroad Retirement Act of 1934, and over 5,000 beneficiaries received payments during the plan's existence.

Neither the retirement program nor the death benefit retarded the growth of the political power of the railroad brotherhoods. While the Santa Fe had contracts with only the Trainmen and the Engineers, the brotherhoods grew in size and strength on other carriers and developed a significant bloc of support in the Congress. Responding to the demands of the railroad unions, Congress passed the Adamson Bill in 1916, establishing the eight-hour day for most railway workers. Despite pleas by railroad managers, President Wilson signed the bill, which became effective on September 2. Ripley's ire against the Adamson Act was such that the annual 10 percent Christmas bonus, some $2,750,000, was granted to all employees with two or more years of service earning $2,500 or less per year, *except* those covered by the new federal law. The act sharply increased labor costs but served only as a prelude to an even more difficult period for the nation's rail network.

As the United States increased sales of munitions and foodstuffs to the Allies in Europe in 1915–1916, the railway network sought to cope with vast shipments of goods to Atlantic and Gulf ports. The strain on the railways in the Northeast began to show in the spring and summer of 1917. The United States entered the war on April 7, 1917, and the rush of cargoes and personnel to Eastern ports reached massive proportions. A car shortage developed as traffic increased 30 percent in 1916 and 43 percent in 1917. The American Railway Association had attempted to draft a plan to cope with such emergencies as early as 1915, but the association could not deal with the traffic jams at ocean terminals. The rampant inflation of 1916–1917 caused the railroad brotherhoods to demand cost-of-living increases, and it raised the specter of a national rail strike. When a decline in available shipping in the ports created additional traffic chaos, the federal government moved to seize the railroads. At noon on December 28, 1917, President Wilson, using an authority granted by the Federal Possession and Control Act, seized the rail system. The Rail-

The "Prairie Mallet"—a nightmare for crews. H. L. Broadbelt

road Control Act of March 1, 1918, established a payment plan to protect the rights of the stockholders and bond owners. The U.S. Railroad Administration operated the system and paid compensation equal to the average net operating income during the previous three years ending June 30, 1917. The USRA also maintained the tracks and repaired the equipment. The companies would be returned to their owners within twenty-one months following the termination of hostilities.

The USRA reorganized the nation's rail system and coordinated the flow of traffic. Secretary of the Treasury William G. McAdoo became the director general of the USRA, and Walker D. Hines, former chairman of the Santa Fe's board of directors, became assistant director general. Former Santa Fe Vice President Edward Chambers served as director of the division of traffic and Ford Harvey became an advisor on dining facilities. Hines actually ran the USRA as McAdoo's Treasury office kept him away from day-to-day operations. Despite his previous role as an opponent of the Adamson Act and governmental regulation of the railroads, Hines changed his views, and later, when he succeeded McAdoo as Director General, came to favor strong public regulation with continued private ownership of the system. He tried to persuade President Wilson to establish as a national goal a coordinated federal rail policy to protect investors, shippers and workers, but the president, too busy with war and peace, did not respond.

Operation of the Santa Fe by the USRA produced mixed results. William Benson Storey became federal manager of the ATSF while Ripley remained president. All off-line offices were closed, and ticket agencies were combined with those of other railways. The railroads routed traffic over their former competitors, and shippers were not allowed to designate routes as the USRA sought to maximize efficiency. Luxury passenger services ended, and terminal operations were combined. Under USRA, railroads were ordered to repair equipment owned by other lines, and Atchison maintenance costs climbed from $22,657,796 in 1916 to $46,020,979 in 1919 and $58,375,927 in 1920. The movement of men and material became the principal operating goal, and, as a result, losses mounted. Ripley and other railway leaders sought higher rates from the ICC in 1917, as profit levels either failed to rise or actually declined. In the *Annual Report* for 1916 Ripley had noted that profits were up only because of the war in Europe and that the percentage of income to property investment had declined even before federalization, as the following figures show.

RATE OF RETURN, 1896–1914[4]

1896 (six months)	.65	1906	5.71
1897	1.57	1907	6.31
1898	2.26	1908	4.73
1899	2.86	1909	6.11
1900	4.19	1910	5.58
1901	5.05	1911	5.59
1902	5.44	1912	5.36
1903	5.07	1913	5.63
1904	5.31	1914	5.08
1905	4.51		

Responding to the pleas of Ripley and other "civilian" executives, the USRA raised rates in June 1918, with increases of 28 percent on freight and 18 percent on passenger rates. Yet the increases in revenues which resulted failed to cover substantial new wage hikes and rising taxes.

The USRA work rules and pay scales caused labor costs to soar. The cost of living rose 40 percent between 1915 and 1917, and the average wage for railroad workers rose from $828 to $1,004. The Railroad Wage Commission of the USRA found that 51 percent of the workers earned $75 per month or less and 80 percent earned $100 or less, and the commission inaugurated a new sliding-wage scale which provided retroactive pay increases from January 1, 1918. McAdoo issued a general order on May 25, 1918, raising the average wage, which reached $1,485 in 1919 and $1,820 in 1920. USRA work rules did establish equal wages for women and end some discrimination against blacks, but other work rules created substantial "featherbedding." The USRA worked closely with the railroad brotherhoods, and negotiated blanket contracts which brought almost total unionization to the Atchison for the first time.

Federal and state tax bills also increased as the government levied a 2 percent corporate income tax, a 4 percent war income tax and an excess profits tax. Between 1916 and 1917 the Atchison's federal tax bill rose from $862,334 to $4,838,283 and state levies from $5,905,821 to $7,094,077, for a total increase of $5,164,205, or an amount equal to 19.79 percent of net operating revenue. These labor and tax costs had to be paid out of the USRA established rate structure, creating a substantial change in the Atchison's transportation ratio, or the ratio of transportation expenses to gross revenue, as seen in the following figures.

TRANSPORTATION RATIO, 1912–1923[5]

Year Ending June 30,	1912	31.31
	1913	30.06
	1914	30.44
	1915	29.60
	1916	28.62
Year Ending December 31,	1917	31.37
	1918	35.48 USRA
	1919	36.05 USRA
	1920	38.75 USRA (8 mo. control)
	1921	35.07
	1922	31.59
	1923	30.82

To compensate the Atchison for use of the system the USRA agreed to a yearly rental of $42,885,310. *The Wall Street Journal* reported that if the ATSF had operated under its own management it would have earned 8.35 percent in 1919. Net operating income declined, however, and the USRA paid only rent, not lost profits. The USRA operation of the Santa Fe was more successful than its use of other lines, and the USRA "lost" only a small sum renting the Atchison. The federalization experience proved to be less than a total success.

In January 1919, the USRA stood in disarray. Hines seemed unable to halt a sharp decline in traffic and earnings, and Wilson, who wanted federal control to end, ordered the railroads returned to their owners on March 1, 1920. His directive pleased no one; the railroad owners demanded fiscal adjustments for USRA operations; the brotherhoods demanded continuation of labor's gains; and shippers sought permanent rate controls and a general tariff reduction. Congress responded with the Transportation Act of 1920 which guaranteed the railroads an income of not less than half the previous rate during the first six months following termination of federal control. The railroads protested the proposed payments, and adjustments were made. (The Atchison, for example, received an additional $21.5 million in 1922.) The additional payments underscored the serious financial losses of the USRA. During World War I, the railroads paid $146 million in federal taxes, while the USRA lost $1.6 billion. These figures would stand in sharp contrast with the $4.2 billion in taxes paid by the railroads during World War II, and without a USRA. The USRA experience forced the federal government to create an entirely new regulatory policy to enable the industry to meet the growing crises. The government's response was the Transportation Act.

The temporary federalization of the industry produced numerous schemes for federal action. The brotherhoods supported the Plumb Plan for federal ownership, a proposal vigorously opposed by the railroads. Congress took a middle course between nationalization and a return to pre–1917 regulation by passing the Transportation Act. The new federal law ended the absolute compulsion for competition and encouraged mergers which were in the public interest. The legislation established a fund to aid financially ailing railways by recapturing all rail profits exceeding 6 percent. Weak roads could borrow from the fund created by taxing the strong carriers. Further, a federal plan to merge the network into several large units was authorized. The ICC would attempt to establish a "fair" rate of return of 5.5 percent and was given control over railway security issues. The federal government would become a positive force in the transportation sector, the sponsors of the law believed, and the ICC responded quickly by increasing rates 33⅓ percent on interterritorial shipments and by 25 percent in the southern territory and 40 percent in the eastern and trunk line regions.

The Transportation Act also created a nine-man Railroad Labor Board to hear labor disputes. Despite the wage hikes under the USRA, the new work rules and the Adamson Act, organized labor remained unhappy, and wildcat strikes, such as that of ATSF shopmen in January 1919, became the norm. The labor board established subsidiary boards to hear disputes and urged board members to render decisions based on reasonable wages and working conditions. The labor board granted a general 22 percent wage increase in 1920; but when falling revenues led to a wage reduction of 12 percent the following year, the railway workers held a strike vote. The carriers, meanwhile, asked for the termination of national work rules and a return to local regulations. A compromise maintained the peace for a brief period, but again in 1922 the shopmen struck in a long and bitter dispute. The strike on the ATSF was "disastrous," and the railway hired new men and brought pensioners out of retirement to keep the shops open. Over 3,000 passengers were marooned in Arizona and California when train crews joined the strikers. A company union replaced the shopmen's union, adding to the bitterness, and when the strike terminated, many men were not rehired. The Railroad Labor Board brought the strike to an end, but not before severe damage to labor-management relations had occurred.

In some respects 1919–1920 served as a watershed in the history of the Atchison. Federal control ended, but labor retained most of its gains. The ICC began to operate with its new guidelines and principles, and the economy entered into a growth period, especially in the Southwest. Significant changes in the Atchison's management took place as directors Henry

William Benson Storey, president of the Atchison from 1920 to 1933. Santa Fe Railway

Clay Frick and Augustus Julliard died in 1919, and President Ripley died on February 4, 1920. They were nineteenth-century railroad men in their thinking and responses, and the ATSF needed, and received, a new generation of junior executives with twentieth-century ideas. These young men felt that railroads had to do more than just carry goods and people. The Atchison needed to increase its aid to farmers along its routes as they fought to survive the vagaries of the marketplace and the weather. Industries meant cargoes, and the ATSF needed to encourage the establishment of plants and factories in its territory. Indeed, facilities must be built by the railway itself to promote traffic growth. These policies required new departments and publications, trained advisors and capital outlays. Ripley had moved forward along these lines before 1920, but his successor, William Benson Storey, reshaped the management and expanded the company's operations and services.

William Benson Storey came aboard with the acquisition of the San Francisco and San Joaquin Valley Railroad in 1901. A native of California, Storey was born in San Francisco in 1857, educated at the University of California, and had been a surveyor and engineer for various Golden State railroads. After joining the Santa Fe, he moved up through the ranks serving as chief engineer on the Eastern Lines, chief engineer for the system, and in 1909, vice president in charge of construction. A year later he became vice president of the construction and operating department. He supervised the rebuilding of the Chicago–Kansas City line, finished the Belen and Coleman cutoffs, managed the Atchison for the USRA, and succeeded Ripley as President on January 1, 1920. Storey saw the need to help develop the economy of the Santa Fe's territory, and he began to emphasize the industrial department, a move symbolic of the changes which took place after 1920.

The Atchison corporate structure included an agriculture department and a livestock department, and in response to the changing economy of the region, the management had added an industrial department. The primary emphasis before 1920 had been on agriculture and colonization, and, in 1910 the agriculture department had been organized to promote the growth of farming along the Santa Fe and to aid farmers in developing scientific methods. Experts toured the region and urged farmers to use better seeds and improved strains of livestock. The ATSF furnished 50,000 bushels of free seeds between 1911 and 1918, asking only that agriculturalists plant ten-acre plots with the seeds in order to make comparisons with varieties previously used. The agricultural department also urged farmers to diversify their production and to substitute alfalfa, milo, barley, maize, kaffir and other grains for wheat and cotton. The experts encouraged expansion of livestock, both for meat and dairy products; and twenty-five demonstration trains toured the line promoting the slogan "A Cow, Sow and Hen." The Santa Fe helped establish organizations of young people similar to 4H Clubs and the Future Farmers of America, and it sponsored the first Kaffir Club in the nation in Nolan County, Texas. The agriculture department also continued the railway's colonization program.

Although the land department had been discontinued in 1897, the railway continued to promote land sales along its routes, particularly in West Texas. Each new farm produced an average of $300 yearly in railway revenue, and C. L. Seagraves, general colonization agent, worked diligently to place colonists near the Atchison's lines. J. D. Tinsley, a soil specialist, and Professor Harry Bainer of the Colorado Agricultural and Mechanical College toured new farms for the ATSF, giving expert advice to the recently arrived colonists. As early as 1911 these men sounded a call for contour plowing and moisture-conserving methods. When the Santa Fe Land Improvement Company purchased 340,000 acres of land between Dodge City and Elkhart, the railway built a new branch into the area. A nation-wide advertising campaign attracted buyers for the farm properties who paid one-eighth down and 6 percent interest on the balance for the farms. In four years 150,000 acres had been sold at an average price of $15.00 per acre. The railway also advertised free federal lands which were available under the Homestead and Desert Land Acts. A Santa Fe publication, *Earth*, issued as many as 100,000 copies each month, and the ATSF distributed some twenty-three bulletins on various agricultural topics.

The colonization and diversification efforts continued after World War I. An ATSF demonstration farm attracted 400,000 visitors in twenty-three months, and six exhibition trains toured the line in 1922–1924. Agricultural colleges in Oklahoma, Texas, Kansas and Colorado furnished speakers, at the railway's expense, and they encouraged farmers to reduce the production of staples and to switch to cows, hogs and poultry. The trains also featured model-farm kitchens and home demonstration agents who aided the wives of the farmers. The Santa Fe encouraged the settlers by moving their effects at low rates, and in 1926 some 3,302 carloads were shipped to Texas, California, Colorado, Kansas and other southwestern states. One estimate suggests that between 1911 and 1946, some 750,000 people attended agricultural programs or visited demonstration trains sponsored by the railway. The agricultural department made significant contributions to carloadings, but its program was essentially the same as that carried on before 1900. The major economic changes in the twentieth century came through the efforts of the industrial department.

The industrial department originated in 1902 but did not become a significant factor in the ATSF's structure until after 1922. By 1912 the department claimed to be bringing to the Santa Fe's lines an average of $16 million per year in investment capital in the form of cement plants, glass works, sugar beet refineries and similar operations. But the promotion of industrial sites did not hit full stride until the twenties. The railway began to publish bulletins on "New Industrial Sites in the West and Southwest," and this emphasis on locational opportunities aided traffic growth along the Santa Fe. Storey and the board became convinced, however, that the railway should invest its own money in commercial operations and committed the ATSF to three major urban projects.

One of the Atchison's first urban developments was the Chicago Produce Terminal. The South Water Street Market in Chicago had long served as a primary distribution point for California and Texas produce and for tropical fruit delivered by the Illinois Central from New Orleans. The construction of Wacker Drive forced the market to move, and another location near the central part of the city had to be found. The Atchison and the IC jointly proposed and developed a new site along the ATSF's tracks. Over 150 merchants moved to the new terminal, which cost the market $17 million and the railroads $8 million. The mile-long market covered 112 acres of land, and the four yards surrounding the building were capable of holding 1,825 refrigerator cars. The terminal partially opened in 1925, with full use achieved on August 15, 1927. The facility handled an unprecedented volume of fruit and vegetables, becoming the second largest such market in the world.

Engine 3937, built by Baldwin in 1927, hauls a freight train in Cajon Pass, California. Santa Fe Railway

Another large-scale urban investment project developed by the Atchison was the Terminal Building in Dallas. Dallas grew from a small town of 38,067 in 1890 to a major city of 158,976 people in 1920. One of the primary businesses of the second largest city in Texas was the distribution of goods, and the Atchison sought to obtain the bulk of that traffic. The ATSF entered Dallas only from the south, providing a poor connection to the Galveston-Chicago line; but this could be partially offset by constructing the best freight distribution facility available. The removal of the Gulf, Colorado and Santa Fe passenger operation to the new Union Station in 1916 opened for development the site of the old passenger station on Commerce Street. Local businessmen opposed a plan by the Dallas city government to route a highway through the site, hoping that it could be utilized for a large commercial project. The ATSF decided to take advantage of the excellent downtown location and turn the plot into an office building and distribution center. In 1923 the Santa Fe organized the Terminal Building Corporation of Dallas to construct the four-unit building. Built of concrete faced with terra-cotta, the terminal consisted of a 19-story office building, two 10-story warehouses, and an 8-story warehouse. A continuous basement below the streets linked the four units which contained 1.2 million square feet of storage area. Submerged railroad tracks passed under the four units, and a steamless locomotive moved cars below the warehouses. Twenty-five elevators moved goods from the tracks into the buildings. The 8-story building contained the largest cold-storage plant in the Southwest. Over 100,000 cubic yards of earth were removed at the four-block-long site, which extended from Commerce to Young Street. Construction commenced on September 1, 1923, and the facility opened in the summer of 1925. The office tower, the Santa Fe Building, housed the University Club of Dallas on its top floor. For thirty years the facility attracted substantial traffic for the ATSF, but the vertical storage concept became obsolete after World War II. The decision to use Atchison capital for urban development, and the successful operations in Chicago and Dallas, led the Storey team to enter an even larger project in Los Angeles.

The city of Los Angeles had boomed after the Santa Fe arrived in the 1880s; and while the rate of growth subsequently slowed, the population swelled to 102,479 in 1900 and to 576,672 in 1920. During the twenties another boom ensued and the population more than doubled, reaching 1,283,048 in 1930. As Los Angeles grew, its chamber of commerce became worried at the lack of a manufacturing base and entered upon a campaign to develop a "balanced prosperity" for the city. The chamber of commerce worked closely with the railroads to develop industrial sites and to attract factories from the East and Midwest. As a result of these promotional efforts, climatic advantages, harbor development and an expanding labor force, employment and production in industry leaped dramatically in the twenties. One of the major contributors to this growth was the Central Manufacturing District. Los Angeles developers began to create the CMD in 1923, with the construction of a $5 million warehouse. The ATSF reached the CMD over the Los Angeles Junction Railroad; and as the district grew, Storey and the board became interested in its potential. The site was six miles long and one mile wide, the largest privately owned industrial district in the world, and was located only four miles from the center of Los Angeles. A large cauliflower farm when purchased by developers, the CMD soon became a massive industrial center. The corporate structure included the land, the 6-story warehouse, the Union Stockyards and the junction railway. By 1928 some 50 acres had been sold, and 74 plants had been built. Storey and the board formed the Western Improvement Company, which purchased the CMD on February 1, 1928. The next year the ATSF added part of the Bandini Estate to the property, which provided 1,135 additional acres for development. The value of buildings in the CMD soon reached $15 million as local and national firms established offices, distribution facilities and manufacturing and assembly plants. The industries included firms in rubber products, automotive supplies, food processing and metal fabrication. The scope of the operation can be seen in the enormous exchange of freight cars between the ATSF

Pullmans and Café cars for the flapper and the "jellybean." Historical Collection, Security Pacific National Bank

and the Junction Railroad; by 1952 the LAJRR provided the Santa Fe with 3.1 percent of *all* cars received from connecting lines. Land sales remained good until the depression of the thirties, but World War II ushered in a boom which continued into the next two decades. The value of the ATSF's holdings reached $16 million by 1952, with operating revenues of $3 million; and Los Angeles became the leading producer of freight revenue and gross earnings on the Atchison, partially as a result of the CMD's growth. The development of the district also helped provide Los Angeles with its widely decentralized industrial base and contributed to its sustained prosperity.

"Coolidge Prosperity" throughout the Southwest created profits which allowed Storey to improve and rebuild the Atchison. Traffic peaked in volume in 1920, slid lower until 1926, but then accelerated until the fall of 1929. Freight traffic held strong throughout most years, but automobiles and buses took passenger traffic away in every year but 1922. When the federal government relinquished control of the system in 1920, the ATSF had a firm base upon which to build; the railway owned 2,159 locomotives, 73,464 freight cars and 1,580 passenger cars. Transportation expenses were, however, much larger than before 1917. In 1923, Storey noted that where the ATSF spent $1.00 for labor in 1915, it spent $2.15 eight years later, and where it had paid $1.00 for taxes, it now paid $3.69. Further, where it had received $1.00 for freight service, consumers paid only $1.39 in 1923. Expenses climbed, making economy and operating improvements the management's goals. Storey had faith in the Atchison and the people the railway served, and he asked the board and the stockholders to approve a massive capital expenditures program to rehabilitate and expand the Santa Fe.

Major reconstruction programs throughout the twenties concentrated on relaying rails, building new bridges, constructing larger terminals and relocating tracks to reduce grades and curvature. In 1924 the Santa Fe had 6,934 miles of 90-pound rail and 2,296 miles of 85-pound rail; but two years later Storey announced that 110-pound rail would become standard on the main line and that 450 miles of new, heavier rail would be laid. In several locations second tracks were laid or long passing sidings constructed. A new terminal facility in Tulsa improved traffic from that growing city; the shops at San Bernardino were expanded; and to serve the growing Panhandle and Santa Fe, a 14-story office building was constructed in Amarillo. The Mississippi River bridge at Fort Madison, built in 1887 and long a bottleneck, was replaced in 1927. The new bridge carried two tracks and a highway across its swing-span of 525 feet, then the longest in the world. The capital expenditures on track, buildings and bridges paralleled outlays for freight equipment needed to carry the diversified traffic of the system.

The economy of the Southwest changed materially in the twenties. Agriculture expanded, though not as rapidly as manufacturing, and timber, stone and minerals declined in importance as industrial and consumer products increased their share of the freight traffic. Petroleum discoveries in California, Texas, Oklahoma and Kansas created a demand for tank cars, and the burgeoning citrus and produce farms of the Southwest demanded more efficient refrigerator cars and faster movement to markets. Storey responded with massive purchases of equipment and substantial modernization of existing cars. The 71,992 cars of 1919 grew to 87,060 during the decade, and the average capacity increased from 36 tons to 40 tons. In 1926, for example, the board allocated over $9 million for 1,500 boxcars, 300 coal cars, 1,000 refrigerator cars, 150 cabooses and 58 passenger cars. The growing economy and the modern freight car fleet enabled Storey to expand and improve freight operations.

The significant developments in freight traffic in the twenties were growing diversification, reduced rates and a decline in the average distance of freight hauls. Copper replaced coal as the leading mineral, while oil and sulphur cargoes jumped from minimal to substantial proportions. Yet gross earnings per train mile slipped from 1.316¢ to 1.234¢, and the average distance for freight hauls declined from 347 miles to 325. Storey responded to these trends with a hard-hitting promotional program. Traffic representatives called on a wide range of customers or potential customers, and the operating department established fast freight runs for special or perishable cargoes. Atchison employees were urged to aid in the solicitation of cargoes, and the *Santa Fe Magazine* published articles about successful efforts to win new traffic. The ATSF held seminars on damage and claim reductions and encouraged employees to be concerned about the way freight was treated. Storey labored to win a more substantial share of California's produce and citrus traffic, especially after the construction of the Chicago Produce Terminal; and soon long lines of orange and yellow "reefers" could be seen on the Belen Cutoff, being rushed to the Midwest and East. Revenues and profits began to reflect Storey's successful efforts to increase traffic and rebuild the system, as shown in following chart.

GROWTH IN THE TWENTIES

	Mileage	*Operating Revenue ($)*	*Net Corporate Income ($)*
1921	11,706	228,925,069	39,331,661
1922	11,709	225,124,544	34,382,370
1923	11,757	238,683,735	42,087,801
1924	11,904	235,410,951	42,151,806
1925	12,068	236,942,528	46,157,934
1926	12,210	259,040,315	60,631,494
1927	12,349	255,617,824	49,754,117
1928	12,383	247,632,836	49,930,430
1929	13,157	267,189,178	61,036,803

By the middle of the decade, the Atchison was being hailed as one of the finest rail properties in the nation.

A financial report issued by Wood, Struthers and Company in 1925 declared the Santa Fe to be in splendid condition. The ATSF had doubled its ownership of refrigerator cars since 1912, and between 1917 and 1923 the railway purchased 348 new locomotives and retired 257 for a 29.2 percent increase in the total tractive effort. The economic boom of the Atchison's territory had contributed to the rate of growth, but the report quoted Professor William Z. Ripley, who said:

> A combination of courage and intelligence has produced a railroad which reaches almost every point that it should and which has such connections hither and thither as to consolidate its strength at all strategic points. Nor is energy dissipated anywhere by useless or unnatural extensions beyond its natural gateways.[6]

The report also declared the ATSF's financial position to be one of undeniable strength, which was quite accurate.

Storey continued E. P. Ripley's conservative financial policy, plowing millions of dollars in earnings back into the property. Assets grew rapidly, but capitalization remained stable. By the end of the decade over $400 million had been reinvested in the system, and assets grew from $1,004,000,000 to $1,260,000,000. The ATSF averaged a return of 5.65 percent on invested capital, and considerable sums were used to redeem bonds and equipment trust certificates. Bond owners continued to convert their holdings into common stock, reducing fixed costs, and Storey paid off the bonds which had been sold for the Oklahoma and Arizona extensions before World War I with an issue of common stock. The board of directors did not ignore the stockholders, who received a dividend on common stock of 5 percent, which was increased to 7 percent in 1924 and to 10 percent in 1928. The price of Atchison common stock on Wall Street rose from 97 in 1924 to 299 prior to the crash. Despite some speculation in Atchison securities, ownership continued to be widespread, and the railway remained independent.

Storey took great pride in the Santa Fe's large body of owners—perhaps a consequence of his experience with the "Valley Road" in the 1890s. He reported in 1922 that the Atchison had 64,643 stockholders of whom 29,820 were men, 29,235 were women and 5,588 were institutions. Atchison stockholders included 122 insurance companies, 108 educational institutions, 93 religious organizations and 89 hospitals, but only 4,409 individuals or institutions owned more than 100 shares. Atchison bondholders numbered 32,000, and individuals with $129,196,000 in bonds represented the largest group of security owners. Insurance companies owned $78,042,000 in bonds and other corporations held $51,339,000. Storey repeatedly declared that there was no water in company securities and that true valuation was considerably above the total issues of stocks and bonds. His contentions, but not his figures, were supported by the valuation report of the Interstate Commerce Commission.

The Interstate Commerce Commission began to conclude its valuation study in the mid-twenties, and its findings were issued in 1925. The tentative valuation of $391,162,318 of the Atchison's owned property was considered entirely too low by Storey, who protested bitterly. He differed with the ICC largely on the definition of carrier property and the charging off of depreciation; Storey contended that the Atchison was worth at least $750 million. The final valuation of $579,057,598 (as of June 30, 1916) failed to persuade Storey, who again protested. A supplementary report raised the figure to $580,613,098 for rate-making purposes. The Santa Fe management noted that in the decade following 1916 the railway had

Albuquerque shops and roundhouse—a major industry of the "Duke City."
Santa Fe Railway

grown from 11,833 miles to 13,302, and while the number of locomotives owned rose only from 2,099 to 2,103, the average weight increased from 97.62 tons to 123.71. Freight cars grew in number from 68,331 to 83,947, and total tonnage carried from 28,219,777 to 42,781,931. Further, the Atchison achieved record earnings on its investment in 1926.

Yet, even Storey admitted that the picture was not totally bright. Earnings in 1927 and 1928 did not equal 1926, passenger revenues continued to fall, and taxes continued to rise. Where the railway had paid $4,438,000 in taxes in 1912, it paid $14,836,500 in 1921 and $17.7 million in 1924. There can be no doubt, however, of the Atchison's strong position before October 1929. It was prosperous, its management remained conservative and stable, and huge capital outlays had created an efficient and modern physical plant. Cash and federal bondholdings gave the Atchison a large degree of liquidity, a major factor in weathering the depression of the thirties. The management had not been so conservative, however, as to halt Ripley's expansion program. Construction of new lines and purchases of smaller railways continued through the decade; but the Atchison refused to participate in some of the consolidation schemes proposed after the passage of the Transportation Act of 1920.

The Transportation Act called for regional consolidations and the absorption of weak carriers by the strong. The Atchison served as the basis for several merger schemes, but none was carried out. Professor W. Z. Ripley proposed in 1921 that the Atchison should merge with the Fort Worth and Rio Grande, absorb a few branches owned by other carriers and gain entrance to New Orleans. The Interstate Commerce Commission merger scheme of that year added the Colorado and Southern, Fort Worth and Denver City, Denver and Rio Grande, Western Pacific, and several western shortlines to the Atchison. Storey found this plan to add a northern transcontinental route to the Santa Fe more appealing, but he urged an entrance into St. Louis. An ICC plan in 1929 would have added the Chicago and Great Western, Kansas City, Mexico and Orient, the Midland Valley and several other shortlines. While the proposal gave the Atchison entrance into the Twin Cities and Omaha, Storey rejected it. Viewing these schemes as either unacceptable or visionary, the Atchison board and Storey embarked on their own acquisition plan, which served to strengthen the Santa Fe's position in its own territory and to withdraw from areas where meaningful competition was impossible.

Initial expansion under Storey consisted of numerous branches in Oklahoma, Kansas and the Texas Panhandle to reach new wheat areas or oil fields. As northwestern Oklahoma and southwestern Kansas wheat acreage expanded, the Santa Fe built lines to serve the farmers. It also acquired a shortline in California to gain access to the agricultural area of the Palo Verde Valley. Additional branches were built in the northern portion of the Texas Panhandle and west from Lubbock toward the New Mexico state line. In 1927 the Santa Fe purchased the Oklahoma, New Mexico and Pacific, a line built by John Ringling and Lee Cruce to serve the Healdton oil field west of Ardmore, Oklahoma. The price of over \$1 million was returned very quickly as additional oil discoveries were made in the area. The previous year the Atchison purchased the New Mexico Central Railway, which operated 115 miles of track in the center of the state. While virtually all of the NMC was eventually abandoned, its acquisition by another railroad could have undermined the Atchison's near monopoly in the northern half of New Mexico.

The Atchison also sought to consolidate its position in California. As the Golden State's economy expanded the ATSF built several branches, pushed into Oakland, and tried to improve operations in the bay area. Storey also moved to prevent the Southern Pacific from strengthening its hold on California traffic. The SP sought in 1925 to acquire the Central California Traction Company, which operated a line 55 miles long from Stockton to Sacramento, largely paralleling the SP. The CCT served as an agricultural feeder for the ATSF, SP and Western Pacific. Between 1920 and 1924 the CCT transferred 17,000 cars of freight to the three larger roads, with 43 percent going to the Santa Fe and 20 percent to the SP. While the SP said it wanted the CCT to avoid double tracking its own line, the ATSF saw the move as an attempt to take the lion's share of the interline freight. After the WP had purchased the Sacramento Northern, a similar electric railway, interchange traffic between the Santa Fe and the SN declined from 204 cars in 1920 to 29 cars in 1924. Storey would not allow such a diversion to occur again. When the Southern Pacific asked for ICC approval to purchase the CCT, the Atchison and WP objected, and the ICC refused to approve the sale. In 1928 the three major carriers reached a compromise, and jointly purchased the CCT, each acquiring one-third, and they agreed not to divert traffic from previous patterns. The Atchison and the SP also resolved a continuing problem in 1928 when the ATSF sold its share of the Northwestern Pacific to the SP. As has been noted earlier, the trans-bay operation had failed to generate traffic or profits.

Similarly, the Atchison tightened its grip on the plains of Oklahoma and Texas. In 1928 the ATSF purchased a railroad linking Clinton and Cheyenne, Oklahoma, and Pampa, Texas, and this line became a significant source of wheat, livestock, and, later, petroleum business. In the south plains the Santa Fe built other branches to reach additional wheat and oil traffic. These acquisitions pale in comparison, however, with the purchase of the Kansas City, Mexico and Orient Railway in 1928.

The flamboyant promoter Arthur Edward Stilwell built the KCM&O shortly after the turn of the century. An enthusiastic and colorful businessman, Stilwell created two rail empires, the Kansas City Southern, running from Kansas City to Port Arthur, Texas, and the KCM&O, only to lose them when the projects fell into the hands of receivers. Born in Rochester, New York, in 1859, Stilwell grew up in that city where his family was important in commercial and political circles. After financial reverses, the family lost its place in Rochester society, and young Arthur became an itinerant salesman. Moving to Kansas City in 1886, he helped promote a belt railway network and then the Kansas City, Pittsburg and Gulf, the predecessor of the Kansas City Southern. The KCP&G project linked Kansas City to a deep-water port on the Gulf of Mexico by a route "straight

as the crow flies." Aided by English and Dutch investors, the indefatiga-
ble Stilwell built the line even during the depression of 1893. The over-
optimistic promoter simultaneously began to develop a connecting rail
system north of Kansas City and the harbor at his namesake city, Port
Arthur. Grossly overextended, the loosely assembled companies collapsed
and fell into the hands of John W. "Bet-a-Million" Gates and the "canni-
bals of Wall Street."

Most of Stilwell's friends felt that he would not recover from the loss,
but the promoter's drive and ambition could not be thwarted. In 1900 he
seized upon a long-discussed project to link Kansas City with the obscure
port of Topolobampo in Sinaloa, Mexico, on the Gulf of California. Topolobampo was the closest Pacific port to Kansas City, closer than either Los
Angeles or San Diego, and since the 1870s several Americans had
dreamed of building a rail line from the Midwest to Topolobampo, which
they envisioned as an entrepot for corn, wheat and manufactured goods
being sent to Japan, China and India. Although the idea had existed for
at least two decades, Stilwell claimed it for his own: "I have designed a
railroad 1600 miles long which will bring the Pacific Ocean 400 miles
nearer to Kansas City than any other present route. Not only that, but it
will be 1600 miles nearer to Central and South America than San Francisco
is."[7] He proposed to build from Kansas City to Wichita, southwest across
Oklahoma Territory through the Texas plains, to Sweetwater and San
Angelo and on to the Rio Grande. In Mexico the projected line stretched
across the northern portion of that country through Chihuahua and the
Sierra Madres to Topolobampo.

"Oriente" wood-burning locomotive of the Kansas City, Mexico and Orient
Railway in Mexico. Santa Fe Railway

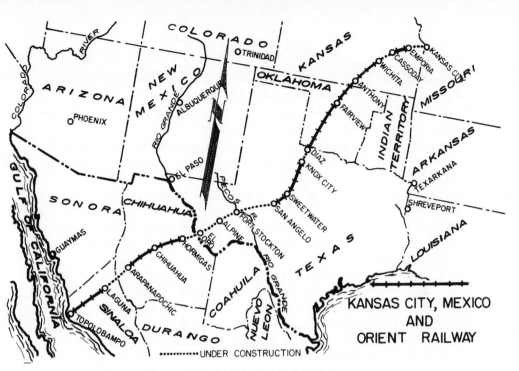

Kansas City, Mexico and Orient Railway

Beguiling Kansas City businessmen and English investors, Stilwell built the KCM&O from Wichita south to San Angelo and constructed lines from Topolobampo east to the Sierra Madres and east and west from Chihuahua for short distances. Investor interest waned by 1907, and Stilwell barely kept the railroad operating. A few miles of track were added each year, but the route remained uncompleted. The coming of revolution to Mexico brought this "entrepreneurial error" to grief. The destruction of the Mexican segments, the termination of capital inflow, and a lack of profits on the line in the United States led to bankruptcy. The KCM&O entered receivership in 1912, and in 1928 it still remained unredeemed. The receivers built an extension to Alpine, Texas, but could not finish the project. The line was foreclosed in 1914 and again in 1924, and even the U.S. Railroad Administration rejected it, at least initially.

Receiver William T. Kemper kept the "Orient" alive, and traffic did increase in the early twenties when petroleum discoveries materially aided Kemper's efforts to avoid additional financial problems. By 1927 almost 50 percent of the road's revenue came from oil. Kemper sought to sell the property to several major railroads, approaching the Southern Pacific; Missouri Pacific; Chicago, Rock Island and Pacific; and Chicago, Burlington & Quincy, as well as the Santa Fe. Storey and the Atchison board looked closely at the "Orient" and concluded that in the hands of another carrier it could be quite damaging. The ATSF's hold on traffic in the south Texas plains was substantial, but losses could occur if another trunk line railroad took the KCM&O and rehabilitated it. Further, portions of the "Orient" could be used as a cutoff for cargoes bound from the plains country for Kansas City or Chicago. The "Orient" operated 735 miles of track in the United States and 320 miles in Mexico, and it owned 75 locomotives in various stages of disrepair, 1,404 freight cars and 32 passenger cars. The rails were light, the roadbed almost nonexistent, and the track in Mexico was barely operable. Nevertheless, the strategic location of the route attracted the Atchison, and its offer of $14 million was accepted by Kemper in 1928.

Storey wanted only the mileage in this country, and in 1929 the Mexican lines were sold to B. F. Johnson, a sugar planter in Sinaloa, for $600,000 in cash and a $900,000 mortgage. Johnson eventually defaulted, and in 1940 the Mexican government acquired the line; the Santa Fe ultimately received $90,000 for the mortgage. Storey authorized the completion of the KCM&O from Alpine to Presidio on the Rio Grande, and a branch from San Angelo to Sonora, Texas, in the Edwards Plateau. The Santa Fe rebuilt the eight intersections of its lines with the "Orient" and began to reroute freight, saving as much as 285 miles on some traffic. The expansion of agricultural production on the plains made the acquisition a valuable feeder. The Mexican government improved the old KCM&O, and in 1958 a program was begun to complete the route from Presidio to Topolobampo. On November 20, 1961, the route to the Gulf of California opened, having cost $88 million. The KCM&O's successor, the Ferrocarril de Chihuahua al Pacifico, began to exchange some freight with the ATSF at Presidio, mainly winter produce. Arthur Stilwell's dream came true, but Topolobampo does not rival Los Angeles and no great international commerce has developed. The purchase of the "Orient" did give the Santa Fe a major branch line and protected its west Texas flank from a rival.

In October 1929, the Atchison stood as one of the fiscal and physical giants of the rail industry. Its territory was growing more rapidly than the rest of the nation; its management had poured millions of dollars into track rebuilding, equipment acquisition and expansion programs; and its treasury held a large cash and negotiable bond reserve. Storey's conservative program placed his company in a solid position to weather the economic catastrophe which followed the crash of '29. Many railroads had been in financial trouble even in the twenties, and many would fall into bankruptcy in the thirties. The Atchison withstood the effects of the Great Depression and emerged ready to contribute to the nation's effort to halt the spread of tyranny around the globe.

10

Depression, War and Technological Change

The facade of prosperity erected during the Roaring Twenties hid serious problems in the national economy. Some industries never recovered from the postwar recession, and agriculture lagged far behind the industrial sector in profits, if not in productivity. The economy of Europe remained sick throughout the decade, and tariff walls erected by the United States shut out a sizable portion of world trade. Speculation in the stock market and in Florida and California real estate drained dollars needed for investment in plants or public works. Yet few economists or Wall Streeters saw the enormous cracks in the false front of "Coolidge Prosperity." The first symptoms of the diseased economy were noted in 1928, but not until "the crash" in October 1929 did the extent of the illness become a national concern. For a few months the economy continued to move forward, if at a slower rate, and the "Santa Fe Southwest" remained somewhat sheltered from the immediate consequences of the slow down. By 1930 the coming of the depression began to affect the Atchison; and when "Mother Nature" placed a huge section of the Santa Fe's territory within the "Dust Bowl", the management initiated programs to deal with the effects of the national economic disaster and the vagaries of the weather. The next decade witnessed a winning fight to survive the depression. Indeed, when war came in 1939, the Santa Fe stood fiscally and physically ready.

Following the crash, President Hoover pleaded with the nation's industries to maintain their projected capital spending outlays and to keep employment at the prevailing level. In its *Annual Report* for 1929, the

Atchison announced that it would spend $85 million for 5,854 freight cars and 49 passenger cars, that it had 172 miles of track under construction, and that it would ask the ICC for permission to build an additional 380 miles of line. Business conditions remained "excellent" in the railway's territory, stated the report, and gross earnings continued to climb. The optimism of April soon disappeared, however, and on June 1, a retrenchment program was instituted. Shop and maintenance crews were reduced in size, although orders for new equipment were not aborted. Profits remained high enough to continue the 10 percent dividend through 1930, but the *Annual Report* did convey to stockholders the extent of the decline in traffic and revenues. The Santa Fe suffered the worst traffic losses in its history as the depression and drought came to the Southwest. Emergency rates on feed and cattle helped move livestock out of the Dust Bowl and save those which remained. Branch-line freight and passenger services were cut back as wheat and corn crops failed. Storey tried to sound optimistic, but warned stockholders of the effect of declining agricultural prices on rail shipments. By December 1931, the management conceded that no economic revival seemed imminent, and the quarterly dividend was reduced from 2½ percent to 1½ percent effective March 1, 1932. The impact of the national economic collapse forced Storey to make a painful recommendation to the board: he urged that all Atchison employees accept a 10 percent reduction in wages. The labor unions agreed to the proposal as did the company officers. Storey hoped that the savings would preclude additional layoffs and allow him to maintain employment levels.

The enormous decline in revenues and profits in 1932 led to the omission of dividends after the first of June. The Atchison's mileage peaked in 1932, and the abandonment of little-used branches signaled another attempt at cost reduction. Yet confidence in the Atchison remained high, and several major insurance companies increased their holdings of the railway's securities. Storey repeatedly announced that maintenance programs would continue and that he had no intention of allowing the property to deteriorate; the wage reduction was extended, and additional savings schemes were introduced. All common stock dividends were omitted in 1933; 126 miles of track were abandoned; capital spending tumbled to $2.5 million; and passenger rates were slashed to 2¢ per mile in coaches. The strain on Storey became excessive, and he simply could not continue to vigorously lead the Atchison as he had since 1920. On May 2, 1933, he retired as president to be succeeded by Samuel T. Bledsoe.

The selection of Bledsoe to lead the Atchison came as no surprise. He already served as chairman of the executive committee and as general counsel, and he had been a leading spokesman for the Santa Fe and the

Samuel T. Bledsoe, president of the Santa Fe from
1933 to 1939. Santa Fe Railway

entire rail industry before the ICC and Congressional committees. His
succession to the presidency marked a significant shift in the road's management, however, as Bledsoe was not a railroadman in the tradition of
Strong, Ripley and Storey, but came to the presidency through the practice of law. Born in Kentucky on May 12, 1868, Bledsoe studied law at
the University of Texas and became an attorney in Indian and Oklahoma
territories, specializing in land and railroad matters. In 1895 he began to
represent the ATSF in Ardmore, eventually becoming general attorney for
the system within the state of Oklahoma. His outstanding work led to his
appointment as general counsel for the Atchison, and then elevation to
executive positions within the management. Although he lacked experi-

ence as a track layer, surveyor or engineer, he possessed a keen sense of railroading and was not reluctant to accept changes in technology and marketing. Under Bledsoe the Atchison would streamline its passenger trains, purchase diesel locomotives for all types of service, and institute new approaches to transportation marketing. Bledsoe's first task, however, was to cope with the depression.

Under Bledsoe's direction, the management continued to reduce expenditures and sought to maximize efficiency and find new sources of traffic. Several hundred miles of track, principally in Oklahoma, Texas and New Mexico, were abandoned. A new branch in the Pecos Valley reached a United States Potash refinery and brought additional traffic to that feeder system. Indeed the net income for 1934 was almost double the earnings for 1933, and a common stock dividend of 2 percent was declared—the first in two years. Capital improvement allocations increased, and Bledsoe told the press he saw a revival of business in the offing. Earnings did continue to improve, and on April 1, 1935, he revoked the wage cuts at a yearly cost of $6,150,000. Bledsoe fought not only the depression but also increasing competition from pipelines and trucks. Despite his efforts, most less-than-carload (LCL) business was lost, and he responded by improving service and by speeding up schedules. Almost $4 million was allocated for 140 miles of new 112-pound rail and for superelevating curves on the Chicago–Los Angeles line. These improvements were made without additional borrowing or by leaving debts unpaid.

By 1936–1937, revenues improved but profits declined. Bledsoe refused to stop his track improvement program, however, and rapidly enlarged the capital expenditures budget. He ordered 155,000 tons of rail, new light-weight passenger cars, 27 locomotives, and over 3,000 freight cars. The equipment order totaled $19.6 million of which an equipment trust covered $13.8, the rest committed from the road's treasury. Bledsoe not only placed the largest order for rails since 1929, but he also launched a vigorous advertising campaign soliciting new business to help pay for it. In 1937 the Santa Fe began to publish freight advertisements independent of those soliciting passenger traffic. Full pages were purchased in *Fortune, Time, News-Week, Nation's Business* and *United States News*. The campaign and a good harvest helped produce the best revenues since 1931, and even passenger revenue showed growth in 1937.

The optimism and hope of 1937 became disappointment and concern the next year as revenues fell sharply. The recession of 1938 came after the federal government substantially reduced expenditures, and as "pump-priming" slowed, so did the national economy. The extent of the decline on the Atchison can be seen in the following figures.

OPERATING STATISTICS, 1929–1941

	Mileage	Operating Revenue ($)	Net Income ($)
1929	13,157	267,189,178	61,036,803
1930	13,312	226,421,044	37,885,314
1931	13,568	181,181,260	23,101,691
1932	13,535	133,133,537	7,545,007
1933	13,427	119,826,436	3,698,671
1934	13,300	128,093,947	7,001,314
1935	13,259	135,686,391	9,554,315
1936	13,226	157,265,504	9,998,125
1937	13,538	170,669,945	7,659,404
1938	13,451	154,323,226	8,228,044
1939	13,445	160,039,966	8,490,832
1940	13,407	170,003,370	12,745,370
1941	13,418	225,043,648	30,236,581

The Santa Fe again omitted common stock dividends, and for the first time failed to pay interest on its general adjustment bonds. Since the interest was payable only if earned, there was no default. Further, the board voted to omit the preferred dividend. The payment of interest on the adjustment bonds resumed in September 1938, but only a slight improvement in revenues and earnings took place the following year.

The worry and strain fell heavily on Bledsoe, who expressed continued concern for the welfare of the Atchison employees and their families. The company suffered a significant loss as Bledsoe became ill, and died on March 8, 1939. Within three weeks the board elected Edward J. Engel to succeed him as president and as chairman of the executive committee. Like Bledsoe, Engel entered the Atchison through the managerial ranks and had not been in construction, a train crewman or in the operating department. Born in Ohio in 1874, he joined the Atchison in 1899 as a stenographer for E. P. Ripley. A graduate of a business school in Sandusky, the quiet but efficient Engel became Ripley's right-hand man. Moving quickly up the executive ladder, Engel became assistant to the president (1910), vice president (1918), and executive vice president (1935). Engel brought to the presidency a broad knowledge of the corporate structure, a determination to achieve the highest level of operating efficiency, and a continuing commitment to Bledsoe's program for the technological advancement of the Atchison. Engel would carry through the program to dieselize motive power, streamline and air condition the passenger trains, and apply the concept of broadcasting to train control and operations.

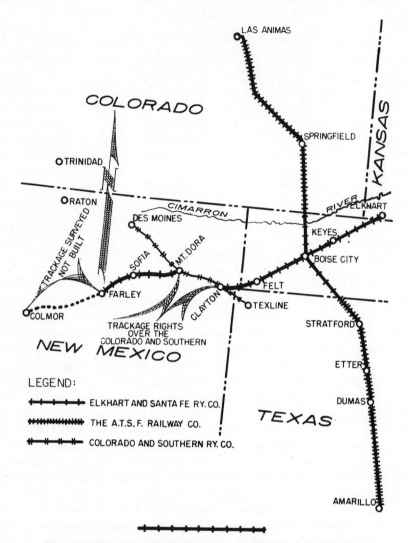

ELKHART AND SANTA FE RAILWAY COMPANY

Elkhart and Santa Fe Railway

Business conditions began to improve in 1939, especially after war broke out in Europe in September. Engel placed over 1,000 shopmen back on a six-day week, and a $2.50 per share dividend on the preferred stock was declared in June. Adverse business conditions in the Southwest eased even though agricultural production continued to lag. The directors authorized almost $25 million in capital improvements in 1939–1940, including large orders for freight and passenger cars and for track rebuilding. The Santa Fe continued to scrap more freight cars than it purchased, but capacity per car rose to an average of 43.65 tons. Major structures, such as Dearborn Station, were remodeled; the Gulf, Colorado and Santa Fe erected a seven-story office building and union station in Galveston in 1931–1932; and from 1933 to 1939, the ATSF participated in the development of the Los Angeles Union station. The Santa Fe paid one-third of the cost of the $9 million Los Angeles terminal, which it built jointly with the Union Pacific and Southern Pacific. Opened on May 7, 1939, the Los Angeles station combined the California Mission architectural style with a highly efficient passenger and express terminal. The fifteen tracks with their umbrella sheds would soon see business on a scale undreamed of in 1939.

The Atchison weathered the financial crises of the depression far more easily than many of its rail neighbors. A substantial number of Granger and western railroads entered bankruptcy, but the conservative managers of the Santa Fe kept it out of danger. The line paid its obligated interest and yielded meager profits. Assets increased slightly as did the amount of bonds outstanding, and investor confidence in the company's securities remained high. Trust bonds sold at a 2.25 percent interest rate in 1936, and 2.5 percent in 1939, with a price of $100.353 on the earlier issue. In August 1939, the Atchison resumed dividend payments, and the common stock made a moderate recovery in the market. The policy of retaining some profits to create a substantial holding of cash and federal securities provided liquidity when it was needed, and a reserve in case the economy worsened. Bledsoe and Engel brought the Atchison out of the depression in a strong financial position, and even in the midst of economic adversity they continued a moderate expansion program.

In the 1870s, when the Santa Fe was still trying to decide how to get out of Kansas and on to New Mexico, A. A. Robinson sought to persuade the board to build along the Cimarron Cutoff of the Santa Fe Trail. The cutoff possessed much lower grades than Raton Pass and was shorter in distance. The Atchison management decided against the topographical advantages the route offered because of the sparse population in the area and the almost desertlike terrain. The opening of the Belen Cutoff and the shift of heavy freight to that line reduced the problems raised by Raton Pass. And yet, some Santa Fe men remained convinced that Robinson had

Edward J. Engel, president of the Santa Fe from 1939 to 1944. Santa Fe Railway

been correct, and, even before the Belen Cutoff had been built, surveyed the route. In 1910 a survey team worked south and west from Dodge City some 228 miles through Elkhart, Kansas, to Clayton, New Mexico, and on to the Atchison main line at Colmor between Las Vegas and Raton. Two years later the Santa Fe built 119 miles from Dodge City to Elkhart to reach a new wheat area. Nothing further was done, although additional surveys were made in 1917 and 1921. The project, which became known as the Colmor Cutoff, received a boost in 1925 when the Elkhart branch was extended into the Oklahoma panhandle to the town of Felt, some 59 miles. Five more years elapsed before the California traffic boom led the management to renew the project. In 1930 the ICC granted the Santa Fe permission to complete the 1 percent grade line by building from Felt through Clayton to Colmor. The Colmor Cutoff would shorten the trans-continental route by 69 miles and provide a much lower grade than over Raton. The Colorado and Southern granted the ATSF trackage rights for 17 miles between Clayton and Mt. Dora, reducing the cost of the project from $7 million to $6.5 million. In 1931, construction crews built 24 miles of track from Felt to Clayton, and from Mt. Dora to Farley, another 36 miles. As the depression worsened and traffic declined, the route became far less appealing, and construction terminated, leaving a gap of 35 miles from Farley to Colmor. The area traversed was hit hard by dust storms, wheat production plummeted, and the line saw twice-weekly service which declined to a once-weekly local from Boise City to Farley in 1940. As demands for scrap metal increased in 1941, the ATSF received permission to abandon the Boise City–Farley line, which was ripped up in 1942. The War Production Board acquired the 96 miles of rails and sent them to Iran for use on the railroad to the Caspian Sea and Russia. The Colmor Cutoff failed to yield profits and can only be considered a mistake, but another project in the same area became a success.

Despite its strong, although not monopolistic, position in the Texas Panhandle–Plains country, the ATSF suffered from the absence of a direct Galveston-Denver route. The Colorado and Southern–Fort Worth and Denver City line took a large share of the traffic between the Gulf and the Rockies. As early as 1893, Chief Engineer James Dun had urged A. A. Robinson to build a connection from the Gulf, Colorado and Santa Fe to the ATSF line in Colorado. Nothing was done, however, until the twenties, when the Texas and Oklahoma panhandles developed large-scale production of wheat and cattle, and oil and natural gas discoveries were made. The Atchison then requested permission from the ICC to build 220 miles of track north from Amarillo through Boise City, Oklahoma, to Las Animas, Colorado. The new line would reduce the Atchison's Colorado-Texas route by 400 miles, and the ICC granted permission in 1930. Construction gangs built north from Amarillo to Boise City, 121 miles, in 1931, but the

Light locomotives provided branch-line power in the 1930s and 1940s. Keith L. Bryant, Sr.

Dust Bowl and the depression terminated work. The advantages of the proposed line became increasingly significant as competition with the C&S/FW&D and truck lines grew. In 1936, the Santa Fe moved to close the 111-mile gap between Boise City and Las Animas. The board approved spending $3,750,000 to build the longest stretch of new railroad to be constructed since the beginning of the depression. On February 1, 1937, the completed route opened giving the ATSF the shortest Amarillo-Denver line by 25 miles. The governor of Colorado rode a special train to Springfield, Colorado, where he drove a "golden spike" to celebrate the opening of the line. The coming of rain to the Dust Bowl, the revival of agriculture and ranching, additional petroleum discoveries, and the development of through-traffic made the Amarillo–Las Animas Cutoff a solid revenue producer.

The Atchison management moved to solidify and strengthen the system in Texas throughout the late twenties and the thirties. Faith in the region and its future growth and the desire to reduce distances combined in 1937 for yet another purchase. The St. Louis–San Francisco Railroad (Frisco) owned a 215-mile branch from Fort Worth southwest through Brownwood to Menard. The line, built as the Fort Worth and Rio Grande Railway by Jay Gould, was not profitable for the Frisco, which was in severe financial straits. The Santa Fe could use the property to reach the Coleman Cutoff at Brownwood from Fort Worth, and reduce the Fort Worth-California haul by 117 miles. The Santa Fe offered the Frisco $1,519,325 for the

branch and asked the ICC for permission to acquire the route. Santa Fe
stockholders approved the proposal, the Frisco trustees accepted, and the
ICC agreed, saying that the ATSF was performing a public service in purchasing the property and assuming its obligations of $15,053,431. The
Santa Fe took possession on March 2, 1937, and immediately began to
rehabilitate the property. The Fort Worth-Brownwood segment soon carried a substantial volume of traffic as Dallas-Fort Worth freight bound for
California or West Texas was shifted to the cutoff. The Bledsoe-Engel
management saw the advantages presented by the low prices of the depression to build or buy properties which gave the Atchison a competitive
advantage. This philosophy even extended to purchasing truck lines—the
rail carrier's growing and threatening competitor.

The expanding truck companies made some inroads into the territory
served by the Santa Fe in the twenties, but the absence of good highways
inhibited the growth of the industry until the early thirties. The first
cargoes seriously affected by trucks were the less-than-carload lots, long a
mainstay on the Atchison. In order to meet truck competition, the ATSF
began to provide pickup and delivery service for LCL shipments in 1931.
This action represented only the first step, and a small one at that, toward
meeting the threat posed by trucks. The rapid expansion of motor-freight
service in the Southwest forced the management to act quickly, which it
did. In September 1935, the ATSF purchased controlling interest in the
Southern Kansas Stage Line, a bus and truck operator. The railway pur-

The "Scout" offered low-cost travel during the Great Depression. Santa Fe
Railway

chased the remainder of the Southern Kansas securities in 1939, and it also acquired other truck operations in its region. A new subsidiary, the Santa Fe Trail Transportation Company, became the operator of the truck routes, which covered the states of Kansas, Oklahoma, Nebraska, Missouri and Arkansas. The truck subsidiary purchased new diesel tractors and stainless steel trailers, coordinated its services with the railway, and provided door-to-door service for the ATSF's LCL customers. The Santa Fe Trail Transportation Company lines were extended west to Arizona and California, and routes grew to 7,300 miles during World War II and to 9,444 miles by 1949. The truck subsidiary became an integral part of the freight services of the Santa Fe; and when the bus operation was sold in 1947, the truck routes were retained. Federal and state regulatory agencies limited the truck line to those areas reached by the ATSF, but this limitation did not prove harmful to the coordinated rail-highway service.

As the depression ended in 1939–1940, the faith of the management, the board of directors and the stockholders was rewarded in the form of rising business and revenue. The Dust Bowl eased in intensity as rains returned to produce bumper wheat crops and grass for the sleek, white-faced cattle. The "Okies" riding the Scout to California were replaced by tourists going to the expositions in San Francisco and San Diego. The region served by the Atchison changed as a result of the depression, and the rate of growth slowed; but signs of a renewed economic and population boom began to appear even before the United States entered World War II. Other rail carriers failed to recover from the depression, however, and the federal government sought to evoke a more positive climate for the rail industry. Loans from the Reconstruction Finance Corporation and favorable rulings from the ICC did not save some roads from bankruptcy, and many still operated under trustees. The Transportation Act of 1920 had failed to meet problems created by the depression, and Congress responded with a new directive for the industry.

The Transportation Act of 1940 sought to eliminate excessive restrictions on the railroads and allow the federal government to play a more positive role in alleviating the industry's problems. Section 32 of the law had a profound impact on the Atchison, and one which was not entirely positive. Under existing federal laws, railroads which had received land grants had to charge lower rates on federal goods and personnel traveling over their lines. Even the Post Office paid a lower rate. Section 32 provided that the U.S. government would begin to pay the prevailing commercial rate on civilians traveling for the government, on nondefense-related federal property and on the mail. In return, the railroads holding land grants had to surrender all claims to unpatented lands. The government retained the 50 percent discount rate for all military traffic. The ATSF agreed to close out its two land grants, which meant surrendering 400,000 acres of unpatented land in Arizona; but any immediate loss would be more than offset by long-range returns on the mail and other federal property moving at full rates. Much of the grant surrendered consisted of poor grazing land, and the Atchison had sought unsuccessfully to sell it throughout the thirties. Anticipating some savings from the arrangement, the Atchison agreed to the plan.

Within two years, the Santa Fe management realized the inadequate relief provided by Section 32. World War II brought a vast increase in military traffic, and the railway suffered huge losses in potential revenue. President Engel declared the military discount rate to be "a serious and growing burden."[1] As military traffic volume grew, the justice of Engel's complaint became obvious, but the 50 percent rate held. Between 1942 and 1946 the Santa Fe discounted $151,243,773 in freight charges and $38,252,191 in passenger fares for a revenue loss of $189,495,964. Even raw materials moving to federally leased plants received the discount. When the railroads complained about the application of the rate in the latter instance, the Supreme Court ruled in the government's favor. Finally, on October 1, 1946, the military discount ended, but the huge losses during the war could not be recaptured.

Public misconception about the size and value of the land grants, largely the result of descriptions and depictions in history textbooks, hindered the railroad's efforts to win political support for repeal of the discount. The Atchison did retain its patented lands in Arizona and New Mexico, and, when the war ended, mounted an effort to sell as much as the market would absorb. In 1948 about one million acres in Arizona and New Mexico remained in the possession of the railroad, but eight years later the Atchison went out of the land business. The land office in Albuquerque closed, leaving the railroad with 151,000 acres unsold. With the termination of land sales, the Santa Fe reported that total revenue from *all* sales had been approximately $25 million to June 30, 1947, but that the railway had granted the federal government $215 million in reduced rates. The myth of fantastic profits remained, however, and as late as June 1971, President John Reed of the Santa Fe found himself explaining the entire land grant question when some U.S. senators called for the return to the federal government of all the land granted to the railroads. At least the Transportation Act of 1940 had called attention to the matter of rate discounts, but only World War II demonstrated the injustice of the military discount.

The effects of the war in Europe became evident in the *Annual Report* for 1940. Agricultural production, particularly wheat, soared, and the management reported that a large number of aircraft plants, shipyards and munitions facilities had been located along ATSF lines. The report noted that the number of stockholders had increased and exceeded the number of employees, 53,000 to 41,300, but dividends of $8,635,700 fell far below the total wages paid—some $81 million. President Engel also announced a $12.5 million equipment order, the largest since 1937. The order included 2,800 freight cars and two additional diesel passenger locomotives. The increase in business continued into 1941, and the operating ratio fell from 76.24 to 69.72, a significant decrease, but modest compared to 1942 when the ratio declined further to 54.92. The traffic in both military and civilian goods became even heavier after December 7, 1941. The war caused the Santa Fe executives to reexamine the value of some branch lines, and over 250 miles of track were abandoned. To support the massive growth in traffic, it became necessary to hire additional employees, and their number swelled from 47,000 to almost 54,000. Stockholders rejoiced when the $9.90-per-share earnings of 1941 hit $27.79 per share in 1942. This windfall did not reoccur as the federal corporate income tax increased, and a stiff wartime excess-profits tax was levied. Engel and the board used large portions of the increased earnings for debt reduction, and they warned stockholders that while profits were excellent, locomotives, cars and trackage were taking a heavy beating, and that no new equipment was available and some maintenance simply had to be deferred. As the burdens of war became larger and larger, the ATSF responded valiantly.

The Santa Fe owned the key line from Chicago to the West Coast, and its double tracks were used to absolute capacity. Ton miles of freight carried almost doubled between 1941 and 1942, and passenger traffic rose by 88 percent. The 82 miles of track between San Bernardino and Barstow, shared with the Union Pacific, carried 20 to 30 freight trains every twenty-four hours. Shortages of manpower meant new employees had to be trained and retirees brought back to active service. Motive-power demands were met by utilizing locomotives far beyond normal mileage, by purchasing steam locomotives from Eastern roads, and by the enormous capabilities of the diesel units. The freight diesels worked from Kansas City to Belen and from Winslow to Barstow, but the passenger units traveled through from Chicago to Los Angeles. The diesels could move sixty cars of freight from Kansas City to Los Angeles, some 3,150 tons in 53 hours. Some steam locomotives in passenger service regularly ran through from Argentine, Kansas, to Los Angeles (1,788 miles) and from Los Angeles to Newton (1,590 miles). The locomotive shops extended their

Although thirty years old, the "Mikados" contributed to the war effort. Santa Fe Railway

operations to two shifts and then to three shifts daily to keep the power serviced and available to meet constantly increasing demands.

One of the most heavily utilized routes was the 118-mile long "surfline" between Los Angeles and San Diego. Both cities became major military centers with aircraft plants, naval installations and nearby army and marine facilities. San Diego depended almost entirely on the ATSF for freight and passenger service; and on July 5, 1942, some 4,919 people moved over the Santa Fe between the two cities, with one train running in seven sections. To maximize track capacity, 24 miles were double tracked and Centralized Traffic Control (CTC) installed over 113 miles of the route.

Military demands fell heavily on the Atchison, which served numerous army, navy and marine installations. Troops moving to the West Coast over the ATSF required dozens of passenger cars and diners; moving one army division required 55 trains totaling some 22 miles of cars. The Santa Fe also provided men and units for the armed services from its own ranks. Some 12,000 former employees joined military units, and many served in railway battalions in India, Burma, Italy, France and North Africa. The 710th, 713th, and 758th Railway Battalions were mainly comprised of former ATSF employees. The 713th, or "Santa Fe Battalion," trained at Clovis in 1942, and worked the Amarillo-Belen line before being sent to Casablanca in 1943. The men operated trains, rebuilt bridges and track and established marshalling yards in Algeria, Tunisia, Italy, France and Germany, following the army all the way to Karlsruhe in 1945. The loss of so many employees, and the wartime labor shortage, led the ATSF to request permission to hire Mexican nationals. The federal government agreed, and of the system's 58,767 employees in 1943, 4,250 were Mexicans working on the railway from Illinois to California.

From 1943 through 1945, the tonnage carried continued to climb and operating revenues increased, but profits actually declined. Higher taxes, higher wages and the military discount kept profits from moving upward. Taxes in 1944 stood 678 percent above 1929, while gross earnings were up only 97 percent. Rates, both passenger and freight, were lower in 1944 than in 1929. As a result, the operating ratio climbed from 57.52 in 1944 to 76.50 in 1945. The Santa Fe management tried to handle the massive volume of traffic with all of the efficiency it could muster, but costs multiplied at a rapid rate. Only 22,700 new boxcars could be purchased, and so older cars were rebuilt. In order to turn equipment around rapidly, more men and unloading devices had to be utilized. The federal government pooled freight cars to meet national needs, but this policy hurt the Atchison because of its large holding of box and refrigerator cars. The payment of overtime or double-time for labor added to operating costs, and yet the traffic had to be moved, and moved quickly.

The demands placed on President Engel grew larger, and in 1944 he retired after 45 years of service. On August 1, 1944, Fred G. Gurley became president and chairman of the executive committee. Born in Sedalia, Missouri, in 1889, Gurley joined the Chicago, Burlington & Quincy in 1906 as a clerk, and for the next 33 years worked his way up on the "Q." By 1925 he had become general superintendent and had caught the eye of CB&Q executive Ralph Budd. Budd made him assistant to the vice president in charge of operations, and later vice president. Gurley helped bring the Zephyr and the diesel to the CB&Q, and his ability attracted the attention of Engel. In 1939 Engel offered him the ATSF's vice presidency, and Gurley came aboard. Engel and Gurley worked well together, sharing an enthusiasm for the diesel, streamlined passenger trains and the application of new technology to rail problems. An expert on motive power and operations, Gurley provided much of the executive leadership needed to meet the demands of World War II.

Gurley saw the necessity of growing with the Southwest, even during the war. He sought to place the Santa Fe in a position to attract greater traffic in developing urban areas, such as Oklahoma City and Long Beach. In Oklahoma City a local interurban line, the Oklahoma Railway, served as a freight feeder to nearby communities and operated a switching service for several industries, most notably the stockyards and adjacent meat-packing plants. In 1943 the Oklahoma Railway offered to sell its freight and switching lines, and the Santa Fe and Rock Island bought them for $373,942. The ATSF bought an eight-mile-long branch to the stockyards, and the Rock Island acquired 13 miles of track in the northern part of the

Fred G. Gurley, president of the Santa Fe from 1944 to 1957. Santa Fe Railway

city. The acquisition gave the ATSF a valuable switch line and access to another industrial area. A similar motivation led the Santa Fe to ask for ICC permission to reach the harbor at Long Beach. That city swelled in size to 250,000 people during the war as the harbor and nearby aircraft plants boomed. The ATSF had tried to reach Long Beach for nearly forty years, and wartime traffic made a connection mandatory. An ICC examiner recommended approval of the request to give the Santa Fe equal access with the Southern Pacific and Union Pacific, and the commission concurred in June 1945. The ICC agreed to allow the ATSF to build two miles of track, but after the decision, the SP and its local affiliate, Pacific Electric, gave the Atchison trackage rights to the harbor and a switching agreement, eliminating the need for new and costly construction. Atchison freight service began on December 15, 1945, and another significant source of freight was tapped.

The Santa Fe needed all of the business it could acquire in late 1945 and early 1946. The end of the war in August 1945 brought about a dramatic decline in freight and passenger business. Operating revenues fell sharply, though profits increased. Maintenance costs jumped drastically and were only partially offset by a reduction in federal taxes. An even greater emphasis on efficiency in 1946 brought about some stability; trains moved farther and faster with less motive power, passengers per train increased, and passenger locomotives covered more miles each day than ever before. Still Gurley battled to combat costs, and the board authorized $24.9 million in capital expenditures in 1946 for equipment, line relocation, grade reduction, new bridges and modern communications devices. The Atchison's financial position remained very strong, and Gurley had capital to spend largely because of sharply decreased fixed charges.

One of the brightest aspects of the Santa Fe's position at the end of the war could be found in its financial reports. Earnings had been very strong, and Engel and Gurley used much of this money to reduce the company's debts. Nearly $100 million in obligations were retired, and by 1945 all callable bonds had been paid. Equipment trusts were eliminated, and a large cash or negotiable bond reserve developed. At the end of the war the railway owed only $8.6 million per year in interest, and the highest interest rate being paid was 4.5 percent. Only the general mortgage bonds of $152 million and the adjustment mortgage bonds of $51 million remained outstanding. The conservative fiscal policies initiated by Ripley continued, and the demands of the postwar years could be dealt with from a solid financial base.

A substantial part of capital expenditures during the war and immediately thereafter was for a modern communications system and for more efficient train dispatching. In 1944 the Santa Fe began to install Centralized Traffic Control in areas with substantial numbers of trains. The use of CTC reduced train-running times by one-third and added as much as 80 percent to the capacity of a single-track line. CTC enabled a dispatcher miles away in a control room to set switches and route trains. Sitting in front of a massive control board on which small lights marked the progress of each train, a dispatcher could arrange meets, place trains on sidings, and regulate the use of second tracks. The initial cost of $13,000 per mile for CTC did not deter the management from rapidly expanding the system, and by 1946 some 520 miles of CTC had been installed. CTC proved highly valuable on the "surfline" to San Diego, on the Belen Cutoff through Abo Canyon in New Mexico, and on the heavily used main line tracks in Kansas.

The operating department also pioneered in the use of radio for rail communications. On June 4, 1944, one of the "Spud Specials," a fast

Switch crews directed by radio increased efficiency in the yards. Santa Fe Railway

freight carrying potatoes from Bakersfield to Chicago, moved across the system using a two-way radio-telephone device. The radio-telephone replaced the hand and whistle system which had been used since the nineteenth century. A radiophone in the locomotive, another in the caboose, and a matching set in a radio-equipped switcher allowed the train to be made up and operated by radio. The positive results of this test encouraged Gurley to rapidly extend the radio-telephone communications system to yard locomotives and cabooses and to create a radio network between Chicago and the West Coast and Chicago and Galveston. The Santa Fe's communications needs grew, and by 1946 the company handled the greatest volume of telephone and telegraph messages of any transportation operation in the world, largely by adopting a high frequency multichannel system. Over 2,700 of its employees worked in communications, and the CTC, radio-telephone and multichannel telegraph systems were extended throughout the Santa Fe, bringing greater efficiency in the utilization of locomotives and freight cars.

Engel and Gurley also spent millions of dollars to eliminate—or at least alleviate—traffic bottlenecks. One obstacle to rapid movement of freight and passengers was the Colorado River bridge near Needles. The cantilever bridge built in 1890 was the largest of its type in the nation, but it featured a low speed restriction, and the approaches contained several sharp curves. Work began in 1942 to construct a new bridge upstream from the old Red Rock bridge. The deepest pneumatic construction work under water yet attempted in the United States, the project located the piers 121 feet below the river level. The seven piers carried eight double-track spans some 1500 feet. When the bridge opened on March 8, 1945, schedules were reduced by ten minutes for passenger trains and twenty minutes for freight trains. Two years later the bridge at Canyon Diablo was also replaced. The existing bridge, built in 1900, had received a gauntlet track in 1913 to raise its capacity, but speed was restricted to ten miles per hour. The narrow but extremely deep canyon had to be rebridged, and engineers selected a site north of the existing bridge. Before the massive concrete piers could be poured, concrete was pumped into the cracks of the limestone walls. A false-work built from both sides of the canyon allowed workmen to erect the steel supports, but huge safety nets were hung below the iron workers as a safety precaution. The bridge consisted of a 300-foot hinged arch with 120-foot simple truss spans at either end for a total length of 544 feet. The roadbed, ballast and rails were continuous over the bridge, which had no speed restriction. The new bridge opened in September 1947.

During the war the Santa Fe and the SP improved the line over Tehachapi Pass, but the terrain limited the degree of efficiency which could be achieved. The 28 miles of track wound through 18 tunnels and up 2.5 percent grades. In 1943 the two roads installed CTC over the pass, but 70-car freight trains still required two 2–10–2 helpers, and speed was limited to 25 miles per hour for passenger trains and 20 miles per hour for freights. The rapid increase in industrial and agricultural production in the San Joaquin Valley placed heavier loads on the route through the pass, and peak use in the summer stretched the capacity of the line to its absolute limit. Significant grade and curve reduction would be delayed, however, for several years.

On its own lines the Atchison embarked upon a massive track-rebuilding and grade-improvement program. By 1945 the Santa Fe had 1,936 miles of double track, 44 miles of triple track, and 10 miles of line had 4 tracks. Further, the weight of new rails being laid was at least 110 pounds.

The installation of heavier rails, reduction of curves and grades and track relocation raised the maximum speed limits to 90 miles per hour on much of the main line. Three dam projects in Texas forced the GCSF to rebuild its tracks near the sites, and the extension of a jet airfield in the Mojave Desert led to a 26-mile relocation project. The engineering department also developed a flood-detection system in the mountains of Arizona to aid section crews in curbing the impact of flash floods. When flooding by several rivers in Kansas in 1951 destroyed miles of track, the replacement lines were built on higher ground with reduced grades and curves.

Throughout the system the improvement of terminal operations received considerable attention and absorbed millions of dollars in capital. Argentine Yard in Kansas City remained a bottleneck until 1947, when a long-planned expansion program began. The old flat yard was replaced by a hump yard containing 56 tracks which reduced switching time by as much as 10 hours for some freight cars. Argentine handled 4,000 cars daily at peak periods, and one-fourth of that volume was interchanged with the city's twelve other carriers. The town of Turner, Kansas, had to be moved to make way for the new yard, with its storage tracks, locomotive terminal and departure yards. Huge towers illuminated the yard at night as radio-equipped switchers assembled trains. A pit with a shatterproof glass covering located below the track enabled yardmen to inspect the running gear of the freight cars as they moved through the hump system. The Argentine Yard emerged as a giant facility, some four miles long and one-half mile wide.

Santa Fe tugs and barges, a common sight on San Francisco Bay. Santa Fe Railway

The Santa Fe "navy" on San Francisco Bay also needed and received attention. The three veteran 1,200-horsepower tugs were augmented by the all-steel tug "Edward J. Engel," and the even larger "John R. Hayden." A fleet of 260-foot-long barges each capable of carrying 14 freight cars moved traffic from Point Richmond to the San Francisco slips. By 1950 the tug fleet had been equipped with radio and radar, substantially improving freight service in the Bay area.

Between 1945 and 1953, the Atchison spent $126 million for improvements. About half of this sum went for new rail, grade improvements and yards, and the remainder was committed to shops, buildings, bridges and communications. Additional track relocation programs in Missouri and Texas raised speed limits and allowed increased tonnage assignments for locomotives. Gurley and the operating department sought to utilize the most modern technological devices and apply them to rail use. The board agreed to large-scale expenditures and to innovations broadly conceived. The federal government thwarted these programs on two occasions, however, restricting the ATSF's efforts to develop a modern and competitive transportation system.

On May 5, 1946, President Gurley announced the formation of Santa Fe Skyway, which would engage in contract air transportation in the territory served by the railway. A fleet of surplus Douglas DC-3 aircraft piloted by war veterans would operate from Chicago to the West Coast and to Texas. The Santa Fe also requested permission from the Civil Aeronautics Board to initiate service as a common carrier. Santa Fe Skyway purchased three DC-3s, established a headquarters at Wichita, Kansas, and inaugurated temporary service on July 1. Skyway named its planes

The inaugural flight of Santa Fe Skyway to Chicago. Santa Fe Railway

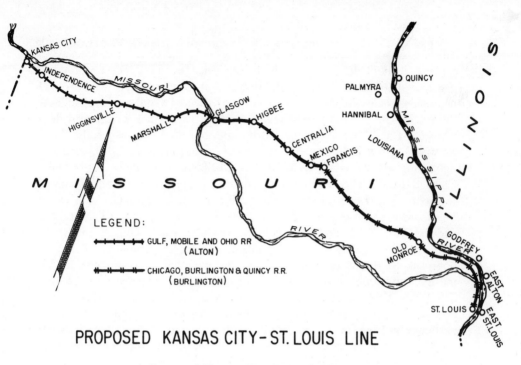

PROPOSED KANSAS CITY–ST. LOUIS LINE

Proposed Kansas City–St. Louis Line

for southwestern Indian tribes, and hired 18 pilots, 15 mechanics and 10 salesmen. The "flying refrigerators" carried strawberries, fish, peaches, melons and fresh flowers from California to the Midwest. The three DC-3s were joined in February 1947 by four C-54s capable of carrying 20,000-pound payloads. Much to the dismay of Gurley and the board, the CAB refused to allow the railroad to operate a common carrier airline, and denied its request. In late 1947, this attempt at a coordinated rail-air service was terminated.

Another attempt to improve rail service and enter a new market also fell victim to a negative decision by a federal regulatory agency. From the days of the Wakarusa Picnic through World War II, the Santa Fe had sought to enter St. Louis. The traffic moving from and through St. Louis to the West Coast was substantial, and the Atchison depended on interchange with other lines to obtain a share of the tonnage. If the ATSF had its own entrance, a larger proportion could be acquired. Gurley, like W. B. Strong before him, sought to gain entrance into St. Louis, and he turned to his old boss at the CB&Q, Ralph Budd, for support. The "Q" also desired to improve its St. Louis–Kansas City route by shortening its line, and also to improve its Chicago–Kansas City mainline. Gurley and Budd proposed a scheme to fulfill the desires of both railroads. In 1945, they proposed to purchase 156 miles of the Gulf, Mobile and Ohio (formerly the Alton) from Kansas City to Mexico, Missouri, and spend $5 million to rehabilitate the track. The GM&O would retain trackage rights and would provide a connection at Mexico with the CB&Q line into St. Louis which the Santa Fe would also use. In addition, the ATSF would give the CB&Q trackage rights over its main line from Bucklin to Sheffield to improve the "Q's" Chicago–Kansas City service. The Santa Fe proposed to use the Terminal Railroad in St. Louis to reach other railroads in the city. The plan called for no new construction and was quickly ratified by the ATSF, CB&Q and GM&O boards and stockholders. In June 1946, Gurley and Budd filed the proposal with the Interstate Commerce Commission for its approval. St. Louis civic leaders and the chamber of commerce lauded the plan and lobbied vigorously for the Atchison's entrance into the city. The Santa Fe brief stressed the improved service which the plan would produce, and won strong public support. Opposition mounted, however, particularly from the Chicago, Rock Island and Pacific, the Missouri Pacific, the Frisco and the Cotton Belt; several of the roads were in receivership, and they feared substantial traffic losses. The ICC examiner reported negatively on the plan, and said that the opposing railroads faced a loss of $10–12 million in annual revenue if the Santa Fe entered St. Louis. The reorganization plans of these railroads would be placed in jeopardy, contended the examiner. On July 6, 1948, the ICC denied the request because of its alleged impact on the financially weak roads. The narrow view taken by the commission prevented the logical expansion of the Santa Fe and denied St. Louis a significant transportation asset, but the two setbacks before the regulatory agencies did not deter Gurley in his determination to create a broadly conceived transportation system based on the Santa Fe Railway.

Between 1945 and 1955, Gurley and the management sought to expand the Santa Fe's sources of freight traffic, and they did so by offering more frequent and faster freight trains, by purchasing specialized cars for specific needs and by encouraging the growth of industry and new mining operations. Traffic analysis soon showed an absolute decline in some freight categories, such as petroleum and live cattle, and a substantial increase in manufactured goods, potash and coal. To enhance on-line loadings, the operating department provided nearly all branches with at least daily service, and timed deliveries to meet shipper needs if possible. Where competition was keen, running times were reduced; between 1946 and 1954 freight train time between Denver and Chicago was reduced by eight hours. Speed also became an essential element in the campaign to capture a larger share of the growing fresh produce market in the Southwest. As early as 1929 the railway obtained about 43 percent of the California citrus business and retained this sizable traffic with the "Green Fruit Express"—its refrigerated car special. Long lines of yellow and orange "reefers" gathered at San Bernardino, to be organized into solid trains of produce and rushed to Chicago. Over 14,000 reefers carried 100,000 loads of perishables from California and Arizona to the East each growing season. These cars consumed millions of tons of ice provided by icing platforms located along the line. Special trains moved the spring potato crop out of the San Joaquin Valley, and in 1949 a "Cotton Special" began to carry West Texas cotton from the Lubbock area to wharves at Houston and Galveston. Some shippers paid premiums of $1.25 per hundred pounds to have cars of produce included in a train which operated from Bakersfield to Chicago on a special 62-hour schedule. Agriculture remained a significant source of traffic for the ATSF, and wheat continued to be the single most significant commodity. Three-fourths of all the agricultural tonnage came from Kansas, Texas and Oklahoma. By the middle of the 1950s, the Atchison had developed a diversified business which enabled the system to cope with the vagaries of the national economy.

Unlike some other large systems heavily dependent on interchange traffic, the Santa Fe loaded and delivered on its own lines almost two-thirds of its tonnage. It also achieved a more balanced flow of carloadings from east to west and from north to south. Between Clovis and Belen, for example, car movement was almost perfectly balanced. The one-third of

Northern 2910 pounds through Kansas with the Fast Mail. Keith L. Bryant, Sr.

the Atchison's traffic acquired through interchange came largely from eastern carriers, and almost half of the cars were exchanged at Kansas City or in the Chicago area. Gurley and the departments responsible for traffic made the system less and less dependent on any one source of revenue and on other railroads.

This successful effort could not have been achieved without the phenomenal growth of the southwestern economy. As the population of California, Texas and Arizona swelled, the Atchison's traffic grew with it. The Santa Fe captured 30 percent of the traffic volume of California, over 90 percent of all rail traffic in New Mexico, 45 percent in Kansas, and 20 percent or more in Oklahoma and Colorado. The system moved slightly less than one-third of all rail freight in the Southwest, and originated nearly one-fourth of the total on its own rails!

The management responded to the alterations and growth of the southwestern economy and made equipment purchases needed to haul new cargoes. As the volume of manufactured goods increased, so did the number of boxcars and the fleet of "damage-free" cars. As "less-than-carload" traffic declined, the railway sought volume replacements. In southeastern New Mexico, the United States Potash Company operation near Carlsbad expanded after 1939 when potash previously acquired from Europe became unavailable. The potash production grew rapidly, and the ATSF built branches to reach the new mines. By the mid-1950s, Carlsbad, New Mexico, became the second largest revenue producing station on the system. The Gurley team coordinated its efforts to solicit new business, expand industrial development and to meet changing traffic requirements.

The advertising department concentrated on expanding passenger traffic before 1940, and freight solicitation was largely in the hands of agents and field representatives. The duties of the advertising department began to change in 1936 with the creation of the public relations department which absorbed the *Santa Fe Magazine* and assumed greater responsibility for broadcasting and interpreting the railway's operations to the public. The film bureau became a part of this operation, providing films and travelogues on transportation history, safety, and train tours to civic groups and schools. The advertising department developed a program of institutional advertising, and it began to place freight-only advertisements on a national scale. Large ads in 950 newspapers, *Look*, *The Saturday Evening Post*, and business journals were aimed primarily at shippers. The campaign stressed the theme that the Santa Fe was "America's New Railroad." The department coordinated its campaign with the increasingly important industrial department.

After 1945, the Atchison enlarged its efforts to attract new industries to sites along the line. The industrial department was expanded to include full-time agents in San Francisco, Los Angeles, Galveston and Topeka; and in 1951 the office of assistant to the president in charge of industrial development was created. The department integrated the system's industrial development activities and created industrial districts or sites at strategic locations. The railway purchased land along the line in a number of cities, leveled existing buildings, constructed utility systems and rail spurs, and solicited sales to mercantile and industrial corporations. In 1952 the Atchison had twenty-one such sites, each with 80 to 160 acres of land available for development. During the previous seven years some 3,100 plants had located along the Santa Fe, generating annual gross revenues of $150 million for the railway. The number of industrial sites continued to grow, and each year the industrial department made substantial contributions to car loadings.

This emphasis on new traffic included building branch lines and purchasing existing feeder railroads. To improve its access to several large manufacturing facilities near Chicago, the Atchison purchased a majority interest in the Illinois Northern Railway. The Illinois Northern owned or leased 19 miles of track, primarily serving the plant of its owner, International Harvester Company. In 1947, IH decided to sell the railway, and the Atchison joined the CB&Q, the New York Central and the Pennsylvania in purchasing the feeder. The Interstate Commerce Commission approved an agreement whereby the ATSF acquired 51 percent of the Illinois Northern, the CB&Q 25 percent and the other two lines 12 percent each. The purchase cost the Santa Fe $489,000, but it protected the company's share of the line's traffic. Similarly, the ATSF built new branches to reach developing industries. In 1957, a branch almost 30 miles long was extended to a Kaiser Steel Plant and a Permanente Cement facility at Hesperia, California. Even more spectacular, costly and productive was the Atchison's new branch into Dallas.

As has been seen, the Atchison's competitive position in Dallas remained weak even after the construction of the terminal warehouse complex. The entry into Dallas via the Cleburne-Dallas-Paris branch delayed freight movements, forced freight to travel a lengthy and circuitous route to reach the Chicago-Houston line at Cleburne, and caused Dallas passengers to be moved to and from Fort Worth by bus. The Dallas chamber of commerce had long sought to have the Santa Fe enter the city from the north to provide direct, one-carrier service to Chicago. Beginning in 1951, the ATSF surveyed possible routes, and in June 1953, Gurley proposed to build 38 miles of new track from the main line at Sawyer to a connection with the Cotton Belt at Addison, and to use the Cotton Belt from Addison to Dallas. The new line would reduce the ATSF's freight haul by 70 miles and would give the railway a 1,001-mile route to Chicago, quite competi-

Switcher 2357 maneuvers a string of tank cars at Argentine Yard. Santa Fe
Railway

tive with the Missouri Pacific–Gulf, Mobile and Ohio line of 995 miles via
St. Louis. Citizens of Dallas joined in requesting ICC approval of the proposal, but the towns of Denton and Richardson asked for relocation of the
proposed new construction so that they too would be served. Gurley
accepted the ICC's decision, which required service to Denton, and restruc-
tured the project as a 46.7-mile all-Santa Fe line from Sanger through
Denton to Garland on the ATSF's Paris-Dallas branch.

Construction began in late 1954, and the line opened on December 1 of
the following year. The longest main line construction in twenty-five years,
the northern entry gave the Santa Fe access to the booming industrial area
north of Dallas. Shippers in Dallas could now route freight directly to
Chicago and save seventy-two hours, and some 55,000 cars of freight were
forecast to move over the line during the first five years of operation. A
new industrial site of 172 acres was opened in northeast Dallas near the
line, and another site on the branch was acquired for development. At a
cost of $7 million, the Santa Fe built a low-gradient, high-density track
into one of the fastest growing cities on the system. The willingness to
spend capital on such projects solidified the confidence of investors in the
Atchison.

An article in *Fortune* in 1948 called the Santa Fe the "Nation's Number
One railroad" and praised its conservative, but progressive, management.
The company's organization was tight, employee morale was high, and
President Gurley was declared to be one of the best executives in the
business. This report called attention to the Santa Fe's size, strategic location, finances, and operations, and noted that in 1946–1948 the road
had earned more than the New York Central, the Pennsylvania and the

Southern Pacific combined. The financial analysis contained praise for the strong cash position of the Atchison and also its dividend policy. Between 1940 and 1947, the Santa Fe earned $344 million, paying dividends of $49.9 million on the preferred and $94.5 million on the common stock. The remaining profits were reinvested. Even though the annual common stock dividend rose to $6.00 with a $2.00 bonus, cash reserves grew to $150 million. The enormous reduction of the Atchison's debt also received favorable notice in this widely circulated journal story.

The Santa Fe enhanced its reputation as a "blue chip" stock under Gurley. Debt reduction and a low interest rate on outstanding bonds freed cash for dividends and capital needs. The debt per mile fell to $17,544 in 1948, and the total annual interest obligation decreased to $8,496,447. Four years later the annual interest payment declined to $6,096,519, compared with the Southern Pacific's obligation of $59,026,256. This strong financial position allowed the Santa Fe to regularly retire bonds and also pay cash for equipment. The only dark spot on the financial report was the enormous increase in taxes.

The level of taxation had peaked during World War II, with the tax bill reaching a sum two and a half times the total income for 1945. A modest decline followed at the beginning of the postwar period, but by 1949 the tax bill equaled $28.47 a share. The coming of the Korean War and an additional excess-profits tax, plus higher state and local property tax bills, drove the total tax payment to $110 million in 1952. The tax bill was $9.28 per share larger than the earnings available on the common stock, and it represented the third largest cost item in the system's budget. Only the payroll (43.4 percent) and the fuel and supply bill (16.2 percent) exceeded the tax levy (15.2 percent). The rising taxes and Gurley's personal conservatism made him an active Republican party member and a staunch supporter of Dwight D. Eisenhower and the Eisenhower administration.

Indeed, the management's conservatism, especially on fiscal matters, provoked a mild stockholder's revolt in 1952. A minority group of common stockholders called for larger dividends; they complained that of the $235 million in profits earned from 1946 to 1950, only 31 percent had been allocated for dividends. These stockholders formed a committee in New York City which demanded a special dividend of $2.80 per share to be paid out of a $12.8 million tax refund the railway was due to receive, and an additional $5.00 per share to be paid out of Western Improvement Company's holding of $50 million in federal bonds. This wholly owned subsidiary held real estate and petroleum properties which had produced extraordinary profits, and these stockholders wanted the profits distributed. The committee also called for increasing the regular dividend from

$1.00 to $1.50 a quarter. Further, they demanded a tax-free distribution of the stock of the nonrail subsidiaries to the railway's stockholders. The majority of stockholders failed to support these demands, but the board did vote an extra dividend of $1.25. This followed a decision of the previous year to double the outstanding common and preferred shares in a two-for-one split; the par value was reduced from $100 to $50 per share. The stock split expanded the already widespread distribution of Atchison stock. In 1953 the geographical distribution of common holdings included 8,600 stockholders in New York, 7,400 in Massachusetts, 700 in Kansas and 350 in Texas. Large blocks continued to be held by insurance companies, foundations, and lending institutions. A further enlargement in the total number of stockholders followed a five-for-one stock split in 1956 and a reduction of par value to $10 per share.

Demands for additional dividends, a demand made by only a small group of investors, were heard less frequently from 1954 until 1957 as operating revenues declined and profits began to slide. Dieselization expenses rose, passenger losses mounted, taxes climbed, and wages soared. In 1955, the board reduced capital expenditures by half following the achievement of dieselization and was faced with a continuing decline in revenue. Rising labor costs led to a substantial reduction in the total number of employees and the purchase of additional labor-saving devices. Nevertheless, the Atchison remained one of the rail industry's leaders.

Ernest S. Marsh, president of the Santa Fe from 1957 to 1967. Santa Fe Railway

The New York Times in 1955 declared: "things hum on the Santa Fe trail." In one of the most perceptive financial analyses to appear during the decade, the *Times* reported that "Largely because motive power had been completely dieselized, and its yards highly mechanized, and because the management has built one of the greatest communications networks in the world, the performance of the Santa Fe has improved strikingly."[2] The article noted the economic growth and vitality of the region served by the Atchison and also the high morale and loyalty of its employees. Such praise was welcomed by Gurley and the Atchison, and it demonstrated continued confidence in the system even as the nation's rail industry as a whole began to deteriorate and receive considerable public and political criticism.

The confidence in and praise for the Atchison reflected the generally positive parade of statistics flowing from the Chicago offices, as the following figures show.

OPERATING STATISTICS, 1940–1963

	Mileage	Operating Revenue ($)	Net Income ($)
1940	13,407	170,003,370	12,745,370
1941	13,418	225,043,648	30,236,581
1942	13,137	361,148,930	73,664,352
1943	13,147	471,119,015	57,440,364
1944	13,092	528,080,530	54,542,634
1945	13,108	528,703,149	29,414,499
1946	13,083	411,604,239	39,015,177
1947	13,103	462,699,237	47,743,744
1948	13,080	526,733,745	62,842,770
1949	13,095	482,753,947	50,042,147
1950	13,073	522,675,610	82,141,791
1951	13,096	570,581,708	73,345,778
1952	13,071	604,512,060	70,737,705
1953	13,092	613,531,290	77,185,997
1954	13,075	532,292,358	66,172,950
1955	13,146	578,034,019	77,564,886
1956	13,149	590,183,170	70,213,171
1957	13,172	610,714,053	61,941,791
1958	13,081	595,289,055	67,235,272
1959	12,992	633,836,363	65,785,901
1960	12,995	614,017,338	51,596,697
1961	12,979	604,523,603	54,850,383
1962	12,970	612,319,707	70,692,449
1963	12,947	616,080,371	67,500,733

When Fred Gurley decided to retire as president in 1957, he could do so with pride and in a year with nearly record operating revenues.

Between 1957 and 1959, the executive leadership of the Atchison underwent a period of transition. On April 1, 1957, Gurley stepped down as president of the railway but remained chairman of the board and chief executive officer. Ernest S. Marsh succeeded him as president. Born in Lynchburg, Virginia, in 1903, Marsh and his family moved to Clovis, New Mexico, and in 1918 he joined the Santa Fe. Moving up through the executive offices, he became chief clerk in the president's office in 1942, assistant to the president two years later, and in 1948 was named vice president for finance. Marsh became a member of the board in 1956, succeeded Gurley as chief executive officer in 1958, and became chairman of the board in 1967. (This position had not been utilized by management from 1959 to 1967.) A graduate of the advanced management program of the Harvard University School of Business Administration, Marsh brought to the presidency a broad background in railroading, especially finance. His skills were sorely taxed during his first three years as president by increasing costs and a declining net.

The vagaries of the national economy, including a recession in 1958, placed great pressure on the management. Rising taxes and wages, and few and modest rate increases placed the Santa Fe, and the rail industry in general, in a difficult position. Losses from passenger service grew, forcing the Santa Fe to make further applications for discontinuances. In order to achieve greater efficiency, larger capital outlays for labor-saving devices became mandatory. The immediate result was a substantial reduction in employees, a reduction of almost 4,000 individuals in 1961 alone. The Santa Fe obtained permission to absorb its Texas subsidiaries, the GCSF and P&SF, thus saving at least $2 million annually. Despite the efforts of Gurley, and then Marsh, the operating ratio could not be significantly reduced, as these figures demonstrate:

OPERATING RATIO, 1953–1966

1953	71.9	1960	78.5
1954	75.1	1961	77.2
1955	71.9	1962	79.2
1956	75.9	1963	80.6
1957	77.6	1964	80.3
1958	74.6	1965	78.4
1959	75.3	1966	76.9

The Atchison's board agreed with Marsh and his executives that the capital spending outlays had to be increased to make the railway competitive not only with other railroads but also with trucks and, hopefully, pipelines. In 1960 a modernization program began with an initial budget of $100 million, the largest in the history of the system. Hundreds of miles of welded rail, new high-horsepower "second-generation" diesels, expansion of the microwave network and 2,500 new freight cars absorbed most of this budget. The federal economic policy of providing a 7 percent investment tax credit encouraged even larger orders for new equipment in 1962. The ATSF bought 700 "shock-control" insulated boxcars, 50 piggyback flatcars, 200 center-flow covered hoppers and 750 boxcars. This impressive order was surpassed in size three years later by a capital budget of $115 million for 225 miles of welded rail, 4,500 freight cars and 100 diesel locomotives. These orders included triple-deck automobile carriers which brought back a large share of the new car and truck business to the railroads. In 1966 the capital budget included a contract of $38 million with the Pullman-Standard works for 2,500 "jumbo" covered hoppers to be used for bulk cargoes such as wheat and potash. This enormous outpouring of funds did cause operating revenues to increase, as did the general prosperity of the period, but the financial burden of the system fairly leaped to new heights.

In 1960, the Atchison owed $198,726,603 in the form of the general mortgage and adjustment bonds ($185,153,000) and equipment trusts ($13,573,603), with $22,870,978 in the voluntary debt retirement fund. Only six years later the debt climbed to $323,898,889 with the general mortgage reduced to $178,838,500, but the equipment trusts soaring to an incredible $134,743,276. The increase of $120 million in equipment obligations is indicative of the total commitment of the management to creating the best-managed and most technologically advanced rail system in the nation. It should be noted that even in 1966 the conservative fiscal policies had not been abandoned by any means—the voluntary debt reduction fund contained $45,549,555.

The commitment to technological advances and to scientific management deepened when John S. Reed became president of the railway. In November 1966, Marsh was elected chairman, and the board selected Reed to become president in January 1967. In many ways Reed brought a new set of experiences to the presidency and a background dissimilar to previous executives. Born in Chicago in 1917, Reed graduated from Hotchkiss School and Yale University before joining the Santa Fe in 1939. After serving as a lieutenant commander in the navy during World War II, he rejoined the ATSF, becoming a test department assistant, trainmaster, and divisional superintendent at Marceline, Missouri. He entered the executive offices as assistant to the vice president in 1954, becoming vice president of the executive department in 1964. A well-educated member

John S. Reed, president of the Railway and Santa Fe Industries. Santa Fe Railway

of an old Chicago family—his grandfather, John Groves Shedd, had donated the Shedd Aquarium to the city—Reed initiated programs for long-range planning, reemphasized the need for more highly trained executives, and demanded greater utilization of equipment, particularly the diesel locomotives.

Under Gurley, the Atchison had initiated a program to provide its personnel with advanced business skills. In 1952, in cooperation with the University of Southern California's School of Commerce, the ATSF established a six-week summer training program for its junior and senior executives. Thirty to forty men between the ages of 28 and 54 gathered on the USC campus for a vigorous study program dealing with managerial and social problems. For eight hours a day, five days a week, these "middle managers" labored in classrooms and seminars. The railway paid their expenses, and the men brought their families along. The individuals selected for the course were often the "juniors" who stood behind an executive in the corporate structure. Further, the Santa Fe began to hire personnel for the executive and operating departments with the technical skills to operate the data processing center in Topeka and the computerized inventory control in purchasing.

Under Reed's direction, the equipment acquisition program was accelerated, as were several line-rebuilding projects. One of the largest sources of new revenue for the Santa Fe was the movement of truck trailers on flatcars (TOFC or "piggybacks") and metal containers on flatcars. In 1952 experiments began with trailers on flats, and several runs were made with Dry Ice trailers containing semiperishable products. By 1954 the program had proven so successful that the Santa Fe offered TOFC service from Chicago to the West Coast and to the Gulf of Mexico. Flatcars carrying two trailers each became common on expedited freight trains, and soon solid TOFC trains became necessary. The railway's truck subsidiary provided many of the trailers, but trucklines and rail-industry-owned trailers predominated. With the growth of TOFC, the Santa Fe built 88-foot-long, depressed-deck flatcars to carry long trailers and to lower the center of gravity. The TOFC business grew from 113,523 trailers in 1968 to 156,262 in 1972. During that same period, transportation of sealed metal containers on flatcars climbed from 1,626 units to 22,749 units. Most of the containers were destined to ports for overseas shipment, and this traffic increased, especially to Japan, following a visit by Reed and other executives to the Orient. The trailer and container business required capital outlays for loading platforms and cranes, but traffic growth more than justified the expenditures.

Similarly, line improvements, while costly, began to generate a return. The Santa Fe embarked on a major effort in 1955 to reduce track maintenance costs, primarily through the installation of welded rail. The program began with the welding of short lengths of rail on the line with welding machinery carried on flatcars. The great success of welded rail in reducing maintenance costs led to the development of fixed facilities to weld ribbons of rail which were then moved to installation sites on trains of flatcars. The grade-reduction effort continued in 1960 with a new line, 44 miles long, west from Williams, Arizona, to Crookton. The new main line cost $20 million, but it eliminated clearance restrictions and established a faster 60-mile-per-hour speed limit for freight trains. A part of the old main line from Williams to Ash Fork remained operative to reach the Phoenix branch. The Ash Fork–Phoenix line, long a major bottleneck, received a $3.5 million face-lift with 38 miles of new track through Skull Valley, cutting the distance to Phoenix by 14 miles and vastly reducing grades and curvature. A similar project in 1972 reduced curves over Cajon Pass from 10 to 4 degrees, but failed to reduce the grade. Nevertheless, running time was trimmed by seven minutes.

Technology was also applied to the continuing problems of moving

Containers on flatcars, a common sight in the 1960s. Santa Fe Railway

freight through yards and of greater utilization of motive power. In 1970 Secretary of Transportation John Volpe attended the opening of the Santa Fe's 48-track computerized yard in Kansas City, which was capable of sorting 8,000 cars daily. Electromagnetic identification scanners guided the cars to the proper track as they moved over the hump and down into the yard. The system reduced the classification time by 50 percent. Also in 1970 the Santa Fe established a centralized control bureau in the Chicago headquarters which directed and coordinated the assignment of diesel units and cabooses. The bureau sought to achieve maximum utilization of the $300 million diesel fleet by centralizing control. A large display board with magnetic markers maintained a continuous record of the location of all locomotives and their availability. The bureau provided the operating department with data on locomotive and caboose requirements for the entire system.

Yet all of the new hardware and technological advances did not eliminate the need for dedicated employees doing jobs similar to those performed in Kansas in the 1870s. Men such as Track Supervisor Charley Mendez still moved over the line checking for flash flood damage and vandalism and making minor repairs. Mendez traveled the 250-mile Mojave Desert line in a two-cylinder motor car, covering 100 miles daily at 10 to 20 miles per hour. Unlike his predecessors, however, Mendez communicated through a radio transmitter when major repairs called for a section crew. But even this important task may be reduced in scope if a Santa Fe and Department of Transportation (DOT) experiment succeeds. In 1970 the railway and the federal government initiated a track research project near Wichita to test track stability for higher speeds and heavier cars. A similar experiment with the DOT near Pueblo tested higher speed ground-transportation devices.

The Atchison began to reemphasize speed in 1968 as it had not done since the days of the first Super Chief. Early that year Reed announced the inaugural run of the "Super C," a hotshot, all-TOFC and container freight train on a 34½-hour schedule from Chicago to Los Angeles. The track-improvement program and new diesels allowed "Super C" to better the old Super Chief schedule. Moving at an average speed of 63.7 miles per hour, "Super C" premiered on January 17 as the world's fastest freight train. Shippers paid a premium rate of $1,400 per trailer, but they received guaranteed fast delivery to Los Angeles or Chicago. In cooperation with an expedited freight train over the Penn-Central from the East Coast, a New York City to Los Angeles trailer could be transported in 54 hours and 20 minutes coast to coast. Despite criticism from some quarters that railroads should sell bulk and not speed, "Super C" became a well-utilized service of the ATSF.

The Kaiser Steel unit trains roar out of York Canyon. Santa Fe Railway

The management did not neglect the development of the railway's potential as conveyor of heavy bulk cargoes at low rates. The concept of the unit-train, a semipermanently coupled body of freight cars and locomotives hauling a single commodity, received two major applications on the system. The hauling of coal on the Santa Fe had declined with the emergence of the diesel locomotive, and only the demands of World War II kept the extensive coal fields near Raton operative. In 1955, the Kaiser Steel Company purchased 202,853 acres of coal land near Raton as a source of fuel for its Fontana, California, plant. Kaiser began to explore its holdings, and by 1964 was ready to open a huge mine at York Canyon in the Sangre de Cristo Mountains. The Santa Fe agreed to build a 37.5-mile heavy-duty branch to the mine and to create a unit coal train to haul the fuel to California. The steel company required 700,000 tons of coal annually, and to meet this need the ATSF purchased 101 coal cars with a capacity of 100 tons each and acquired 11 diesel units for power. The unit train could carry 8,400 tons of coal to the plant every four days. The new branch cost $4 million, and the unit train represented an investment of an additional $2 million. On September 28, 1966, the operation began with the train making a 2,164-mile round trip, the longest distance covered by a unit train on a single railroad.

A unit train of sulphur from the plains of Texas bound for Galveston. Santa Fe Railway

Three years later the ATSF created another unit train at a more advanced level of technology. The Duval Corporation planned to develop a sulphur mine at Rustler Springs, Texas, not far from the Santa Fe's Coleman Cutoff. The Duval Corporation desired to transport the sulphur to Galveston for shipment by water. Sulphur is a commodity which is difficult to move by rail, and the Santa Fe and the Duval Corporation engineers devised a method of shipping the mineral in a molten state. The sulphur was heated to 290 degrees, then fed into large tank cars, and hauled to Galveston, where enough heat remained in the cars to allow the sulphur to be easily unloaded. The Santa Fe built a 30-mile spur to the plant, and purchased three unit trains of 66 cars each to make the 930-mile run to Galveston. Four diesel units powered each train as it traveled from the mine to Galveston and returned in a continuous movement. Again, the Santa Fe proved its willingness to use technology and spend capital to attract new business. The cost of the Rustler Springs branch and the three unit trains represented only a fraction of the $2 billion in capital spent by the Santa Fe between 1945 and 1972.

In the post-Korean War years the Atchison acquired new lines and constructed branches. The ATSF sought to purchase lines which could feed additional cars into the system, or strengthen its competitive position. One example of this policy was the acquisition of the Toledo, Peoria and Western Railroad. The TP&W operated 239 miles of track from Lomax, Illinois, on the ATSF, through Peoria to Effner, Indiana, on the Pennsylvania Railroad. The TP&W served as a bridge line, bypassing the traffic congestion of Chicago. The road hauled 120,000 cars yearly and switched an additional 18,000. In 1955, when the Santa Fe made its first offer to purchase the line, it had had a checkered history. The TP&W had gone through a period of violent conflict between its owners and employees, and the federal government had been forced to operate the railroad from 1942 to 1945. It had been dieselized, however, and had 41 miles of welded rail and 7,500 acres of industrial land along its route. The Atchison offered $135 per share for 82 percent of the common stock, and when the Pennsylvania asked to be included in the purchase, the management agreed to a 50–50 division of the stock. The ICC agreed to the purchase arrangement in 1957, but final transfer did not occur until 1960. At a cost of $6,075,000, the Santa Fe obtained half-interest in a physically modern bridge line which became an important transcontinental link bypassing Chicago.

Two years later the Atchison purchased the 105-mile-long Oklahoma City–Ada–Atoka Railway, operating from Oklahoma City through Ada to Tupelo, Oklahoma. The OC-A-A had been a part of the "Muskogee lines" (including the Kansas, Oklahoma and Gulf and the Midland Valley), and when the Missouri Pacific's subsidiary the Texas and Pacific Railway bought the "Muskogee lines," the Santa Fe offered to purchase the OC-A-A for $1 million. The T&P accepted, and the ICC approved the sale. The Santa Fe bought the OC-A-A to obtain access to Tinker Airforce Base and to enable the ATSF to abandon some of its own branches. The OC-A-A operated directly to Ada, and the Santa Fe abandoned parts of its lines in the Shawnee-Ada area, continuing a program of track reduction in central and northern Oklahoma.

The Atchison's success in making these purchases was not repeated when it attempted to buy the Western Pacific Railroad. The WP operated from Oakland to Salt Lake City, competing directly with the Southern Pacific. Built by George Gould as a part of a proposed transcontinental railroad, the WP had been in and out of bankruptcy several times. It did have several assets, notably a low-grade freight line through the Sierra Nevada, a substantial interchange at Salt Lake City with the Union Pacific and the Denver and Rio Grande Western, extensive branches in the East Bay-Sacramento area, and a part of the "Bieber Route." The latter line was an interior route from the Pacific Northwest to southern California using the Great Northern from Seattle and Portland south to Bieber, California, the WP from Bieber to Stockton, and the ATSF from

Stockton to Los Angeles and San Diego. The "Bieber Route" prevented the SP from establishing a north-south rail monopoly in California. The Atchison and GN had a significant stake in maintaining the WP's independence, but that independence was gravely threatened when the Southern Pacific announced in 1960 that it planned to acquire the WP and merge it into the SP.

Immediately following the SP's announcement, the Santa Fe moved to protect itself. An Atchison subsidiary, the Chanslor-Western Oil and Development Company, purchased 365,000 shares of WP common, 20 percent of the outstanding shares, and placed them in a trust. The Santa Fe then offered to exchange 1¼ shares of ATSF common for one share of WP, and announced its intention to purchase the Western Pacific. The SP owned 10 percent of the WP stock, and to protect their interests, the GN bought 8.6 percent and the Union Pacific 9.9 percent of the WP shares. The ICC then began a lengthy series of hearings on the plans put forth by the SP and the ATSF. The GN and the WP management favored the Santa Fe, but the UP, Missouri Pacific, DRG&W, Milwaukee Road and the Rock Island favored the Espee. President Marsh of the Santa Fe told an ICC hearing officer that SP control would seriously diminish rail competition in northern California. The Justice Department announced its opposition to any external control of the WP, and urged its continued independence as did the state governments of Arizona, California, Nevada, Oregon, Washington and New Mexico. President Frederick B. Whitman of the WP pleaded for ICC approval of the Santa Fe plan, and the examiner so recommended. The ICC ruled against either plan, however, and in 1965 ordered the Santa Fe to sell its WP holdings. The shares were sold for a profit of over $5.5 million. The ICC's decision to maintain the independence of the WP prevented the SP from gaining additional strength in the Bay area and in northern California, but for the Santa Fe, as Marsh said, "naturally there is disappointment."[3]

The entire merger question became increasingly significant after 1960. In the East and South, mergers and merger plans incorporated nearly every major carrier in the two regions. Merger became synonymous with improved financial strength and economy of operation. In the Midwest several of the "Granger" roads remained "sick," and merger plans began to be developed there. The Norfolk and Western took the Wabash, and the Chicago and Northwestern acquired the Minneapolis and St. Louis and the Chicago Great Western; but the "sickman of Granger roads"—the Chicago, Rock Island and Pacific—remained independent and financially ailing. This strategically located railway, with its Chicago-Omaha, Chicago-Houston, Chicago-Tucumcari, Minneapolis-Kansas City, and Memphis-Tucumcari routes, touched nearly every major city between Canada

Branch-line "doodlebugs" continued into the postwar decade. Keith L. Bryant, Sr.

and the Gulf of Mexico and became sought after by the Union Pacific, the Southern Pacific, the Chicago and Northwestern and the Santa Fe. The UP proposed to purchase all of the Rock Island north of Kansas City and sell the remainder to the SP. The CNW countered with an offer to purchase the CRI&P, sell the Santa Fe everything south of Kansas City except the line to Tucumcari, and give the Santa Fe trackage rights into St. Louis. Every railroad in the region filed an interested party position, and the ICC began the most complex hearings in its history. While volumes of testimony were taken, the whole merger psychology was shaken by the financial collapse of the Penn-Central; some of the roads became stronger, others weaker, and the CNW became separated from its former holding company. After seven years of studies and hearings, the ICC examiner issued a report which favored the CNW/ATSF plan in principle, but urged a series of massive mergers for the entire area west of the Mississippi River. The report proposed the creation of four super-railroads, with the Santa Fe to acquire not only part of the Rock Island but also the Missouri Pacific, the Western Pacific and the DRG&W. While the fate of the proposal was before the ICC, the management of the Santa Fe attempted to find its own merger partners.

In 1963–1965, the Atchison began a series of exploratory talks first with the Missouri Pacific Railroad and then the St. Louis–San Francisco Railroad (Frisco) in contemplation of possible mergers. The Mississippi River Corporation, which controlled the MP, urged the merger of the two systems, but the Santa Fe management became concerned over the snares and tangles of the MP's securities, and the talks collapsed. Negotiations with the Santa Fe's old partner the Frisco commenced, much to the annoyance of the Missouri Pacific. Talks with the Frisco ended, however, when the price appeared to be far higher than the Atchison was willing to pay. William Marbury of the MP urged a continuation of earlier discussions, but the Santa Fe decided to halt the merger negotiations.

The ATSF board of directors and officers failed to anticipate the persistence of the MP and noted with alarm the sale of 851,500 shares of ATSF preferred stock in February 1966. Marbury soon announced that the MP held over 2 million shares of the Atchison's preferred and planned to buy the Santa Fe! The MP became the largest single holder of Atchison stock, prompting an immediate protest by the ATSF before the ICC. In June, the MP asked the ICC for permission to acquire control of the Atchison, and the MoPac countered the Atchison's protest by purchasing an additional 200,000 shares of stock. The MP maintained that a merger would aid both roads and that the Santa Fe's stockholders favored such a move. The ICC refused to block the MP's proposal, but continued sharp opposition by the Santa Fe and the enormous cost involved led the MoPac to drop its request in 1968.

One reason for the conclusion of the merger talks and the strenuous opposition to outside control was a decision by the board and the management to shift, somewhat, the Atchison's historic position. The railway had long been a diversified corporation with rail, truck, oil, real estate, lumber and other activities. With the profits of the railroad stationary or reduced, while the other interests increased in profitability, the decision was made to create a new holding company of which the railway would be only one part. To escape from the restrictions placed on the railway, to gain possible tax advantages, and to enter new and, hopefully, more profitable fields, the board authorized the formation of Santa Fe Industries in November 1967. Another era for the Atchison, Topeka and Santa Fe Railway began.

11

The Coming of the Diesel

Following the end of World War I and control by the U.S. Railroad Administration, the Atchison, Topeka and Santa Fe Railway entered into another era in its continuing development of the steam locomotive. The "mania" for mallets and compounding ended, and the company began to stress speed and efficiency rather than size. For the next thirty years the motive power department developed its own designs for new steam locomotives and constantly upgraded older power with devices which raised their level of performance. In the midst of this program, the Santa Fe became captivated by the potential of the diesel motor and its adaptation to railroading. Working with several locomotive builders, the Atchison became a pioneer in the use of diesel-electric power. By 1957 the age of steam on the Santa Fe had ended as the diesel took over all aspects of motive-power use—switching, freight trains and passenger trains. This technological revolution profoundly affected labor relations on the railway and dramatically altered life in the small railroad towns along the line. The number of locomotives declined, though not as rapidly as the number of employees, and some "railroad towns" died from dieselization. The motive-power revolution occurred gradually, and for a few years it was possible to observe an antique 4–4–0 standing in a yard with a 5,400-horsepower diesel freight locomotive; but the long-range impact of dieselization was substantial.

The arrival of a new era in the employment of steam locomotives became apparent very early in the twenties. The number of locomotives

Extensive rebuilding kept No. 1600 working until the age of steam ended.
Keith L. Bryant, Sr.

owned declined from 2,195 in 1920 to 1,993 in 1929, but the total tractive effort rose by 25 percent. The average tractive effort climbed from
36,741 pounds in 1919 to 49,736 in 1929. The operating department
worked with Santa Fe engineers to design new locomotives to meet specific problems. This led to the use of heavier Pacifics (4–6–2), Mountains
(4–8–2), Mikados (2–8–2), Berkshires (2–8–4), Hudsons (4–6–4), and
Santa Fe types (2–10–2). These locomotives received the most recently
developed equipment and apparatus designed to achieve efficiency, including power reverse, feedwater and superheaters, and automatic coal stok-
ers, and many engines were converted from coal to oil burners. The
conversion from coal to oil came so quickly that huge electric-operated
concrete coal tipples constructed along the line in 1921–1922 were never
filled with a single lump of coal. The Santa Fe scrapped the light-weight
remnants of its pre-1914 power, especially the Tenwheelers, and most of
the mallets. The modernization effort was primarily a function of the company shops, with new power obtained from the Baldwin locomotive
works.

After 1915 the Atchison established its own specifications for new
steam locomotives, and furnished drawings and detailed requirements to
Baldwin. The Atchison placed its own inspectors from the mechanical
engineering office in the builder's shops to insure compliance with the specifications. The Santa Fe continued its close relations with Baldwin, and
the two firms developed several classes of fine, serviceable power.

The backbone of the mainline freight locomotive roster in the twenties
was the 2–10–2. Baldwin delivered 30 of these outstanding locomotives
in 1919, and they demonstrated the full potential of the type. The 3800
Class, as they were designated, were rugged and fast. With their 63-inch
drivers, 30 by 32-inch cylinders and tractive effort of 81,500 pounds, they
could move long freight drags across the Belen cutoff or down the GCSF

line to Galveston. The Atchison's admiration for the 2–10–2 led to subsequent orders nearly every year from 1919 to 1927 and brought the number of the 3800 and 3900 Classes to 140. The locomotives of 1924, 1926 and 1927 were slightly larger in size, and some were equipped with booster engines raising their top speed to 55 miles per hour. The last Santa Fe types were ordered in 1927, but throughout the next two decades they received constant design changes. During World War II the 2–10–2s labored for many months of continuous use in transcontinental freight service, with few mechanical failures. Many were rebuilt after 1945 and received roller bearings and lightweight drive rods; some survived until the end of the steam era.

For shorter freight trains on secondary lines, the Santa Fe selected the 2–8–2, or Mikado. The famous USRA 2–8–2 design failed to attract the Atchison, which developed its own concept in 1917 and refined it further in 1921. The locomotives of 1917–1920 were much larger than earlier 2–8–2s and were comparable to the L-1 Class on the Pennsylvania. An even larger Mikado design came from Baldwin in 1921–1926, the 4000 Class. The 101 units of this class had 63-inch drivers, weighed 330,500 pounds, and could hold their own on the main lines. These rugged but conservative locomotives also continued in service until after 1945.

The need for larger passenger power to pull longer trains of heavier steel cars led to the expansion of the fleet of Mountain types (4–8–2). The design originated on the Chesapeake and Ohio in 1911, and it was generally used on passenger trains in mountain service or for manifest freight. In 1918 the Atchison purchased its first 4–8–2s, and during the next six years added to its roster of Mountains. The 3700 Class became very popular with both trainmen and the operating department, and some 51 units were to be found on the ATSF with the delivery of the last

A workhorse of the passenger fleet—Mountain-type No. 3700. H. L. Broadbelt

group in 1924. The Santa Fe's Mountains had large cylinders and boilers and could generate a substantial tractive effort as they conquered the system's long, continuous grades. Extra power was essential because of the substantial number of mail and baggage cars on Santa Fe passenger trains and the need for steam in the diners and lounges. The last order received disk drivers, and nearly all the Mountains operated with feedwater heaters. Because of their limited speed, the Mountains lost out to a second generation of heavy passenger locomotives, and by the thirties they were largely in fast freight service. World War II brought them back to the passenger trains, especially troop trains, and they performed magnificently in the service for which they were designed.

Just as the mountain divisions needed heavier power, a larger, faster freight locomotive was needed between Chicago and Kansas City to replace the Mikados, which were becoming inadequate to meet the ever-increasing demands of the freight schedules. In 1927 the Santa Fe purchased the first of 22 Berkshires, or 2–8–4s, primarily for the Missouri division. The 4101 Class came with 63-inch drivers, a larger grate area and a tractive effort of 69,200 pounds. Little more than expanded Mikados, the 2–8–4s pulled "hotshot" freights of less than 75 cars from Chicago west as far as La Junta or Wellington. The Berkshire fleet was not enlarged, however, as these engines simply did not have the size needed for long freight trains. During World War II the Santa Fe purchased seven more Berkshires from the Boston and Maine, but the design did not warrant a reorder in the twenties.

With the expansion of passenger services in the twenties, and with many trains operating in multiple sections, the Santa Fe added to its fleet of Pacifics, ordering more 4–6–2s in the period from 1919 to 1924. The Baldwin-built Pacifics belied their simple appearance; although the 3400 Class seemed quite ordinary, they were very modern, and the Santa Fe constantly improved them with larger drivers and superheaters and raised their capacity and speed. Although they could not exceed 70 to 75 miles per hour, they were to be found in California and on the gulf lines pulling secondary passenger trains during World War II. Indeed, only 87 of the 274 units owned by the Santa Fe had been scrapped before 1941. Despite these improvements, however, the Atchison still needed a faster passenger locomotive, especially east of La Junta.

Baldwin and Santa Fe engineers collaborated on a new design in 1927 to respond to this need, and they produced the 10 Hudsons (4–6–4) of the 3450 Class. The Hudson type became very popular in the East, particularly on the New York Central and the Pennsylvania, but never achieved widespread use in the West. Although the 3450 Class replaced the heavy Pacifics and produced greater speed and tractive efforts, the

A modern Pacific from Baldwin, often found on the Coast and Gulf lines.
H. L. Broadbelt

design was less than a total success, and in the 1930s, the Hudsons were
rebuilt and given disc drivers. Of far greater importance in the evolution
of modern steam power on the Santa Fe was the arrival of the first
Northern (4–8–4) in 1927.

During the previous year Santa Fe engineers worked on a design for a
4–8–4, and Number 3751, built from ATSF specifications, arrived from
Baldwin to enter a strenuous testing program. The Northern won great
respect from trainmen throughout the country, and Atchison engineers
found 3751 to be a highly successful locomotive. For almost a year 3751
ran between Albuquerque and La Junta over Raton Pass. In comparison
with the Mountains then in use, 3751 could pull a one-third heavier load
with almost 20 percent less fuel. It could start a train of 26 passenger cars
and pull 9 of them over Raton without a helper. The Atchison ordered 13
more! In 1927–1929, the Northerns arrived with 73-inch drivers, superheaters, one-piece steel cylinders and feedwater heaters. They won praises
from all departments and received additional modernization features. Converted to oil burners, they acquired 80-inch drivers, roller bearings and
larger tenders with roller bearings. These improvements allowed the Northern to operate from Kansas City to Los Angeles, 1,776 miles. These
locomotives substantially improved operations in the mountain divisions,
but the coming of the depression drastically reduced the locomotive
requirements of the operating department.

Between 1922 and 1932, the Atchison spent over $25 million for new
locomotives, but from 1933 until 1938, expenditures fell to $9 million; only
$31,000 was spent in 1933. And yet throughout the thirties the Santa Fe
and Baldwin created some of the finest steam power in the country. While

Backbone of the steam fleet, the Northerns delivered speed and efficiency. Keith L. Bryant, Sr.

appropriations for new locomotives were greatly reduced, work in the engineering offices continued, and in 1930, a design emerged which produced record-breaking performances.

In 1919 Baldwin created the first 2–10–4 ever built with a separate tender for the Santa Fe, and Number 3829 became the first large American-built locomotive with a two axle trailing truck. The Atchison did not reorder the design, but it remained interested especially as the 2–10–2s won additional accolades. Eleven years later, Santa Fe engineers asked Baldwin to construct Number 5000, or "Madame Queen" as she would become known. More modern in design than a similar Chesapeake and Ohio 2–10–4, Number 5000 with 69-inch drivers and 93,000-pound tractive effort could haul 15 percent more tonnage on 17 percent less fuel in 9 percent less time between Clovis and Belen than a 3800 Class 2–10–2. After testing Number 5000 for several years with similar positive results, an order was placed in 1936 for five more 2–10–4s, to become 5001–5005. Delivered in 1937, these coal burners were basically copies of 5000. They had 74-inch drivers, 30 by 34-inch cylinders, weighed 545,260 pounds, and their tenders held 23 tons of coal. These clean-lined beauties performed with such splendid results that the Santa Fe placed an order for five more oil-burning 2–10–4s, which Baldwin delivered in 1939. Almost identical to the first group, these 2–10–4s pulled tenders carrying some 21,000 gallons of oil. With tractive efforts almost equal to a mallet, these ten giant locomotives could produce 5,600 horsepower at 40 miles per hour and could pull a train of 80 cars with relative ease. Only the coming of the diesel freight locomotive and the Second World War prevented immediate additions to this class.

At the time the Santa Fe placed the order for the first group of 2–10–4s, it also purchased another class of 4–8–4s. The earlier Northerns continued to do yeoman service pulling both freight and passenger trains, and by the early thirties they were covering two or three divisions in a run. Some traveled from La Junta to Los Angeles, 1,234 miles, with nine crew changes. The engineering department improved the design in 1936, and the Santa Fe ordered eleven more 4–8–4s, largely for passenger service. The 3765 Class arrived from Baldwin graceful in appearance but capable of enormous work. Three years later another order came from Baldwin, Numbers 3776–3785, almost identical to the 3765 Class. These Northerns carried a nickel-steel boiler above their 80-inch drivers and could generate a tractive effort of 66,000 pounds. In passenger operation they could be serviced and made ready for a return trip in as few as three hours. Capable of attaining 90 miles an hour, they pulled the Chief from La Junta to the West Coast, using a helper over Raton Pass. East of La Junta the Chief and other passenger trains were headed by sisters of the Northerns, a class of Hudsons also ordered in 1937.

The Santa Fe needed additional passenger power capable of reaching high speeds with lengthy trains, and the 3460 Class of 4–6–4s was purchased to do the job. Large and heavy, with 84-inch drivers, the Hudsons could achieve 90 miles per hour. The six engines in the class had huge tenders to make the 992-mile Chicago–La Junta run with as few stops as possible. One of the group, 3460, arrived with a streamlined shroud painted in several shades of blue, and became the "Blue Goose" to its

"Madame Queen", the first of the 2–10–4s. H. L. Broadbelt

No. 3460 heads the "Chicagóan" on a cold Oklahoma morning. Keith L.
Bryant, Sr.

crews. The Hudsons did not achieve the same high level of performance
as their sister 2–10–4s and 4–8–4s, but with tractive efforts of 49,300
pounds and roller bearings they met the requirement for long, sustained
runs at high speed, and they easily replaced the heavy Pacifics previously
used. One of this class, Number 3461, left Los Angeles on December 12,
1937, and pulled mail train Number 8 to Chicago in 49 hours and 5 minutes using helpers twice and stopping for water 18 times and fuel 5 times.
The locomotive was serviced, turned around, and sent back west.

The steam locomotives delivered in 1937–1941 continually set records
for speed, distance and economy of operation. All three types—4–8–4,
4–6–4 and 2–10–4—had interchangeable parts, reducing maintenance
costs. They operated over longer distances aided by larger tenders, more
effective lubricants, and roller bearings. These locomotives averaged
9,000 miles of revenue service a month in passenger use and 6,000 miles
per month in freight assignments. Their utility and flexibility enabled the
mechanical department to reallocate its resources. The number of locomotives declined in the thirties from 1,993 to 1,600, and the average tractive effort rose from 49,736 pounds to 54,042 pounds. But the great success of these steam locomotives only temporarily beclouded the Santa Fe's
interest in other types of power. The gas-electric "doodlebugs" in branch
line passenger service proved valuable, but not until 1935 did the Atchi-

son acquire a true diesel locomotive, Number 2300, a 600-horsepower diesel switcher built by the American Locomotive Company (Alco).

Named for its inventor, Rudolph Diesel, the diesel motor came into prominence in railroading in the mid-1930s. Rudolph Diesel, a German engineer, developed an engine which operated on a mixture of compressed air and oil which exploded to create energy. In railroad use, the diesel engine powered a generator which fed electric current to traction motors located on the axles of the locomotive's wheels. The diesel motors were constructed of lightweight metals, the crankshafts were forgings of high carbon steel, and the pistons were of drop-forged aluminum. The first applications of the diesel-electric concept were in small yard switchers, but the CB&Q's streamlined Zephyrs showed the diesel's potential in long-run, high-speed passenger service.

In 1934 the Electro-Motive Corporation tested a nonarticulated diesel locomotive on the Santa Fe which generated 1,800 horsepower, and the successful results led the railway to order a two-unit locomotive for the Super Chief. The Santa Fe purchased a 3,600-horsepower twin-unit diesel

The first Santa Fe diesels take the Super Chief west in 1936. Santa Fe Railway

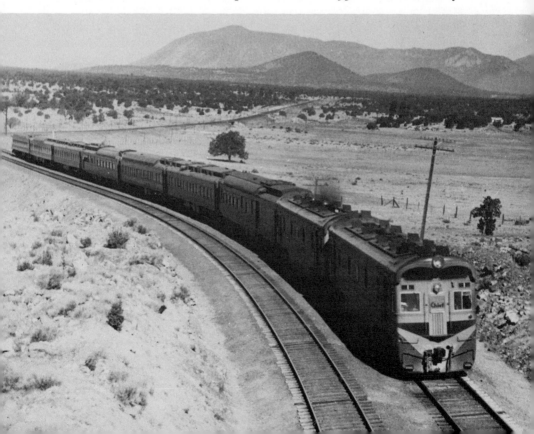

from EMC which subcontracted part of the work. St. Louis Car Company built the bodies while EMC powered the units with two V–12 Winton diesels. The locomotives were capable of attaining a speed of 107 miles per hour, and cabs at either end of the units controlled the 127-foot-long diesels, which weighed 240 tons. Steam generators heated and air conditioned the passenger cars. Units 1A and 1B arrived in August 1935, and during the testing period, which lasted until May 1936, EMC engineers and Santa Fe officials worked out numerous "bugs": the engines rode roughly, the diesel motors overheated, the steam boilers were inadequate, and some wheels cracked under stress. But the performance level could hardly be believed. The units pulled well, hit high speeds readily, and moved over mountain grades easily. When the units demonstrated their ability to operate at sustained speeds week after week pulling the Santa Fe's famous Super Chief, the railway ordered additional diesels for some of its other passenger trains. Dieselization had begun.

The passenger diesels ordered in 1937 and 1938 were also built by EMC, and the efficiency of the units which that firm produced led to additional orders. By mid-1938 the Santa Fe operated ten new streamlined passenger trains powered by the silver and brilliant red diesels. In addition, the railway bought 30 diesel switchers in 1938. The Santa Fe soon owned the largest fleet of diesels in the world, with 39 switchers and fifteen passenger road diesels. The diesel-electric locomotive accelerated faster than a steam locomotive, took curves at higher speeds because of its lower center of gravity, traveled longer without servicing, and replaced as many as fifteen steam locomotives on a transcontinental train. The impact on the railway can almost be described as revolutionary, particularly when the Atchison became the first railroad to utilize the diesel locomotive in revenue freight service.

President Engel and Vice President Fred Gurley, encouraged by J. P. Morris of the mechanical department, became extremely enthusiastic about the possible use of diesels in all aspects of railroading. EMC, which became the EM Division of General Motors, built the first diesel freight locomotive and brought it to the Santa Fe for testing in February 1938. The 5,400-horsepower locomotive had four units containing 64 cylinders, 14 generators and 16 motors. On its first run the locomotive hauled 66 cars of freight from Argentine Yard in Kansas City to Los Angeles. Bypassing water stops, crossing passes without helpers, and moving at a high rate of speed, the experimental units established an unexcelled performance level, leading to the first order for freight diesels by any railroad in the United States. The experimental units surpassed the 2–10–4s of the 5001 Class and yet used less fuel, had lower maintenance costs and had greater dependability.

The nation's first freight diesels climb Cajon Pass. Santa Fe Railway

The first of the blue and bright yellow 100 Class of freight diesels arrived in early 1941, and they entered revenue service. On the initial westbound run a diesel locomotive pulled 110 freight cars from Chicago to the West Coast and reduced the running time from six days to four. Number 100 ran through from Chicago to Los Angeles with only five brief stops; a similar train with steam power required nine locomotives and 35 water and fuel stops. The blue and yellow freight diesels eliminated the terrible water problem in the desert country, but their dynamic brake system proved even more important. The freight diesels received a regenerative brake system which greatly reduced hotbox problems on downgrades. Normally a long freight train developed hot brakes as it moved downgrade, requiring frequent stops to cool the wheels. This practice wasted time and power. The dynamic brake system converted the traction motors to generators. The drag thus created slowed the train without the application of the air brakes. The electric current generated by the traction motors, while in dynamic braking, dissipated as heat through a system of resistors cooled by high-velocity blowers. The 464-ton diesels could hold a freight train on the 2 percent descending grade between Cajon and San Bernardino with only a slight application of the brakes. The saving in brake shoes alone soon reached millions of dollars annually.

The diesel units compiled fantastic records on the Belen Cutoff and the desert runs in California. The units pulled trains of 100 cars over 500 miles without a stop. The diesels established a 95 percent on-time record, and their fuel costs were an incredibly low .25¢ per mile. The 5,400-horsepower diesels could achieve a speed of 75 miles per hour while pulling a sizable freight train. The Atchison's success with these freight units led to orders for similar diesels by the Southern, Great Northern and the Milwaukee Road by the end of 1941; but the Santa Fe became the first railroad to employ Rudolph Diesel's conception in all areas of locomotive service.

The costs of dieselization did not deter Engel and Gurley despite the enormous capital outlays required. With financial courage and vision they built the first all-diesel shop and erected diesel-servicing facilities along the system. Training programs for crews and maintenance men were organized with dispatch as the diesels began to arrive in large numbers; over 2,500 shopmen received new skills, and supervisors attended a two-week training and familiarization session at the EMC plant at La Grange, Illinois. Roundhouses had to be converted for use by the diesels, and wash racks and fuel oil facilities had to be built. The Santa Fe created large diesel shops at San Bernardino and Cleburne with smaller shops at several other locations. Some steam facilities were abandoned or cannibalized, and some, such as the large water tanks and water treatment plants, were given to the towns in which they were located. Expansion of dieselization received a setback, however, with the outset of war in December 1941.

The enormous traffic demands placed on the Atchison during the war strained the locomotive roster to the utmost. Orders for additional diesels and for new steam locomotives were placed in December 1941 and February 1942, but wartime restrictions precluded receiving the power which was so acutely needed. In the period from 1939 to 1942, only 117 new locomotives were acquired while 78 were scrapped; but of the 117 units, 86 were diesels, and this was a godsend. The diesels were assigned to the Argentine-Belen and Winslow-San Bernardino runs, and they quickly earned their costs many times over. Power requirements reached such a high level that the federal government authorized the Santa Fe to purchase additional steam locomotives in 1942 and 1943. In May 1943, Baldwin delivered 2–10–4s Numbers 5011–5034. While excellent locomotives, the Atchison would have preferred additional diesels. In 1943–1944, Baldwin built 30 more 4–8–4s of the 2900 Class, and with their 80-inch drivers and roller bearings, they began to make some of the longest steam runs in the history of railroading. With carbon-steel boiler plates and main and side rods, they were the heaviest Northerns ever built, weighing 510,150 pounds. Operating between Kansas City and Clovis, the 2900s established themselves as the outstanding steam machines on the

No. 2905 and her sisters bolster the engine roster in the dark days of World War II. Keith L. Bryant, Sr.

Santa Fe. Power needs continued to grow during the war, forcing the Santa Fe to purchase second-hand mallets from the Norfolk and Western and used Berkshires from the Boston and Maine. Yet, the stellar performers were the diesels, and as revenue train-miles leaped from 40,900,000 in 1938 to 70,700,000 in 1945, the diesels contributed more than their share to meeting the traffic demands of the war effort.

The freight diesels in California and Arizona operated from Winslow to Barstow or San Bernardino over the desert and Cajon Pass. Grades ranged from 1.4 percent to 2.2 percent, but the diesels never stopped. The "Battle of the Arizona Divide" was won by the blue and yellow diesels as they often ran up to 10,000 miles each month. The steam engines handed in fine performances too, and throughout the war received additional improvements. Some of the older Northerns acquired larger drivers and feedwater systems, and all the motive power received constant attention to keep it running at a wartime peak. The degree of utilization can be seen by the mileage on the early passenger diesels; by May 8, 1945, several units had operated over 20 million miles.

The war experience convinced Gurley, if he needed convincing, to convert totally to diesels. Clearly this could not be accomplished in a brief period because of the enormous cost, but a definite phasing out of steam began. In the fall of 1945 the Santa Fe owned 1,567 steam locomotives, 103 road diesels and 144 diesel switchers. Within five years the figures changed to produce a roster of 1,199 steam engines and 627 road diesels. Though it became the largest user of diesels in the world, the Atchison continued to upgrade its remaining steam power. Older, lighter steam locomotives went to the scrap dealers, but the 2–10–4s, 4–8–4s and

4–6–4s were in constant use. The Northerns built in 1927–1929 were modernized with welded-steel cylinders, new fireboxes, and force-feed lubrication systems. Larger tenders with greater fuel and water capacities allowed even longer runs, and only two locomotive changes were necessary for most transcontinental trains. The steam switch engines were not upgraded, and in this area, the diesel became supreme. With diesel units arriving almost daily during the next decade, the steam roster declined to only 96 engines in 1956. The diesels drove the steamers into storage, and long lines of inactive engines filled the yards at Clovis, Amarillo, Wellington and Albuquerque. On August 27, 1957, the age of steam ended on the Atchison. Over eighty-eight years of tradition terminated, and only a few exhibit locomotives remained to recall the glory of steam in motion. Many

Diesel-servicing facilities at Barstow, California, and a variety of units. Santa
Fe Railway

Santa Fe locomotives were donated to city parks and exhibits, and the
giant of them all, "Madame Queen," found a home in Santa Fe Park in
Amarillo.

Between 1943 and 1952, the Atchison added 1,261 diesels or an average of one new unit approximately every three days. The next year saw
222 more units arrive, and over 70 percent of all runs were made by
diesels. The new diesel units also represented several sizes and builders.
In 1946 the Santa Fe began to purchase large numbers of passenger diesels
from Alco. These huge units generated 6,000 horsepower, could reach 120
miles per hour, and heading the Super Chief over Raton Pass the Alcos
needed no helpers. With their enormous noses painted in the bright red
"warchief" style of the Santa Fe, the Alcos became spectacular sights on

the western runs. Several of the Alcos ran for one million miles without an overhaul. New freight units with higher horsepower ratings could pull long trains over the Belen and Arizona grades without helpers, and some dual-purpose units arrived with gearing ratios allowing a top speed of 100 miles per hour. The extensive use of diesels required additional training programs, and an instruction car traveled over the system to teach shopmen and maintenance men how to service the new motors. The instruction car contained a cutaway model of an EMD engine and was equipped with a diesel's electrical equipment. The instructors taught a variety of courses dealing with electrical and mechanical maintenance. This training program had to reach even the smallest shops and roundhouses as the diesels spread over the system, becoming the primary power on even the shortest and least-used branches.

After 1950, both EMD and Alco developed general purpose diesel units capable of independent operation on branchlines or multiple use on the mainline. The general purpose units could also be employed in switching service, and some, with steam generators, were used on short passenger runs. The horsepower of the "geeps," as they became known, rose until models with 2,250 or 2,400 horsepower became common. The Alco 800 Class and the EMD 900 Class of 1959 came with short noses, 75-mile-per-hour speed, and were actually road engines capable of other uses. The "geeps" lacked the familiar streamlined front end cab of the original diesels, and their narrow carbodies just covered the motors and equipment. Access to the power train on the newer or "second generation" diesels was made easier by reducing the expanse of sheet metal. The low-hooded "geeps" became the primary means by which total dieselization was achieved.

The dieselization program brought significant changes to the Atchison. By 1952 the operating ratio had declined to 70.03, fewer engines and crews were doing more work, and even the road's physical appearance had changed. In 1949 the Santa Fe closed one of the Raton tunnels and tore up part of the second track over the summit as CTC and the diesel made them unnecessary. New shops in Chicago, Barstow and Argentine began to service the diesels using buildings with two levels which enabled maintenance crews to work above and under the locomotives. Water and fuel supplies were preheated before being placed in the diesels to improve efficiency, and the railway began to reclaim the used crankcase oil. Even passenger trains began to appear with new units from the "second generation." Beginning in the mid-1960s, the Santa Fe acquired passenger power from General Electric, and these diesels, the u28cs, became the first nonstreamlined cab units in passenger colors. The u28cs developed 2,800 horsepower with a top speed of 94 miles per hour.

Ugly but utilitarian, the "geeps" dieselized the branch lines. Santa Fe Railway

The acquisition program continued with 90 more units arriving in 1969 and 120 units in 1970. These diesels reflected the trend toward higher horsepower ratings and dual-service potential. The EMD GP38s generated 2,000 horsepower, but the SD45s produced 3,600. General Electric's U23Bs delivered 2,250 horsepower, but a C-C series in 1967 produced 3,600 horsepower. Several of these newer models came with semi-streamlining for dual-purpose use and were painted in passenger colors. The older diesels were usually not traded-in, rather, a rebuilding program was instituted to convert them into road switchers with new "geep-type" bodies. All of the diesel units came under the direction of the Centralized Control Bureau in Chicago, giving the Atchison not only a modern diesel fleet, but the most efficient means to use its new and rebuilt power.

The dieselization program, other technological advances and labor shortages during World War II made profound impacts on employee-management relations and the composition of the Santa Fe's workers. Perhaps the most dramatic change was the decline in the total number of employees. In 1900 the Santa Fe employed nearly 30,000 people, a figure which continually increased until November 1920, when there were 82,059 in the Santa Fe "family." The peak figure then began to decline, and even before 1929 reached 70,000. The depression accelerated payroll reductions, and by May 1938, only 33,613 people remained in the system. World War II brought a substantial increase in employees; by 1944 some 64,000 people worked for the Santa Fe, including a large number of women. During the decade following the end of the war, the number of workers declined, but not substantially. Dieselization and labor-saving devises began to reduce somewhat the number of employees in train crews and in maintenance work, but the company's rising wage bill led to further substantial reductions, as the following figures show.

AVERAGE NUMBER OF EMPLOYEES

1954	56,600	1961	45,877	1967	43,374
1955	57,146	1962	44,976	1968	41,052
1956	56,127	1963	43,889	1969	39,680
1957	55,491	1964	46,496	1970	39,025
1958	49,419	1965	44,680	1971	36,778
1959	50,422	1966	44,821	1972	36,651
1960	49,617				

The drastic reductions in 1957–1958 and in 1960–1961 can be attributed largely to the impact of the diesel, mechanization of tie replacement and other maintenance chores, and sharply curtailed passenger-train service. These significant reductions produced some interesting results in the operating ratio. In 1958, for example, the ratio fell from 77.59 to 74.58 when the number of employees declined by over 6,000. In 1971 the ratio fell from 79.9 to 77.7 when the average number of workers declined by over 2,000. The management of the Santa Fe recognized the serious impact of its growing labor bill on the company's profits and, like other railroads, sought to change the work rules to fit modern operating conditions.

The railway work rules had been established when steam locomotives and crews moved about 100 miles per day. The diesel covered many more miles in a day, but crews either had to be changed or paid overtime when they worked through several divisions. The pay base for train crews in 1958 was 12.5 miles per hour; this meant a full day's pay for a few hours of work. Attempts to gain additional efficiency and productivity were limited by these archaic rules, by the higher wages received by passenger train crews, and by the maximum miles each crew was allowed to travel. The stringent seniority system prevented the advancement of younger men and precluded wage increases based on merit. Another area of strenuous contention between the railroads and the unions was the role of fireman on a diesel locomotive. The railways argued that the fireman's position had become obsolete, but the unions contended that the fireman acted as a safety device or a "co-pilot" in emergencies. The battle over the work rules and the fireman's position continued until 1972, with first President John F. Kennedy and then President Lyndon B. Johnson

Second-generation diesels, such as the 3600-horsepower SD-45s, took over the main-line chores. Santa Fe Railway

appointing federal commissions to attempt to arbitrate the dispute. Strikes, or the threat of a strike, precluded a settlement until it became evident that unless some relief was given the industry, many roads faced financial disaster. The settlement reached in 1972 meant that some 800 firemen on the Atchison would be phased out or transferred to other jobs. The Santa Fe also stopped replacing many crewmen at the time of their death or retirement, and some were encouraged to retire early. In these ways the payroll was reduced.

The effect of the decline in employment hit the "railroad towns" very hard; one observer called it "death by dieselization." An example of this form of "death" could be seen at Purcell, Oklahoma. Purcell served not only as the junction point for the ATSF and the GCSF, but also was one of the junctions of the "Grand Divisions." The Santa Fe facility at Purcell stretched for several miles along the South Canadian River and included a large yard, a roundhouse, minor repair facilities, and a modern station which contained facilities for the many crewmen who terminated their runs there. Some men lived in the small county seat town located on the bluff above the river. Then came the diesel. The roundhouse soon stood empty, the lines of freight cars in the yards began to dwindle, and nearby branches were abandoned or came under other jurisdictions. When the Santa Fe eliminated one of the grand divisions, many crewmen were transferred elsewhere. Freight trains began to move through Purcell without stopping, and the switch engines were reassigned elsewhere. In October

1971 the last switch engine departed and, as a railroad town, Purcell died. The experience of this one central Oklahoma community was repeated throughout the system.

Not only did the number of workers decline, but the composition of the labor force also continued to shift. In the twentieth century the traditional Irish railroad workers began to disappear, and local labor supplies filled the gap. In the Southwest the crews became heavily Mexican or Indian, with some Orientals on the California lines. Train crews remained largely Caucasian, however, with most of the Mexicans and Indians employed in section crews and as laborers. In Kansas, Oklahoma and Texas the section gangs had a large minority of blacks, and throughout the system passenger crews contained significant numbers of blacks. During World War II the labor shortage led to the employment of 7,000 Mexican nationals, some 16 percent of all employees, and by 1942 over 3,500 women were to be found on the Santa Fe with one-third in jobs previously held by men. The Indian workers were largely Navajos, and by 1952 the Santa Fe employed 7,614 Indians, some 12 percent of its total work force. The employment of minority workers was not just a product of the war, but had been a part of the Santa Fe tradition since its founding.

In 1874 the Santa Fe hired Mrs. Caroline Prentis as a clerk in Topeka, and she remained with the system until 1881. Mrs. Prentis was only the first of many women on the railway, and as early as 1925 the line employed 2,000 females. Most women began as clerical help or stenographers, but through the years they became telegraphers, station agents, signal tower operators, yard clerks and even machinists. Some of the women who came to the Atchison in the 1940s stayed with the railway to become career employees. The management recognized their ability to do equal, or even better work, and created a separate women's personnel department to encourage them to pursue a career in railroading. Even before 1941, M. L. Lyles, assistant to the president of the Santa Fe, noted that railroading was not just a man's field but that job opportunities existed for women; after all, 57 percent of the stock of the ATSF was held by women and the largest single stockholder was a woman, why shouldn't the owners hire women? The Santa Fe continued to employ substantial numbers of females, but as late as 1972 few were to be found in executive positions.

The Santa Fe also sought additional employees among the Indians of Arizona and New Mexico. Navajos, Apaches and Mojaves worked in section gangs and in the Barstow, San Bernardino and Albuquerque shops. Many were transferred to the gulf lines and to Chicago as their skills were needed throughout the system. When President Gurley spoke to the Inter-Tribal Ceremonial at Gallup, New Mexico, in 1952, he praised the Indian workers who were becoming machinists, boilermakers, diesel mechanics and car inspectors. Of the 13,704 Indians working for American railroads in 1952, over half were on the Santa Fe. To facilitate the advancement and promotion of Indian workers, the company provided a special instruction car for Indian crewmen. The instructors taught the men new skills and to read and write using tapes and slides. By 1966 some line crews were more than 90 percent Navajo, and the laying of welded rail was being done by Navajo "hard hat" crane operators, welders, track layers and foremen. The Santa Fe took great pride in its record as an employer of members of minority groups, but in 1971 President John Reed called attention to the continuing problem of discrimination:

> Railroad payrolls have probably paid for more college educations, paid off more home mortgages, and provided more of life's necessities for minority groups than have the payrolls of any other industry. Unfortunately, however, railroad minority employment has frequently been concentrated in lower-paying-job categories, largely due to inadequate education and training.[1]

The Santa Fe attempted to meet this problem by expanding its apprentice program and by seeking members of minority groups as students.

Navajo track gangs are found throughout the system. Santa Fe Railway

Labor relations on the system continued to reflect the paternalistic, antiunion position of Ripley and Storey well into the middle of the century. Strikes and labor negotiations became largely national in scope, however, and Santa Fe employees received wages and worked hours established by the national agreements. Wage disputes in 1937, 1941, and 1942–1943 brought federal arbitration in which the Atchison was only one of many railroads involved. When train crews struck the nation's rail network in 1946, and President Truman seized the railroads, the Santa Fe management deplored both acts, but did not take an independent course. The Santa Fe became one of several roads struck by the unions under a policy of selective strikes; in 1950 the ATSF and three other roads were struck during the long work rule dispute. The maneuverability of the Santa Fe management vis-à-vis labor became quite narrow as the nationalization of labor relations took away the options of individual carriers. Even the company's retirement plan and death benefits were discontinued after similar federal programs became operative.

Under the New Deal, a series of federal laws created retirement programs and death benefits for workers in the rail industry. The initial Retirement Act of 1934 was declared unconstitutional, however, and the Railroad Retirement Act of 1935 became the basis for a national plan. The railroads and employees each contributed 3.5 percent of the first $300 a month the worker received to a retirement fund. The first year the scheme cost the ATSF over $2.2 million. The railroad workers were also placed in the unemployment portion of the Social Security Act, and this cost the Santa Fe $1.3 million in 1937. The Santa Fe canceled its own company benefits with the enactment of these federal laws, and the lump-sum death benefits under the new program proved to be less than those previously paid by the ATSF. The company retirement plan ended on May 31, 1937, and workers reaching the age of 65 came under the Railroad Retirement Act, receiving a maximum of $120 a month in benefits. The benefits were larger than those paid by the ATSF, but now the workers paid half the cost where before all of the financial burden fell on the company. Like the Social Security system, younger railway workers paid payroll taxes to support retired railroaders. The federal plan did allow men changing positions from one carrier to another to continue retirement benefits without interruption. The Railroad Retirement Board also assumed responsibility for unemployment compensation in 1939, with the initial cost to each railroad being a 3 percent tax on their total payroll. So large were the sums raised, the board reduced the levy to .5 percent in 1948, with provisions for a sliding scale based on unemployment figures. The railroad retirement system fell into fiscal disarray after 1950, as employment in the industry fell sharply and the number of retirees and

the costs of their pensions rose. Indeed, the fund faced bankruptcy despite
the fact that the system cost the workers and the railroads twice as much
as Social Security. Only congressional intervention seemed likely to prevent
depletion of the fund or levying enormously higher taxes on the railroads
and their remaining employees.

The Atchison management viewed the trend toward federal intervention in railroad labor relations with considerable dismay. President Gurley,
a staunch conservative, favored the so-called right-to-work laws passed
by several states served by the system. The Atchison stood in 1954 as one
of the last railroads holding out against union shop contracts. Fourteen
Santa Fe employees in Texas filed a court case against the railroad brotherhoods to prevent the establishment of the union shop on the railway,
and Gurley supported their suit. He declared that the union shop "does
violence to my very deep-seated beliefs in personal liberty, freedom of
choice, and the rights and dignity of the individual."[2] The federal courts
ruled in favor of the Atchison and its employees, and created a permanent
injunction against the union shop on the Santa Fe in Texas. Three years
later the management refused to sign a union contract which would have
allowed dues to be used for political purposes. This led to yet another
confrontation with the Railroad Brotherhoods.

The issues between the Atchison and the unions became less philo-
sophical in the mid-1960s, and centered largely on the work rules. Wage
disputes tended to be resolved in Washington through mediation for the
entire industry. When mediation failed, Congress often acted to prevent
strikes from decimating what appeared to be a seriously ailing industry.
A few issues continued to fall under local jurisdiction, but increasingly the
rail industry turned to the federal government for relief. Technological
changes, such as dieselization, produced human-relations problems for
the rail network as a whole; and labor matters and issues such as continued passenger train service became larger than just the Atchison or its
employees or its customers. When such questions could not be resolved
in Chicago or Topeka, or in Austin, Santa Fe, Phoenix or Sacramento,
both sides turned to Washington. Eventually even the Santa Fe's "Chico"
sought relief from the federal government in the operation of the Atchison's passenger trains.

12

The Chiefs and Chico

James Pratt of Wakarusa, Kansas, purchased the first passenger ticket on the Atchison, Topeka and Santa Fe Railroad in 1869. The last ticket sold on a Santa Fe-owned and operated passenger train crossed the station counter on May 2, 1971. When Number 24, the old Grand Canyon Limited, pulled into Dearborn Station at 9:00 A.M., 103 years of ATSF passenger service ended. During the more than a century of Santa Fe passenger operations, the railroad progressed from a short-haul prairie line to one of the most famous passenger-oriented railway companies in the country. Santa Fe became synonymous with deluxe equipment, fast schedules, delicious food, courteous service and the word "Chief." Indeed, Chief began as a noun but Hollywood made it a verb, and Gloria Swanson and other "stars" reported to the press they had just "Chiefed" in from Chicago. Symbol of the ATSF's passenger service was a young Navajo Indian boy named "Chico." Chico represented the spirit of the Santa Fe, and he became not only the feature of national advertising campaigns but also the mascot of the traffic department. Chico never lost a kid's love of passenger trains, and neither did the management of the Santa Fe Railway.

During the first two decades of the company's operations, passenger service received second-class treatment. The trains were short, slow and less than major contributors to earnings. Spindly 4–4–0s moved across Kansas at a top speed of 20 miles per hour with two or three wooden coaches and a baggage or mail car. The coaches lacked vestibules, and crossing the open platforms from car to car called for considerable courage. Coal stoves produced furnacelike temperatures for passengers seated nearby but very little warmth for those at the opposite end of the car. Oil lamps cast a pale yellow light over the rows of low-backed seats. Sleeping cars did not arrive on the ATSF until 1876, and they offered only a modest degree of privacy, with only slightly more comfort. A concerted effort to develop substantial passenger traffic began with the entrance into Colorado, but not until the ATSF reached California did the passenger department become truly important.

Beginning with the opening of the Santa Fe's own line into Los Angeles, the company initiated a hard-sell passenger campaign. Fares were slashed to compete with the Southern Pacific, and the wooing of the tourist and the settler began in earnest. In the early 1890s C. A. Higgins wrote a series of books, pamphlets and brochures about the railroad and its passenger service. The "New Guide to the Pacific Coast: Santa Fe Route" described the line, almost mile by mile; while "Grand Canyon of the Colorado" painted word pictures of the glories of this giant chasm. Tourists might become permanent settlers, and much of Higgins's work sought to entice visitors to invest in California properties. His "The Land of Sunshine" and "To California and Back" extolled the virtues of southern California, its beaches, orange groves and Mediterranean climate. He promoted tours of the Indian villages of New Mexico and Arizona, emphasized the Spanish culture of the Southwest, and described the fine passenger accommodations of the Santa Fe and its partner, Fred Harvey. To capitalize on the effect of the advertising campaign, the Santa Fe launched its first true luxury train.

The California Limited crosses the desert. State Historical Society of Colorado, William Jackson Collection

Snow covered the street in front of Dearborn Station on November 27, 1892, and the passengers on the inaugural run of the California Limited hurried inside to escape from the bitter cold. The new Pullman/Chair car train offered direct service from Chicago to Los Angeles and San Diego, with a car from St. Louis joining the consist in Kansas City. A Fred Harvey diner operated in the train to Fort Madison, and meals beyond Kansas City were provided at Harvey Houses. The new passenger cars offered comfort and luxury; the lounge car featured a library with leather chairs. The decor was southwestern and Indian, based on a color scheme of muted browns, blues and orange. Alas, the depression of 1893 reduced traffic on the Limited, which was discontinued on May 3, 1896. E. P. Ripley's regime restored the train as a biweekly the following year. Departing from Chicago on Wednesdays and Saturdays at 6:00 P.M., the Limited arrived in Los Angeles seventy-two hours later. The train consisted of three Pullmans, a diner, and a buffet/smoking car, and the deluxe equipment had vestibules and Pintsch gas lighting. Very quickly the Limited became *the* train to the West Coast. At Cajon Pass a uniformed young boy, Fay Blackburn, greeted the train, which paused long enough for him to present each lady passenger a bouquet of roses, violets and carnations and each gentleman an alligator wallet. The Limited developed a personality and a style, and for fifty years it offered fine service. The train did not accept travelers on passes and featured only Pullman accommodations. Within a few years the Limited operated in as many as seven sections, each with ten or eleven sleepers; they departed at half-hour intervals from Dearborn. The record California Limited operation encompassed 22 sections westbound and 23 eastbound, each section requiring 15 locomotives and crews enroute.

By the turn of the century the Limited acquired vapor-steam-heated cars with "dust-free" ventilation. Green plush seats, inlaid wood paneling and thick carpets created a Victorian atmosphere in the cars. Eventually electric lamps of brass, circulating ice water and a soda fountain in the lounge signified the coming of "modern" equipment. The Fred Harvey diners extended their runs farther west, and for the Limited exquisite menus graced the tables. A typical Limited dinner might include the following:

Little Neck Clams   Olives, Radishes
Consommé
Roast Squab au Cresson
New Potatoes in Cream
Stringless Beans
Lettuce Salad
Pistachio Ice Cream
Neufchatel Cheese   Fruit   Coffee

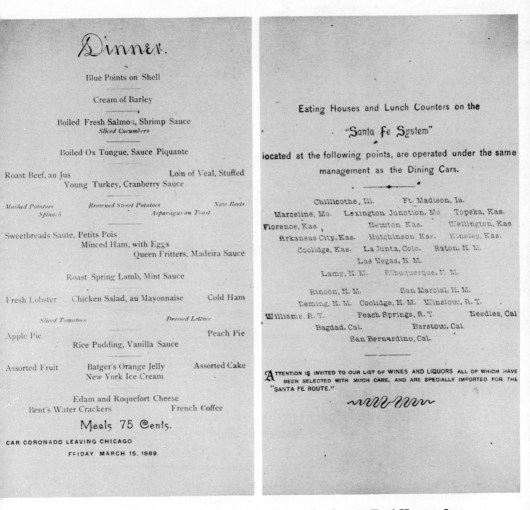

The dinner menu of the car Coronado in 1889—and only 75¢. Fred Harvey, Inc.

The Limited began a tradition of outstanding passenger service on the Santa Fe. By 1906 the Limited operated from Chicago to San Francisco, a distance of 2,577 miles, as well as to Los Angeles and San Diego, and averaged 33.5 miles per hour as it crossed the West.

Ripley promoted the Limited and passenger services throughout the system. Between 1897 and 1917 passenger traffic increased in volume by 600 percent even as rates fell from 2.293¢ per mile to 2.276¢. The number of passengers carried rose dramatically from 3,536,968 to 14,200,421. From this period to the end of passenger service, the Santa Fe enjoyed a business which featured long-distance travelers; the average journey on the line had reached 101.23 miles by 1917. The railroad also expanded its fleet of passenger cars from 641 to 1,719. The enormous growth of passen-

The first "streamliners," the McKeen cars of 1910. Santa Fe Railway

ger traffic can be attributed to the vast population explosion in the South-west and to the vigorous promotional efforts of the company. Tourists, prospective settlers and businessmen poured into Santa Fe country, with California and the Grand Canyon becoming the major attractions. The boom in California, accentuated by the expositions of 1915, caused the Santa Fe to add additional trains. The Missionary joined the fleet on March 1, 1915, offering sleepers, chair cars, a diner and an observation-parlor. It even carried through Pullmans from California to New Orleans, via connecting trains, and passengers could travel to San Diego on a Chicago-Los Angeles ticket without an additional fare. Within California the ATSF inaugurated the Saint and the Angel from Los Angeles to San Francisco via Barstow and Bakersfield. This overnight train included splendidly ornate parlor cars featuring wicker chairs, gothic arch windows with leaded glass and a brass-railed observation platform. The company recognized the value of its passenger traffic and emphasized the best in service.

The Santa Fe did not neglect the branch lines, and it experimented with the most modern accommodations for short hauls. In 1910 the rail-road purchased two self-propelled motor cars from the McKeen Motor Car

Company of Omaha. The gasoline-powered McKeen cars were considered the finest in branch-line equipment. Their "wind resistant design" included a sharply pointed nose, a tapered rear end, porthole windows and a twelve-gauge steel body. The cars seated seventy-five passengers, weighed 60,000 pounds and soon were dashing across the Kansas prairie from Chanute to Pittsburg and across Cajon Pass from Los Angeles to San Bernardino. Their initial success led the ATSF to purchase two additional McKeen cars in 1911, and these also included a baggage compartment. The four cars, painted maroon with gold steps and olive green trucks, were the beginning of an effort to replace costly branch-line passenger trains with self-propelled cars which, though economical, were also of a high quality. As the Model T took an increasing number of passengers off the rails, more motor cars would be acquired by the Santa Fe.

The last significant passenger development on the Santa Fe prior to World War I occurred on December 12, 1911, when the weekly Deluxe began to operate from Chicago to Los Angeles. This extra-fare train, the first on the Santa Fe, charged an additional $25.00 each way for the 63-hour trip. The services on the Deluxe more than compensated for the surcharge; travelers discovered a barber shop, ladies' maid, library, stenographer, daily market reports, bathing facilities, and telephone connections at the terminals. The 63-hour schedule reduced the previous time by 5½ hours westbound and 7¾ hours eastbound. The Deluxe departed from Dearborn at 8:00 P.M. and arrived at La Grande in Los Angeles at 9:00 A.M. on the third day. The six-car trains included a club car, diner, and four Pullmans which contained compartments and drawing rooms with brass beds. The seventy passengers enjoyed first-class accommodations in the Pullmans—"Puite," "Pima," "Pampa," and "Prado,"—while exquisite food could be obtained in the "air conditioned" thirty-seat diner, with its wicker chairs and vermillion mahogany paneling. The extensive wine list reinforced the "snob appeal" of the Deluxe, and the train was one of the few ever to have its own luggage sticker. For America's idle, and not so idle rich, the Deluxe became *the* way to reach Los Angeles.

Travel restrictions during World War I ended the Deluxe, but the Santa Fe's normal passenger services expanded rapidly. Because of the concentration of troops and material on the East Coast, the ATSF's military burden was less than that of the Eastern trunk lines. Nevertheless, Fred Harvey had to call many of the "Girls" out of retirement to help in the houses along the Santa Fe. The Harvey system had followed the Ripley expansion program, and the houses along the Coleman and Belen cutoffs were particularly overtaxed by troop trains going to nearby military installations. Harvey also serviced the new Kansas City Union Station, where demands on the eating facilities became massive. Dining rooms with seats for 152 and 250 could not cope with the enormous increase in travelers, and even a basket-lunch room failed to relieve the crush of business. But throughout the war, the Harvey system maintained the standard.

Harvey's high standards applied to customers as well as to employees. Fred Harvey's rule that men must wear coats in the dining rooms was continued by his sons, and Harvey Houses kept a supply of black alpaca coats for men entering without their own coats. Harvey set out to establish a sedate and genteel environment for his guests, especially the ladies. Most customers accepted the rule without debate, but in 1921 the Harvey coat rule became the subject of extensive litigation. In September of that year, the manager of the Harvey House at Purcell, Oklahoma, refused to allow Campbell Russell to eat without a coat. The incensed Russell, a member of the Oklahoma Corporation Commission, persuaded that regulatory agency to order Harvey to terminate the coat rule. Harvey appealed the ruling to the Oklahoma supreme court, which decided in 1924 that society set rules in first-class establishments and that coats were an accepted part of masculine attire. The court lauded Harvey service and upheld the coat rule.

While this minor skirmish could be counted a victory, the larger battle to retain passengers produced mixed results. Henry Ford's Model T created not only a new morality, but also a new mode of long-distance travel. Farmers and tourists abandoned the train for the car. The Santa Fe had not suffered greatly from the competition of electric interurbans as had trunk carriers in the East and Midwest, but the automobile forced the company to strenuously promote its passenger trains, and to offer a larger range of services. Many older cars were scrapped and the passenger fleet declined from 1,057 cars in 1920 to 823 in 1929. The ATSF added larger diners, more lounge cars, and eliminated worn-out coaches and some smoking cars. The short-haul passenger almost disappeared as the average distance traveled rose from 139 miles to 291. Rates also increased slightly from 2.899¢ per mile to 3.057¢, but per-train-mile revenue fell to $1.56 from $2.45, and total passenger revenue dropped from $60 million to less than $40 million. To counter these figures, the Santa Fe launched a program of fare reductions, tours, innovative equipment and new trains.

The Atchison widely advertised the glories of New Mexico and Arizona throughout the nation. Calendars, brochures and magazine advertisements featured the geographical wonders of the Southwest and California. The Santa Fe and Harvey initiated a series of "Indian Detours" in 1925 for tourists interested in the Indian culture. A coordinated train-bus service took tourists from Lamy or Santa Fe to Taos and the Puyé pueblos. Guides from the area escorted the buses over the poor roads of the region.

Santa Fe
de -Luxe
to Chicago
Kansas City
and a quick
way to
New York

tuesdays
Limited
to sixty
p e o p l e
extra fare
twenty-five
d o l l a r s

Santa Fe Deluxe, all extrafare
speedster. Santa Fe Railway

Cloudbursts and washouts often disrupted the bus trips, but the detours
became justifiably famous and popular. The Santa Fe also promoted
Carlsbad Caverns National Park in southeastern New Mexico, and train-
bus tours linked the Scout to the caverns. Harvey refurbished the lodges at
Grand Canyon, and the Santa Fe operated the Grand Canyon Limited
with direct sleepers and coaches to the south rim. All ATSF passenger
trains on the western run paused in Albuquerque so that tourists could
purchase Indian artifacts from the Museum Shop of the Alvarado Hotel or
from vendors who lined up along the train platforms. The railroad and
Harvey both gained from the advertising and the expansion of services.

As the number of tourists increased, the Santa Fe felt compelled to
offer trains less expensive than the California Limited. The Navajo was
established as a tourist accommodation along the northern route while the
Scout served primarily the southern route via Amarillo. Yet, each train

operated in multiple sections even after the addition of the Grand Canyon Limited in 1929. On May 15, 1923, the California Limited operated with six sections out of Los Angeles, the Navajo with three, the Scout with three and the Missionary with two; the Los Angeles office booked 225 Pullman cars in seven days. Even Byron Harvey's twin-unit diners could not cope with the demands made by increased business to California. The Atchison then decided to revive the Deluxe concept, and a new train was born which would become the railroad's hallmark for over a decade.

The Santa Fe announced the inception of an "extra fast, extra fine, extra fare" all-Pullman train—the Chief. On November 14, 1926, the Chief departed Dearborn with the stars of M-G-M's "War Paint" on board. Tim McCoy and the other celebrities gathered at the rear of the Chief to be photographed with the new train's drumhead, initiating a publicity gimmick to be repeated for thirty years. The daily service included a barber, valet service, ladies' maid, soda fountain, cigar store and bathing facilities. The $10.00 extra fare, plus the first-class Pullman charge, excluded the average traveler, but the Chief sought a particular clientele. The train's seven cars were carefully selected to provide the best accommodations. Fred Harvey operated the diner and club car for the occupants of the four Pullmans and the observation-lounge. Compartments and drawing rooms with freshly cut flowers catered to the tastes of the Chief's customers. In 1928 new buffet/library cars and diners were added, with the former carrying names such as "Santana," "Old Wolf" and "Geronimo." Rising competition with deluxe trains on the Union Pacific and Southern Pacific led to a complete reequipping of the Chief in 1930 with new Pullmans and three lounges. The original 63-hour schedule, the same as the Deluxe of 1911, was reduced to 58 hours in 1929 and to 56 hours the next year. Larger, faster motive power and fewer fueling stops allowed for the reductions. A further reduction in 1934 put the Chief into Los Angeles four hours ahead of its rivals on the UP and SP.

Speed became the order of the day in the 1920s, and by the end of the decade, the fledgling airlines began to offer irregular daytime service limited drastically by weather conditions. Lindbergh's flight to Paris and the coming of larger aircraft generated public interest and rising confidence in air travel. Recognizing the value of speed, and the publicity possibilities, the Santa Fe, the New York Central and the Pennsylvania railroads joined with two airlines to provide direct New York–Los Angeles air-train service. Unable to fly at night, the airlines would put their passengers aboard the trains for that portion of the trip made in darkness. On July 7, 1929, Colonel Charles A. Lindbergh took the controls of a Ford Trimotor owned by Transcontinental Air Transport and flew his passengers, including Amelia Earhart, from Columbus, Ohio, to St. Louis, Kansas

City and Waynoka, Oklahoma. The coast-to-coast travelers had ridden the Pennsylvania Railroad from New York to Columbus, and at Waynoka they were placed onboard Santa Fe Pullmans bound for Clovis, New Mexico. There another TAT plane carried them on to Los Angeles. The train-plane–train-plane connections reduced transcontinental travel from 100 hours to 80 hours. A similar service coordinated New York Central trains, Universal Air Line flights and Santa Fe passenger trains with transfers at Cleveland, Garden City, Kansas, and Albuquerque. The service terminated with the coming of planes designed to fly through the night, but it represented an attempt by the ATSF to cope with and utilize advances in technology.

The inauguration of the air-train service preceded by only a few months the "Great Crash" and the coming of the depression. As has been seen, the territory served by the ATSF suffered severe economic deprivation and climatic catastrophe in the years 1929 to 1939. The vast movement of people to California slowed, branch-line passenger traffic collapsed, and the sales of first-class tickets declined sharply. Fares had to be reduced, new cheaper services provided, and rising competition with other railroads, buses, airplanes and the private car had to be met. The management watched in horror as passenger revenues slid; the revenue for 1934 stood at one-third the 1929 level. State regulatory agencies and the ICC ordered rate cuts, and the 1929 average rate of 3.057¢ per mile declined to 1.77¢ ten years later. Passenger Traffic Manager W. V. Black announced new fares from Chicago to the West Coast in 1931, reducing coach tickets to $40.00, tourist sleeper prices to $65.00, and first-class fares to $79.84. This reduction did produce more passengers, if less revenue. The loss of riders on branches, the elimination of short-run trains and the continued movement of passengers to the West produced an increasingly longer average length of travel. The average ticket sold on the Atchison covered 292 miles in 1929 and 398 miles in 1939. The latter figure was eight times the national average. Passenger revenues, however, did not grow to any significant extent throughout the thirties.

To meet rising competition, and in an attempt to cope with the extremely hot temperatures, dust storms and drought found in the area it traversed, the ATSF began a program to air condition its passenger cars in the early thirties. In August 1930 the first air-conditioned diner began to operate on the West Coast run. Refrigerator coils cooled outside air which was pumped into the Chief's diner. The first attempt to use mechanical refrigeration proved highly successful, and additional equipment was ordered. Not only was the air cooled, but it was also dehumidified, and windows could be closed to keep out dust and smoke. The air-conditioning system utilized steam from the locomotive to operate the refrigerator units, and all of the equipment except the water tanks was placed on the roof of the car. Within three years, most Santa Fe diners, lounges and café cars received air-conditioning, and units were then ordered for coaches and sleepers. In 1934 the company spent almost $2 million to air condition nearly all cars used on its principal trains. This newest improvement became a strong element in the advertising department's campaign to win additional passengers.

The passenger department also sought to attract the less-than-flush traveler with a low-cost economy train—the Scout. In 1936 the ATSF announced that the Scout would receive refurbished coaches and tourist sleepers and would include Harvey diners and lounge cars. The department reserved one chair car for women and children and placed a courier-nurse in attendance. This car became a rolling nightmare of diapers, midnight feedings and a constant parade of women moving back and forth to the diner seeking bottles of warm milk. The Scout coach services included radios, drinking cups and free pillows, and the Harvey diner provided budget meals: breakfast cost 25¢, lunch 30¢, and dinner only 35¢, as the railway sought to emphasize the low cost of train travel. Even the schedule of the Scout was reduced to 60 hours westbound and 58½ hours eastbound to move the running time close to that of the Chief.

The reduced prices in the Harvey diner signified the sharp decline in income and customers for the Santa Fe's partner in the passenger operation. Byron Harvey, who replaced his brother Ford as head of the family business in 1928, attempted to deal with the effects of the depression. At the outbreak of the economic slump Harvey operated 25 hotels, 54 lunchrooms, 50 diners and café cars, and employed 5,000 people. In 1930 Harvey opened another off-line restaurant in the Union Terminal in Cleveland and La Posada Hotel in Winslow, Arizona. These additions were the last for many years, and retrenchment became the order of the day. The small lunchrooms faced increasing competition in the towns, and many were closed. Newer hotels took away tourists and salesmen, forcing many of the Harvey hotels to be phased out. The dairy and poultry operations terminated, and the Harvey facilities in Santa Fe and Newton began to provide food for both bus and train passengers. The closing of the smaller Harvey rooms symbolized the slow death of the branch-line passenger train which had accelerated during the twenties and continued into the thirties.

The Santa Fe initiated a cost reduction program in passenger service in the 1920s by widespread use of "doodlebugs" or self-propelled rail cars. These cars usually contained sections for passengers, mail and baggage and could operate with two-man crews. They replaced a locomotive, several passenger cars and a crew of four or five used on branch-line trains.

Motor Car No. 119 with trailer flies down the old "Orient" line. Keith L.
Bryant, Sr.

The McKeen car experiments of 1909–1910 led to the purchase of gasoline-powered rail cars manufactured by Electro-Motive Corporation and
J. G. Brill. Most of the gas-electrics were assigned to branches in Kansas,
Oklahoma, Texas and California. President Storey announced that passenger service was being reduced by 5.3 million miles in 1932, with motor
cars replacing several trains, and that these changes would provide "great
economies." The units surprised the operating department as their 400-
to 535-horsepower motors could not only move the car but also trailers or a
few boxcars, and several of the gas-electrics were placed in mixed train
service. Some of the "doodlebugs" became famous because of their dura-
bility and power. Motor 160, for example, covered the Wichita-San
Angelo branch, some 519 miles, for the longest such run in the country.
Motor 190, an articulated unit and the largest ever built, contained a
900-horsepower motor and operated in both freight and passenger service
with a top speed of 90 miles per hour. Known affectionately as "The Old
Heifer," and later as the "Pride of the Pecos," Number 190 ended her
career painted in streamline passenger colors. Between 1930 and 1932 the
Atchison purchased over forty-five additional gas-electrics as the replacement of branch-line trains accelerated. While some passengers lamented
the coming of the "doodlebug," these units with their leather seats, toilets
and storm windows kept decent passenger service available to many small
communities far longer than was economically warranted.

The gas-electrics allowed the ATSF to compete with the rapidly growing bus systems in its region, but the management soon capitulated and
decided that if you can't beat them, buy them. On September 22, 1935,
President Bledsoe revealed that the Santa Fe had purchased controlling
interest in the Southern Kansas Stage Line Company, which operated a bus
and truck network in Kansas, Oklahoma, Missouri and Colorado, and

owned interests in other lines in Missouri, Illinois, New Mexico, Arizona and California. An ATSF subsidiary, General Improvement Company, bought 46,000 of the 90,500 shares of the Stage Line for $644,000. The bus system extended from Chicago to California and south to Oklahoma City. Three years later another subsidiary, the Santa Fe Trail Transportation Company, acquired buslines in Arizona, New Mexico and Utah; and the following year the railway acquired the remaining stock of the Southern Kansas system. The bus network extended south to Little Rock and St. Louis, north to Lincoln, and in the West from El Paso to Salt Lake City. The railway coordinated its bus and rail services and reduced duplication to a minimum. The acquisitions not only enhanced passenger revenues, but also blocked expansion of bus operations owned by other railroads. The Santa Fe bus routes reached a peak of 12,000 miles in 1948, with most routes included in either the Santa Fe Trail Transportation Company or the Southern Kansas system. The bus operation became a fiscal drain after World War II, and the ICC refused to allow the bus subsidiary to expand beyond the Santa Fe's territory. The Atchison decided to sell its operating rights and property to the Transcontinental Bus System, which created a nationwide network from three large regional carriers. The Atchison received $2,647,940 in bonds and 39.1 percent of the stock of the Transcontinental Bus System, but the railway later disposed of this security holding.

Even as the Santa Fe sought to reduce costs, increasing competition from other railroads forced the management to review its premium services. The Chicago, Burlington & Quincy inaugurated its fleet of diesel-powered, stainless steel Zephyrs, and challenged the Atchison in several key markets. The Union Pacific extended its "City" fleet of diesel-powered, articulated streamliners to Denver and Los Angeles, and the Atchison moved to meet the challenges. President Bledsoe ordered $3 million in track improvements in 1935 to allow for faster schedules between Chicago and Los Angeles. The Chief's running time was cut twice and its Pullmans refurbished, but Bledsoe's preparations were for a whole new train on the fastest timecard ever, using the recently developed diesel passenger locomotive. Santa Fe trains would be second to none.

Motive-power expert John Purcell and Vice President W. K. Etter pushed hard for the use of diesel power in passenger service, and together with engineers from Electro-Motive Corporation they evolved an acceptable design. The diesel eliminated most water and fuel stops, providing not only a faster schedule but also much greater economy and efficiency. The two-unit diesel locomotive generated 3,600 horsepower and could reach a top speed of 107 miles per hour. The cabs contained illuminated instrument panels and controlled an intricate system of safety devices. Numbers 1A and 1B received a garish exterior paint scheme of black, cobalt blue, Saratoga blue, golden olive and pimpernel scarlet, while the side panels included the Santa Fe emblem and a painting of an Indian head-dress. Electro-Motive delivered the units in August 1935, and several short testing trips proceeded a Chicago-Los Angeles run during the second week of October. The units took nine standard heavyweight passenger cars 2,227 miles in a record-shattering 39 hours and 34 minutes, some 15 hours less than the Chief's schedule and 23 minutes less than the Union Pacific's lightweight streamliner. Santa Fe officials disclaimed that any special effort had been made to enable the train to average 56.5 miles per hour, but Bledsoe ordered an additional $1,500,000 spent on improv-ing the right-of-way. The passenger department also disavowed any hopes to establish a regular schedule of 39 hours; but preparations began imme-diately for just such an effort.

The *Super* Chief. A massive public relations and advertising effort focused public attention on the new darling of the ATSF. Recalling the glamor of the Deluxe, the Super Chief would operate once a week on a schedule of just over 39 hours. The gaudy diesels and nine Pullmans departed from Dearborn on May 12, 1936, on the maiden run. The royal purple and scarlet drumhead on the rear car became a dusty blur as the train raced across the prairies. The total success of the locomotive units and the train led to the placement of an order for the most luxurious set of passenger cars yet built in the United States.

Santa Fe executives found the virtually maintenance-free stainless steel cars of the CB&Q's Zephyrs most appealing, but disliked the lack of flexibility of articulated units. A series of conferences with the Edward G. Budd Company of Philadelphia produced designs for lightweight, non-articulated, stainless steel passenger equipment, and a contract for nine cars costing $662,078.98, was signed in August 1936. The cars weighed only 83,000 pounds compared with a standard passenger car's 160,000 pounds, but their lower center of gravity and new trucks produced a smoother ride. The cars would be air conditioned, feature large picture windows, and be interchangeable with other equipment. The nine cars would accommodate 104 passengers and a crew of twelve in incredibly beautiful surroundings.

Philadelphia architect Paul F. Cret, Chicago designer S. B. McDonald and ATSF Advertising Manager Roger W. Birdseye collaborated on the interior decor. They decorated the interiors of the five Pullmans, the diner and the lounge car (the baggage and mail cars received only the stainless steel exteriors). The designers decided at the outset to use an Indian motif, with Indian names for the cars, southwestern colors and an array of wood veneers. There was some standardization in that the cars

The "second Super Chief" is readied for passengers at the Chicago terminal.
Santa Fe Railway

generally received ivory ceilings, 3/16th-inch jaspé linoleum floors and gray-green frieze upholstery. The sleepers ("Isleta," "Taos," "Oraibi," and "Laguna") contained paneling of avodire from the Ivory Coast, satinwood from Ceylon, rosewood, sycamore, holly, ebony, cypress and teak. The lounge "Acoma," with its barbershop and crew dormitory, contained a bar of zingana wood, a Navajo rug, and was painted in biege, brown, blue and orange. The observation-sleeper "Navajo" carried out the Indian motif with turquoise ceiling, goatskin lampshades, sand paintings encased in glass, and upholstery based on Navajo designs. The rear of the tear-drop observation carried the purple and scarlet drumhead. The diner "Cochiti" received a color scheme of warm brown, orange and brick red. Mary

Elizabeth Coulter, a thirty-five-year veteran of the Harvey system, designed the china and silver, basing her concepts on the fish characters of the Mimbreno Indians of southern New Mexico. Steward Peter Tausch prepared a "yard long" menu, which included beluga cavier, larded tenderloin ($.95), mountain trout, raisin pie and cheshire cheese. A sirloin for two cost $2.75. The diner and lounge contained 78 seats, quite ample for the passengers, in 16 sections, 13 bedrooms, 11 compartments, and 8 drawing rooms. The Budd craftsmen finished the cars in the spring of 1937, and trial runs began on April 15. A thirty-day tour of the system generated significant publicity and public interest.

Mrs. Eddie Cantor, her daughters and actress Eleanor Powell christened the Super Chief before the maiden voyage on May 18. The train stretched 857 feet under the Dearborn shed, and the publicity releases reminded viewers and passengers of the total bill, $941,698. The Super Chief departed at 7:15 P.M. and began its race toward the old La Grande depot. The consist averaged 60.5 miles per hour and hit 87.2 between Dodge City and La Junta. The Super Chief's time of 36 hours and 49 minutes set a record and beat the advertised schedule. On one ten-

The dining car and commissary crews stock the diner before departure. Santa Fe Railway

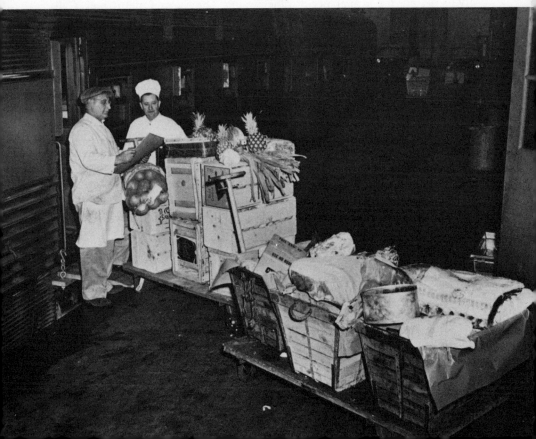

mile segment in Colorado, the "Super" reached 108 miles per hour. The speed record and the luxury train produced only superlatives. The reservations desks could not handle all the requests for tickets, which included a $10.00 extra fare, and revenues of $2.22 per train-mile bettered estimates made by the management. The Super Chief became an instant tradition.

Hollywood adopted the Super Chief, which became its primary mode of travel as well as the subject of novels and motion pictures. In *The Hucksters* one is told that only talent agents and kept women rode the Chief, but that the Super Chief was an exclusive club for New York–Hollywood commuters. The mysterious proceedings behind closed compartment doors created an aura, and as one character suggested, an aphrodisiac. The train became an "extra-fare, extra-exclusive, superdeluxe commuter special that makes Toots Shor's handy to Romanoff's, that connects Sunset Boulevard with Wall Street."[1] To have "Chiefed" West was the only way to travel.

The success of the Super Chief produced a revolution in Santa Fe passenger operations. The company announced that the Chief would be reequipped with stainless steel cars to include single rooms or roomettes. Orders to Budd (twenty-two cars) and Pullman-Standard (forty-five cars) initiated a massive infusion of lightweight streamlined equipment. The increase in traffic often forced the Chief to operate in three or more sections despite the availability of other trains. The Super Chief, Chief, California Limited and Grand Canyon Limited operated west via Raton with the Navajo and Scout via Amarillo. The Ranger and Antelope covered the Chicago-Texas runs with the Oil Flyer to Tulsa. Other trains operated from Texas to California, Denver to El Paso, and Phoenix to Chicago and Los Angeles. A reviving economy, the growth of tourism, and the publicity meant ever-expanding services and ridership.

On February 22, 1938, a "second set" of sleepers from Pullman-Standard allowed for a twice-weekly Super Chief. The six P-S Pullmans were not as luxurious as the original Budd cars, but they continued the Indian motif. Sleepers "Talwiwi," "Tchirege," and "Tsankawi" were typical of the unpronounceable names selected. Additional diesels came from Electro-Motive for the newest Super Chief. This train symbolized the banner year for passenger service on the Atchison, for 1938 marked the coming of the streamliner to the entire system.

The Santa Fe announced the acquisition of the largest fleet of stainless steel cars in the nation and the launching of twelve new streamliners. New trains between Chicago and Los Angeles, Los Angeles and San Diego and Chicago and Kansas City would soon ply the rails. The Chief would operate daily with twelve trains, each with ten new cars, on a 51-hour schedule. The Chief's equipment was part of an order for 151

The San Diegan near San Clemente on the surfline. Santa Fe Railway

stainless steel cars. Further, the same kind of luxury travel available to first-class passengers would also be provided for those traveling by coach.

On February 22, the new all-coach El Capitan left Dearborn. This once-a-week train of five cars included a baggage-dormitory coach, two chair cars, a lunch-counter car and chair observation. A 1,800-horsepower diesel headed the extra-fare streamliner, which carried 192 passengers on the same schedule as the Super Chief.

The next month, on March 27, the San Diegan service between San Diego and Los Angeles began. Making two round trips daily, this six-car diesel-powered train included four coaches, a tavern/lunch-counter car and a parlor observation. The 2½-hour schedule provided strenuous competition for bus operators. The popularity of the San Diegan led to the addition of a second set of equipment on the run in 1940.

In the Chicago-Kansas City market the CB&Q Zephyr cut deeply into the Santa Fe's patronage, and the ATSF responded with two new trains, the Chicagoan and the Kansas Citian. They covered the 451 miles in a time quite competitive with the "Q," and they offered three chair cars, a club-lounge and a parlor observation. The $700,000 investment in each train could not be supported by Kansas City-Chicago traffic, so the run was extended to Wichita on an 11¾-hour schedule. This, too, proved less than profitable, and the passenger department extended the trains to Oklahoma City on December 10, 1939, covering 850 miles in 15 hours. The trains also received a Tulsa connection at Kansas City, making that 707-mile run in 12 hours, 40 minutes. The Santa Fe trains invaded a market long dominated by the Frisco, Katy and Rock Island, and captured the lion's share of the business with the new daytime speedsters to the Southwest. A through Pullman to Dallas and Fort Worth challenged the Rock Island's Rocket and the Missouri Pacific's Sunshine Special.

The competition in the Southwest pales in comparison with the epochal battle which developed in California when the Santa Fe attempted to invade the Los Angeles-San Francisco market, long a virtual Southern Pacific monopoly. The Santa Fe's serpentine rail route between the two cities extended from Los Angeles northeast to Barstow, then up the San Joaquin Valley to Oakland, where passengers took the ferry to San Francisco. The Southern Pacific's coast line, far shorter in mileage, gave the SP a significant edge. The expansion of the California highway network, however, gave the Santa Fe management a chance to seize a larger share of the traffic. A new highway opened from Los Angeles across the mountains to Bakersfield on the Santa Fe, and a new bridge linked Oakland with San Francisco. The Santa Fe proposed a rail-bus coordinated service with new, air-conditioned 36-seat buses between Los Angeles and Bakersfield and between Oakland and San Francisco, connecting with a new streamliner, the Golden Gate, between Bakersfield and Oakland. The route reduced the all-rail distance by 170 miles and 5 hours' time. Further, the fare on the new service would be $6.00, or 1½¢ per mile. The SP charged $9.47, and Pacific Greyhound $6.75, and both filed briefs against the proposed service with the California Railroad Commission.

For almost two years the battle raged, with several labor unions supporting the SP and Greyhound and consumer groups aiding the Santa Fe. The SP argued that the ATSF did not have the right to operate intrastate buses; the Santa Fe attacked the SP "monopoly." On April 18, 1938, the commission approved the proposal and extended the coordinated service to San Diego, Needles and Barstow. The 1½¢ per mile fare was approved, as was the 9 hour 35 minute schedule. The commission ordered service to begin within 90 days, and on July 1, the Golden Gates commenced operation. The five-car stainless steel, diesel-powered trains carried almost 200 passengers on the 313-mile Bakersfield-Oakland segment. Buses operated out of a new downtown San Francisco terminal, and the Los Angeles buses reached Hollywood, Glendale, Burbank and Pasadena, offering a service not provided by the SP.

The public response to the Golden Gates overwhelmed the train's capacity, forcing the Santa Fe to add the Valley Flyer on the route in June 1939. The Flyer consisted of six rebuilt and air-conditioned heavyweight cars pulled by a semistreamlined Pacific, Number 1369. The consist, painted bright red, yellow and silver, included a baggage-club car, diner, lounge, and coaches. The buffet-lounge "Chief Geronimo," formerly on the Chief, added a note of luxury. The Flyer became a favorite of the valley residents and did yeoman service during World War II.

President Engel not only desired the best passenger trains for the Santa Fe, but he also placed them on the fastest schedules possible. He wanted ATSF passenger trains to enter and depart from new or modernized terminal facilities. Engel put the entire system on one schedule to avoid forcing freight trains onto sidings when overtaken by passenger trains. Freights often operated as second sections of passenger trains, running only a few minutes behind the passenger schedule. Track improvements continued, especially from Chicago to La Junta. Between these two points, some 990 miles, the track rose 3,465 feet in elevation, but trains covered the distance in 15½ hours. (A similar 950-mile run on the "water level" route between New York and Chicago took 16 to 18 hours.) The Santa Fe also joined the Union Pacific and Southern Pacific in constructing a new Union Station in Los Angeles. The city had long urged such a move, and the ATSF's old La Grande depot needed to be replaced. The Santa Fe spent almost $3 million as its share of the cost, but became a partner in one of the finest depots in the country. The Spanish-style building with its

No. 1369 and the "Valley Flyer," resplendent in yellow, silver and red. Santa Fe Railway

125-foot clock tower was an architectural gem. The facility included sixteen tracks connected by a 500-foot subway concourse, and a postal terminal annex which contributed to the station's income. Large crowds came to view the station at its opening on Sunday, May 7, 1939. Remodeling of Chicago's Dearborn Station did not enhance its architectural style, but it did improve the facilities for the thousands of passengers using the venerable depot.

The expanded passenger train fleet and the improved facilities found far greater use than the Atchison ever anticipated. War began in Europe in the fall of 1939, and President Roosevelt's rearmament program placed larger and larger burdens on the Santa Fe. Throughout the system the

impact of the military expansion could be seen as men in khaki and blue uniforms began to crowd the trains. The Atchison served stations at or near Fort Riley, Fort Hood, the San Diego Naval and Marine bases, Tinker Field, and many more. With the attack on Pearl Harbor in December 1941, the flow of personnel to the West Coast accelerated, and the Santa Fe responded with more cars, troop trains, and attempts to maintain high-quality service.

Passenger operations during the war reached massive proportions as the increase in passengers carried approached 600 percent. Restrictions on raw materials limited purchases of new equipment; the system added 26 cars in 1941, 41 in 1942, but only one car in 1943. Retired units were reconditioned and put back into service, but ten diners added to the roster failed to meet the demand for food service. Finally, the passenger department reopened the long-closed Harvey Houses and reinstituted the train stop for meals. West Coast trains operated in multiple sections, often carrying 4,000 to 5,000 passengers. The rationing of tires and gasoline caused civilians to turn to trains, adding to the crush, and job seekers going to California or Texas defense plants swelled the throngs on Santa Fe trains.

Fred Harvey valiantly attempted to cope with the demands made by military and civilian travel. The diner fleet was doubled, and older "Harvey Girls" again came out of retirement to work in the reopened houses. The number of Harvey employees rose to 5,000, and then to 7,000. Self-service facilities for ATSF employees released some Harvey operatives for the dining rooms. Harvey news agents on the trains were soon selling 150,000 bottles of milk and 500,000 sandwiches a month; on one trip, the passengers on the Scout consumed 4,400 sandwiches. To explain its dilemma to the public, the Harvey system ran large advertisements featuring "Private Pringle," who tried to convey the enormity of Harvey's services. Standard 36-seat diners fed 350 people in ten sittings of 30 minutes each, and frying 50 to 60 dozen eggs for breakfast became a routine for the cooks—the eggs were always fresh, never cold storage. Harvey curtailed its resort operations and ended the "bottomless cup of

coffee," but kept the standard of quality as high as possible. In 1945 the Harvey houses, diners and news agents served 5 million pounds of potatoes, 1.7 million dozen eggs, 20 million cups of coffee and 1 million gallons of milk and cream. The railway added equipment to aid its partner and expanded the houses where possible; but Harvey operated all of the food services. The railway and the still family-owned Harvey system remained compatible partners through the "duration" and met the challenges of the war boom.

When the war ended in 1945, the Santa Fe's new president, Fred Gurley, determined to continue the program begun in 1938, ordered new equipment, instituted new schedules and prepared to respond to a projected boom in passenger travel. The Atchison and every other major railroad foresaw an increase in rail travel, and spent millions of dollars to meet the anticipated demand. The vast expansion of federal and state highway building, the ever-growing number of private automobiles and the development of an extensive air network were scarcely recognized and their impact wholly underestimated. The result was an enormous investment in locomotives and cars to meet a public demand which never materialized.

In 1946 the Atchison, in cooperation with the Pennsylvania Railroad and the New York Central, began to operate coast-to-coast Pullmans via

The "Texas Chief" along the Washita River in the Arbuckle Mountains. Santa Fe Railway

Chicago. Cars from the Broadway Limited and the Twentieth Century Limited were added to the Chief on a daily basis. A similar arrangement took a car from the Baltimore and Ohio's Capital Limited from Washington on to Los Angeles via the Chief. Further, in the fall of 1946, the Super Chief and El Capitan began to operate every other day instead of twice weekly, and went back to the pre-war 39 hour 45 minute schedule. To operate the trains more frequently the railway purchased 164 lightweight cars, and brought the fleet of streamliners to 424 units. Within two years the purchase of additional equipment made it possible to operate both trains daily. The new Pullmans for the Super Chief contained only rooms, no sections, and included radios, nonfogging windows, a softer and quieter ride, and more efficient air conditioning. The new coaches for El Capitan had reclining seats, and each car carried an attendant. El Capitan also included a lunch-counter diner offering budget meals.

In 1948 the ATSF made a successful effort to break into the Chicago-Oklahoma-Texas market. The old flagship on the Chicago-Galveston run, the Ranger, had acquired streamlined cars, but the ATSF needed a new train and a new image to challenge the Missouri Pacific's Eagle and the Frisco-Katy Texas Special. The new service began on April 3, 1948, when the Texas Chief departed from Dearborn on a schedule reducing the Chicago-gulf time by ten hours. The Texas Chief included new coaches, sleepers, diner and lounge, and the train provided a courier nurse in the coaches and radios in the Pullmans. The new train soon became a favorite in the Southwest and developed an admiring and enthusiastic clientele. With the opening of the Santa Fe's direct rail route into Dallas in 1955, a Chicago-Dallas section of the Texas Chief was added. The remodeled cars for the Texas Chief's addition carried out a Texas motif with a copper frieze in the diner featuring blue bonnets and the Lone Star. The lounge contained murals of hammered copper using Texas themes of cowboys and oil wells, and tooled leather plaques with designs derived from Texas cattle brands. The Texas Chief's popularity became a primary factor in the ultimate withdrawal of the Texas Special by the Katy and the Frisco.

Another new train, though far less successful, was launched in 1950. The Kansas City Chief operated on an overnight schedule between Chicago and Kansas City, competing against the CB&Q's Zephyr. The newest Chief departed at 10:00 P.M. and arrived at 7:45 A.M. and its Gay Nineties style Centennial Club Car offered passengers a late drink or snack and an early breakfast. The Kansas City Chief could not generate enough business, and eventually was withdrawn.

This modest setback failed to deter the management's decisions to support a broad range of passenger services, to embark on a program to reequip the Super Chief, Chief and El Capitan, and provide new cars and accommodations on other trains. In 1952 the ATSF placed an order for 118 cars with the Budd Company, and their delivery gave the passenger department 519 post-1946 units, with an additional 51 units remaining on order. The stainless steel cars had roller-bearing trucks and air conditioning, and the 48-seat coaches provided more leg room and lounge space. Eight cars in the Budd order attracted considerable attention in the industry. They were full-length domes, based on the vista dome concept but were much larger. They seated 103 passengers including 28 in a lounge below the dome seats and 18 in a lounge directly under the glass dome. These giants weighed 103½ tons and were assigned to the El Capitan, Chicagoan and Kansas Citian. A special thermostatic control regulated the dome car's interior temperature taking into account the effect of the sun on the vast expanse of glass. Indian designs etched in glass panels, hammered metal plaques, and a color scheme of Mesa Red, Zuni Turquoise and Pueblo Beige decorated the cars.

The Super Chief was not neglected in the acquisition of luxury equipment. Largely reequipped in 1946–1947, the train received new cars again in 1951. New sleepers and diners built by Pullman-Standard, Budd and American Car and Foundry were added, but the prizes of the package were the Pleasure Dome Lounge cars. The Dome Lounge included a private dining facility—the Turquoise Room—a sunken cocktail lounge seating ten, a large main lounge, a dome-parlor, a writing desk and a bar. Advertisements called the Dome the "top of the Super, next to the stars." The new trains toured the system and 35,000 people in seven cities came aboard to see the facilities. On January 28, 1951, the equipment went into regular service; the five sets of cars cost over $8 million, an indication of the Santa Fe's commitment to passenger service.

Even more striking was the decision to launch yet another transcontinental streamliner. In 1953 the management decided to substantially upgrade its service between Chicago and San Francisco, entering a market dominated by the CB&Q–DRG&W–WP California Zephyr and the UP–SP City of San Francisco. The San Francisco Chief went into operation on June 6, 1954, offering the only one-railroad train between the two cities. Further, the newest Chief used the Amarillo-Clovis route, and at Clovis a section of the train moved over the Coleman Cutoff to Houston, Fort Worth and Dallas. Equipment for the new Chief included coaches with reclining seats, all room Pullmans, a full-length dome lounge and a Harvey diner. Services, such as the courier-nurse, were similar to those on the Los Angeles run, and the San Francisco Chief's schedule of 47 hours and 20 minutes from Chicago to San Francisco compared favorably with other trains on the route. The train required six sets of equipment, and the new cars vastly improved service on the Santa Fe between Texas and California. Public response was not overwhelming, but the management launched an advertising campaign to support the new service.

Across Muir Trestle—the "San Francisco Chief," with its Hi-level cars and full-length dome. Santa Fe Railway

By the mid-1950s, several railroads began to withdraw from passenger operations, not in a massive way, but mainly by reducing the number of trains and some types of services. The Santa Fe continued its commitment, however, and constantly experimented with new equipment. By 1954 the "bread and butter" train on the ATSF was El Capitan. Its coaches were full most of the time; its early morning arrivals, comfortable coaches and fast schedules attracted patronage even during normally slow periods, and it was a primary source of revenue. The train often could not meet reservation requests, and second and third sections were not feasible given the high cost of equipment to be used only at peak periods. The 80-foot-long coaches could seat a limited number of passengers because of the extra leg room required on the long-distance train and the need for large restrooms and space for a car attendant or conductor. In an attempt to increase the train's capacity, the Santa Fe experimented for two years with a new two-level car design which was based on the contours of the full-length dome lounges. The Budd Company built coaches of a similar configuration which provided a greater seating capacity per car and, thereby, increased revenue. The new Hi-level chair cars, lounges and diners stood 15½ feet high, two feet taller than conventional equipment. Seats were located on the second level, eight feet above the rails, but below on the first floor were the platform-level doors, baggage space, restrooms and rooms for nurses, conductors and attendants; all of the second floor was occupied by revenue producing seats. The ends of the cars did not have vestibules but, rather, direct car-to-car connections were provided, thus saving additional space. Each Hi-level car seated 28 more passengers than a conventional coach, and the new nine-car El Capitan consisting of Hi-level coaches, diner and "Top of the Cap" Lounge held 496 passengers compared to 350 on the previously used equipment. The new cars could be serviced from the outside, the interior materials required less maintenance, and the cars weighed less per passenger. The Hi-level diner seated 80 people and used a dumbwaiter to reach the kitchen, which was located on the lower level. Passenger response was highly favorable both to the experimental cars and to the exhibition train which toured the system in June and July 1956. Service on the Hi-level El Capitans began July 8, and the inaugural trains met in Albuquerque to help celebrate the city's 250th anniversary. The Santa Fe invested $13 million in the Hi-level trains, and advertised them lavishly. El Capitan offered new family fares, inexpensive meals and discount meal tickets.

The Santa Fe management, working through the advertising department and the passenger department, promoted passenger services with national and regional media campaigns, and with a variety of ticket prices and attractions. In 1948 and 1949 at the Chicago Railroad Fair the ATSF exhibit included an Indian village centered on a large pueblo. Hopi, Zuni and Navajo Indians worked in the village, and buildings representing a Navajo hogan and an Apache wickiup were included in the exhibit. Between 120 and 125 Indians carried on various crafts and performed dances at the Village. The Wheels a'Rolling pageant used an ATSF 0–4–0 named "Little Buttercup" in a scene which celebrated the Harvey Girls and the settling of the West. The Santa Fe also exhibited a 2–10–4, a 5,400-horsepower diesel and four cars from the Super Chief. A 250-seat movie tent drew large crowds to view travel films of the Southwest. Throughout the 1940s and 1950s, the advertising department produced attractive copy for *Holiday*, *The Saturday Evening Post* and other national journals, and sponsored radio programs, rented billboards, and sent agents to speak to civic groups about the railroad's passenger trains.

The passenger department revived the courier-nurse service after 1946, providing aid to mothers with young children, the elderly and invalids. The department hired three members of the Zuni Pueblo to ride El Capitan and the Super Chief between Gallup and Raton. Wearing tribal costumes, they described the Indian villages and pueblos along the route. As early as 1953 the system developed the family-plan fare, with one adult paying the full ticket price, the second adult two-thirds fare, and children paying half price. Originally limited to Pullman passengers on Monday, Tuesday and Wednesday departures, the fare was expanded to include both sleeper and coach tickets and all departure dates. In 1970 the ATSF offered "Flexi-fares," a one-price ticket which included meals and

The Hi-level "El Capitan" winds through Apache Canyon. Santa Fe Railway

accommodations. The Flexi-fare rate for sleeping accommodations was the same as coach plus the room charge. The Santa Fe also accepted a variety of charge cards. Throughout the period the department offered many tours —Indian Detours, ski trips to New Mexico, and tours to Carlsbad Caverns and Grand Canyon and special trains for football games, school trips and political candidates. The operating department cooperated fully with the passenger department, and speed reductions which were taking place on other railroads were not paralleled on the Atchison. The Super Chief still averaged 82.1 miles per hour from Garden City to Lamar, and the San Francisco Chief reached 71.2 miles per hour between Shopton and Carrollton. Despite these arduous and costly attempts to attract passengers, nearly every year the total number of riders declined and passenger revenues fell.

First to feel the rapid decline in riders after 1946 was the Harvey system. As late as 1949, Harvey retained nearly 7,000 employees, but soon had to close the houses at Newton, Dodge City, La Junta and Las Vegas. The hotels at Grand Canyon remained popular, and 70 rooms were added to La Fonda in Santa Fe, but others were closed. La Posada in Winslow, for example, became a division headquarters for the ATSF. In an attempt to save the houses in 1950–1952, the California Limited began to stop for meals west of Albuquerque, reviving the old custom, but this modest effort failed. The houses kept quality at a high level and prices low—an excellent lamb stew cost 90¢ at Newton on July 1, 1953, and ten different desserts were available for a maximum price of 35¢ each. The number of Harvey employees declined to 2,000, and most were involved in preparing food for the 122 dining and lunch-counter cars. Harvey still operated its chicken ranch and bottling plant at Newton and the bakery in Chicago, but patronage in the diners declined, income fell and losses mounted. Standards were not lowered; fresh fruit, freshly baked pies, live mountain trout and hot rolls still flowed into the diners from the commissaries. An attempt at cost reduction on the El Paso-Albuquerque connection in the form of a "Lunch-o-mat" did not meet expectations. The Santa Fe remodeled the Alvarado Hotel in 1954, but declining patronage led to its demolition in 1970. The Harvey system became a public corporation in 1966, entered the interstate highway market, expanded its nonrail food services, and soon parted with the Santa Fe. On December 31, 1968, Harvey operation of the ATSF dining cars terminated. Before the long association ended, only the supervisory personnel from Harvey were non-ATSF employees, and the transition to "Santa Fe All the Way" went largely unnoticed by passengers. Food quality remained high, the same waiters and dining car stewards served the cars, and fresh yellow roses still graced the tables.

The general collapse in passenger traffic could also be seen on the branch lines. Even the doodlebugs and their trailers cost far more to operate than revenues could sustain. The Santa Fe began to curtail their operation, or if they continued, to use them as connections with mainline trains. The company invested in two Budd-built Rail Diesel Cars, and put them on the San Diego-Los Angeles run. They made two round trips, nonstop, with a running time of 2 hours and 15 minutes. The RDCs each contained 80 seats and two 275-horsepower diesel engines. When patronage increased beyond their seating capacity, and after a serious accident, the RDCs were sent to a Kansas run, and the San Diegans took over their schedule. Several doodlebugs received diesel motors, silver and red paint schemes and pulled stainless steel trailers between Amarillo and Lubbock

Streamlined rail cars failed to reduce passenger losses. Santa Fe Railway

and from Clovis to Carlsbad. Even these connecting trains had to be discontinued as ridership declined.

The management refused to accept the long-rumored and hotly debated "death" of the passenger train. As other major passenger haulers retreated, sold their diners and Pullmans, and padded schedules, the ATSF pressed on to improve its trains. In September 1962, the Santa Fe announced that $8 million in new equipment would be purchased, including twenty-four more Hi-level chair cars. They arrived in the spring of 1964, and joined twelve newly rebuilt Pullman cars containing eleven bedrooms each. The new equipment went to the San Francisco Chief, the Super Chief and El Capitan. The Super Chief and El Capitan were now combined as one train, except during the summer months and holiday periods, in a further attempt to reduce costs.

The entire area of passenger train profits, losses and operating costs is an accountant's dream—or nightmare. The computations based on the

Interstate Commerce Commission formula offer one set of figures and direct, out-of-pocket costs produce other data. Regardless of the accounting method used, the Atchison management saw passenger train operations move from a "generally profitable" situation in 1950 to a "substantial loss" in 1965. Revenues exceeded directly related expenses between 1950 and 1965 in all years but 1954–1958 and 1965. The ICC formula showed much higher losses as early as 1950 when each revenue dollar cost $1.20 in expenses. The management remained optimistic, but cut off those trains with large losses. Passenger train miles fell from 24 million in 1950 to 15 million in 1965. The average journey increased, however, from 520 miles to 713, and the average train load rose from 79.6 to 116.4. The fixed costs, ever-increasing wages for passenger crews, and air and car competition began to take their toll.

The doodlebug between Atchison and Topeka made its last run on March 15, 1958, symbolic of the cutbacks which became necessary. The Chief acquired coaches, a new schedule and lost its New York City Pullmans. The Golden Gates were terminated in 1965 to give the San Francisco Chief more riders in the San Joaquin Valley. Only the Post Office Department's patronage kept losses from soaring beyond possible support levels. The Atchison remained the major mail rail carrier west of Chicago and ranked third in the nation in volume of Post Office traffic. All passenger trains had mail facilities, and Numbers 7 and 8 carried mail exclusively. But, the bottom dropped out in September 1967, when the Postmaster General announced the termination of virtually all contracts with rail carriers. The crushing blow had been delivered.

On October 4, 1967, President John Reed delivered a eulogy to the Chiefs. He announced that within forty-eight hours all but two railway Post Office cars would cease operation, producing a loss of $35 million in yearly revenue. This, plus a 17.3 percent decline in patronage during the first eight months of the year, created an ICC formula loss of $32 million, which was more than the ATSF could bear. Since 1946 the Santa Fe had spent $136 million for cars and locomotives for passenger service, but losses had mounted. The ATSF supported the third largest passenger operation in the nation, a luxury it could no longer afford. Therefore, Reed announced, the ATSF would ask for permission to terminate all passenger service except the Super Chief/El Capitan, San Francisco Chief, Texas Chief and San Diegans. Fourteen trains, including half of the dining and sleeper service, would be discontinued. "The Santa Fe has not abandoned the traveling public—travelers show an increasing preference to drive or fly," Reed declared.[2] There were, as one journal said, too many Chiefs and not enough passengers. The Santa Fe tried to operate too many trains for too long.

After a long and hotly contested series of hearings, the Chief made its last run on May 13, 1968. The El Pasoans had been terminated on April 9, and the Dallas connection of the Texas Chief was discontinued on July 19. Service between Texas and California ended, and by 1971 only the Denver-La Junta and Kansas City-Tulsa runs and Numbers 23 and 24 between Chicago and Los Angeles were still pending termination. The remaining trains continued to offer the very best in accommodations. After the contract with the Pullman Company ended, the sleeper service became the sole responsibility of the passenger department, which fought hard to retain and expand patronage on the remaining trains. Rave notices in the *Chicago Tribune, Trains, Sunset Magazine,* and *Esquire* praised the Super Chief and notified the potential traveler that the Santa Fe still wanted them. The losses on the San Francisco Chief led the management to ask that the train be shifted to the Chicago-Los Angeles run, that all service in the San Joaquin Valley end, and that Numbers 23 and 24 be discontinued. The request was denied. Revenues continued to fall, and the Santa Fe joined other passenger carriers in supporting Railpax, a plan for a national corporation to operate noncommuter passenger service.

Congress responded to the pleas of the railroads, and created the National Railroad Passenger Corporation. The NRPC entered into negotiations with the Atchison and other carriers for absorption of selected routes and the purchase of equipment. Amtrak, the NRPC's operating division, formulated a route structure, inspected available equipment and signed contracts with the railroads for operating NRPC trains. Amtrak retained the Chicago-Los Angeles, Chicago-Houston and Los Angeles-San Diego routes and train names, and offered to purchase a substantial number of Santa Fe passenger cars. The railway sold a group of Hi-level cars to Auto-train for service between Virginia and Florida, and sold 526 cars to Amtrak. Amtrak purchased baggage cars, sleepers, coaches, diners, domes, and lounges, some of which were from the original Super Chief of 1937. The Santa Fe's maintenance program had kept the equipment in excellent condition, and the company provided a major share of Amtrak's fleet of 1,200 cars. Amtrak also contracted with the Santa Fe to service and repair passenger cars.

The contract with Amtrak relieved the Atchison of its passenger losses, but at a price. To become a part of Amtrak, Santa Fe paid NRPC $21,054,000 in thirty-six payments, but refused to accept NRPC common stock. Severance pay to passenger train crews reached an additional $12 million. NRPC paid the railway $12,324,000 for the passenger cars, spare parts and supplies, creating a bookkeeping loss of $30,755,000. The total cost reached $64.5 million with only $31 million used as a federal tax credit. President Reed explained that the immediate losses had to be accepted to gain relief from the enormous drain on the railway's treasury.

"Madame Queen" gives the Super Chief some help to conquer Raton Pass.
Santa Fe Railway

Amtrak passenger operations began on May 1, 1971, and the last Santa Fe passenger train arrived in Dearborn Station at 9:00 P.M. on May 2. The Dearborn Station agent erased the chalked entry on the arrival board, "On Time." The agents locked up Dearborn, and the Amtrak Chiefs moved over to Union Station. An era ended—the names remained, but airline-type tickets, uniformed hostesses and stewards, and red, silver and blue cars proclaimed the demise of "Santa Fe All The Way." The happy little Navajo boy Chico retired from passenger promotion; he left behind fond memories and many friends.

Epilogue:
Santa Fe Industries

By the mid-1960s, the crisis in the nation's rail industry had reached massive proportions. A half-dozen carriers in the Northeast faced bankruptcy, and profit margins of the "healthy" railways of the South and West sank lower and lower. Between 1929 and 1960 the railroad industry's share of inter-city freight declined from 74.9 percent to 44.1 percent. The loss of freight to trucks, barges and pipelines paralleled, although not as precipitously, the loss of passengers to private automobiles, buses and airplanes. Wages continued to absorb larger proportions of earnings as hourly rates rose, and the carriers failed to gain relief from the archaic work rules. The average hourly wage for railway workers increased from $2.66 in 1960 to $4.14 in 1970. The Interstate Commerce Commission moved with a snail-like pace in granting, or rejecting, requests for rate increases, passenger train discontinuances, and abandonment of unprofitable branch lines. Millions of dollars of potential revenue were lost due to lengthy delays in approvals of rate increases. While the railroads continued to shoulder a major share of local and state property taxes, in addition to their federal tax obligations, rival carriers received tax benefits in the form of federal and state highway and airport building programs. The romance of the rails failed to prevent an increasingly tarnished image in the mind of the public, which equated the health of the railways with the cleanliness of their passenger cars and continuous dividend checks. Young people saw a business career with the railways as a deadend. Faced with these seemingly insurmountable problems, the boards of directors of many railways determined to move into nonrail enterprises to raise the level of profitability. Some of the companies still had capital to invest or had nonrail assets which they began to emphasize. To facilitate this movement toward non-rail enterprises, many carriers reorganized their corporate structures and became "conglomerates" or holding companies.

The trend in American business organization toward holding companies, or "conglomerates," accelerated in the 1960s, and the managers of many railways found the advantages of such corporate structures attractive. The decision in 1967 by the board of directors of the Atchison, Topeka and Santa Fe Railway to create a holding company reflected this national trend and a new approach to the development of the railway's long-existing diversified holdings. The reorganized corporate structure facilitated additional acquisitions in both transportation and nontransportation fields, and, hopefully, would enhance earnings. In 1968 Santa Fe Industries emerged as a holding company for the railway and its subsidiaries.

The stockholders of the railway voted overwhelmingly to exchange their securities on a one-for-one basis for stock in Santa Fe Industries. On

The second-generation diesels helped to reduce the operating ratio. Santa Fe Railway

August 21, 1968, the exchange was effected. Santa Fe Industries quickly regrouped the railway's subsidiaries, and trade journals soon commented on the infusion of young executives entering managerial positions in "Industries." The officers of "Industries" sought to simplify the vast corporate structure that they had inherited. Many of the subsidiaries represented only responses to legal problems created by state and federal regulatory agencies and by archaic state laws, but others were large, profitable concerns. The corporate maze had been reduced several times earlier, but considerable pruning remained to be done. As early as 1940–1943, some sixteen subsidiaries had been dissolved and later the assets of fourteen more had been transferred to other Santa Fe-owned firms. Nevertheless, in 1968 the number and scope of the railway's subsidiaries remained very large indeed.

As has been seen, the Santa Fe railroad had acquired nonrail properties almost from the beginning of its existence. By the mid-1920s, the value of investments in other corporations was carried on the books at $30,285,000, but these stocks and bonds actually represented a considerably larger asset. The holdings included land, coal mines, timber, producing oil wells, tie and lumber processing plants, and interests in several small railroads, as well as the large operating rail subsidiaries. The acquisition of truck and bus lines in the 1930s, and urban real estate in the late 1920s and thereafter, increased the value of the railway's properties. By 1962 the Atchison's books showed its nonrail investments to be worth $18,440,000, and its oil and mineral properties were carried at $12.1 million, but both areas were seriously undervalued. Nonrail assets were estimated to be worth at least $160 million, and the Atchison also held $92 million in federal bonds and special bank deposits. As a good-will gesture, and to gain a tax advantage, the ATSF owned $11,100,000 in municipal and county bonds issued by governments along its routes. Non-operating sources produced approximately one-fourth of the railway's total income before taxes. The largest and most profitable of the subsidiaries was the Chanslor-Western Oil and Development Company, which held most of the petroleum properties and real estate investments.

The Atchison entered the oil business in 1904–1905, when it began to purchase stock in the Chanslor-Canfield Midway Oil Company of California. Even earlier, in 1896, the railway had purchased 320 acres of land in Orange County which appeared to have potential as a source of petroleum. The ATSF and its oil subsidiary acquired additional land in Orange and Kern Counties, and oilman E. L. Doheny developed the property. The Santa Fe later purchased the Petroleum Development Company and merged it into Chanslor-Canfield Midway, and by 1916 the two properties had produced over 36 million barrels of oil. The petroleum

Chanslor-Western oil field at Rincon, California. Santa Fe Railway

operation encompassed 12,750 acres of land either owned or leased by the subsidiaries. Nine years later Chanslor-Canfield Midway's assets reached $94,768,000 in value, and net earnings in 1923 were $6,144,000. From its holding of 79 percent of the oil firm's stock, the Atchison had received $19,360,000 in dividends by 1923. During the next twenty-five years, the oil company added to its properties, and the annual production of petroleum reached 2.4 million barrels from 558 producing wells.

The Santa Fe expanded its petroleum holding in 1916, when it purchased the Coline Oil Company of Oklahoma. The Coline Oil Company owned producing wells in the Healdton Field west of Ardmore, and became a source of fuel oil for the Gulf, Colorado and Santa Fe. In five years Coline Oil paid the Atchison $2,711,000 in dividends. Other petroleum properties were acquired in Texas, and together with those in Oklahoma and California produced profits of $9.2 million in 1952.

The following year the Atchison formed the Chanslor-Western Oil and Development Company, which brought together the Western Improvement Company's real estate holdings and the various oil subsidiaries. Chanslor-Western some eleven years later began a secondary recovery program on its California holdings and subsequently extended its exploratory operations into Colorado, Montana and Wyoming. Chanslor-Western also managed the Santa Fe Pacific Railroad Company, the owner of the Santa Fe portion of the remaining A&P land in Arizona and New Mexico, and the mineral rights to lands previously sold. The Santa Fe Pacific leased 550,000 acres to Tenneco Oil Company in 1970, and Shell Oil Company leased 250,000 acres in 1972. Petroleum became the Santa Fe's largest single source of nonrail income very early in the twentieth century, and remained so under "Industries."

Another source of revenue for Santa Fe Industries was the Santa Fe Trail Transportation Company. "Trail" expanded the truck subsidiaries first acquired in the 1930s and by 1970 operated routes of over 17,000 miles with 5,656 pieces of equipment. As "piggyback" service expanded on the ATSF, the truck subsidiary became a major source of trailers. In 1970 "Trail" purchased $13.5 million in new equipment, largely trailers, and substantially augmented its existing "piggyback" fleet. The "Trail" operation relieved the Atchison of its obligation to provide LCL service, but because of its considerable short-haul operations, the motor carrier activities of "Trail" are unprofitable.

Kirby Lumber Company was formed in 1901 by John Henry Kirby and other Texas lumber men. Kirby Lumber owned sawmills and timber land north and east of Beaumont in Texas and Louisiana. The firm entered bankruptcy in 1933, and three years later was reorganized as Kirby Lumber Corporation. Following the reorganization, the Atchison, as a major creditor, became the owner of 60 percent of the stock. This holding grew to 95 percent, and Kirby became a part of Chanslor-Western. By 1970 Kirby employed 925 people and owned a tree farm of 560,000 acres and mineral rights on 314,000 acres which produced substantial oil and gas royalties. The firm entered a sustained yield program under a scientifically managed plan which produced 78 million feet of lumber and 117 million square feet of plywood annually. Kirby built a large plywood mill and a plant to make precut lumber for housing, and in 1972 gross revenue reached $23.6 million. Expanding plywood production soon increased revenues to an even higher level.

Not all of the subsidiaries became major sources of revenue and profits. In 1952 a Navajo Indian sheep herder discovered uranium near Grants, New Mexico, on land where the mineral rights were held by the Santa Fe Pacific Railroad Company. The ATSF organized the Haystack Mountain

Sustained-yield forests feed the Kirby Lumber plywood plant at Silsbee, Texas.
Santa Fe Railway

Development Company to explore the discovery, but the uranium ore boom failed to turn Haystack into a major producer. Returns from the company were meager.

The Santa Fe also entered the air freight forwarding business, an investment which proved to be less than a total success. In 1967 Chanslor-Western agreed to purchase 49 percent of the stock of Express Air Freight, Inc., an air freight forwarder, and three years later the Civil Aeronautics Board approved the purchase. Chanslor-Western then acquired all of the stock of the firm, and transferred its headquarters from New Jersey to the Wichita, Kansas, offices of "Trail." The forwarding subsidiary became Santa Fe Air Freight Company, and an aggressive sales campaign began. The results were not rewarding, however, and the operations were discontinued in December 1973.

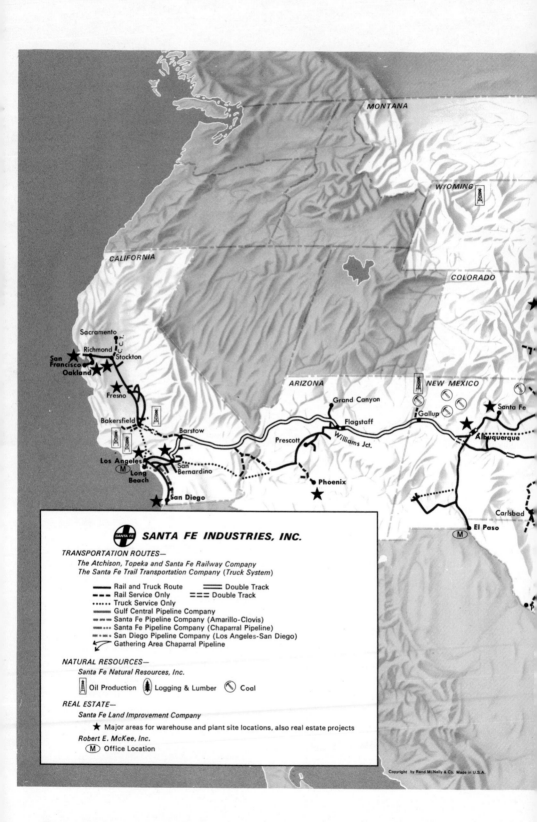

MONTANA

WYOMING

CALIFORNIA

COLORADO

Sacramento
Richmond
Stockton
San Francisco
Oakland

Fresno

Bakersfield

Barstow

ARIZONA

NEW MEXICO

Grand Canyon

Flagstaff

Gallup

Santa Fe

Prescott

Williams Jct.

Albuquerque

Los Angeles
Long Beach
San Bernardino

Phoenix

San Diego

Carlsbad

El Paso

SANTA FE INDUSTRIES, INC.

TRANSPORTATION ROUTES—

The Atchison, Topeka and Santa Fe Railway Company
The Santa Fe Trail Transportation Company (Truck System)

Rail and Truck Route	Double Track
Rail Service Only	Double Track
Truck Service Only	

Gulf Central Pipeline Company
Santa Fe Pipeline Company (Amarillo-Clovis)
Santa Fe Pipeline Company (Chaparral Pipeline)
San Diego Pipeline Company (Los Angeles-San Diego)
Gathering Area Chaparral Pipeline

NATURAL RESOURCES—

Santa Fe Natural Resources, Inc.

Oil Production   Logging & Lumber   Coal

REAL ESTATE—

Santa Fe Land Improvement Company

★ Major areas for warehouse and plant site locations, also real estate projects

Robert E. McKee, Inc.

Ⓜ Office Location

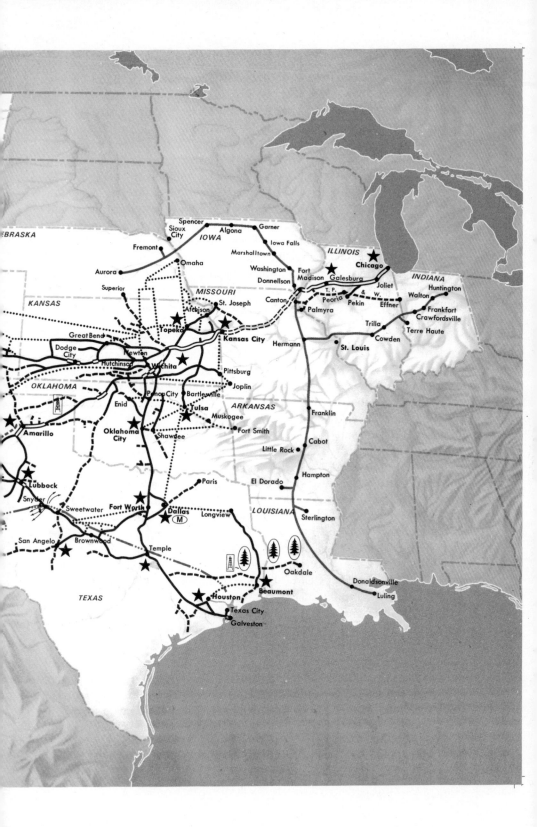

Another area of diversification produced mixed results in the profit and loss columns. In June 1970, Santa Fe Pipeline Company initiated construction of the 675-mile-long Chaparral pipeline from the Snyder area of west Texas to Houston. The Chaparral project was designed to transport natural gas liquids from a number of processing plants in the Permian Basin to the Gulf of Mexico. The new enterprise was financed by selling $40 million in 8¾ percent senior debentures due in 1980, which were guaranteed by Santa Fe Industries. Completed in February 1971, this pipeline operation had its first profit in 1973. Santa Fe Pipeline Company also constructed and operated a 108-mile-long pipeline from Amarillo to Clovis to supply jet fuel to Cannon Air Force Base at Clovis and to transport Santa Fe Railway diesel fuel. Santa Fe Pipeline Inc. (Delaware) held half interest in the San Diego Pipeline Company, which supplied fuel to the San Diego area from Los Angeles. In recent years these pipelines have produced modest income, but a massive pipeline project in the Mississippi Valley proved to be the source of substantial losses.

In 1968 Gulf Central Pipeline Company, a subsidiary of Chanslor-Western, began construction of a 1,880-mile-long pipeline and related terminal facilities to transport anhydrous ammonia from the Gulf coast of Louisiana to Missouri, Indiana, Iowa, Illinois and Nebraska. Limited service became available in October 1969 in Arkansas and Louisiana, and the entire system was completed in November 1970. The pipeline and terminal storage centers could supply 1.1 million tons of anhydrous ammonia annually to the farmers of the Midwest. The system cost $105 million, but in 1970 it produced revenues of only $1 million. The severe shortage of natural gas in Louisiana precluded the construction of additional anhydrous ammonia plants, leading to substantial losses in 1971 and 1972. While the volume of production handled increased late in 1973, it appears unlikely that operations will be profitable in the near future. The Santa Fe management has retained outside consultants in an attempt to find alternative uses for the Pipeline or another source of anhydrous ammonia. Together, Gulf Central Pipeline and Santa Fe Air Freight had an adverse effect of $4 million in 1972.

One of the bright spots in the *Annual Reports* of Santa Fe Industries was real estate. The railway's industrial site department continued to sell large parcels of land for new plants. By 1968 "Industries" and its subsidiaries held 22,000 acres of industrial land in seventy locations, and continued its program of land acquisition throughout the railway's territory. Some sites, such as the Red Bird Industrial District in Dallas, grew very rapidly. Santa Fe Land Improvement Company also began to convert some of the railway's land holdings in the East Bay area of San Francisco into commercial and residential property. A $25 million water-front village

Coordinated rail-truck freight service covers most of the system. Santa Fe Railway

project on 30 acres of ATSF land in Oakland was initiated in 1971. In this project the Santa Fe Land Improvement Company became an equity partner. The real estate holdings of Santa Fe Industries prompted another substantial acquisition.

In 1972, Santa Fe Industries purchased Robert E. McKee, Inc., a general contractor and real estate developer, and the Zia Company, a maintenance firm. For a total cost of $19,650,000 (represented by 561,560 shares of common stock and $1,858,400 in 6¼ percent debentures), "Industries" acquired 100 percent of McKee and Zia. McKee had been a general contractor in El Paso since 1913, had built large buildings throughout the Santa Fe Southwest, and held $167 million in construction contracts in 1972. Zia served as the maintenance contractor for the Atomic Energy Commission's Los Alamos project, and both acquisitions strengthened the increasingly profitable real estate and land operations.

The diversification effort by Marsh and Reed broadened the base of Santa Fe Industries by emphasizing the nonrail subsidiaries which had produced 22 percent of the railway's profits in 1966 and 33.1 percent in 1967. One of the most lucrative investments was Golden Gate Fields, a race track in the East Bay located on Santa Fe land, which paid substantial rent and a share of the paremutuals. Plans for greater diversification were thwarted, however, by the unstable nature of the national economy, and by high interest rates. The decline in the price of "Industries" common stock precluded exchanging stock in mergers because it would dilute the stockholders' interests. Additional diversification plans may also have been postponed because of the larger profits being produced by the railway, and the substantial capital requirements needed to continue the modernization program on the ATSF.

Capital spending on the railway and nonrail enterprises remained very high after the formation of Santa Fe Industries. The large capital budget of $190 million in 1969 declined slightly the following year to $170 million and substantially in 1972 to $119 million, following completion of the major pipeline projects. The projection for 1973 was an incredible $200 million. The vast sums allocated for capital expenditures on the railway, $97 million in 1971 for example, included orders for additional second generation diesels, for rebuilding older "F" diesel units into general purpose locomotives, and for new freight cars. In 1972 the railway acquired 52 new 3,600-horsepower diesels and 1,629 freight cars, and placed orders for 64 more diesels and 2,466 freight cars. Additional piggyback terminals, new grade separations and hundreds of miles of welded rail absorbed part of the budget. The microwave communications system was extended from Beaumont to Longview and Oakdale, and the Pueblo-Denver line received centralized traffic control. The new equipment, line improvements, an expanding economy, additional services, and cost reductions produced record revenues.

The railway's operating ratio of 82.5 in 1968 had represented the greatest problem faced by the management of "Industries." A cost reduction program of an unprecedented nature ensued. The continuing effort to extend mechanization together with major reductions in passenger train operations led to another large decline in the total number of employees; there were only 36,651 in the "family" in 1972. In 1970, in a further attempt to reduce expenses, the Board of Directors approved a plan to abandon 815 miles of unprofitable branchlines. Within two years some 369 miles had been taken out of service, and the average mileage operated declined from 12,862 in 1968 to 12,569 in 1972. The abandonment program led to an immediate tax write-off of some $7.7 million, and only delays in responses by regulatory agencies to applications for abandonments prevented a more rapid decline in mileage. The most substantial drain on the railway, passenger train losses, terminated in May 1971, and the management declared an extraordinary cost of $30 million to join Amtrak, but this figure was less than the projected passenger losses of $70 million for the next three years. Additional losses were suffered because of the bankruptcy of the Penn-Central and other eastern lines, and an adverse decision in the Transcontinental Divisions Case of 1967. The reduction in employees and mileage and termination of passen-

"Super C," the world's fastest freight train, in Cajon Pass. Santa Fe Railway

ger service, however, caused the operating ratio to fall to 79.9 in 1970, and to 77.6 in 1972. Simultaneously the Santa Fe expanded services and established new cost reduction programs.

The railway management created several new operations to generate additional revenues. In July 1970, the Santa Fe initiated a direct daily freight train between Richmond, Virginia, and Richmond, California. The train moved over the Seaboard Coast Line, the Frisco and the Santa Fe, covering the 3,494 miles in four days. This service, plus "Super C" and the "land bridge" concept, began to attract new business. The "land bridge" operation took metal containers from ships arriving in New Jer-

One-hundred-ton hopper cars in Corwith Yard enroute to the wheat fields of the Plains. Santa Fe Railway

sey from Europe, and moved them by rail to the West Coast where they were placed on ships for ports around the Pacific. Santa Fe Industries opened an office in Tokyo to develop Japanese traffic for the "land bridge." In 1971 the ICC granted the request of the Norfolk and Western to operate over thirty miles of the ATSF between Camden, Missouri, and the Argentine Yard. This connection expedited service from the West Coast to the East, particularly to Detroit, and reduced some shipping times by twenty-four hours. Service was also improved at Pueblo for traffic routed over the Denver and Rio Grande Western and the Western Pacific, and connections were improved at Amarillo for cars moving to and from Memphis over the Chicago, Rock Island and Pacific. The Santa Fe built a branch line to the barge facility at Tulsa's Port of Catoosa on the Arkansas River. New services, rate increases, the growth of TOFC and containers, and massive export grain shipments led to record revenues in 1972 and 1973, and the railway continued to be the primary business and the largest source of income of Santa Fe Industries. During the first six months of 1972, the railway earned $35.7 million of "Industries' " $50.6 million in profits, and in the first six months of 1973, the railway produced $34.7 million of the $60.0 million earned by "Industries."

The financial record of Santa Fe Industries became stronger as the railway's earning ability improved, and the financial reports of 1968–1972 produced the following trends:

	1968	1969	1970	1971	1972
Revenues and Sales	763,617,000	819,015,000	859,713,000	896,841,000	972,841,000
(Railway Revenue)	673,400,000)	719,200,000	755,200,000	779,400,000	831,700,000
Net Income	45,388,000	60,760,000	40,216,000	33,143,000	80,966,000
(Net Railway Operating Income)	47,000,000)	64,600,000	60,600,000	95,000,000	103,000,000
Per Share (Undiluted)	1.81	2.43	1.59	1.31	3.23
Capital Expenditures	122,149,000	180,537,000	146,777,000	123,284,000	119,732,000
Current Assets	200,889,000	214,782,000	250,264,000	272,294,000	309,782,000
Current Liabilities	139,663,000	156,799,000	201,535,000	191,188,000	191,076,000
Stockholders (Preferred)	6,044	6,258	6,342	6,249	6,013
(Common)	113,641	117,449	121,329	111,683	104,549
Wages, Salaries, Benefits	411,938,000	428,906,000	451,729,000	474,242,000	537,713,000

These figures helped hold sales of Santa Fe Industries bonds close to 100, although with ever-increasing interest rates. The 6¼ bonds sold at 106 in October 1971. Common and preferred stock prices rose and fell in a rhythm reflecting the general fluctuation of the stock market. Common stock prices between 1966 and 1972 ranged from 16½ to 42, and at a price of 30 yielded 5.3 percent annually. The annual dividend rate of $1.60 remained constant except for an added 5¢ per share paid in the first quarter of 1973. The preferred stock price held steady at 7 to 9, and returned 5.6 percent at 9. Several leading market reports described Santa Fe Industries securities in positive terms, especially as the net income figures rose.

By 1971 the only words of caution expressed in several quarters concerned the growing long-term indebtedness. "Industries" borrowed $107.3 million in 1970 and $63 million the following year, and the total debt at the end of 1971 reached $559.3 million, a slight decline from 1970. In 1971 the long-term debt represented 30 percent of the total capitalization. The financial situation began to improve that year, with cash and short-term investments rising by $25.1 million to $152.3 million, and working capital rose to $81 million, an increase of $32.4 million. The improvements came after the ICC granted several additional rate-increase requests, and Congress reestablished the 7 percent investment tax credit, which significantly reduced federal income taxes. "Industries" also restructured its basic organization in 1971, redeploying capital requirements and operations.

After 1968 it became increasingly clear to the management and the board that the corporate structure remained too complex and diffuse for optimum returns. Duplication and overlapping areas of interest and responsibility reduced efficiency. In 1971, the "Industries'" subsidiaries were reorganized into distinct areas. Santa Fe Natural Resources, Inc., served as a holding company for the forest, oil and mineral subsidiaries including Chanslor-Western and Kirby Lumber. Santa Fe Air Freight was transferred to "Industries," and became a part of the transportation group made up of the railway, Santa Fe Trail Transportation and Santa Fe Pipelines. The latter became the parent for all of the pipeline and related companies. A real estate group brought together the construction, development and services operations. Allocations of and development of resources became manifestly easier with the new structure.

The management began to report significant improvements in earnings in May 1972, and both revenues and profits began to climb. The transportation group had a 72.6 percent gain in net income in 1971, with pipelines increasing by 16.2 percent, and the other areas by 11.2 percent. Oil Development Company of Texas accelerated exploration activities, leading to a discovery in Sheridan County, Montana, with production at 800 barrels of oil per day. The railway-produced net income in 1972 was 73.5 percent of "Industries' " total, compared with only 54 percent in 1968. The proportion of income generated by petroleum fell from 24.1 percent to 18.7, and real estate's contribution declined from 10.8 percent to 7.5 percent. The pipelines continued to report overall losses. In his message to the stockholders in the 1972 *Annual Report*, John Reed described a "bright and encouraging" picture for "Industries." Record net income, tax credits, general business improvement and rate hikes had created a healthy set of statistics.

At the outset of 1973, the "Industries' " board of directors elected Reed to succeed Marsh as chairman, and Reed also became chief executive officer for "Industries." He continued as president of both corporations. Reed reported to the stockholders that in 1972 revenues and profits reached new records, and the first quarter of 1973 exceeded the first quarter of 1972. The railway continued to generate the largest revenues and profits, and ATSF carloadings were up 9 percent and revenue-ton-miles increased by 12 percent. Kirby Lumber turned in a stellar performance in the resources group, but real estate showed the largest percentage increase in income before taxes. Capital spending for 1973 was set at $200 million, with $145 million allocated for the railway. Another sign of the rapid improvement in the railway's picture was Reed's report that the Santa Fe had compiled the best safety record among major American railroads for the third consecutive year. Reed concluded, "Although there are problems, Santa Fe has the physical assets, the financial strength, and the people to continue to improve and take full advantage of the opportunities which lie ahead."[1] Only a significant alteration of the national economy seemed likely to upset the prediction of record revenue for the coming year.

Colonel Holliday would have found his railroad a very different kind of corporation in 1973, with undreamed of locomotives, cars and services. No longer could a passenger travel by train from Atchison to Topeka or to Santa Fe, but natural gas and petroleum passed through Santa Fe pipelines, people lived and shopped in Santa Fe real estate, and Santa Fe oil and plywood helped meet the nation's thirst for power and homes. Perhaps the "Sage of Emporia," William Allen White, best summarized the contributions of the Atchison, Topeka and Santa Fe Railway when he wrote in *The Emporia Gazette*:

> The Santa Fe is the best thing that ever happened to Emporia. It is one of the best things that ever happened to Kansas. It is easily one of the best things that ever happened to this land; a just, efficient and far-sighted transportation system linking indissolvably the great industrial civilization of the east with the agricultural civilization of the boundless west.[2]

Colonel Holliday's dreams, visions and prophecies, which he so eloquently stated at the Wakarusa Picnic, not only became reality, but also proved to be limited, if only because of the scientific and technological advances of the following century. The "Old Man" would have been proud.

Notes

Chapter 1

1. William S. Hinkley, *The Early Days of the Santa Fe* (Topeka, Kan.: Crane & Co., Printers, n.d.), p. 13.
2. *Crawford Democrat*, February 20, 1855.
3. L. L. Waters, *Steel Trails to Santa Fe* (Lawrence: University of Kansas Press, 1950), p. 24.
4. *Topeka Record*, November 24, 1860.
5. *Kansas State Record*, October 7, 1868.
6. Steam locomotives are classified into types by the number and the locations of the wheels. Fredric Whyte devised a system, which bears his name, for classification that uses numerical symbols for .wheels. In the Whyte system, the first numeral represents the total number of lead wheels, the second numeral the driving wheels, and the third the trailing wheels. Thus, a 4–4–0 has four lead wheels, four drivers, and no trailing wheels, and a 4–6–2 has four lead wheels, six drivers, and two trailing wheels.
7. *Osage Chronicle*, May 15, 1869.
8. *Ibid.*, September 18, 1869.
9. In their excellent analysis of Bostonian investors, Arthur M. Johnson and Barry E. Supple defined ."developmental" investors as those who placed their capital in land transportation for long-run economic development and profits, while "opportunistic" capitalists invested funds for immediate returns or for manipulative gains. See their *Boston Capitalists and Western Railroads* (Cambridge, Mass.: Harvard University Press, 1967), p. 9.
10. "Santa Fe Splinters," vol. 18, compiled by Joseph Weidel, 1940. Offices of the Atchison, Topeka and Santa Fe Railway, Chicago, Illinois.
11. *Daily Commonwealth*, December 29, 1872.

Chapter 2

1. *Pueblo Chieftain*, quoted in William I. Hinkley, *The Early Days of the Santa Fe* (Topeka, Kan.: Crane & Co., Printers, n.d.), pp. 27–28.
2. *Pueblo Chieftain*, March 2 and March 16, 1876.
3. J. G. Pangburn, *The Rocky Mountain Tourist: The Tour from the Banks of the Missouri to the Base of the Rockies* (Topeka, Kan.: T. J. Anderson, Publisher, 1877, 2nd ed.).
4. Atchison, Topeka and Santa Fe Railroad, *Annual Report for 1877*.
5. *Ibid.*
6. C. K. Holliday to Thomas Nickerson, quoted in L. L. Waters, *Steel Trails to Santa Fe* (Lawrence: University of Kansas Press, 1950), pp. 57–58.
7. Robert G. Athearn, *Rebel of the Rockies* (New Haven, Conn.: Yale University Press, 1962), p. 50.
8. *Ibid.*, p. 58.
9. A. A. Robinson and W. R. Morley to W. B. Strong, January 10, 1879, copy in "Santa Fe Splinters," vol. 20, compiled by Joseph Weidel, 1940. Offices of the Atchison, Topeka and Santa Fe Railway, Chicago, Illinois.

Chapter 3

1. *Kansas in 1875, Strong and Impartial Testimony of the Wonderful Productiveness of the Cottonwood and Arkansas Valleys* (Topeka, 1875), quoted in Gilbert C. Fite, *The Farmers' Frontier, 1865–1900* (New York: Holt, Rinehart and Winston, 1966), p. 30.
2. "500,000 Acres of the Best Farming and Fruit Lands . . . in and Adjacent to the Cottonwood Valley," Land Department, Atchison, Topeka and Santa Fe Railroad (Topeka, 1874).
3. "How and Where to Get a Living Sketch of 'The Garden Of the West' Presenting Facts Worth Knowing Concerning the Lands of the Atchison, Topeka and Santa Fe Railroad Company" (Boston: Published by the Company, 1876).
4. "Memorial of the Atchison, Topeka and Santa Fe . . . to the Senate and the House of Representatives of the State of Kansas" (Boston: n.p., 1881), quoted in Ira G. Clark, *Then Came the Railroads* (Norman: University of Oklahoma Press, 1958), pp. 87–88.
5. T. Jefferson Coolidge, *The Autobiography of T. Jefferson Coolidge, 1831–1920* (Boston: Houghton Mifflin Co., 1923), pp. 87–88.
6. Quoted in Julius Grodinsky, *Transcontinental Railway Strategy, 1869–1893: A Study of Businessmen* (Philadelphia: University of Pennsylvania Press, 1962), p. 157.
7. Charles E. Perkins to Peter Geddes, May 15, 1880, quoted in Arthur M. Johnson and Barry E. Supple, *Boston Capitalists and Western Railroads* (Cambridge, Mass.: Harvard University Press, 1967), p. 309.
8. Atchison, Topeka and Santa Fe Railroad, *Annual Report for 1884*.

9. Atchison, Topeka and Santa Fe Railroad, *Annual Report for 1882.*

10. Charles Crocker to Collis P. Huntington, April 27, 1882, quoted in Grodinsky, *Transcontinental Railway Strategy*, p. 194.

11. William B. Strong to Kidder, Peabody & Company and Lee, Higginson & Company, April 15, 1882, quoted in Johnson and Supple, *Boston Capitalists and Western Railroads*, p. 304.

12. *Arizona Journal-Miner* [Prescott], quoted in William S. Greever, "Railway Development in the Southwest," *New Mexico Historical Review* XXXII (April 1957), 168–169.

13. Circular, dated January 1881, signed by Thomas Nickerson, President of the California Southern Railroad Company.

14. James Marshall, *Santa Fe: The Railroad That Built an Empire* (New York: Random House, 1945), p. 191.

15. *Railroad Gazette*, February 26, 1886, quoted in Grodinsky, *Transcontinental Railway Strategy*, p. 318.

Chapter 4

1. Harold L. Henderson, "Frederick Henry Harvey," (Master's thesis, University of Kansas City, 1942), p. 19.

2. Irvin S. Cobb, *Roughing It De Luxe* (New York: George H. Doran Co., 1913), p. 26.

3. Henderson, "Frederick Henry Harvey," p. 40.

4. William E. Curtis, "Hotels in West Owe Excellence to Fred Harvey," *Chicago Record-Herald*, April 27, 1911.

5. Edna Ferber, "Our Very Best People," in *Mother Knows Best* (Garden City, N.Y.: Doubleday Doran & Co., 1928), p. 175.

6. Patrice Smart, "Those Harvey Girls . . . ," *Railroad Magazine* LXXVI (December 1964), p. 14.

7. S. E. Kiser, "The Harvey Girl," *Santa Fe Magazine* I (January 1907), p. 10.

8. Noble R. Prentis, *Southwestern Letters* (Topeka: Kansas Publishing House, 1882), p. 34.

9. "Impressions of El Ortiz," *Santa Fe Magazine* VI (October 1910), 55–56.

10. Henry T. Fink, *Food and Flavor* (New York: The Century Co., 1913), p. 8, quoted in Henderson, "Frederick Henry Harvey," p. 49.

Chapter 5

1. Atchison, Topeka and Santa Fe Railroad, *Annual Report for 1888.*

2. *Kansas Daily State Journal* (Topeka), April 15, 1886, quoted in H. Craig Miner, *The St. Louis–San Francisco Transcontinental Railroad* (Lawrence: University Press of Kansas, 1972), p. 166.

3. Atchison, Topeka and Santa Fe Railroad, *Annual Report for 1880.*

4. Atchison, Topeka and Santa Fe Railroad, *Annual Report for 1885.*

5. Glenn Danford Bradley, *The Story of the Santa Fe* (Boston: Richard C. Badger, 1920), p. 258.
6. *Boston Herald*, November 16, 1880, and *The Commercial and Financial Chronicle*, December 18, 1880, both quoted in Arthur M. Johnson and Barry E. Supple, *Boston Capitalists and Western Railroads* (Cambridge, Mass.: Harvard University Press, 1967), p. 318.
7. Charles Francis Adams, "The Canal and Railroad Enterprise of Boston," in *The Memorial History of Boston*, ed. Justin Winsor (Boston, 1883), IV: 147, cited by Johnson and Supple, *Boston Capitalists and Western Railroads*, p. 381.
8. *The New York Times*, August 2, 1887.
9. *Railway Age*, vol. XII (1887), 325, quoted by Stuart Daggett, *Railroad Reorganization* (Cambridge, Mass.: Harvard University Press, 1908), p. 198.
10. S. F. Van Oss, *American Railroads as Investments* (New York: G. P. Putnam's Sons, 1893), pp. 563–564.

Chapter 6

1. *The Times* (London), May 23, 1892.
2. Ira G. Clark, *Then Came the Railroads* (Norman: University of Oklahoma Press, 1958), p. 223.
3. *Topeka Daily Capital* and *Topeka State Journal*, January 10, 1893, quoted in Karel Denis Bicha, "Jerry Simpson: Populist Without Principle," *The Journal of American History LIV* (September 1967), 297.
4. *The New York Times*, September 18, 1897.
5. *San Francisco Examiner*, January 30, 1895.

Chapter 7

1. Albro Martin, *Enterprise Denied: Origins of the Decline of the American Railroads, 1897–1917* (New York: Columbia University Press, 1971), p. 169.
2. E. P. Ripley to James Dun, January 24, 1899, "Santa Fe Splinters," vol. 22, compiled by Joseph Weidel, 1940. Offices of the Atchison, Topeka and Santa Fe Railway, Chicago, Illinois.
3. H. L. Marvin to A. A. Robinson, May 20, 1884, "Santa Fe Splinters," vol. 7.
4. Carl Snyder, *American Railways as Investments* (New York: The Moody Corp., 1907), p. 82.
5. Albert Atwood, "Sound Properties: The Atchison," *Harper's Weekly LIV* (July 18, 1914), 72.
6. *Ibid.*, p. 71.
7. Martin, *Enterprise Denied*, pp. 128–130.
8. *Ibid.*, pp. 200–201.

9. *The Commercial and Financial Chronicle*, August 16, 1913.
10. E. P. Ripley, "How I Got Customers to See My Side," *System* XXIX (April 1916), 345.
11. Quoted in "A Harmony Special," *The Outlook* CVI (September 8, 1915), 60–61.
12. *The Commercial and Financial Chronicle*, October 10, 1914.

Chapter 8

1. L. L. Waters, *Steel Trails to Santa Fe* (Lawrence: University of Kansas Press, 1950), p. 391.
2. The tractive effort is the force exerted by a locomotive in turning its wheels by the action of the steam against the pistons, causing the locomotive to move along the rails. The effort is calculated from the engine's dimensions.
3. A Mallet-articulated locomotive had two sets of frames connected by a hinged joint. Each frame had a set of drivers, the rear set operating with high-pressure cylinders, and the front drivers with low-pressure cylinders.

Chapter 9

1. Atchison, Topeka and Santa Fe Railway, *Annual Report for 1914*.
2. S. E. Busser, "The Santa Fe Reading-Room System," *Santa Fe Magazine* III (July 1909), 867.
3. Atchison, Topeka and Santa Fe Railway, *Annual Report for 1914*.
4. *Ibid.*
5. Wood, Struthers and Company, "ATSF Railway System," (New York: Wood, Struthers and Company, 1925).
6. *Ibid.*
7. Arthur E. Stilwell and James R. Crowell, "I Had a Hunch," *The Saturday Evening Post* CC (February 4, 1928), 38, 44; quoted in Keith L. Bryant, Jr., *Arthur E. Stilwell, Promoter with a Hunch* (Nashville, Tenn.: Vanderbilt University Press, 1971), p. 170.

Chapter 10

1. *The New York Times*, April 1, 1942.
2. *Ibid.*, October 23, 1955.
3. *Santa Fe Magazine* LVIII (April 1965), 15.

Chapter 11

1. Quoted in *Trains* XXI (April 1971), 9.
2. "The Right Not to Join," *Time* LXII (February 1, 1954), 62.

Chapter 12

1. Frederic Wakeman, *The Hucksters* (New York: Rinehart and Co., 1946), p. 275.
2. *Santa Fe Magazine* LX (October 1967), 11-12.

Epilogue

1. "To Santa Fe Industries' Stockholders," May 25, 1973.
2. William Allen White, "The Santa Fe," *The Emporia Gazette*, quoted in *Santa Fe Magazine* XX (February 1926), 21.

Bibliographical Essay

The records of most large corporations are voluminous, and the archives of the nation's major railroads are often measured not in cubic feet or linear feet of shelf space, but by the number of warehouses. The corporate archives of the Santa Fe Railway, largely concentrated in the Chicago headquarters and at the offices in Topeka, are immense, and no single historian, or even group of scholars, could ever hope to see all of the manuscripts, receipt books, stock transfers, freight reports, and other records. The historian who would attempt to write the history of a railway is, therefore, forced to limit the types of sources utilized, and hopes that the essence of the story can be related from the documents selected. The secondary literature about the ATSF, while also vast, is generally accessible and has been a significant aid in the preparation of this book. The "Bibliographical Essay" does not encompass all the materials utilized but is a selection of those materials found to be most valuable.

The Chicago headquarters of Santa Fe Industries, located in the Railway Exchange Building, contains the basic materials relative to the history of the Atchison, Topeka and Santa Fe Railroad and Railway. The corporate offices house virtually complete files of the *Annual Reports* of the ATSF, many of its predecessors and subsidiaries, and most company publications such as the *Santa Fe Magazine, The Santa Fe Today*, and *Earth*. One of the major sources for historical research is the "Santa Fe Splinters," thirty-four typescript volumes compiled by Joseph Weidel in 1940. Weidel collected a monumental body of primary sources from company records, newspaper accounts and interviews, and gathered them into topically arranged volumes. Corporate charters, presidential letters, survey and engineering reports, operation statistics and governmental documents found in the "Splinters" were indispensable to this project. The Chicago office also holds many pamphlets, brochures, passenger publications and other materials published by the railroad. (Fugitive sources of this nature were often located at the Newberry Library in Chicago.) The reports of the receivers of the 1890s, the railroad's charter, the federal and state land grants and other legal documents can be found in the Fred G. Gurley Collection in the Chicago offices. The records of the former corporate offices in New York City are now at the Kansas State Historical Society in Topeka. Some of the legal papers were published as *Documents Relating to the Atchison, Topeka and Santa Fe Railroad Company* (Boston, 1890), in four volumes. The only significant corporate records not made available to the author were the minutes of the meetings of the board of directors.

Several collections of manuscript materials relating to the ATSF were used. The E. I. DuPont De Nemours and Company Collection at the Eleutherian Mills Historical Library contains letters from Santa Fe officials soliciting traffic, and demonstrates the intense rivalry which existed between the Atchison and the Southern Pacific in the 1880s. The Cornell University Library Collection of Regional History holds the Johnson Family Papers (Benjamin Johnson) and the Turner Family Papers (Avery Turner) containing letters from two Santa Fe employees in the 1870s and 1880s which describe the life of the railroader and provide yet another dimension to the railway's history.

The published primary sources relating to the Santa Fe, though ranging from the essential to the trivial, proved to be a major contribution to the research for this volume. The letters of Cyrus K. Holliday and articles about Holliday making use of primary materials are to be found in *The Kansas Historical Quarterly* including Lela Barnes (ed.), "Letters of Cyrus Kurtz Holliday, 1854–1859," VI (1937), 241–294; and Frederick F. Seely, "The Early Career of C. K. Holliday: A Founder of Topeka and the Santa Fe Railroad," XXVIII (1961) 193–200. See also Milton Tabor, "Cyrus Kurtz Holliday," *Shawnee County Historical Society Bulletin* II (December 1948), 104–113. *The Kansas Historical Quarterly* has also published a two-part collection of newspaper articles about the early days of the ATSF; Joseph W. Snell and Don W. Wilson, eds., "The Birth of the Atchison, Topeka, and Santa Fe Railroad," IV (Summer 1968), and IV (Fall 1968). An indispensable memoir, written by one of the company's first employees, is William S. Hinkley, *The Early Days of the Santa Fe* (Topeka, Kansas, n.d.).

Several presidents of the railroad or the railway published memoirs about their experiences or became contributors to business and railroad journals while in office, and these were found to be highly useful. The best of these accounts are T. Jefferson Coolidge, *The Autobiography of T. Jefferson Coolidge, 1831–1920* (Boston, 1923); E. P. Ripley, "Why Railroads Need Higher Rates" (n.p., 1910), and "How I Got Customers to See My Side," *System*, XXIX (April 1916), 339–345; and W. B. Storey, "A History of the ATSF Railway System," *Shipper and Carrier* VI (June 1925), 5–11. See also, "William Benson Storey—Civil Engineer and Railroad Executive," *Journal of the Western Society of Engineers* XLV (February 1940), 31–39. Several employees of the Santa Fe or its predecessors have written memoirs from yet another perspective, and the best of these accounts are Walter Justin Sherman, "Early Days on the Texas Santa Fe," *Northwestern Ohio Historical Society Quarterly Bulletin* VI

(1934), 7–9; and Joseph A. Noble, *From Cab to Caboose: Fifty Years of Railroading* (Norman, Oklahoma, 1964).

The secondary literature about the Santa Fe includes solid historical works and materials aimed largely at railroad "buffs." No study of the ATSF can proceed without consulting Glenn Danford Bradley's pioneer study entitled *The Story of the Santa Fe* (Boston, 1920). The history of the Atchison by L. L. Waters, *Steel Trails to Santa Fe* (Lawrence, Kansas, 1950), despite occasional stylistic turgidity, stands as a substantial research effort and was most helpful in the writing of this volume. The popular history of the ATSF written by James Marshall, *Santa Fe, the Railroad That Built an Empire* (New York, 1945), while based on Waters's research, suffers from factual errors and significant omissions. Merle Armitage's *Operations Santa Fe* (New York, 1948) is not only a beautiful book but also is highly informative. The standard history of the development of the railroad network of the south central states is Ira G. Clark, *Then Came the Railroads* (Norman, Oklahoma, 1958). Three unpublished studies containing substantial statistical data are: Thomas Doniphan Best, "The Role of the Atchison Topeka and Santa Fe Railway System in the Economic Development of the Southwestern States, 1859–1954," (Ph.D. dissertation, Northwestern University, 1959); John Walker Barriger, IV, "The Development of the Santa Fe, 1935–1948," (B.S. thesis, Massachusetts Institute of Technology, 1949); and John Byron McCall, "An Economic Study of Railroad Passenger Services: The Santa Fe and Southern Pacific Railroads, 1950–1965," (Ph.D. dissertation, Oklahoma State University, 1968). The contribution of Ray Morley to the growth of the Santa Fe is described in Norman Cleaveland's *The Morleys—Young Upstarts on the Southwest Frontier* (Albuquerque, 1972). Two volumes written primarily for railroad buffs but containing some important materials are Donald Duke and Stan Kistler, *Santa Fe . . . Steel Rails Through California* (San Marino, California, 1963), and David F. Myrick, *New Mexico's Railroads* (Golden, Colorado, 1970). Frederic Wakeman's novel *The Hucksters* (New York, 1946) provides a fictional view of the romance of the Atchison's streamliners during the 1940s.

The financial history of the Atchison has been drawn from *The Commercial and Financial Chronicle, Moody's Magazine, Poor's Manual of Railroads, The Wall Street Journal, The New York Times, Business Week, Financial World, Fortune, Modern Railroads*, and *The Nation's Business*. The reports of several brokerage houses have been consulted, including those circulated by Wood, Struthers and Company; Rand, Avery and Frye; Kidder, Peabody and Company; and Lee, Higgenson and Company. The Interstate Commerce Commission, *Valuation Docket 625* (May 3, 1927) of 847 pages was an invaluable aid. The study of the financial condition of the system following its collapse in 1893, written by Stephen Little, reveals the massive losses entailed by the unwise expansion of the previous five years. The Atchison's financial condition before and after its reorganization and rehabilitation is analyzed in three useful volumes: S. F. Van Oss, *American Railroads as Investments* (New York, 1893); Carl Snyder, *American Railways as Investments* (New York, 1907); and Albert W. Atwood, "Sound Properties: The Atchison," *Harper's Weekly*

BIBLIOGRAPHICAL ESSAY

LIX (July 18, 1914), 71–72. No study of the Atchison in the nineteenth century can be written without incurring considerable indebtedness to the outstanding work of Arthur M. Johnson and Barry E. Supple in *Boston Capitalists and Western Railroads* (Cambridge, Massachusetts, 1967). Their analysis of the investment practices of Bostonians proved to be crucial to this volume.

The history of the Santa Fe's motive power appears in the virtually definitive *Iron Horses of the Santa Fe Trail* (Dallas, 1965), by E. D. Worley. Other valuable accounts of steam locomotives on the system include Sylvan R. Wood, "The Locomotives of the AT&SF Railway System," *Bulletin No. 75*, Railway and Locomotive Historical Society, (Boston, 1949); Alfred W. Bruce, *The Steam Locomotive in America* (New York, 1952); and Baldwin Locomotive Works, *The AT&SF Railway System, Record of Recent Construction, Number 56* (Philadelphia, 1906). The engineering history of early steam power can be found in John H. White, Jr.'s definitive *American Locomotives: An Engineering History, 1830–1880* (Baltimore, 1968).

The long and often acrimonious debate over the merits of the federal land grants to a few of the nation's railways continues. Four studies of the Atchison's land grants in Kansas, Arizona and New Mexico bring some order to the chaos of conflicting records and legal cases. For thoughtful analyses of the Atchison's land grants see: Paul Wallace Gates, *Fifty Million Acres* (Ithaca, New York, 1954); Sanford A. Mosk, *Land Tenure Problems in the Santa Fe Railroad Land Grant Area* (Berkeley, California, 1944); Leslie E. Decker, *Railroads, Lands and Politics* (Providence, Rhode Island, 1964); and William S. Greever, *Arid Domain: The Santa Fe Railway and Its Western Land Grant* (Palo Alto, California, 1954). See also Greever's "Two Arizona Forest Lieu Land Exchanges," *Pacific Historical Review* XIX (May 1950), 137–149.

The literature about the "Russian" Mennonites and their migration to Kansas under the auspices of the Santa Fe tends toward the romantic and the antiquarian. Several studies based on substantial research or translations of primary sources provided information about the coming of the Mennonites and their contributions to the economy of Kansas. These include Kendall Bailes, "The Mennonites Come to Kansas," *American Heritage* X (August 1959), 30–33, 102–105; Helen B. Shipley, "The Migration of the Mennonites from Russia, 1873–1883, and Their Settlement in Kansas," (M.A. thesis, University of Minnesota, 1954); Melvin Gingerich, "Mennonites in Kansas," *Mennonite Quarterly* XXVIII (1954), 307–309; and J. Neale Carman, "German Settlements Along the Atchison, Topeka and Santa Fe Railway: A Translation from the German," *The Kansas Historical Quarterly* XXVIII (1962), 310–316.

The relationship between Fred Harvey and the Santa Fe cannot be thoroughly analyzed until the early records of the Harvey system, if they exist, are made available to scholars. Because of the closely guarded privacy of this long-time family-owned corporation, few primary sources are available. The account in this study draws primarily upon publications of the Harvey system, and the fine study by Harold L. Henderson, "Frederick Henry Harvey," (M.A. thesis, University of Kansas City, 1942).

Other sources consulted include:

Avery, Whitefield. "The Dining Room That Is Two Thousand Miles Long." *Capper's Magazine*, September 1930, 23–24.

Beebe, Lucius. "The Santa Fe's Ineffable Deluxe." *American West* II (Summer 1965), 13–18.

————. "Purveyor to the West: Harvey House." *American Heritage* XVIII (February 1967), 28–31.

————, and Charles Clegg. *The Trains We Rode*. Berkeley, 1965, vol. I.

Curtis, William E. "Hotels in West Owe Excellence to Fred Harvey." *Chicago Record-Herald*, April 27, 1911.

Ferber, Edna. "Our Very Best People," in *Mother Knows Best*. Garden City, New York, 1928.

Fergusson, Erna. "Fred Harvey—Civilizer," in *Our Southwest*. New York, 1940.

Henderson, James D. "Meals by Fred Harvey." *Arizona and the West* VIII (Winter 1966), 305–322.

Hungerford, Edward. "Dining-Car Problems." *The Saturday Evening Post* (October 7, 1911), 34–37.

Hurd, Charles W. "The Fred Harvey System." *The Colorado Magazine* XXVI (July 1949), 176–183.

Smart, Patrice. "Those Harvey Girls . . ." *Railroad Magazine* LXXIV (December 1964), 13–16.

The secondary literature concerning the history of American railroads, business history in the late nineteenth century and the twentieth century, and the Santa Fe Southwest represents an enormous body of books and articles. A complete list of the sources utilized in this volume would extend for many pages without suggesting their relative importance. The following works were used extensively or contained substantial material about the Atchison not available elsewhere:

Anderson, George L. *Kansas West*. San Marino, California, 1963.

Athearn, Robert G. *Rebel of the Rockies*. New Haven, 1962.

Bryant, Keith L., Jr. *Arthur E. Stilwell, Promoter with a Hunch*. Nashville, 1971.

Carr, Clark Ezra. *History of Bringing the Atchison, Topeka and Santa Fe Railway to Galesburg*. Galesburg, Illinois, 1913.

Cochran, Thomas C. *Railroad Leaders, 1845–1890*. New York, 1965.

Cole, Arthur H. *Business Enterprise in Its Social Setting*. Cambridge, Massachusetts, 1959.

Daggett, Stuart. *Railroad Consolidation West of the Mississippi River*. Berkeley, 1933.

————. *Chapters on the History of the Southern Pacific*. New York, 1966.

————. *Railroad Reorganization*. Cambridge, Massachusetts, 1908.

Dykstra, Robert R. *The Cattle Towns*. New York, 1968.

Going, Charles Buxton. *Methods of the Santa Fe*. New York, 1909.

Grodinsky, Julius. *Jay Gould*. Philadelphia, 1957.

———. *Railroad Consolidation*. New York, 1930.

———. *Transcontinental Railway Strategy*. Philadelphia, 1962.

Kennan, George. *E. H. Harriman: A Biography*. Boston, 1922.

Kirkland, Edward Chase. *Dream and Thought in the Business Community. 1860–1900*. Chicago, 1964.

———. *Industry Comes of Age*. Chicago, 1967.

Kolko, Gabriel. *Railroads and Regulation, 1877–1916*. Princeton, New Jersey, 1965.

Martin, Albro. *Enterprise Denied*. New York, 1971.

Miner, H. Craig. *The St. Louis–San Francisco Transcontinental Railroad*. Lawrence, Kansas, 1972.

Overton, Richard C. *Burlington Route*. New York, 1965.

———. *Gulf to the Rockies*. Austin, Texas, 1953.

Petrowski, William Robinson. "The Kansas Pacific Railroad: A Study in Railroad Promotion." Ph.D. dissertation, University of Wisconsin, 1965.

Riegel, Robert Edgar. *The Story of the Western Railroads*. Lincoln, Nebraska, 1964.

Ripley, William Z. *Railroads: Finance and Organization*. New York, 1915.

———. *Railroads: Rates and Regulations*. New York, 1912.

———. *Railway Problems*. Boston, 1907.

———. *Trusts, Pools and Corporations*. Boston, 1905.

Index